OECD/G20 Base Erosion and Profit Shifting Project

Harmful Tax Practices – 2018 Peer Review Reports on the Exchange of Information on Tax Rulings

INCLUSIVE FRAMEWORK ON BEPS: ACTION 5

OECD
BETTER POLICIES FOR BETTER LIVES

Please cite this publication as:
OECD (2019), *Harmful Tax Practices – 2018 Peer Review Reports on the Exchange of Information on Tax Rulings: Inclusive Framework on BEPS: Action 5*, OECD/G20 Base Erosion and Profit Shifting Project, OECD Publishing, Paris, *https://doi.org/10.1787/7cc5b1a2-en*.

ISBN 978-92-64-52945-8 (print)
ISBN 978-92-64-39513-8 (pdf)

OECD/G20 Base Erosion and Profit Shifting Project
ISSN 2313-2604 (print)
ISSN 2313-2612 (online)

Corrigenda to publications may be found on line at: *www.oecd.org/about/publishing/corrigenda.htm*.

Foreword

The integration of national economies and markets has increased substantially in recent years, putting a strain on the international tax rules, which were designed more than a century ago. Weaknesses in the current rules create opportunities for base erosion and profit shifting (BEPS), requiring bold moves by policy makers to restore confidence in the system and ensure that profits are taxed where economic activities take place and value is created.

Following the release of the report Addressing Base Erosion and Profit Shifting in February 2013, OECD and G20 countries adopted a 15-point Action Plan to address BEPS in September 2013. The Action Plan identified 15 actions along three key pillars: introducing coherence in the domestic rules that affect cross-border activities, reinforcing substance requirements in the existing international standards, and improving transparency as well as certainty.

After two years of work, measures in response to the 15 actions were delivered to G20 Leaders in Antalya in November 2015. All the different outputs, including those delivered in an interim form in 2014, were consolidated into a comprehensive package. The BEPS package of measures represents the first substantial renovation of the international tax rules in almost a century. Once the new measures become applicable, it is expected that profits will be reported where the economic activities that generate them are carried out and where value is created. BEPS planning strategies that rely on outdated rules or on poorly co-ordinated domestic measures will be rendered ineffective.

Implementation is now the focus of this work. The BEPS package is designed to be implemented via changes in domestic law and practices, and in tax treaties. With the negotiation of a multilateral instrument (MLI) having been finalised in 2016 to facilitate the implementation of the treaty related BEPS measures, over 90 jurisdictions are covered by the MLI. The entry into force of the MLI on 1 July 2018 paves the way for swift implementation of the treaty related measures. OECD and G20 countries also agreed to continue to work together to ensure a consistent and co-ordinated implementation of the BEPS recommendations and to make the project more inclusive. Globalisation requires that global solutions and a global dialogue be established which go beyond OECD and G20 countries.

A better understanding of how the BEPS recommendations are implemented in practice could reduce misunderstandings and disputes between governments. Greater focus on implementation and tax administration should therefore be mutually beneficial to governments and business. Proposed improvements to data and analysis will help support ongoing evaluation of the quantitative impact of BEPS, as well as evaluating the impact of the countermeasures developed under the BEPS Project.

As a result, the OECD established the OECD/G20 Inclusive Framework on BEPS (Inclusive Framework), bringing all interested and committed countries and jurisdictions on an equal footing in the Committee on Fiscal Affairs and all its subsidiary bodies. The Inclusive Framework, which already has more than 135 members, is monitoring and peer reviewing the implementation of the minimum standards as well as completing the work on standard setting to address BEPS issues. In addition to BEPS members, other international organisations and regional tax bodies are involved in the work of the Inclusive Framework, which also consults business and the civil society on its different work streams.

This report was approved by the Inclusive Framework on 11 December 2019 and prepared for publication by the OECD Secretariat.

Table of contents

Follow OECD Publications on:

http://twitter.com/OECD_Pubs

http://www.facebook.com/OECDPublications

http://www.linkedin.com/groups/OECD-Publications-4645871

http://www.youtube.com/oecdilibrary

http://www.oecd.org/oecddirect/

Abbreviations and acronyms

APA	Advance pricing arrangement
ATR	Advance tax ruling
ATO	Australian Taxation Office
BEPS	Base Erosion and Profit Shifting
BRA	Barbados Revenue Authority
CRA	Canada Revenue Agency
DFI	International Tax Department (Uruguay)
DGI	Large Taxpayer Division within the Tax Administration (Uruguay)
EOI	Exchange of Information
EU	European Union
FHTP	Forum on Harmful Tax Practices
FIOT	Fiscal Intelligence and Fraud Team
HMRC	Her Majesty's Revenue and Customs
IFSC	International financial services company
IP	Intellectual Property
IRBM	Inland Revenue Board Malaysia
ITO	International Tax Office (Kenya)
LIAATM	Law on International Administrative Assistance in Tax Matters
MHQ	Multinational Companies Headquarters
MLI	Multilateral Instrument
MNE	Multinational Enterprise
NCTA	National Tax and Customs Administration (Hungary)
NTA	National Tax Agency (Japan)
NTS	National Tax Service (Korea)
OECD	Organization for Economic Co-operation and Development
PE	Permanent Establishment
R&D	Research and Development

RFN	Receita Federal do Brazil (Brazilian Tax Administration)
SAARC	South Asian Association for Regional Cooperation
SRC	Seychelles Revenue Commission
STA	Swedish Tax Agency
TAAO	Tax Administrative Assistance Ordinance
ToR	Terms of reference
TRNC	Turkish Republic of Northern Cyprus
XML	Extensible Mark-Up Language

Executive Summary

Context for the exchange of information on tax rulings (the "transparency framework")

The BEPS Action 5 minimum standard on the compulsory spontaneous exchange of information on tax rulings (the "transparency framework") provides tax administrations with timely information on rulings that have been granted to a foreign related party of their resident taxpayer or a permanent establishment, which can be used in conducting risk assessments and which, in the absence of exchange, could give rise to BEPS concerns.

The transparency framework requires spontaneous exchange of information on five categories of taxpayer-specific rulings: (i) rulings related to certain preferential regimes, (ii) unilateral advance pricing arrangements (APAs) or other cross-border unilateral rulings in respect of transfer pricing, (iii) rulings providing for a downward adjustment of taxable profits, (iv) permanent establishment (PE) rulings; and (v) related party conduit rulings.[1] The requirement to exchange information on the rulings in the above categories includes certain past rulings as well as future rulings, pursuant to pre-defined periods which are outlined in each jurisdiction's report and that varies according to the time when a certain jurisdiction has joined the Inclusive Framework or has been identified as a Jurisdiction of Relevance. The exchanges occur pursuant to international exchange of information agreements, which provide the legal conditions under which exchanges take place, including the need to ensure taxpayer confidentiality.

The inclusion of the above categories of rulings in the scope of the transparency framework is not intended to suggest that the issuance of such rulings constitutes a preferential regime or a harmful tax practice. In practice, tax rulings can be an effective way to provide certainty to taxpayers and reduce the risk of disputes. Rather, the need for transparency on rulings is that a tax administration's lack of knowledge or information on the tax treatment of a taxpayer in another jurisdiction can impact the treatment of transactions or arrangements undertaken with a related taxpayer resident in their own jurisdiction and thus lead to BEPS concerns. The availability of timely and targeted information about such rulings, as agreed in the template in Annex C of the Action 5 Report, *Countering Harmful Tax Practices More Effectively, Taking Into Account Transparency and Substance* (OECD, 2015[1]), is intended to better equip tax authorities to quickly identify risk areas.

This framework was designed with a view to finding a balance between ensuring that the information exchanged is relevant to other tax administrations and that it does not impose an unnecessary administrative burden on either the country exchanging the information or the country receiving it.

Scope of this review

This is the third annual peer review of the transparency framework. It covers individual reports for 112 jurisdictions, including 20 jurisdictions reviewed for the first time. This comprises all Inclusive Framework members that joined prior to 30 June 2018 and Jurisdictions of Relevance identified by the Inclusive

Framework prior to 30 June 2018, as well as being the first review for certain developing countries that had requested additional time and were deferred from the previous years' peer reviews.

Eight other members of the Inclusive Framework have not been assessed under the transparency framework, namely Anguilla, the Bahamas, Bahrain, Bermuda, the British Virgin Islands, the Cayman Islands, the Turks and Caicos Islands and the United Arab Emirates. These jurisdictions do not impose any corporate income tax, and therefore cannot legally issue rulings within the scope of the transparency framework and nor do Inclusive Framework members exchange information on rulings with them. Therefore, these jurisdictions are considered to be outside the scope of the transparency framework. In addition, Sint Maarten was affected by a natural disaster and therefore it was considered appropriate that the peer review of the jurisdiction be deferred to the next annual review.

The reviews contained in this annual report cover the steps jurisdictions have taken to implement the transparency framework during the calendar year 2018. The reviews have been prepared using information from each reviewed jurisdiction, input from peers who received exchanges of information under the transparency framework, and input from the delegates of the Forum on Harmful Tax Practices ("FHTP").

Key findings

Key findings from this third peer review include:

- As at 31 December 2018, almost 18 000 tax rulings in the scope of the transparency framework had been issued by the jurisdictions being reviewed. This is the cumulative figure, including certain past rulings issued since 2010.
- Almost 30 000 exchanges of information took place by 31 December 2018, with almost 9 000 exchanges undertaken during 2018, almost 14 000 exchanges undertaken during 2017 and over 6 000 exchanges during 2016.
- Most of the jurisdictions already have undertaken steps to implement the necessary legal framework for spontaneous exchange of information on rulings for the year in review.
- 80 jurisdictions did not receive any recommendations, as they have met all the terms of reference.
- 55 recommendations for improvement have been made for the year in review.
- Action is being taken to respond to the recommendations. Of the 60 recommendations for improvement made to the 92 jurisdictions in the previous year peer review, 21 recommendations have been actioned and removed during the year in review. In a number of other cases, plans are in place in respect of the remaining recommendations and it is expected they will be removed in next year's review.
- However, there are nine recommendations made to OECD and G20 countries which are recommendations issued for the third time, because action has not yet been taken in respect of a number of cases. This is particularly with regard to the transparency obligations that apply to grandfathered IP regimes. Where recommendations are recurring from previous years, this is noted in the report. These members are urged to take action to ensure these recommendations are removed for the fourth and final review under this methodology. The Secretariat has offered its advice to support these jurisdictions, where relevant.
- 106 peer input questionnaires were submitted providing feedback on the conduct of the exchanges by Inclusive Framework members. Peer input is not mandatory, but in cases where it was provided it has in a number of cases allowed jurisdictions to revise their processes and improve the clarity of templates.
- In a number of cases, the peer review process has assisted jurisdictions in identifying areas where improvement is required, and jurisdictions have been able to take action to implement changes over 2019 while the peer review was ongoing. Where these changes were implemented in 2019,

they are generally not taken into account in the recommendations issued for the year 2018. However, these changes will be reviewed in the subsequent peer review.

A compilation of the recommendations made is provided below.

Aspect of the implementation of the transparency framework that should be improved	Recommendation for improvement
Andorra	
Andorra experienced difficulties in identifying all potential exchange jurisdictions for future rulings.	Andorra is recommended to ensure that all potential exchange jurisdictions are identified swiftly for all future rulings. This recommendation remains unchanged since the prior year peer review report.
Andorra did not undertake spontaneous exchange of information on tax rulings within scope of the transparency framework during the year in review.	Andorra is recommended to continue its efforts to complete the templates for all relevant rulings and to ensure that all information on past and future rulings is exchanged as soon as possible. This recommendation remains unchanged since the prior year peer review report.
Angola	
Angola has not yet finalised the steps to have in place its necessary information and gathering process.	Angola is recommended to finalise its information gathering process for identifying all past and future rulings and all potential exchange jurisdictions, with a review and supervision mechanism, as soon as possible. This recommendation remains unchanged since the prior year peer review report.
Angola has not yet finalised the steps to have effective compulsory spontaneous exchange of information on the tax rulings within the scope of the transparency framework.	Angola is recommended to continue to put in place a domestic legal framework allowing spontaneous exchange of information on rulings and to continue its efforts to complete the templates for all relevant rulings and to ensure that the exchanges of information on rulings occur as soon as possible. This recommendation remains unchanged since the prior year peer review report.
Argentina	
	No recommendations are made.
Aruba	
	No recommendations are made.
Australia	
	No recommendations are made.
Austria	
	No recommendations are made.
Barbados	
Barbados has experienced delays in the exchange of information on rulings.	Barbados is recommended to continue its efforts to ensure that all information on past and future rulings is exchanged as soon as possible. This recommendation remains unchanged since the prior year peer review report.
Barbados did not identify or exchange information on new entrants to the grandfathered IP regime.	Barbados is recommended to identify and exchange information on all new entrants to the grandfathered IP regime as soon as possible.
Belgium	
	No recommendations are made.
Belize	
	No recommendations are made.
Benin	
Benin has not yet finalised the steps to have in place its necessary information and gathering process.	Benin is recommended to finalise its information gathering process, with a review and supervision mechanism, as soon as possible.
Benin has not yet finalised the steps to have effective compulsory spontaneous exchange of information on the tax rulings within the scope of the transparency framework.	Benin is recommended to continue to put in place a domestic legal framework allowing spontaneous exchange of information on rulings and to continue its efforts to complete the templates for all relevant rulings and to ensure that the exchanges of information on rulings occur as soon as possible.

Botswana	
Botswana has not yet finalised the steps to have in place its necessary information and gathering process.	Botswana is recommended to apply the best efforts approach to identify all potential exchange jurisdictions for APA and PE rulings and to put in place a review and supervision mechanism, as soon as possible.
Botswana does not yet have the necessary legal framework in place for exchanging information on rulings and a process in place to ensure the timely exchange of information on rulings in the form required by the transparency framework.	Botswana is recommended to continue to put in place a domestic legal framework allowing spontaneous exchange of information on rulings and to ensure the timely exchange of information on rulings in the form required by the transparency framework.
Brazil	
	No recommendations are made.
Brunei Darussalam	
	No recommendations are made.
Bulgaria	
	No recommendations are made.
Burkina Faso	
	No recommendations are made.
Cameroon	
	No recommendations are made.
Canada	
Canada experienced some delays in exchanging information on future rulings.	No recommendation is made because Canada has since completed exchanges on the delayed future rulings in the year in review and this is not a recurring issue.
Chile	
	No recommendations are made.
China (People's Republic of)	
	No recommendations are made.
Colombia	
	No recommendations are made.
Congo	
Congo has not yet finalised the steps to have in place its necessary information and gathering process.	Congo is recommended to finalise its information gathering process, with a review and supervision mechanism, as soon as possible.
Congo has not yet finalised the steps to have effective compulsory spontaneous exchange of information on the tax rulings within the scope of the transparency framework.	Congo is recommended to continue to put in place a domestic legal framework allowing spontaneous exchange of information on rulings and to continue its efforts to complete the templates for all relevant rulings and to ensure the timely exchange of information on rulings in the form required by the transparency framework.
Costa Rica	
Costa Rica experienced difficulties in ensuring that all relevant information is captured adequately and identified additional past and future rulings that were not previously captured.	Costa Rica is recommended to strengthen its review and supervision mechanism to ensure that the information gathering process is working effectively.
Costa Rica experienced difficulties in ensuring that information on rulings is transmitted to the Competent Authority responsible for international exchange of information without undue delay.	Costa Rica is recommended to continue its efforts to ensure that information on rulings is transmitted to the Competent Authority without undue delay. This recommendation remains unchanged since the prior year peer review report.
Côte d'Ivoire	
	No recommendations are made.
Croatia	
Croatia experienced some delays in exchanging information on one future ruling.	No recommendation is made because Croatia has since completed exchanges on the delayed future ruling quickly after the issues were identified and resolved, and this is not a recurring issue.
Curaçao	
The information gathering process is still underway in Curaçao with respect to past and future rulings in scope of the transparency framework and the classification of these rulings under each category.	Curaçao is recommended to finalise its information gathering process for identifying all past and future rulings in scope of the transparency framework as soon as possible. This recommendation remains unchanged since the prior year peer review report.
Curaçao experienced delays in exchanging information on past and future rulings.	Curaçao is recommended to continue its efforts to ensure that all information on past and future rulings is exchanged as soon as possible. This recommendation remains unchanged since the prior year peer

	review report.
Czech Republic	
The Czech Republic experienced delays in the exchange of information on future rulings due to the application of the timelines set out in the EU Directive 2011/16/EU.	The Czech Republic is recommended to ensure that all information on future rulings is exchanged as soon as possible. This recommendation remains unchanged since the 2016 peer review report and the 2017 peer review report.
Democratic Republic of Congo	
	No recommendations are made.
Denmark	
	No recommendations are made.
Djibouti	
	No recommendations are made.
Egypt	
Egypt does not have in place the information gathering process as required under the transparency framework.	Egypt is recommended to ensure that it has put in place an effective information gathering process to identify all relevant past and future rulings and all potential exchange jurisdictions and to implement a review and supervision mechanism, as soon as possible.
Egypt does not have in place a process to ensure the timely exchange of information on rulings in the form required by the transparency framework.	Egypt is recommended to develop a process to complete the templates on relevant rulings and to ensure that the exchanges of information on rulings occur in accordance with the form and timelines under the transparency framework.
Estonia	
	No recommendations are made.
Finland	
	No recommendations are made.
France	
France did not identify or exchange information on new entrants to the IP regime or taxpayers benefitting from the third category of IP asset with respect to the former IP regime.	France is recommended to identify and exchange information on all new entrants to the IP regime, and to identify and exchange information on taxpayers benefitting from the third category of IP assets. This recommendation remains unchanged since the 2016 peer review report and the 2017 peer review report.
Gabon	
Gabon has not yet finalised the steps to have in place its necessary information and gathering process.	Gabon is recommended to finalise its information gathering process, with a review and supervision mechanism, as soon as possible.
Gabon has not yet finalised the steps to have effective compulsory spontaneous exchange of information on the tax rulings within the scope of the transparency framework.	Gabon is recommended to continue to put in place a domestic legal framework allowing spontaneous exchange of information on rulings and to ensure the timely exchange of information on rulings in the form required by the transparency framework.
Georgia	
	No recommendations are made.
Germany	
	No recommendations are made.
Greece	
	No recommendations are made.
Guernsey	
	No recommendations are made.
Haiti	
	No recommendations are made.
Hong Kong (China)	
	No recommendations are made.
Hungary	
Hungary did not yet apply the "best efforts approach" to indemnify potential exchange jurisdictions for all past rulings.	Hungary is recommended to continue to apply the "best efforts approach" to identify potential exchange jurisdictions for all past rulings. This recommendation remains unchanged since the 2016 peer review report and the 2017 peer review report.
Hungary did not identify or exchange information on new entrants to the grandfathered IP regime.	Hungary is recommended to continue its efforts to identify and exchange information on all new entrants to the grandfathered IP regime. This recommendation remains unchanged since the 2016 peer

	review report and the 2017 peer review report.
Iceland	
	No recommendations are made.
India	
India experienced delays in the exchange of information on future APAs.	India is recommended to continue its efforts to ensure that all information on future APAs is exchanged as soon as possible. This recommendation remains unchanged since the prior year peer review report.
Indonesia	
	No recommendations are made.
Ireland	
Ireland experienced some delays in exchanging information on future rulings.	No recommendation is made because Ireland has quickly remedied the issue, completed exchanges on the delayed future rulings in the year in review and is not a recurring issue.
Isle of Man	
	No recommendations are made.
Israel	
During the year in review, Israel continued to experience delays in the provision of rulings to the Competent Authority.	Israel is recommended to continue its efforts to reduce the timelines for providing the information on future rulings to the Competent Authority. This recommendation remains unchanged since the prior year peer review report.
Israel continued to encounter delays in the exchange of information for all future rulings within the scope of the transparency framework.	Israel is recommended to ensure that all information on future rulings is exchanged as soon as possible. This recommendation remains unchanged since the 2016 peer review report and the 2017 peer review report.
Italy	
During the year of review Italy continued to experience delays when forwarding information to the Competent Authority.	Italy is recommended to continue its efforts to continue its efforts to apply reduced timelines for providing the information on future rulings to the Competent Authority. This recommendation remains unchanged since the 2016 peer review report and the 2017 peer review report.
Italy has completed the exchange of information on new entrants to the grandfathered IP regime that obtained benefits with respect to trademarks in mid-2019.	As the exchange was done by mid-2019 (after the year in review), the recommendation to complete the exchanges on the new entrants is retained, though this is not a recurring issue. A recommendation on this issue remains since the 2016 peer review report and the 2017 peer review report.
Jamaica	
	No recommendations are made.
Japan	
	No recommendations are made.
Jersey	
	No recommendations are made.
Jordan	
	No recommendations are made.
Kazakhstan	
Kazakhstan does not have information gathering process in place.	Kazakhstan is recommended to finalise its information gathering process for identifying all relevant past and future rulings and all potential exchange jurisdictions and to implement a review and supervision mechanism, as soon as possible.
Kazakhstan does not have a domestic legal framework allowing spontaneous exchange of information on rulings and has in place a process for completion of templates and exchange of information on rulings.	Kazakhstan is recommended to put in place a domestic legal framework allowing spontaneous exchange of information on rulings and to ensure the timely exchange of information on rulings in the form required by the transparency framework.
Kenya	
	No recommendations are made.
Korea	
	No recommendations are made.
Latvia	
	No recommendations are made.

Liberia	
	No recommendations are made.
Liechtenstein	
	No recommendations are made.
Lithuania	
	No recommendations are made.
Luxembourg	
	No recommendations are made.
Macau (China)	
	No recommendations are made.
Malaysia	
Malaysia experienced delays in the provision of rulings to the Competent Authority and did not undertake spontaneous exchange of information on all tax rulings within scope of the transparency framework during the year in review.	Malaysia is recommended to continue its efforts to reduce the timelines for providing the information on rulings to the Competent Authority and to complete the templates for all relevant rulings and to ensure that the exchanges of information on rulings occur as soon as possible. This recommendation remains unchanged since the prior year peer review report.
Malaysia did not identify or exchange information on new entrants to the grandfathered IP regime.	Malaysia is recommended to identify and exchange information on all new entrants to the grandfathered IP regime.
Maldives	
	No recommendations are made.
Malta	
	No recommendations are made.
Mauritius	
Mauritius experienced some delays in exchanging information on one future ruling.	No recommendation is made because Mauritius completed exchanges on the delayed future ruling quickly after the issues were identified and resolved, and this is not a recurring issue.
Mexico	
	No recommendations are made.
Monaco	
	No recommendations are made.
Mongolia	
	No recommendations are made.
Montserrat	
	No recommendations are made.
The Netherlands	
	No recommendations are made.
New Zealand	
	No recommendations are made.
Nigeria	
	No recommendations are made.
Norway	
	No recommendations are made.
Oman	
	No recommendations are made.
Pakistan	
	No recommendations are made.
Panama	
Panama did not identify the jurisdictions of residence of related parties to transactions for which a preferential treatment is granted or which gives rise to income from related parties benefiting from a preferential treatment with regard to the one identified past ruling. This issue was not identified through the review and supervision mechanism.	Panama is recommended to strengthen its review and supervision mechanism to ensure that the information gathering process is working effectively.
Panama experienced some delays in exchanging information on the one identified past ruling due to an error in the review and supervision mechanism with regard to the information gathering process as well as	No recommendation is made because Panama completed the exchanges on the one identified past ruling quickly after the issues were identified and resolved, and this is not a recurring issue.

uncertainty in the determination of the effective application of the information exchange instruments.	
Papua New Guinea	
	No recommendations are made.
Paraguay	
	No recommendations are made.
Peru	
	No recommendations are made.
The Philippines	
The Philippines does not currently collect information on all potential exchange jurisdictions, particularly the ultimate parent company for past rulings.	The Philippines is recommended to apply the "best efforts approach" to identify potential exchange jurisdictions for all past rulings.
The Philippines does not currently collect information on all potential exchange jurisdictions, particularly the ultimate parent company for future rulings.	The Philippines is recommended to ensure that all potential exchange jurisdictions are identified swiftly for all future rulings.
The Philippines does not have a review and supervision mechanism in place to ensure that all relevant information on the identification of rulings and potential exchange jurisdictions is captured adequately.	The Philippines is recommended to have in place a review and supervision mechanism to ensure that the information gathering process is working effectively.
The Philippines does not yet have the necessary domestic legal framework in place for exchanging information on rulings or a process in place to ensure the timely exchange of information on rulings in the form required by the transparency framework.	The Philippines is recommended to continue to put in place a domestic legal framework allowing spontaneous exchange of information on rulings and to ensure the timely exchange of information on rulings in the form required by the transparency framework.
Poland	
During the year in review, Poland encountered delays in identifying all potential exchange jurisdictions for future rulings other than APAs.	Poland is recommended to ensure that all potential exchange jurisdictions are identified swiftly for all future rulings other than APAs. This recommendation remains unchanged since the 2016 peer review report and the 2017 peer review report.
Portugal	
	No recommendations are made.
Qatar	
	No recommendations are made.
Romania	
Romania experienced delays in the exchange of all past rulings and future rulings since written procedures on exchange of information have only been recently introduced.	Romania is recommended to ensure that all information on past and future rulings is exchanged as soon as possible. This recommendation remains unchanged since the prior year peer review report.
Russian Federation	
	No recommendations are made.
Saint Kitts and Nevis	
	No recommendations are made.
Saint Lucia	
Saint Lucia has not yet finalised the steps to have in place its necessary information and gathering process.	Saint Lucia is recommended to finalise its information gathering process for identifying future rulings and potential exchange jurisdictions, with a review and supervision mechanism, as soon as possible.
Saint Lucia does not have a process to complete the templates on relevant rulings, to make them available to the Competent Authority for exchange of information, and to exchange them with relevant jurisdictions.	Saint Lucia is recommended to develop a process to complete the templates on relevant rulings and to ensure that the exchanges of information on rulings occur in accordance with the form and timelines under the transparency framework.
Saint Lucia did not identify or exchange information on new entrants to the IP regime or taxpayers benefitting from the third category of IP asset.	Saint Lucia is recommended to identify and exchange information on all new entrants to the IP regime, and to identify and exchange information on taxpayers benefitting from the third category of IP assets.
San Marino	
San Marino does not yet have in place a process to identify all information on potential exchange jurisdictions for future rulings.	San Marino is recommended to finalise its information gathering process for identifying all past and future rulings and potential exchange jurisdictions, with a review and supervision mechanism, as soon as possible.
San Marino does not yet have in place a process for completion of templates and exchange of information on rulings.	San Marino is recommended to develop a process to complete the templates on relevant rulings and to ensure that the exchanges of information on rulings occur in accordance with the form and timelines

	under the transparency framework.
San Marino has not exchanged all information on new taxpayers benefitting from the grandfathered IP regime, and new assets of existing taxpayers benefitting from the grandfathered regime as this information was not able to be collected during the year in review.	San Marino is recommended to continue its efforts to identify and exchange information on new entrants to the grandfathered IP regime.
Saudi Arabia	
	No recommendations are made.
Senegal	
Senegal has not yet finalised the steps to have in place its necessary information and gathering process.	Senegal is recommended to finalise its information gathering process, with a review and supervision mechanism, as soon as possible.
Senegal does not have a process to complete the templates on relevant rulings, to make them available to the Competent Authority for exchange of information, and to exchange them with relevant jurisdictions.	Senegal is recommended to develop a process to complete the templates on relevant rulings and to ensure that the exchanges of information on rulings occur in accordance with the form and timelines under the transparency framework.
Serbia	
	No recommendations are made.
Seychelles	
	No recommendations are made.
Sierra Leone	
	No recommendations are made.
Singapore	
	No recommendations are made.
Sint Maarten	
	Review deferred, as the jurisdiction suffered a natural disaster.
Slovak Republic	
	No recommendations are made.
Slovenia	
	No recommendations are made.
South Africa	
	No recommendations are made.
Spain	
Spain has not exchanged information on new assets of existing taxpayers benefitting from the grandfathered regime as this information was not available during the year in review. It is noted that Spain has already started to take steps to amend the tax form adopted in August 2017 to address this, but the tax form was appealed before the National Court and proceedings remained underway for the year in review.	Spain is recommended to continue its efforts to identify and exchange relevant information on new assets of existing taxpayers benefitting from the grandfathered IP regime. This recommendation remains unchanged since the prior year peer review report.
Sri Lanka	
It is not known whether Sri Lanka has an information gathering process in place.	Sri Lanka is recommended to ensure that it has put in place an effective information gathering process to identify all relevant past and future rulings and all potential exchange jurisdictions and to implement a review and supervision mechanism, as soon as possible. This recommendation remains unchanged since the prior year peer review report.
It is not known whether Sri Lanka has a domestic legal framework allowing spontaneous exchange of information on rulings if needed and has a process in place to ensure the timely exchange of information on rulings in the form required by the transparency framework.	Sri Lanka is recommended to put in place a domestic legal framework allowing spontaneous exchange of information on rulings if needed and to ensure the timely exchange of information on rulings in the form required by the transparency framework. This recommendation remains unchanged since the prior year peer review report.
Sweden	
Sweden experienced delays in identifying all potential exchange jurisdictions for future rulings.	Sweden is recommended to continue its efforts to amend its rulings practice to require taxpayers to provide information on all potential exchange jurisdictions for future rulings as soon as possible. This recommendation remains unchanged since the 2016 peer review report and the 2017 peer review report.
Switzerland	
Switzerland experienced some delays in exchanging information on	No recommendation is made because Switzerland completed

past rulings.	exchanges on the delayed past rulings in early 2019 and this is not a recurring issue.
Thailand	
Thailand did not undertake spontaneous exchange of information on all tax rulings within scope of the transparency framework during the year in review.	Thailand is recommended to continue its efforts to complete the templates on relevant rulings and to ensure that the exchanges of information on rulings occur as soon as possible.
Trinidad and Tobago	
	No recommendations are made.
Tunisia	
	No recommendations are made.
Turkey	
Turkey has not been able to identify and exchange information on new entrants to the grandfathered IP regime or to exchange information on all taxpayers benefitting from the third category of assets in the IP regime.	Turkey is recommended to identify and exchange information on new entrants to the grandfathered IP regime and to exchange information on taxpayers benefitting from the third category of IP assets as soon as possible. This recommendation remains unchanged since the prior year peer review report.
Ukraine	
	No recommendations are made.
United Kingdom	
The United Kingdom experienced some delays in exchanging information on future rulings.	No recommendation is made because the United Kingdom has remedied the issue and completed exchanges on the delayed future rulings in the year in review and this is not expected to be a recurring issue.
United States	
	No recommendations are made.
Uruguay	
	No recommendations are made.
Viet Nam	
Viet Nam is currently putting in place a process for completion of templates and exchange of information on rulings.	Viet Nam is recommended to develop a process to complete the templates on relevant rulings and to ensure that the exchanges of information on rulings occur in accordance with the form and timelines under the transparency framework. This recommendation remains unchanged since the prior year peer review report.
Zambia	
	No recommendations are made.

Next steps

The peer review is an annual process that has taken place in 2017, 2018 and 2019, with a fourth review scheduled to take place in 2020. The next annual peer review will continue to track the progress of jurisdictions and the actions taken to respond to any remaining recommendations, and an update on statistics on the exchanges of information. The carrying out of any subsequent reviews after 2020 will be subject to the agreement of the Inclusive Framework on BEPS. First discussions on the effectiveness of the rulings standard, and the format for any further peer review process, will take place in 2020.

Notes

[1] The Action 5 Report, *Countering Harmful Tax Practices More Effectively, Taking Into Account Transparency and Substance* also provides that additional types of rulings could be added to the scope of the transparency framework in the future, where the FHTP and the Inclusive Framework agree that such a ruling could lead to BEPS concerns in the absence of spontaneous information exchange.

1 The review of the BEPS Action 5 standard on the exchange of information on certain tax rulings

Overview of the peer review on the exchange of information on tax rulings

The Action 5 Report (OECD, 2015) is one of the four BEPS minimum standards. It involves two distinct aspects: a review of certain preferential tax regimes and substantial activities in no or only nominal tax jurisdictions to ensure they are not harmful, and the transparency framework. Each of the four BEPS minimum standards is subject to peer review in order to ensure timely and accurate implementation and thus safeguard the level playing field. All members of the Inclusive Framework on BEPS commit to implementing the Action 5 minimum standard and to participating in the peer review, on an equal footing. The peer review of the Action 5 minimum standard is undertaken by the FHTP and approved by the Inclusive Framework on BEPS.

The purpose of a peer review is to ensure the effective and consistent implementation of an agreed standard and to recognise progress made by jurisdictions in this regard. The peer review evaluates the implementation of the standard against an agreed set of criteria. These criteria are set out in terms of reference, which include each of the elements that a jurisdiction needs to demonstrate it has fulfilled in order to show effective implementation of the standard.[1]

The peer review has been conducted in accordance with the agreed methodology. The methodology sets out the process for undertaking the peer review, including the process for collecting the relevant data, the preparation and approval of annual reports, the outputs of the review and the follow up process.

The terms of reference and agreed methodology do not alter the Action 5 minimum standard. Any terms used in the terms of reference or methodology take their meaning from the language and context of the Action 5 Report (OECD, 2015) and the references therein. Any terms in this report which are not included in the glossary take their meaning from the language and context of the Action 5 Report (OECD, 2015).

Outline of the key aspects assessed in the annual report

This annual report contains the findings of the third annual peer review of jurisdictions' compliance with the transparency framework, conducted over the course of 2019. It assesses the implementation of the transparency framework during the 1 January 2018 - 31 December 2018 period.

One of the terms of reference is related to confidentiality (ToR III). Each jurisdiction that receives information on rulings under the transparency framework should ensure that the information received is kept confidential. The confidentiality aspect is reviewed by making sure that the international information exchange mechanisms being used by the jurisdictions include a confidentiality provision that restricts the use of information on rulings and there is the necessary domestic law and information security practices in place to give effect to such restrictions. Given its expertise in this area, the reviews of confidentiality in connection with the transparency framework defer to the work of the Global Forum on Transparency and Exchange of Information for Tax Purposes ("Global Forum") in connection with the standard on Automatic Exchange of Financial Account Information for Tax Purposes. The outcomes of that work are not published and no further references to the review of confidentiality are made in this peer review document.

Where a jurisdiction has not been assessed by the Global Forum, they have been requested to complete the confidentiality and data safeguards questionnaire used as the basis of those assessments, and this has been made available to FHTP members to inform their decision as to which jurisdictions it should exchange with.

The reports on each reviewed jurisdiction cover each of the aspects of the terms of reference, except for confidentiality, which are broken down into three elements. A fourth element applies to jurisdictions which offer IP regimes. These capture the key elements of the transparency framework which are briefly described below. Where recommendations from prior years' peer review reports were not addressed, the report specifically notes this. Jurisdictions are urged to address these recommendations that have remained in place for more than one review.

A. The information gathering process

This involves assessing the processes in place in each of the jurisdictions for identifying past and future rulings that fall within the scope of the transparency framework, and for each of these rulings, identifying the jurisdictions with which the information should be exchanged. With respect to past rulings which do not contain information to identify those jurisdictions for which the tax rulings would be relevant, the jurisdiction issuing the ruling should apply the "best efforts approach" to try to identify this information. The review of the information gathering process also covers any supervision mechanism that the jurisdiction has in place to ensure that all relevant information is captured adequately.

B. The exchange of information

The exchange of information requires the legal and administrative framework to be in place to allow spontaneous exchange of information on the relevant tax rulings and subsequent exchange of the relevant rulings where a valid exchange of information request is received. Information on past rulings was to be spontaneously exchanged pursuant to the relevant deadline outlined in each jurisdiction's report.[2] Information on future rulings is to be spontaneously exchanged as soon as possible and no later than three months after the date on which the ruling becomes available to the Competent Authority for exchange of information. The exchange of information should occur in the agreed standardised form, either using the template contained in Annex C of the Action 5 Report (OECD, 2015), or the OECD XML Schema. Adequate completion of the summary section in the Annex C template or the OECD XML Schema should be ensured through adherence to the instruction sheet to the summary section or the internal FHTP suggested guidance, or an alternate process that allows the summary section to contain sufficient detail for the receiving jurisdiction's tax administration to appropriately assess the potential base erosion and profit shifting risks posed by the ruling where applicable.

The peer review includes reviewing (i) that there is a sufficient domestic and international legal framework for the exchange information related to rulings; (ii) that the summary templates for information on rulings being exchanged are complete and in the appropriate form; and (iii) that the systems are in place to ensure that information on rulings is transmitted to the jurisdiction's Competent Authority for exchange of information without undue delay and exchanged with relevant jurisdictions in accordance with the appropriate timelines.

With respect to the international exchange of information, the terms of reference required jurisdictions to exchange information with Inclusive Framework members being reviewed for the same year, to the extent that an exchange of information agreement was in force for such exchanges and subject to the recipient jurisdiction demonstrating that it would keep the information received confidential.[3]

C. Statistics

Each jurisdiction is required to report statistics on the exchange of information under the transparency framework including (i) the total number of spontaneous exchanges sent, (ii) the number of spontaneous exchanges under each category of ruling and (iii) a list of jurisdictions with which the information was exchanged for each type of ruling.

D. Exchange of information on IP regimes

The review of the transparency framework also includes a review of the spontaneous exchanges of information which are required to occur in respect of certain features of IP regimes, as set out in the Action 5 "nexus approach." This includes, irrespective of whether a tax ruling is provided, identifying and exchanging information on taxpayers which benefit from the third category of IP assets (as defined in paragraph 37 of the Action 5 Report), and taxpayers making use of the option to treat the nexus ratio as a rebuttable presumption (as defined in paragraphs 67- 69 of the Action 5 Report). This aspect of the review is only relevant for those jurisdictions which offer IP regimes, and the minimum standard does not require any jurisdiction to introduce such a regime.

Spontaneous exchange of information is also required with respect to new entrants benefiting from grandfathered IP regimes (regardless of whether a ruling is provided). This applies with respect to IP regimes that were not compliant with the nexus approach, and where jurisdictions have taken steps to abolish the regime, or amend it, as part of the FHTP's regime review process. In some cases, when introducing those legislative changes, jurisdictions have chosen to provide grandfathering to existing taxpayers to provide time to transition to the new rules. Additional spontaneous exchange of information on the taxpayers benefiting from this grandfathering is required where taxpayers or new IP assets were transferred into a non-nexus IP regime in the period between the announcement of forthcoming changes and those changes taking place. The timelines for which these enhanced transparency vary according to the time at which the FHTP reviewed the regime, and are set out in Annex A of the 2017 Progress Report on Preferential Regimes (OECD, 2017[2]).

Response to the report

In addition, jurisdictions had the option to include a response to the report and update on recent developments which occurred after the 2018 year in review. Where included, this reflects the individual jurisdiction's views, and not those of the FHTP or the OECD Secretariat.

Notes

[1] Terms of Reference and Methodology for the review available at www.oecd.org/tax/beps/beps-action-5-harmful-tax-practices-peer-review-transparency-framework.pdf (OECD, 2017).

[2] The Action 5 Report (OECD, 2015) acknowledged that some jurisdictions may need to put in place the domestic or international legal framework in order to comply with the obligations under Action 5. In such cases the timelines for exchange of information on rulings are subject to a jurisdiction's legal framework.

[3] Where a ruling related only to tax years which were not covered by the relevant exchange of information agreement, no exchange of information would be required to occur in respect of that ruling. No negative inference is drawn in the peer review where an exchange was not permitted to occur because of the absence of, or the tax years covered by, an exchange of information agreement, although Inclusive Framework members are encouraged to expand their exchange of information agreements where relevant.

2 Country profiles

Andorra

Andorra has met all aspects of the terms of reference (OECD, 2017[3]) (ToR) for the calendar year 2018 (year in review), except for identifying potential exchange jurisdictions for future rulings (ToR I.4.2.1) and for undertaking spontaneous exchange of information on rulings (ToR II.5). Andorra receives two recommendations on these points for the year in review.

In the prior year report, Andorra received three recommendations. One of these recommendations has been addressed and is removed. The other two recommendations have not been addressed and remain in place.

Andorra can legally issue five types of rulings within the scope of the transparency framework. In practice, Andorra issued rulings within the scope of the transparency framework as follows:

- 177 past rulings;
- For the period 1 April 2017 - 31 December 2017: 44 future rulings; and
- For the year in review: 51 future rulings.

Rulings issued in the form of written inquiries (binding consultations) are published online in anonymised form. Rulings issued in the form of special agreements are published in the Andorran official gazette.[1]

As no exchanges took place, no peer input was received in respect of the exchanges of information on rulings received from Andorra.

Introduction

This peer review covers Andorra's implementation of the BEPS Action 5 transparency framework for the year 2018. The report has four parts, each relating to a key part of the ToR. Each part is discussed in turn. A summary of recommendations is included at the end of this report.

A. The information gathering process

Andorra can legally issue the following five types of rulings within the scope of the transparency framework: (i) preferential regimes;[2] (ii) cross-border unilateral advance pricing arrangements (APAs) and any other cross-border unilateral tax rulings (such as an advance tax ruling) covering transfer pricing or the application of transfer pricing principles; (iii) rulings providing for unilateral downward adjustments; (iv) permanent establishment rulings; and (v) related party conduit rulings.

Past rulings (ToR I.4.1.1, I.4.1.2, I.4.2.1, I.4.2.2)

For Andorra, past rulings are any tax rulings within scope that are issued either: (i) on or after 1 January 2015 but before 1 April 2017; or (ii) on or after 1 January 2012 but before 1 January 2015, provided they were still in effect as at 1 January 2015.

In the prior year peer review report, it was determined that past rulings were able to be identified but that Andorra was not able to obtain information on potential exchange jurisdictions.

For the year in review, the tax authority and the EOI division reviewed the database list of issued rulings, the information contained in the ruling request and related annexes in order to extract information about the potential exchange jurisdictions. Andorra also used information from third-party sources (e.g. official registers). Andorra has used the "best efforts approach" for all past rulings and the recommendation is removed. In addition, although Andorra was able to obtain all relevant information in most cases using the best efforts approach, Andorra is considering taking steps beyond the best efforts approach, by approaching the taxpayer to obtain any outstanding information on potential exchange jurisdictions.

Future rulings (ToR I.4.1.1, I.4.1.2, I.4.2.1)

For Andorra, future rulings are any tax rulings within scope that are issued on or after 1 April 2017.

In the prior year peer review report, it was determined future rulings were able to be identified, but that the information on potential exchange jurisdictions was not always being collected, and instead this was being performed by the application of the "best efforts approach." The prior year report noted that Andorra intended to amend the application process to require the taxpayer to identify all relevant jurisdictions when requesting the ruling. However, this amendment did not take place during the year in review. Andorra is therefore recommended to continue its efforts to ensure that all potential exchange jurisdictions are identified swiftly for all future rulings.

Review and supervision (ToR I.4.3)

In the prior year peer review reports, it was determined that Andorra's review and supervision mechanism was sufficient to meet the minimum standard. Andorra's implementation in this regard remains unchanged, and therefore continues to meet the minimum standard.

Conclusion on section A

Andorra has met all of the ToR for the information gathering process except for identifying all potential exchange jurisdictions for future rulings (ToR I.4.2.1). Andorra is recommended to ensure that all potential exchange jurisdictions are identified swiftly for all future rulings.

B. The exchange of information

Legal basis for spontaneous exchange of information (ToR II.5.1, II.5.2)

Andorra has the necessary domestic legal basis to exchange information spontaneously. Andorra notes that there are no legal or practical impediments that prevent the spontaneous exchange of information on rulings as contemplated in the Action 5 minimum standard.

Andorra has international agreements permitting spontaneous exchange of information, including being a party to the (i) *Multilateral Convention on Mutual Administrative Assistance in Tax Matters: Amended by the 2010 Protocol* (OECD/Council of Europe, 2011[4]) ("the Convention") and (ii) double tax agreements in force with 27 jurisdictions.[3]

Completion and exchange of templates (ToR II.5.3, II.5.4, II.5.5, II.5.6, II.5.7)

In the prior year peer review report, it was determined that Andorra's process for the completion and exchange of temples met the ToR, except for undertaking spontaneous exchange of information on tax rulings within scope of the transparency framework (ToR II.5). Therefore, Andorra was recommended to complete the templates for all relevant rulings and to ensure that the exchanges of information on rulings occur as soon as possible.

During the year in review, no further steps were taken to finalise the completion and exchange of templates. Andorra intends to require taxpayers to provide all relevant information needed to complete the template contained in Annex C of the 2015 Action 5 Report. This obligation is being considered for inclusion in an amendment to the relevant regulations in 2019. Andorra also intends to prepare an internal note to ensure that information on rulings is made available to the Competent Authority responsible for exchange of information without undue delay.

As there were no exchanges for the year in review, no data on the timeliness of exchanges can be reported.

Conclusion on section B

Andorra has met all of the ToR for the information gathering process except for undertaking spontaneous exchange of information on tax rulings within scope of the transparency framework (ToR II.5) and Andorra is recommended to complete the templates for all relevant rulings and to ensure that all information on past and future rulings is exchanged as soon as possible.

C. Statistics (ToR IV)

As there was no information on rulings exchanged by Andorra for the year in review, no statistics can be reported.

D. Matters related to intellectual property regimes (ToR I.4.1.3)

Andorra offers an intellectual property regime (IP regime)[4] that is subject to the transparency requirements under the Action 5 Report (OECD, 2015[5]). It states that the identification of the benefitting taxpayers will occur as follows:

- ***New entrants benefitting from the grandfathered IP regime***: No enhanced transparency requirements apply, as follows. During the year in review, Andorra amended the IP regime by implementing the nexus approach. The previous regime has been closed-off, and although grandfathering was provided, it only applies to entrants that benefited from the regime prior to the relevant date from which enhanced transparency obligations would apply.
- ***Third category of IP assets***: not applicable as the regime does not allow the third category of IP assets to qualify for the benefits.
- ***Taxpayers making use of the option to treat the nexus ratio as a rebuttable presumption***: not applicable as the regime does not allow the nexus ratio to be treated as a rebuttable presumption.

Summary of recommendations on implementation of the transparency framework

Aspect of implementation of the transparency framework that should be improved	Recommendation for improvement
Andorra experienced difficulties in identifying all potential exchange jurisdictions for future rulings.	Andorra is recommended to ensure that all potential exchange jurisdictions are identified swiftly for all future rulings. This recommendation remains unchanged since the prior year peer review report.
Andorra did not undertake spontaneous exchange of information on tax rulings within scope of the transparency framework during the year in review.	Andorra is recommended to continue its efforts to complete the templates for all relevant rulings and to ensure that all information on past and future rulings is exchanged as soon as possible. This recommendation remains unchanged since the prior year peer review report.

Notes

[1] Available at https://www.impostos.ad/comunicats-tecnics-i-consultes-vinculants

[2] With respect to the following preferential regimes: 1) Holding company regime, 2) Intercompany and financing regime, 3) Companies involved in international trade and 4) Companies involved in the international exploitation of intangible assets regime.

[3] Parties to the Convention are available here: www.oecd.org/tax/exchange-of-tax-information/convention-on-mutual-administrative-assistance-in-tax-matters.htm Andorra also has double tax agreements with Argentina, Australia, Austria, Belgium, Czech Republic, Denmark, Faroe Islands, Finland, France, Germany, Greenland, Iceland, Italy, Korea, Liechtenstein, Luxembourg, Malta, Monaco, Netherlands, Norway, Poland, Portugal, San Marino, Spain, Sweden, Switzerland and United Arab Emirates.

[4] Special regime for exploitation of certain intangible assets.

Angola

Angola is taking steps to implement the legal basis for the transparency framework and to commence administrative preparations (in line with the terms of reference (OECD, 2017[3]) (ToR)) to ensure that it finalises its information gathering process (ToR I.4), and information on rulings will be identified and exchanged in a timely manner (ToR II.5). Angola receives two recommendations on these points for the year in review.

In the prior year report, Angola had received two recommendations. As they have not been addressed, these recommendations remain in place.

Angola can legally issue five types of rulings within the scope of the transparency framework. In practice, Angola issued rulings within the scope of the transparency framework as follows:

- No past rulings;
- For the period 1 April 2017 - 31 December 2017: one future ruling; and
- For the year in review: no future rulings.

As no exchanges took place, no peer input was received in respect of the exchanges of information on rulings received from Angola.

Introduction

This peer review covers Angola's implementation of the BEPS Action 5 transparency framework for the year 2018. The report has four parts, each relating to a key part of the ToR. Each part is discussed in turn. A summary of recommendations is included at the end of this report.

A. The information gathering process

Angola can legally issue the five following types of rulings within the scope of the transparency framework: (i) cross-border unilateral advance pricing agreements (APAs) and any other cross-border unilateral tax rulings (such as an advance tax ruling) covering transfer pricing or the application of transfer pricing principles; (ii) rulings providing a downward adjustment of taxable profits; (iii) permanent establishment rulings; and (iv) related party conduit rulings.

Past rulings (ToR I.4.1.1, I.4.1.2, I.4.2.1, I.4.2.2)

For Angola, past rulings are any tax rulings within scope that are issued either: (i) on or after 1 January 2015 but before 1 April 2017; or (ii) on or after 1 January 2012 but before 1 January 2015, provided they were still in effect as at 1 January 2015.

In the prior year peer review report, it was determined that Angola has not recorded the information on the tax rulings issued with the necessary level of detail to meet the standard of the transparency framework and that the necessary information on past rulings is unlikely to be found on the available records. Angola noted that it would seek to apply the best efforts approach once all past rulings have been identified. Therefore, Angola was recommended to finalise its information gathering process for identifying all past rulings and potential exchange jurisdictions.

During the year in review, no additional implementation steps were taken.

Future rulings (ToR I.4.1.1, I.4.1.2, I.4.2.1)

For Angola, future rulings are any tax rulings within scope that are issued on or after 1 April 2017.

In the prior year peer review report, it was determined that Angola was following guidelines covering which rulings would fall in the scope of the transparency framework and what information should be kept in order to meet the level of detail required by the transparency framework. Angola noted that it is developing a system to record and track all future rulings in order to be able to conduct an effective analysis of future rulings issued.

During the year in review, no additional implementation steps were taken.

Review and supervision (ToR I.4.3)

In the prior year peer review report, it was determined that Angola did not yet have a review and supervision mechanism for past rulings under the transparency framework. Angola started to implement a review and supervision mechanism for future rulings by requiring that the information on tax rulings be recorded in hard copy and electronically in spreadsheets with the name, date and topic of the information requested or issue being complained or appealed. However, during the year in review, no additional implementation steps were taken.

Conclusion on section A

Angola is recommended to finalise its information gathering process for identifying all past and future rulings and all potential exchange jurisdictions, with a review and supervision mechanism, as soon as possible (ToR I.4).

B. The exchange of information

Legal basis for spontaneous exchange of information (ToR II.5.1, II.5.2)

Angola is currently in the process of putting in place the necessary domestic legal basis to exchange information spontaneously.

Angola does not have currently in effect an agreement that would allow for spontaneous exchange of information under the transparency framework. Angola is not a Party to the *Multilateral Convention on Mutual Administrative Assistance in Tax Matters: Amended by the 2010 Protocol* (OECD/Council of Europe, 2011) ("the Convention"). Angola is encouraged to continue its efforts to expand its international exchange of information instruments to be able to exchange rulings. It is however noted that jurisdictions are assessed on their compliance with the transparency framework in respect of the exchange of information network in effect for the year of the particular annual review.

Completion and exchange of templates (ToR II.5.3, II.5.4, II.5.5, II.5.6, II.5.7)

In the prior year peer review report, it was determined that Angola is still developing a process to complete the templates on relevant rulings, to make them available to the Competent Authority for exchange of information and to exchange them with relevant jurisdictions. Angola explained in the prior year review that an information exchange unit had been recently created to assume the role of the Competent Authority and legislation and procedures for the functioning of the unit are being developed. During the year in review, no update has been provided on this.

As Angola did not have the necessary legal basis to conduct exchanges, no data on the timeliness of exchanges can be reported.

Conclusion on section B

Angola is recommended to continue to put in place a domestic legal framework allowing spontaneous exchange of information on rulings and to continue its efforts to complete the templates for all relevant rulings and to ensure that the exchanges of information on rulings occur as soon as possible (ToR II.5).

C. Statistics (ToR IV)

As there was no information on rulings exchanged by Angola for the year in review, no statistics can be reported.

D. Matters related to intellectual property regimes (ToR I.4.1.3)

Angola does not offer an intellectual property regime for which transparency requirements under the Action 5 Report (OECD, 2015[5]) were imposed.

Summary of recommendations on implementation of the transparency framework

Aspect of implementation of the transparency framework that should be improved	Recommendation for improvement
Angola has not yet finalised the steps to have in place its necessary information and gathering process.	Angola is recommended to finalise its information gathering process for identifying all past and future rulings and all potential exchange jurisdictions, with a review and supervision mechanism, as soon as possible. This recommendation remains unchanged since the prior year peer review report.
Angola has not yet finalised the steps to have effective compulsory spontaneous exchange of information on the tax rulings within the scope of the transparency framework.	Angola is recommended to continue to put in place a domestic legal framework allowing spontaneous exchange of information on rulings and to continue its efforts to complete the templates for all relevant rulings and to ensure that the exchanges of information on rulings occur as soon as possible. This recommendation remains unchanged since the prior year peer review report.

Argentina

Argentina has met all aspects of the terms of reference (OECD, 2017[3]) (ToR) for the calendar year 2018 (year in review) and no recommendations are made.

In the prior year report, Argentina had received one recommendation. Argentina has resolved this issue and therefore the prior year recommendation is removed.

Argentina can legally issue five types of rulings within the scope of the transparency framework. In practice, Argentina issued rulings within the scope of the transparency framework as follows:

- Two past rulings;
- For the period 1 April 2016 - 31 December 2016: no future rulings;
- For the calendar year 2017: one future ruling, and
- For the year in review: no future rulings.

These rulings are published in anonymised form.[1]

As no exchanges were required to take place during the year in review, no peer input was received in respect of the exchanges of information on rulings received from Argentina.

Introduction

This peer review covers Argentina's implementation of the BEPS Action 5 transparency framework for the year 2018. The report has four parts, each relating to a key part of the ToR. Each part is discussed in turn. A summary of recommendations is included at the end of this report.

A. The information gathering process

Argentina can legally issue five types of ruling within the scope of the transparency framework: (i) rulings related to preferential regimes[2]; (ii) cross-border unilateral advance pricing agreements (APAs) and any other cross-border unilateral tax rulings (such as an advance tax ruling) covering transfer pricing or the application of transfer pricing principles; (iii) cross-border rulings giving a unilateral downward adjustment to the taxpayer's taxable profits in the country giving the ruling; (iv) permanent establishment rulings; and (v) related party conduit rulings.

Past rulings (ToR I.4.1.1, I.4.1.2, I.4.2.1, I.4.2.2)

For Argentina, past rulings are any tax rulings within scope that are issued either: (i) on or after 1 January 2014 but before 1 April 2016; or (ii) on or after 1 January 2010 but before 1 January 2014, provided they were still in effect as at 1 January 2014.

In the prior years' peer review reports, it was determined that Argentina's undertakings to identify past rulings and all potential exchange jurisdictions were sufficient to meet the minimum standard. Argentina's implementation in this regard remains unchanged, and therefore continues to meet the minimum standard.

Future rulings (ToR I.4.1.1, I.4.1.2, I.4.2.1)

For Argentina, future rulings are any tax rulings within scope that are issued on or after 1 April 2016.

In the prior year peer review report, it was determined that Argentina's undertakings to identify future rulings and all potential exchange jurisdictions met all the ToR, except for identifying one future ruling (ToR I.4.1.2). Therefore, Argentina was recommended to continue its work to improve its information-gathering process on future rulings as soon as possible.

The process for identifying future rulings involves coordination between the Deputy General Direction for Technical and Legal Tax Matters (which is responsible for issuing rulings) and the Directorate for International Affairs, and verification against the public repository of rulings. During the year in review, Argentina took steps to enhance the co-ordination with the relevant areas to ensure that the identification of future rulings is made in a timely manner, and to ensure that the error made in the prior year would not be repeated. In light of this, the recommendation on identifying future rulings is removed.

Argentina further noted that the Argentinian Tax Administration is finalising the modifications to its rulings regulation to formalise the process, including to require taxpayers to provide the relevant information on potential exchange jurisdictions upon submitting an application for a ruling, instead of drawing on information in the file and the use of its powers to request additional information from the taxpayer. This will be reviewed in the subsequent peer review.

Review and supervision (ToR I.4.3)

In the prior years' peer review reports, it was determined that Argentina's review and supervision mechanism was sufficient to meet the minimum standard. Argentina's implementation in this regard remains unchanged, and therefore continues to meet the minimum standard.

Conclusion on section A

Argentina has met all of the ToR for the information gathering process and no recommendations are made.

B. The exchange of information

Legal basis for spontaneous exchange of information (ToR II.5.1, II.5.2)

Argentina has the necessary domestic legal basis to exchange information spontaneously. Argentina notes that there are no legal or practical impediments that prevent the spontaneous exchange of information on rulings as contemplated in the Action 5 minimum standard.

Argentina has international agreements permitting spontaneous exchange of information, including being a party to the (i) *Multilateral Convention on Mutual Administrative Assistance in Tax Matters: Amended by the 2010 Protocol* (OECD/Council of Europe, 2011[4]) ("the Convention"), (ii) bilateral agreements in force with 23 jurisdictions.[3]

Completion and exchange of templates (ToR II.5.3, II.5.4, II.5.5, II.5.6, II.5.7)

In the prior years' peer review reports, it was determined that Argentina's process for the completion and exchange of templates were sufficient to meet the minimum standard. Argentina's implementation in this regard remains unchanged and therefore continues to meet the minimum standard.

As Argentina did not issue any rulings in scope of the transparency framework in the relevant period, Argentina was not required to exchange any information on rulings in the year in review and no data on the timeliness of exchanges can be reported.

Conclusion on section B

Argentina has the necessary legal basis for spontaneous exchange of information, and a process for completing the templates in a timely way. Argentina has met all of the ToR for the exchange of information process and no recommendations are made.

C. Statistics (ToR IV)

As there was no information on rulings exchanged by Argentina for the year in review, no statistical data can be reported.

D. Matters related to intellectual property regimes (ToR I.4.1.3)

Argentina does not offer an intellectual property regime for which transparency requirements under the Action 5 Report (OECD, 2015[5]) were imposed.

Summary of recommendations on implementation of the transparency framework

Aspect of implementation of the transparency framework that should be improved	Recommendation for improvement
	No recommendations are made.

Notes

[1] Available at http://biblioteca.afip.gob.ar/search/query/BoletinesDGI.aspx (accessed 8 July 2019) and http://biblioteca.afip.gob.ar/estaticos/consultasVinculantes/index.aspx (accessed 8 July 2019).

[2] With respect to the following preferential regime: Promotional Regime for Software Industry.

[3] Parties to the Convention are available here: www.oecd.org/tax/exchange-of-tax-information/convention-on-mutual-administrative-assistance-in-tax-matters.htm. Argentina also has double tax agreements with Aruba, Australia, Azerbaijan, Belgium, Bolivia, Brazil, Canada, Chile, Denmark, Ecuador, Finland, France, Italy, Mexico, Netherlands, Norway, Peru, Russia, Spain, Sweden, United States, United Kingdom and Venezuela.

Aruba

Aruba has met all aspects of the terms of reference (OECD, 2017[3]) (ToR) for the calendar year 2018 (year in review) that can be met in the absence of rulings being issued.

This is Aruba's first review of implementation of the transparency framework.

Aruba can legally issue five types of rulings within the scope of the transparency framework but in practice has not issued any rulings within the scope of the transparency framework.

As no rulings have been issued in practice, no exchanges of information were required to be conducted. Therefore no peer input was received in respect of the exchanges of information on rulings received from Aruba.

Introduction

This peer review covers Aruba's implementation of the BEPS Action 5 transparency framework for the year 2018. The report has four parts, each relating to a key part of the ToR. Each part is discussed in turn. A summary of recommendations is included at the end of this report.

A. The information gathering process

Aruba can legally issue the following five types of rulings within the scope of the transparency framework: (i) preferential regimes;[1] (ii) cross-border unilateral APAs and any other cross-border unilateral tax rulings (such as an advance tax ruling) covering transfer pricing or the application of transfer pricing principles; (iii) rulings providing for unilateral downward adjustments; and (iv) permanent establishment rulings; and (v) related party conduit rulings. Rulings are issued by the Inspector of Taxes upon appropriate application by a taxpayer.

Past rulings (ToR I.4.1.1, I.4.1.2, I.4.2.1, I.4.2.2)

For Aruba, past rulings are any tax rulings issued prior to 1 September 2018. However, there is no obligation under the terms of the transparency framework for Aruba to conduct spontaneous exchange information on past rulings under the terms of the peer review.

Future rulings (ToR I.4.1.1, I.4.1.2, I.4.2.1)

For Aruba, future rulings are any tax rulings within scope that are issued on or after 1 September 2018.

No rulings were issued by Aruba during the future rulings period in the year of review. However, Aruba indicates that there are processes in place for the issuance, review and record keeping of rulings for the purposes of the transparency framework.

Applications for rulings in Aruba must be accompanied by prescribed information, such as the kind of ruling being sought, organisational structure chart of the taxpayer, a complete description of the relevant facts and the purpose of the proposed transactions, and an indication of the effect of the transaction in other jurisdictions. All tax rulings are stored in a database with the issuance date, administrative reference details, and marked according to the type of ruling under the transparency framework. When a taxpayer applies for a ruling, the application must include all information on relevant exchange jurisdictions, which would cover all potential exchange jurisdictions for the purposes of the transparency framework.

Review and supervision (ToR I.4.3)

The accuracy of the information gathering process and the identification of rulings in scope of the transparency framework is supervised by the Inspector of Taxes and the Director of Taxes. The Director of Taxes is the Competent Authority for exchange of information in Aruba.

Conclusion on section A

Aruba has met all of the ToR for the information gathering process and no recommendations are made.

B. The exchange of information

Legal basis for spontaneous exchange of information (ToR II.5.1, II.5.2)

Aruba has the necessary domestic legal basis to exchange information spontaneously. Aruba notes that there are no legal or practical impediments that prevent the spontaneous exchange of information on rulings as contemplated in the Action 5 minimum standard.

Aruba is a party to international agreements permitting spontaneous exchange of information, including (i) the *Multilateral Convention on Mutual Administrative Assistance in Tax Matters: Amended by the 2010 Protocol* (OECD/Council of Europe, 2011) ("the Convention"), and (ii) double tax agreements and tax information exchange agreements in force with 25 jurisdictions.[2]

Completion and exchange of templates (ToR II.5.3, II.5.4, II.5.5, II.5.6, II.5.7)

Aruba notes that the Inspector of Taxes would be responsible for the completion of the information required in the template contained in Annex C of the Action 5 Report (OECD, 2015), which would include providing a detailed summary of the ruling following the instructions in Annex C. Final review of the template would be conducted by the Director of Taxes. After the Director of Taxes is satisfied with the template, the Director of Taxes would instruct the Fiscal Intelligence and Fraud Team (FIOT) to conduct the spontaneous exchange of information with relevant exchange jurisdictions. As the Director of Taxes is also the Competent Authority in Aruba, all tax rulings would be readily available to the Competent Authority and no delays are expected.

As Aruba did not issue any rulings in scope of the transparency framework in the relevant period, Aruba was not required to exchange any information on rulings in the year in review and no data on the timeliness of exchanges can be reported.

Conclusion on section B

Aruba has the necessary legal basis to undertake spontaneous exchange of information. Aruba has met all of the ToR for the exchange of information process that can be met in the absence of rulings being issued and exchanged in practice and no recommendations are made.

C. Statistics (ToR IV)

As there was no information on rulings exchanged by Aruba for the year in review, no statistics can be reported.

D. Matters related to intellectual property regimes (ToR I.4.1.3)

Aruba offers an intellectual property regime (IP regime).[3] However, for the year in review no transparency requirements under the Action 5 Report (OECD, 2015[5]) were relevant, as follows:

- ***New entrants benefitting from the grandfathered IP regime***: not applicable for the year in review, because Aruba is currently in the process of eliminating/amending the regime and has not taken a decision yet on whether it will provide grandfathering to existing taxpayers.
- ***Third category of IP assets***: not applicable to this regime, which was in the year in review in the process of being eliminated/amended.

- ***Taxpayers making use of the option to treat the nexus ratio as a rebuttable presumption***: not applicable to this regime, which was in the year in review in the process of being eliminated/amended.

Summary of recommendations on implementation of the transparency framework

Aspect of implementation of the transparency framework that should be improved	Recommendation for improvement
	No recommendations are made.

Notes

[1] With respect to the following preferential regimes: 1) Exempt companies, 2) Investment promotion, 3) Free zone, 4) Transparency regime and 5) Shipping regime.

[2] Parties to the Convention are available here: www.oecd.org/tax/exchange-of-tax-information/convention-on-mutual-administrative-assistance-in-tax-matters.htm Aruba also has double tax agreements with Antigua and Barbuda, Argentina, Australia, Bahamas, Bermuda, British Virgin Islands, Canada, Cayman Islands, Czech Republic, Denmark, Faroe Islands, Finland, France, Greenland, Iceland, Mexico, Netherlands, Norway, Saint Kitts and Nevis, Saint Lucia, Saint Vincent and the Grenadines, Spain, Sweden, United Kingdom and United States.

[3] Exempt company.

Australia

Australia has met all aspects of the terms of reference (ToR) for the calendar year 2018 (year in review) and no recommendations are made.

In the prior year report, Australia did not receive any recommendations.

Australia can legally issue four types of rulings within the scope of the transparency framework. In practice, Australia has issued rulings within the scope of the transparency framework as follows:[1]

- 202 past rulings;
- For the period 1 April 2016 - 31 December 2016: 15 future rulings;
- For the calendar year 2017: 13 future rulings, and
- For the year in review: 10 future rulings.

Australia publishes edited anonymised versions of private rulings on the ATO Legal Database (excluding the unilateral APAs which are not published due to privacy reasons).[2]

Peer input was received from five jurisdictions in respect of the exchanges of information on rulings received from Australia. The input was generally positive, noting that information was complete, in a correct format and almost all received in a timely manner.

Introduction

This peer review covers Australia's implementation of the BEPS Action 5 transparency framework for the year 2018. The report has four parts, each relating to a key part of the ToR. Each part is discussed in turn. A summary of recommendations is included at the end of this report.

A. The information gathering process

Australia can legally issue the four following types of rulings within the scope of the transparency framework: (i) rulings related to preferential regimes;[3] (ii) cross-border unilateral advance pricing arrangements (APAs) and any other cross-border unilateral tax rulings (such as an advance tax ruling) covering transfer pricing or the application of transfer pricing principles; (iii) permanent establishment rulings; and (iv) related party conduit rulings.

Past rulings (ToR I.4.1.1, I.4.1.2, I.4.2.1, I.4.2.2)

For Australia, past rulings are any tax rulings within scope that are issued either: (i) on or after 1 January 2014 but before 1 April 2016; or (ii) on or after 1 January 2010 but before 1 January 2014, provided they were still in effect as at 1 January 2014.

In the prior years' peer review reports, it was determined that Australia's undertakings to identify past rulings and all potential exchange jurisdictions were sufficient to meet the minimum standard. Australia's implementation in this regard remains unchanged, and therefore continues to meet the minimum standard.

Future rulings (ToR I.4.1.1, I.4.1.2, I.4.2.1)

For Australia, future rulings are any tax rulings within scope that are issued on or after 1 April 2016.

In the prior years' peer review reports, it was determined that Australia's undertakings to identify future rulings and all potential exchange jurisdictions were sufficient to meet the minimum standard. Australia's implementation in this regard remains unchanged, and therefore continues to meet the minimum standard.

Review and supervision (ToR I.4.3)

In the prior years' peer review reports, it was determined that the Australia's review and supervision mechanism was sufficient to meet the minimum standard. The Australia's implementation in this regard remains unchanged, and therefore continues to meet the minimum standard.

Conclusion on section A

Australia has met all of the ToR for the information gathering process and no recommendations are made.

B. The exchange of information

Legal basis for spontaneous exchange of information (ToR II.5.1, II.5.2)

Australia has the necessary domestic legal basis to exchange information spontaneously. Australia notes that there are no legal or practical impediments that prevent the spontaneous exchange of information on rulings as contemplated in the Action 5 minimum standard.

Australia is a party to international agreements permitting spontaneous exchange of information, including (i) the *Multilateral Convention on Mutual Administrative Assistance in Tax Matters: Amended by the 2010 Protocol* (OECD/Council of Europe, 2011) ("the Convention") and (ii) double tax agreements in force with 43 jurisdictions.[4]

Completion and exchange of templates (ToR II.5.3, II.5.4, II.5.5, II.5.6, II.5.7)

In the prior years' peer review reports, it was determined that Australia's completion and exchange of templates were sufficient to meet the minimum standard. Australia's implementation in this regard remains unchanged, and therefore continues to meet the minimum standard.

For the year in review, the timeliness of exchanges is as follows:

Past rulings in the scope of the transparency framework	Number of exchanges transmitted by 31 December 2018	Delayed exchanges		
		Number of exchanges not transmitted by 31 December 2018	Reasons for the delays	Any other comments
	77	2	N/A	The exchanges on past rulings includes 50 delayed exchanges from the prior year report.
Future rulings in the scope of the transparency framework	Number of exchanges transmitted within three months of the information becoming available to the competent authority or immediately after legal impediments have been lifted	Delayed exchanges		
		Number of exchanges transmitted later than three months of the information on rulings becoming available to the competent authority	Reasons for the delays	Any other comments
	45	2	A small amount of delayed rulings result from minor administrative oversight.	N/A
Total	122	4		

Follow up requests received for exchange of the ruling	Number	Average time to provide response	Number of requests not answered
	0	N/A	N/A

Conclusion on section B

Australia has the necessary legal basis for spontaneous exchange of information and a process for completing the templates in a timely way. Australia has completed exchanges in a timely manner generally, with some minor delays due to minor administrative oversight or the recipient jurisdiction not having confirmed whether there are systems in place to receive exchanges. Australia has met all of the ToR for the exchange of information process and no recommendations are made.

C. Statistics (ToR IV)

The statistics for the year in review are as follows:

Category of ruling	Number of exchanges	Jurisdictions exchanged with
Ruling related to a preferential regime	2	*De minimis* rule applies
Cross-border unilateral advance pricing agreements (APAs) and any other cross-border unilateral tax rulings (such as an advance tax ruling) covering transfer pricing or the application of transfer pricing principles	98	Argentina, Brazil, Canada, China (People's Republic of), Denmark, France, Germany, Guernsey, India, Ireland, Israel, Italy, Jersey, Korea, Luxembourg, Malaysia, Malta, Netherlands, Philippines, Russia, Singapore, Switzerland, United Kingdom, United States
Cross-border rulings providing for a unilateral downward adjustment to the taxpayer's taxable profits that is not directly reflected in the taxpayer's financial / commercial accounts	0	N/A
Permanent establishment rulings	21	Denmark, France, Germany, Ireland, New Zealand, Singapore, Switzerland, United States
Related party conduit rulings	1	*De minimis* rule applies
De minimis rule	N/A	N/A
IP regimes: total exchanges on taxpayers benefitting from the third category of IP assets, new entrants benefitting from grandfathered IP regimes; and taxpayers making use of the option to treat the nexus ratio as a rebuttable presumption	N/A	N/A
Total	122	

D. Matters related to intellectual property regimes (ToR I.4.1.3)

Australia does not offer an intellectual property regime for which transparency requirements under the Action 5 Report (OECD, 2015[5]) were imposed.

Summary of recommendations on implementation of the transparency framework

Aspect of implementation of the transparency framework that should be improved	Recommendation for improvement
	No recommendations are made.

Notes

[1] In the prior years' peer review reports, Australia reported that it had 208 past rulings, nine future rulings for the period 1 April 2016 – 31 December 2016, and 22 future rulings for the calendar year 2017. However, upon subsequent review, Australia has provided revised number of rulings for both past and future rulings due to a record-keeping error. This clerical error with regard to statistics does not impact the correct

identification and exchange of the relevant rulings. This issue has been rectified, and all rulings in scope of the transparency framework will now be recorded on one register.

[2] Available at https://www.ato.gov.au/law/#Law.

[3] With respect to the following preferential regimes: 1) Offshore banking unit regime and 2) Conduit foreign income regime.

[4] Parties to the Convention are available here: www.oecd.org/tax/exchange-of-tax-information/convention-on-mutual-administrative-assistance-in-tax-matters.htm. Australia also has bilateral agreements with Argentina, Austria, Belgium, Canada, Chile, China (People's Republic of), Czech Republic, Denmark, Fiji, Finland, France, Germany, Hungary, India, Indonesia, Ireland, Italy, Japan, Kiribati, Korea, Malaysia, Malta, Mexico, Netherlands, New Zealand, Norway, Papua New Guinea, Philippines, Poland, Romania, Russia, Singapore, Slovak Republic, South Africa, Spain, Sri Lanka, Sweden, Switzerland, Chinese Taipei, Thailand, Turkey, United Kingdom, United States and Viet Nam.

Austria

Austria has met all aspects of the terms of reference (OECD, 2017[3]) (ToR) for the calendar year 2018 (year in review) and no recommendations are made.

In the prior year report, Austria had received one recommendation for the timely exchange of information on past and future rulings (ToR II.5.6). This recommendation has been addressed and is removed.

Austria can legally issue one type of ruling within the scope of the transparency framework. In practice, Austria issued rulings within the scope of the transparency framework as follows:

- 59 past rulings;
- For the period 1 April 2016 - 31 December 2016: 13 future rulings;
- For the calendar year 2017: 10 future rulings, and
- For the year in review: nine future rulings.

Peer input was received from one jurisdiction in respect of the exchanges of information on rulings received from Austria. The input was positive, although it indicated one error where information was missing. Austria quickly resolved the issue and provided the completed information.

Introduction

This peer review covers Austria's implementation of the BEPS Action 5 transparency framework for the year 2018. The report has four parts, each relating to a key part of the ToR. Each part is discussed in turn. A summary of recommendations is included at the end of this report.

A. The information gathering process

Austria can legally issue one type of ruling within the scope of the transparency framework: cross-border unilateral advance pricing arrangements (APAs) and any other cross-border unilateral tax rulings (such as an advance tax ruling) covering transfer pricing or the application of transfer pricing principles

Past rulings (ToR I.4.1.1, I.4.1.2, I.4.2.1, I.4.2.2)

For Austria, past rulings are any tax rulings within scope that are issued either: (i) on or after 1 January 2014 but before 1 April 2016; or (ii) on or after 1 January 2010 but before 1 January 2014, provided they were still in effect as at 1 January 2014.

In the prior years' peer review reports, it was determined that Austria's undertakings to identify past rulings and all potential exchange jurisdictions were sufficient to meet the minimum standard. Austria's implementation in this regard remains unchanged, and therefore continues to meet the minimum standard.

Future rulings (ToR I.4.1.1, I.4.1.2, I.4.2.1)

For Austria, future rulings are any tax rulings within scope that are issued on or after 1 April 2016.

In the prior year peer review report, it was determined that Austria's undertakings to identify future rulings and all potential exchange jurisdictions were sufficient to meet the minimum standard. Austria's implementation in this regard remains unchanged, and therefore continues to meet the minimum standard.

Review and supervision (ToR I.4.3)

In the prior years' peer review reports, it was determined that Austria's review and supervision mechanism was sufficient to meet the minimum standard. Austria's implementation in this regard remains unchanged, and therefore continues to meet the minimum standard.

Conclusion on section A

Austria has met all of the ToR for the information gathering process and no recommendations are made.

B. The exchange of information

Legal basis for spontaneous exchange of information (ToR II.5.1, II.5.2)

Austria has the necessary domestic legal basis to exchange information spontaneously. Austria notes that there are no legal or practical impediments that prevent the spontaneous exchange of information on rulings as contemplated in the Action 5 minimum standard.

Austria has international agreements permitting spontaneous exchange of information, including being a party to the (i) *Multilateral Convention on Mutual Administrative Assistance in Tax Matters: Amended by the 2010 Protocol* (OECD/Council of Europe, 2011[4]) ("the Convention"), (ii) the Directive 2011/16/EU with all other European Union Member States, (iii) double tax agreements in force with 70 jurisdictions and (iv) tax information exchange agreements with seven jurisdictions.[1]

Completion and exchange of templates (ToR II.5.3, II.5.4, II.5.5, II.5.6, II.5.7)

In the prior years' peer review reports, it was determined that Austria's process for the completion and exchange of templates were sufficient to meet the minimum standard. Austria's implementation in this regard remains unchanged and therefore continues to meet the minimum standard.

For the year in review, the timeliness of exchanges is as follows:

Past rulings in the scope of the transparency framework	Number of exchanges transmitted by 31 December 2018	Delayed exchanges		
		Number of exchanges not transmitted by 31 December 2018	Reasons for the delays	Any other comments
	0	0	N/A	N/A
Future rulings in the scope of the transparency framework	Number of exchanges transmitted within three months of the information becoming available to the competent authority or immediately after legal impediments have been lifted	Delayed exchanges		
		Number of exchanges transmitted later than three months of the information on rulings becoming available to the competent authority	Reasons for the delays	Any other comments
	66	0	N/A	N/A
Total	102	0		

Follow up requests received for exchange of the ruling	Number	Average time to provide response	Number of requests not answered
	1	60 days	0

The prior year peer review report determined that Austria had experienced some delays in exchanging information on past and future rulings. These issues have now been resolved and all outstanding information has been exchanged, and no further delays have been encountered. As such the prior year recommendation has been removed.

Conclusion on section B

Austria has the necessary legal basis for spontaneous exchange of information, a process for completing the templates in a timely way and has completed all exchanges. Austria has met all of the ToR for the exchange of information process and no recommendations are made.

C. Statistics (ToR IV)

The statistics for the year in review are as follows:

Category of ruling	Number of exchanges	Jurisdictions exchanged with
Ruling related to a preferential regime	N/A	N/A
Cross-border unilateral advance pricing agreements (APAs) and any other cross-border unilateral tax rulings (such as an advance tax ruling) covering transfer pricing or the application of	102	Australia, Brazil, Czech Republic, Germany, Hungary, Ireland, Italy, Korea, Liechtenstein, Luxembourg, Netherlands, Russia, Slovenia, Spain, Sweden, Switzerland, United Kingdom,

transfer pricing principles		United States
Cross-border rulings providing for a unilateral downward adjustment to the taxpayer's taxable profits that is not directly reflected in the taxpayer's financial / commercial accounts	N/A	N/A
Permanent establishment rulings	N/A	N/A
Related party conduit rulings	N/A	N/A
De minimis rule	N/A	N/A
IP regimes: total exchanges on taxpayers benefitting from the third category of IP assets, new entrants benefitting from grandfathered IP regimes; and taxpayers making use of the option to treat the nexus ratio as a rebuttable presumption	N/A	N/A
Total	102	

D. Matters related to intellectual property regimes (ToR I.4.1.3)

Austria does not offer an intellectual property regime for which transparency requirements under the Action 5 Report (OECD, 2015[5]) were imposed.

Summary of recommendations on implementation of the transparency framework

Aspect of implementation of the transparency framework that should be improved	Recommendation for improvement
	No recommendations are made.

Notes

[1] Parties to the Convention are available here: www.oecd.org/tax/exchange-of-tax-information/convention-on-mutual-administrative-assistance-in-tax-matters.htm. Austria also has bilateral agreements in force with Algeria, Armenia, Bahamas, Bahrain, Belarus, Bosnia and Herzegovina, Brunei Darussalam, Burkina Faso, Dominican Republic, Egypt, El Salvador, Gabon, Guatemala, Hong Kong (China), Jamaica, Kenya, Kuwait, Montenegro, North Macedonia, Morocco, Peru, Philippines, Qatar, Serbia, Chinese Taipei, Tajikistan, Thailand, Turkey, Turkmenistan, United Arab Emirates, United States, Venezuela and Viet Nam.

Barbados

Barbados has met all aspects of the terms of reference (OECD, 2017[3]) (ToR) for the calendar year 2018 (year in review) except for identifying and exchanging information on all new entrants to the grandfathered IP regime (ToR I.4.1.3) and the timely exchange of information on rulings (ToR II.5). Barbados receives two recommendations on these points for the year in review.

In the prior year report, Barbados received two recommendations. One of these recommendations has been addressed and is removed. The second recommendation has not been addressed and remains in place and a new recommendation is added.

Barbados can legally issue five types of rulings within the scope of the transparency framework. In practice, Barbados has issued rulings within the scope of the transparency framework as follows:

- Two past rulings;
- For the period 1 September 2017 – 31 December 2017: no future rulings; and
- For the year in review: one future ruling.

No peer input was received in respect of the exchanges of information on rulings received from Barbados.

Introduction

This peer review covers Barbados' implementation of the BEPS Action 5 transparency framework for the year 2018. The report has four parts, each relating to a key part of the ToR. Each part is discussed in turn. A summary of recommendations is included at the end of this report.

A. The information gathering process

Barbados can legally issue the five following types of rulings within the scope of the transparency framework: (i) rulings related to preferential regimes;[1] (ii) cross-border unilateral advance pricing arrangements (APAs) and any other cross-border unilateral tax rulings (such as an advance tax ruling) covering transfer pricing or the application of transfer pricing principles; (iii) rulings providing for unilateral downward adjustments; (iv) permanent establishment rulings; and (v) related party conduit rulings.

Past rulings (ToR I.4.1.1, I.4.1.2, I.4.2.1, I.4.2.2)

For Barbados, past rulings are any tax rulings within scope that are issued either: (i) on or after 1 January 2015 but before 1 September 2017; or (ii) on or after 1 January 2012 but before 1 January 2015, provided they were still in effect as at 1 January 2015.

In the year in review, Barbados' process for identifying past rulings were conducted as follows. The Legal Department of the Barbados Revenue Authority ("BRA") is constituted as one centralised office. All physical files relating to rulings are maintained within one area of the Legal Department. Due to the small number of rulings issued by Barbados, the Legal Department staff members therefore conducted a manual review of all files pertaining to tax rulings to identify past rulings in scope. Each physical file was manually read and reviewed to determine whether it fell into any of the five rulings categories.

In order to identify potential exchange jurisdictions, the BRA reviewed the available information in the taxpayer's files. Barbados was able to ascertain the relevant exchange jurisdiction from the information on file. Barbados reports that the "best efforts approach" was not utilised as all the information regarding relevant exchange jurisdictions was contained within the ruling request in the file.

Future rulings (ToR I.4.1.1, I.4.1.2, I.4.2.1)

For Barbados, future rulings are any tax rulings within scope that are issued on or after 1 September 2017.

During the year in review, Barbados implemented a new process to identify and flag future rulings as being within scope of the transparency framework. Each ruling is manually read to determine whether it is in scope of the five types of rulings that Barbados can legally issue under the transparency framework. This process for future rulings is identical to the process for past rulings above. For future rulings, information regarding potential exchange jurisdictions is to be acquired during the ruling request process. A ruling request would not be processed without the relevant information being obtained from the taxpayer.

Review and supervision (ToR I.4.3)

The BRA is a centralised office that also serves as Competent Authority of Barbados. The legal officers within the BRA Legal Department, who are briefed on the Action 5 transparency framework requirements, compile the rulings information. This information is then reviewed by the General Counsel and by the Senior Manager of the Policy, Planning and Governance Department who has the ultimate responsibility for matters of international taxation.

Conclusion on section A

In the prior year peer review report, it was determined that Barbados's undertakings on the information gathering process have met the ToR except that Barbados was recommended to finalise the identification of all past and future rulings and potential exchange jurisdictions, with a review and supervision mechanism, as soon as possible (ToR I.4). During the year in review, Barbados has addressed this recommendation and the recommendation is now removed. Barbados has met all of the ToR for the information gathering process and no recommendations are made.

B. The exchange of information

Legal basis for spontaneous exchange of information (ToR II.5.1, II.5.2)

Barbados has the necessary domestic legal basis to exchange information spontaneously. Barbados notes that there are no legal or practical impediments that prevent the spontaneous exchange of information on rulings as contemplated in the Action 5 minimum standard.

Barbados is a party to international agreements permitting spontaneous exchange of information, including (i) the *Multilateral Convention on Mutual Administrative Assistance in Tax Matters: Amended by the 2010 Protocol* (OECD/Council of Europe, 2011) ("the Convention") and (ii) double taxation agreements in force with 40 jurisdictions.[2]

Completion and exchange of templates (ToR II.5.3, II.5.4, II.5.5, II.5.6, II.5.7)

Barbados notes that a Legal Officer in the Legal Department would be responsible for the completion of the information required in the template contained in Annex C of the Action 5 Report (OECD, 2015), which would include providing a detailed summary of the ruling following the instructions in Annex C. Final review of the template would be conducted by the General Counsel of the Legal Department. The process is supervised by the Senior Manager of the Policy, Planning and Governance Department who oversees the International Taxation Unit responsible for conducting the spontaneous exchange of information. All of these departments are within the BRA which is the Competent Authority for Barbados, and therefore, all rulings are made available to the Competent Authority with immediacy.

For the year in review, the timeliness of exchanges is as follows:

Past rulings in the scope of the transparency framework	Number of exchanges transmitted by 31 December 2018	Delayed exchanges		
		Number of exchanges not transmitted by 31 December 2018	Reasons for the delays	Any other comments
	0	2	Barbados was in the process of developing a new framework to implement the standard which resulted in delayed exchanges.	Internal procedures were finalised in 2019 for the exchange of information on rulings going forward.
Future rulings in the scope of the transparency framework	Number of exchanges transmitted within three months of the information becoming available to the competent authority or immediately after legal	Delayed exchanges		
		Number of exchanges transmitted later than three months of the information on rulings becoming available to the competent authority	Reasons for the delays	Any other comments

	impediments have been lifted			
	0	1	Barbados was in the process of developing a new framework to implement the standard which resulted in delayed exchanges.	Internal procedures were finalised in 2019 for the exchange of information on rulings going forward.
Total	0	3		

Follow up requests received for exchange of the ruling	Number	Average time to provide response	Number of requests not answered
	0	N/A	N/A

The Legal Department was in the process of developing its framework to exchange information on rulings, which resulted in the delayed exchanges. All exchanges for past and future rulings were completed in early 2019. The Legal Department finalised its internal procedures in 2019, and therefore exchanges are expected to be conducted in a timely manner in future.

Conclusion on section B

Barbados has the necessary legal basis to undertake spontaneous exchange of information and a process for completing the templates, but experienced delays in the exchange process. Barbados has met all of the ToR for the exchange of information process except for the timeliness of exchanges, and is recommended to continue its efforts to ensure that all information on past and future rulings is exchanged as soon as possible (ToR II.5).

C. Statistics (ToR IV)

As there was no information on rulings exchanged by Barbados for the year in review, no statistics can be reported.

D. Matters related to intellectual property regimes (ToR I.4.1.3)

Barbados offered two intellectual property regimes (IP regime)[3] that were abolished from 1 July 2018 and are subject to transparency requirements under the Action 5 Report (OECD, 2015[5]). It states that the identification of the benefitting taxpayers will occur as follows:

- ***New entrants benefitting from the grandfathered IP regime***: Transparency obligations apply for the two regimes, because grandfathering is provided to entrants that entered the regime after the relevant date from which enhanced transparency obligations apply. Barbados is currently in the process of developing mechanisms to identify these new entrants. Barbados is therefore recommended to identify and exchange information on all new entrants to the grandfathered IP regime as soon as possible (ToR I.4.1.3).
- ***Third category of IP assets***: not applicable as the IP regimes have been abolished.
- ***Taxpayers making use of the option to treat the nexus ratio as a rebuttable presumption***: not applicable as the IP regimes have been abolished.

Summary of recommendations on implementation of the transparency framework

Aspect of implementation of the transparency framework that should be improved	Recommendation for improvement
Barbados has experienced delays in the exchange of information on rulings.	Barbados is recommended to continue its efforts to ensure that all information on past and future rulings is exchanged as soon as possible. This recommendation remains unchanged since the prior year peer review report.
Barbados did not identify or exchange information on new entrants to the grandfathered IP regime.	Barbados is recommended to identify and exchange information on all new entrants to the grandfathered IP regime as soon as possible.

Notes

[1] With respect to the following preferential regime: Credit for foreign currency earnings.

[2] Parties to the Convention are available here: www.oecd.org/tax/exchange-of-tax-information/convention-on-mutual-administrative-assistance-in-tax-matters.htm. Barbados also has bilateral agreements in force with Antigua, Austria, Bahrain, Belize, Botswana, Canada, China (People's Republic of), Cyprus, Cuba, Czech Republic, Dominica, Finland, Grenada, Guyana, Iceland, Italy, Jamaica, Luxembourg, Malta, Mauritius, Mexico, Netherlands, Norway, Panama, Portugal, Saint Kitts and Nevis, Saint Lucia, Saint Vincent and the Grenadines, San Marino, Seychelles, Singapore, Spain, Sweden, Switzerland, Trinidad & Tobago, Qatar, United Arab Emirates, United Kingdom, United States and Venezuela.

Note by Turkey: The information in this document with reference to "Cyprus" relates to the southern part of the Island. There is no single authority representing both Turkish and Greek Cypriot people on the Island. Turkey recognises the Turkish Republic of Northern Cyprus (TRNC). Until a lasting and equitable solution is found within the context of the United Nations, Turkey shall preserve its position concerning the "Cyprus issue".

Note by all the European Union Member States of the OECD and the European Union. The Republic of Cyprus is recognised by all members of the United Nations with the exception of Turkey. The information in this document relates to the area under the effective control of the Government of the Republic of Cyprus.

[3] 1) International business companies and 2) International societies with restricted liability

Belgium

Belgium has met all aspects of the terms of reference (ToR) for the calendar year 2018 (year in review) and no recommendations are made.

In the prior year report, Belgium received one recommendation to continue its efforts to identify and exchange information on new entrants to the grandfathered IP regime (ToR I.4.1.3). This recommendation has been addressed and is removed.

Belgium can legally issue four types of rulings within the scope of the transparency framework. In practice, Belgium has issued rulings within the scope of the transparency framework as follows:

- 586 past rulings;
- For the period 1 April 2016 - 31 December 2016: 57 future rulings;
- For the calendar year 2017: 107 future rulings, and
- For the year in review: 103 future rulings.

Peer input was received from six jurisdictions in respect of the exchanges of information on rulings received from Belgium. The input was generally positive, noting that information was complete, in a correct format and almost all received in a timely manner.

Introduction

This peer review covers Belgium's implementation of the BEPS Action 5 transparency framework for the year 2018. The report has four parts, each relating to a key part of the ToR. Each part is discussed in turn. A summary of recommendations is included at the end of this report.

A. The information gathering process

Belgium can legally issue the following four types of rulings within the scope of the transparency framework: (i) rulings related to preferential regimes;[1] (ii) cross-border unilateral advance pricing agreements (APAs) and any other cross-border unilateral tax rulings (such as an advance tax ruling) covering transfer pricing or the application of transfer pricing principles; (iii) rulings providing for unilateral downward adjustments; and (iv) permanent establishment rulings.

Past rulings (ToR I.4.1.1, I.4.1.2, I.4.2.1, I.4.2.2)

For Belgium, past rulings are any tax rulings within scope that are issued either: (i) on or after 1 January 2014 but before 1 April 2016; or (ii) on or after 1 January 2010 but before 1 January 2014, provided they were still in effect as at 1 January 2014.

In the prior year peer review report, it was determined that the Belgian tax administration's undertakings to identify past rulings and all potential exchange jurisdictions were sufficient to meet the minimum standard. The Belgian tax administration's implementation in this regard remains unchanged, and therefore continues to meet the minimum standard.

Future rulings (ToR I.4.1.1, I.4.1.2, I.4.2.1)

For Belgium, future rulings are any tax rulings within scope that are issued on or after 1 April 2016.

In the prior year peer review report, it was determined that the Belgian Tax Administration's implementation of a system to identify future rulings and all potential exchange jurisdictions was sufficient to meet the minimum standard. The Belgian Tax Administration's implementation in this regard remains unchanged, and therefore continues to meet the minimum standard.

Review and supervision (ToR I.4.3)

In the prior year peer review report, it was determined that the Belgian Tax Administration's review and supervision mechanism was sufficient to meet the minimum standard. The Belgian Tax Administration's implementation in this regard remains unchanged, and therefore continues to meet the minimum standard.

Conclusion on section A

Belgium has met all of the ToR for the information gathering process and no recommendations are made.

B. The exchange of information

Legal basis for spontaneous exchange of information (ToR II.5.1, II.5.2)

Belgium has the necessary domestic legal basis to exchange information spontaneously. Belgium notes that there are no legal or practical impediments that prevent the spontaneous exchange of information on rulings as contemplated in the Action 5 minimum standard.

Belgium is a party to international agreements permitting spontaneous exchange of information, including (i) the *Multilateral Convention on Mutual Administrative Assistance in Tax Matters: Amended by the 2010 Protocol* (OECD/Council of Europe, 2011) ("the Convention"), (ii) the Directive 2011/16/EU with all other European Union Member States and (iii) double tax agreements in force with 70 jurisdictions.[2]

Completion and exchange of templates (ToR II.5.3, II.5.4, II.5.5, II.5.6, II.5.7)

In the prior year peer review report, it was determined that the Belgian Tax Administration's completion and exchange of templates was sufficient to meet the minimum standard. Belgium's implementation in this regard remains unchanged, and therefore continues to meet the minimum standard.

For the year in review, the timeliness of exchanges is as follows:

Past rulings in the scope of the transparency framework	Number of exchanges transmitted by 31 December 2018	Delayed exchanges		
		Number of exchanges not transmitted by 31 December 2018	Reasons for the delays	Any other comments
	63	0	N/A	These past rulings were exchanged with four jurisdictions with whom the legal basis for exchange did not enter into force until 2018, and one developing country (non-financial centre) that received a deferral. As such these exchanges were not delayed as they were only legally permitted to occur or required by the ToR to occur in 2018.
Future rulings in the scope of the transparency framework	Number of exchanges transmitted within three months of the information becoming available to the competent authority or immediately after legal impediments have been lifted	Delayed exchanges		
		Number of exchanges transmitted later than three months of the information on rulings becoming available to the competent authority	Reasons for the delays	Any other comments
	354	0	N/A	N/A
Total	417	0		

Follow up requests received for exchange of the ruling	Number	Average time to provide response	Number of requests not answered
	2	1 day	0

Conclusion on section B

Belgium has the necessary legal basis for spontaneous exchange of information, a process for completing the templates in a timely way and has completed all exchanges on time. Belgium has met all of the ToR for the exchange of information process and no recommendations are made.

C. Statistics (ToR IV)

The statistics for the year in review are as follows:

Category of ruling	Number of exchanges	Jurisdictions exchanged with
Ruling related to a preferential regime	42	Australia, Brazil, Canada, Chile, China (People's Republic of), Denmark, France, Germany, Indonesia, India, Italy, Mexico, Netherlands, Poland, Romania, Russia, Sweden, Slovenia, South Africa, Spain, Switzerland, Turkey, Ukraine, United Kingdom, United States
Cross-border unilateral advance pricing agreements (APAs) and any other cross-border unilateral tax rulings (such as an advance tax ruling) covering transfer pricing or the application of transfer pricing principles	348	Australia, Austria, Barbados, Bulgaria, Canada, China (People's Republic of), Czech Republic, Denmark, Egypt, Finland, France, Germany, Greece, Hungary, Indonesia, Ireland, Italy, Japan, Jersey, Liechtenstein, Luxembourg, Malaysia, Malta, Mexico, Netherlands, Panama, Poland, Portugal, Romania, Russia, Saudi Arabia, Singapore, Slovenia, South Africa, Spain, Sweden, Tunisia, Turkey, Ukraine, United Kingdom, United States
Cross-border rulings providing for a unilateral downward adjustment to the taxpayer's taxable profits that is not directly reflected in the taxpayer's financial / commercial accounts	0	N/A
Permanent establishment rulings	75	Australia, Austria, Finland, France, Germany, Ireland, Italy, Japan, Jersey, Lithuania, Luxembourg, Netherlands, Poland, Spain, Switzerland, Ukraine, United Kingdom, United States
Related party conduit rulings	0	N/A
De minimis rule	N/A	N/A
IP regimes: total exchanges on taxpayers benefitting from the third category of IP assets, new entrants benefitting from grandfathered IP regimes; and taxpayers making use of the option to treat the nexus ratio as a rebuttable presumption	1	*De minimis* rule applies
Total	466[3]	

D. Matters related to intellectual property regimes (ToR I.4.1.3)

Belgium has an intellectual property regime (IP regime) that is subject to transparency requirements under the Action 5 Report (OECD, 2015[5]).[4] The identification of the benefitting taxpayers will occur as follows:

- ***New entrants benefitting from the grandfathered IP regime***: In the prior year peer review report, Belgium received a recommendation to continue its efforts to identify and exchange information on new entrants to the grandfathered IP regime. For taxpayers filing tax returns in calendar year 2017 (regarding tax year 2016), Belgium introduced a new requirement in the tax return form to identify new entrants that entered the regime after the relevant date from which enhanced transparency obligations apply. New entrants included both (i) new taxpayers not previously benefiting from the regime and (ii) new IP assets owned by taxpayers already benefiting from the regime. As described in the prior year peer review report, the Belgian Tax Administration has finalised the tax return assessment process to establish which taxpayers are in scope for enhanced transparency under the Standard. The exchanges were completed in February 2019. Belgium acknowledges that these exchanges were approximately five months delayed, given that tax returns were received by the Belgian Tax Administration in September 2017 and it is expected under the Standard that the exchanges should have taken place by September 2018. Belgium has now completed the identification and exchange of all new entrants to the grandfathered IP regime and the prior year recommendation is now removed.
- ***Third category of IP assets***: not applicable as the regime does not allow the third category of IP assets to qualify for the benefits.
- ***Taxpayers making use of the option to treat the nexus ratio as a rebuttable presumption***: Belgium confirms that no taxpayer elected to treat the nexus approach as a rebuttable presumption.

Summary of recommendations on implementation of the transparency framework

Aspect of implementation of the transparency framework that should be improved	Recommendation for improvement
	No recommendations are made.

Belize

Belize has met all aspects of the terms of reference (ToR) for the calendar year 2018 (year in review).

In the prior year report, Belize did not receive any recommendations.

Belize indicates that it cannot legally issue any type of rulings within the scope of the transparency framework.

As no exchanges took place, no peer input was received in respect of the exchanges of information on rulings received from Belize.

Introduction

This peer review covers Belize's implementation of the BEPS Action 5 transparency framework for the year 2018. The report has four parts, each relating to a key part of the ToR. Each part is discussed in turn. A summary of recommendations is included at the end of this report.

A. The information gathering process

As no rulings are issued, this section is not assessed.

B. The exchange of information

As no rulings are issued, this section is not assessed.

C. Statistics (ToR IV)

As no rulings are issued, no statistics can be reported.

D. Matters related to intellectual property regimes (ToR I.4.1.3)

Belize offered an intellectual property regime (IP regime)[5] that was abolished from 1 July 2018. The regime is not subject to the transparency requirements under the Action 5 Report (OECD, 2015[5]), because:

- ***New entrants benefitting from the grandfathered IP regime***: No enhanced transparency requirements apply, as follows. The regime has been closed-off, and although grandfathering was provided, it only applies to entrants that benefited from the regime prior to the relevant date from which enhanced transparency obligations would apply.
- ***Third category of IP assets***: not applicable as the IP regime has been abolished.
- ***Taxpayers making use of the option to treat the nexus ratio as a rebuttable presumption***: not applicable as the IP regime has been abolished.

Summary of recommendations on implementation of the transparency framework

Aspect of implementation of the transparency framework that should be improved	Recommendation for improvement
	No recommendations are made.

Notes

[1] With respect to the following preferential regimes: 1) Patent income deduction, 2) Tax shelter regime for maritime exploitation and 3) Excess profits.

[2] Parties to the Convention are available here: www.oecd.org/tax/exchange-of-tax-information/convention-on-mutual-administrative-assistance-in-tax-matters.htm. Belgium also has bilateral agreements in force with Albania, Algeria, Andorra, Antigua and Barbuda, Argentina, Armenia, Australia, Azerbaijan, Bahrain, Bangladesh, Belarus, Brazil, Belize, Bosnia and Herzegovina, Canada, Chile, China (People's Republic of), Côte d'Ivoire, Democratic Republic of the Congo, Ecuador, Egypt, Gabon, Georgia, Ghana, Hong Kong (China), Iceland, India, Indonesia, Israel, Japan, Kazakhstan, Korea, Kosovo, Kyrgyzstan, Kuwait, Malaysia, Mauritius, Mexico, Moldova, Mongolia, Montenegro, Morocco, New Zealand, Nigeria, North Macedonia, Norway, Pakistan, Philippines, Russia, Rwanda, San Marino, Senegal, Serbia, Seychelles, Singapore, South Africa, Sri Lanka, Switzerland, Tajikistan, Chinese Taipei, Thailand, Tunisia, Turkey, Turkmenistan, Ukraine, United Arab Emirates, United States, Uruguay, Uzbekistan, Venezuela and Viet Nam.

[3] There were 417 exchanges as defined under footnote 13 of the Terms of Reference. The total of number of exchanges given in this table is higher than 417 due to the fact that some exchanges fall under more than one category of ruling.

[4] Deduction for innovation income.

[5] International business companies.

Benin

Benin is taking steps to implement the legal basis for the transparency framework and to commence administrative preparations to ensure that information on rulings will be exchanged in a timely manner, in line with the terms of reference (OECD, 2017[3]) (ToR). Benin is recommended to ensure that it has put in place an effective information gathering process and to implement a review and supervision mechanism, as soon as possible (ToR I.4). In addition, Benin is recommended to develop a process to complete the templates on relevant rulings, to ensure that the exchanges of information on rulings occur in accordance with the form and timelines under the transparency framework going forward (ToR II.5).

Benin can legally issue one type of rulings within the scope of the transparency framework. In the prior year peer review report, it was noted that Benin did not issue rulings within the scope the transparency framework. However, it has since been confirmed that Benin can issue rulings to which the transparency framework applies.

In practice, Benin has issued no rulings in the year in review. As no exchanges were required to take place, no peer input was received in respect of the exchanges of information on rulings received from Benin.

Introduction

This peer review covers Benin's implementation of the BEPS Action 5 transparency framework for the year 2018. The report has four parts, each relating to a key part of the ToR. Each part is discussed in turn. A summary of recommendations is included at the end of this report.

A. The information gathering process

Benin can legally issue one type of rulings within the scope of the transparency framework: permanent establishment rulings.

Past rulings (ToR I.4.1.1, I.4.1.2, I.4.2.1, I.4.2.2)

For Benin, past rulings are any tax rulings within scope that are issued either: (i) on or after 1 January 2015 but before 1 April 2017; and (ii) on or after 1 January 2012 but before 1 January 2015, provided still in effect as at 1 January 2015.

In Benin, rulings are issued by the directorate of Legislation and Litigation, within the Tax Administration. This unit is responsible for storing and reviewing such rulings and has reviewed its files, being able to confirm that no past rulings have been issued. To date, no rulings in scope of the transparency framework have been issued. As such there was no need to identify potential exchange jurisdictions.

Future rulings (ToR I.4.1.1, I.4.1.2, I.4.2.1)

For Benin, future rulings are any tax rulings within scope that are issued on or after 1 April 2017.

No rulings were issued by Benin during the future rulings period in the year of review. However, Benin indicates that there are no processes in place for the record keeping of rulings for the purposes of the transparency framework. It is noted that Benin intends to implement guidelines and practices to make sure the necessary information to meet the requirements of the transparency framework is required in all cases.

Review and supervision (ToR I.4.3)

Benin did not yet have a review and supervision mechanism under the transparency framework for the year in review. Benin is discussing the implementation of a revision and supervision mechanism for ensuring implementation of the transparency framework.

Conclusion on section A

Benin is recommended to finalise its information gathering process, with a review and supervision mechanism, as soon as possible (ToR I.4).

B. The exchange of information

Legal basis for spontaneous exchange of information (ToR II.5.1, II.5.2)

Benin is currently in the process of putting in place the necessary domestic legal basis to exchange information spontaneously.

Benin is not a Party to the *Multilateral Convention on Mutual Administrative Assistance in Tax Matters: Amended by the 2010 Protocol* (OECD/Council of Europe, 2011) ("the Convention"). Benin is encouraged to continue its efforts to expand its international exchange of information instruments to be able to exchange rulings. It is however noted that jurisdictions are assessed on their compliance with the transparency framework in respect of the exchange of information network in effect for the year of the particular annual review.

Completion and exchange of templates (ToR II.5.3, II.5.4, II.5.5, II.5.6, II.5.7)

Benin is still developing a process to complete the templates on relevant rulings, to make them available to the Competent Authority for exchange of information, and to exchange them with relevant jurisdictions.

As no exchanges were required to take place in the year of review, no data on the timeliness of exchanges can be reported.

Conclusion on section B

Benin is recommended to put in place a domestic legal framework allowing spontaneous exchange of information on rulings and to continue its efforts to complete the templates for all relevant rulings and to ensure that the exchanges of information on rulings occur as soon as possible (ToR II.5).

C. Statistics (ToR IV)

As no rulings are issued, no statistics can be reported.

D. Matters related to intellectual property regimes (ToR I.4.1.3)

Benin does not offer an intellectual property regime for which transparency requirements under the Action 5 Report (OECD, 2015[5]) were imposed.

Summary of recommendations on implementation of the transparency framework

Aspect of implementation of the transparency framework that should be improved	Recommendation for improvement
Benin has not yet finalised the steps to have in place its necessary information and gathering process.	Benin is recommended to finalise its information gathering process, with a review and supervision mechanism, as soon as possible.
Benin has not yet finalised the steps to have effective compulsory spontaneous exchange of information on the tax rulings within the scope of the transparency framework.	Benin is recommended to continue to put in place a domestic legal framework allowing spontaneous exchange of information on rulings and to continue its efforts to complete the templates for all relevant rulings and to ensure that the exchanges of information on rulings occur as soon as possible.

Botswana

Botswana is taking steps to implement the legal basis for the transparency framework and to commence administrative preparations (in line with the terms of reference (OECD, 2017[3]) (ToR)) to ensure that it finalises its information gathering process (ToR I.4) and information on rulings will be identified and exchanged in a timely manner (ToR II.5). Botswana receives two recommendations on these points for the year in review.

This is Botswana's first review of implementation of the transparency framework.

Botswana can legally issue three types of rulings within the scope of the transparency framework. In practice, Botswana issued rulings within the scope of the transparency framework as follows:

- 10 past rulings;
- For the period 1 April 2018 - 31 December 2018: one future ruling.

As no exchanges took place, no peer input was received in respect of the exchanges of information on rulings received from Botswana.

Introduction

This peer review covers Botswana's implementation of the BEPS Action 5 transparency framework for the year 2018. The report has four parts, each relating to a key part of the ToR. Each part is discussed in turn. A summary of recommendations is included at the end of this report.

A. The information gathering process

Botswana can legally issue the following three types of rulings within the scope of the transparency framework: (i) preferential regimes;[1] (ii) cross-border unilateral APAs and any other cross-border unilateral tax rulings (such as an advance tax ruling) covering transfer pricing or the application of transfer pricing principles; and (iii) permanent establishment rulings. Both the Tax Authority and the Ministry of Finance and Economic Development can issue rulings.

Past rulings (ToR I.4.1.1, I.4.1.2, I.4.2.1, I.4.2.2)

For Botswana, past rulings are any tax rulings within scope that are issued either (i) on or after 1 January 2016 but before 1 April 2018; and (ii) on or after 1 January 2014 but before 1 January 2016, provided still in effect as at 1 January 2016.

Rulings with respect to the International financial services company ("IFSC") regime are issued by the Minister of Finance and Economic Development ("the Minister"). Companies apply for the IFSC certificate with the IFSC Certification Committee. The Committee will assess the application according to the criteria laid out under the Income Tax Act and then make a recommendation to the Minister. The Minister will then approve the application and issue the IFSC certificate. A copy of the certificate is kept by the Minister and by the IFSC Certification Committee. The Tax Policy (International Tax Unit) team manually reviewed the file of the certificates to identify the rulings falling within the period of validity defined as past rulings.

When an IFSC applies for a certificate, it is required to disclose the relevant structure including all related companies and parent companies. As such, information on all potential exchange jurisdictions was available and Botswana did not need to apply the "best efforts approach" for these rulings.

APAs and permanent establishment rulings fall under scope of the Commissioner General, who considers and processes the requests and stores them in a manual filing system. The Tax Treaties and Agreements team in the tax administration reviewed all the files according to the date of issue to identify rulings falling within the period of validity defined as past rulings. Botswana does not have a process in place for identifying the potential exchange jurisdictions for APAs and permanent establishment rulings and did not yet apply the best efforts approach.

Future rulings (ToR I.4.1.1, I.4.1.2, I.4.2.1)

For Botswana, future rulings are any tax rulings within scope that are issued on or after 1 April 2018.

The process for future rulings is similar to the process for past rulings. Each time an IFSC certificate is issued, the Tax Policy (International Tax Unit) team will flag it as being relevant for the purposes of the transparency framework, and would verify that the information on the potential exchange jurisdictions has been obtained.

With respect to APAs and PE rulings, the Tax Treaties and Agreements team would identify the ruling at the point it is issued to flag it as being relevant for the purposes of the transparency framework. The ruling application process does not require the taxpayer to provide information on all potential exchange jurisdictions. The Commissioner General has the authority to require this information from the taxpayer and would do so to obtain information on all potential exchange jurisdictions.

Review and supervision (ToR I.4.3)

Botswana did not yet have a review and supervision mechanism for past or future rulings under the transparency framework for the year in review. Botswana is discussing the implementation of a revision and supervision mechanism for future rulings, including appropriate training for the relevant tax officers.

Conclusion on section A

Botswana is recommended to apply the best efforts approach to identify all potential exchange jurisdictions for APA and PE rulings and to put in place a review and supervision mechanism, as soon as possible (ToR I.4).

B. The exchange of information

Legal basis for spontaneous exchange of information (ToR II.5.1, II.5.2)

Botswana does not have the necessary domestic legal basis to exchange information spontaneously. Botswana can only exchange information on request. Botswana is undergoing a comprehensive reform of its tax laws. Botswana notes that new tax laws, including with respect to the spontaneous exchange of information, will likely be implemented in July 2020.

Botswana has international agreements permitting spontaneous exchange of information, including bilateral agreements in force with 24 jurisdictions.[2] Botswana is encouraged to continue its efforts to expand its international exchange of information instruments to be able to exchange rulings. It is however noted that jurisdictions are assessed on their compliance with the transparency framework in respect of the exchange of information network in effect for the year of the particular annual review.

Completion and exchange of templates (ToR II.5.3, II.5.4, II.5.5, II.5.6, II.5.7)

Botswana is currently developing a process to complete the templates on relevant rulings, to make them available to the Competent Authority for exchange of information, and to exchange them with relevant jurisdictions.

As no exchanges took place for the year in review, no data on the timeliness of exchanges can be reported.

Conclusion on section B

Botswana is recommended to continue to put in place a domestic legal framework allowing spontaneous exchange of information on rulings and to ensure the timely exchange of information on rulings in the form required by the transparency framework (ToR II.5).

C. Statistics (ToR IV)

As there was no information on rulings exchanged by Botswana for the year in review, no statistics can be reported.

D. Matters related to intellectual property regimes (ToR I.4.1.3)

Botswana offered an intellectual property regime (IP regime)[3] that was abolished as of 1 January 2019 and that is not subject to the transparency requirements under the Action 5 Report (OECD, 2015[5]), because:

- ***New entrants benefitting from the grandfathered IP regime***: as there were no taxpayers benefitting from the IP regime and no grandfathering provisions have been provided, and therefore no enhanced transparency requirements apply.
- ***Third category of IP assets***: not applicable as the IP regime has been abolished.
- ***Taxpayers making use of the option to treat the nexus ratio as a rebuttable presumption***: not applicable as the IP regime has been abolished.

Summary of recommendations on implementation of the transparency framework

Aspect of implementation of the transparency framework that should be improved	Recommendation for improvement
Botswana has not yet finalised the steps to have in place its necessary information and gathering process.	Botswana is recommended to apply the best efforts approach to identify all potential exchange jurisdictions for APA and PE rulings and to put in place a review and supervision mechanism, as soon as possible.
Botswana does not yet have the necessary legal framework in place for exchanging information on rulings and a process in place to ensure the timely exchange of information on rulings in the form required by the transparency framework.	Botswana is recommended to continue to put in place a domestic legal framework allowing spontaneous exchange of information on rulings and to ensure the timely exchange of information on rulings in the form required by the transparency framework.

Notes

[1] With respect to the following preferential regime: International financial services company.

[2] Botswana has bilateral agreements with Barbados, China (People's Republic of), Denmark, Eswatini, Faroe Islands, Finland, France, Greenland, Iceland, India, Ireland, Isle of Man, Malta, Mauritius, Mozambique, Namibia, Norway, Russia, Seychelles, South Africa, Sweden, United Kingdom, Zambia and Zimbabwe.

[3] International financial services company.

Brazil

Brazil has met all aspects of the terms of reference (OECD, 2017[3]) (ToR) for the calendar year 2018 (year in review) and no recommendations are made.

In the prior year report, Brazil did not receive any recommendations.

Brazil can legally issue two types of rulings within the scope of the transparency framework. In practice, Brazil issued rulings within the scope of the transparency framework as follows:

- 10 past rulings;
- For the period 1 April 2016 - 31 December 2016: no future rulings;
- For the calendar year 2017: no future rulings, and
- For the year in review: six future rulings.

These rulings are published on the Receita Federal do Brazil's ("RFB") website in a redacted form.[1]

No peer input was received in respect of the exchanges of information on rulings received from Brazil.

Introduction

This peer review covers Brazil's implementation of the BEPS Action 5 transparency framework for the year 2018. The report has four parts, each relating to a key part of the ToR. Each part is discussed in turn. A summary of recommendations is included at the end of this report.

A. The information gathering process

Brazil can legally issue two types of ruling within the scope of the transparency framework: (i) rulings related to preferential regimes[2] and (ii) cross-border unilateral advance pricing agreements (APAs) and any other cross-border unilateral tax rulings (such as an advance tax ruling) covering transfer pricing or the application of transfer pricing principles.

Past rulings (ToR I.4.1.1, I.4.1.2, I.4.2.1, I.4.2.2)

For Brazil, past rulings are any tax rulings within scope that are issued either: (i) on or after 1 January 2014 but before 1 April 2016; or (ii) on or after 1 January 2010 but before 1 January 2014, provided they were still in effect as at 1 January 2014.

In the prior years' peer review reports, it was determined that Brazil's undertakings to identify past rulings and all potential exchange jurisdictions were sufficient to meet the minimum standard. Brazil's implementation in this regard remains unchanged, and therefore continues to meet the minimum standard.

Future rulings (ToR I.4.1.1, I.4.1.2, I.4.2.1)

For Brazil, future rulings are any tax rulings within scope that are issued on or after 1 April 2016.

In the prior years' peer review reports, it was determined that Brazil's undertakings to identify future rulings and all potential exchange jurisdictions have met all the ToR. Brazil's implementation in this regard remains unchanged, and therefore continues to meet the minimum standard.

Review and supervision (ToR I.4.3)

In the prior years' peer review reports, it was determined that Brazil's review and supervision mechanism was sufficient to meet the minimum standard. Brazil's implementation in this regard remains unchanged, and therefore continues to meet the minimum standard.

Conclusion on section A

Brazil has met all of the ToR for the information gathering process and no recommendations are made.

B. The exchange of information

Legal basis for spontaneous exchange of information (ToR II.5.1, II.5.2)

Brazil has the necessary domestic legal basis to exchange information spontaneously. Brazil notes that there are no legal or practical impediments that prevent the spontaneous exchange of information on rulings as contemplated in the Action 5 minimum standard.

Brazil has international agreements permitting spontaneous exchange of information, including being a party to the (i) *Multilateral Convention on Mutual Administrative Assistance in Tax Matters: Amended by the 2010 Protocol* (OECD/Council of Europe, 2011[4]) ("the Convention"), (ii) bilateral agreements in force with 33 jurisdictions.[3]

Completion and exchange of templates (ToR II.5.3, II.5.4, II.5.5, II.5.6, II.5.7)

In the prior years' peer review reports, it was determined that Brazil's process for the completion and exchange of templates were sufficient to meet the minimum standard. Brazil's implementation in this regard remains unchanged and therefore continues to meet the minimum standard.

For the year in review, the timeliness of exchanges is as follows:

Past rulings in the scope of the transparency framework	Number of exchanges transmitted by 31 December 2018	Delayed exchanges		
		Number of exchanges not transmitted by 31 December 2018	Reasons for the delays	Any other comments
	0	0	N/A	N/A
Future rulings in the scope of the transparency framework	Number of exchanges transmitted within three months of the information becoming available to the competent authority or immediately after legal impediments have been lifted	Delayed exchanges		
		Number of exchanges transmitted later than three months of the information on rulings becoming available to the competent authority	Reasons for the delays	Any other comments
	8	0	N/A	N/A
Total	8	0		

Follow up requests received for exchange of the ruling	Number	Average time to provide response	Number of requests not answered
	0	N/A	N/A

Conclusion on section B

Brazil has the necessary legal basis for spontaneous exchange of information, a process for completing the templates in a timely way. Brazil has met all of the ToR for the exchange of information process and no recommendations are made.

C. Statistics (ToR IV)

The statistics for the year in review are as follows:

Category of ruling	Number of exchanges	Jurisdictions exchanged with
Ruling related to a preferential regime	1	*De minimis* rule applies
Cross-border unilateral advance pricing agreements (APAs) and any other cross-border unilateral tax rulings (such as an advance tax ruling) covering transfer pricing or the application of transfer pricing principles	7	Belgium, China (People's Republic of), Finland, Germany, Netherlands, United States
Cross-border rulings providing for a unilateral downward adjustment to the taxpayer's taxable profits that is not directly reflected in the taxpayer's financial / commercial accounts	N/A	N/A

Permanent establishment rulings	N/A	N/A
Related party conduit rulings	N/A	N/A
De minimis rule	N/A	N/A
IP regimes: total exchanges on taxpayers benefitting from the third category of IP assets, new entrants benefitting from grandfathered IP regimes; and taxpayers making use of the option to treat the nexus ratio as a rebuttable presumption	N/A	N/A
Total	8	

D. Matters related to intellectual property regimes (ToR I.4.1.3)

Brazil does not offer an intellectual property regime for which transparency requirements under the Action 5 Report (OECD, 2015[5]) were imposed.

Summary of recommendations on implementation of the transparency framework

Aspect of implementation of the transparency framework that should be improved	Recommendation for improvement
	No recommendations are made.

Notes

[1] Available at: https://idg.receita.fazenda.gov.br/acesso-rapido/legislacao

[2] With respect to the following preferential regime: PADIS – Semiconductors Industry.

[3] Parties to the Convention are available here: www.oecd.org/tax/exchange-of-tax-information/convention-on-mutual-administrative-assistance-in-tax-matters.htm. Brazil also has bilateral agreements in force with Argentina, Austria, Belgium, Canada, Chile, China (People's Republic of), Czech Republic, Denmark, Equator, Finland, France, Hungary, India, Israel, Italy, Japan, Korea, Luxembourg, Mexico, Norway, Netherlands, Peru, Portugal, Philippines, Slovak Republic, Russia, South Africa, Spain, Sweden, Trinidad and Tobago, Turkey, Ukraine and Venezuela.

Brunei Darussalam

Brunei Darussalam has met all aspects of the terms of reference (OECD, 2017[3]) (ToR) for the calendar year 2018 (year in review) that can be met in the absence of rulings being issued in practice.

In the prior year report, Brunei Darussalam did not receive any recommendations.

Brunei Darussalam can legally issue five types of rulings within the scope of the transparency framework. In practice, Brunei Darussalam has not issued any rulings within the scope of the transparency framework.

As no exchanges were required to take place, no peer input was received in respect of the exchanges of information on rulings received from Brunei Darussalam.

Introduction

This peer review covers Brunei Darussalam's implementation of the BEPS Action 5 transparency framework for the year 2018. The report has four parts, each relating to a key part of the ToR. Each part is discussed in turn. A summary of recommendations is included at the end of this report.

A. The information gathering process

Brunei Darussalam can legally issue the following five types of ruling within the scope of the transparency framework: (i) rulings related to preferential regimes;[1] (ii) cross-border unilateral advance pricing arrangements (APAs) and any other cross-border unilateral tax rulings (such as an advance tax ruling) covering transfer pricing or the application of transfer pricing principles; (iii) cross-border rulings giving a unilateral downward adjustment; (iv) permanent establishment rulings; and (v) related party conduit rulings.

Past rulings (ToR I.4.1.1, I.4.1.2, I.4.2.1, I.4.2.2)

For Brunei Darussalam, past rulings are any tax rulings within scope that are issued either: (i) on or after 1 January 2015 but before 1 April 2017; or (ii) on or after 1 January 2012 but before 1 January 2015, provided they were still in effect as at 1 January 2015.

In the prior year peer review report, it was determined that Brunei Darussalam's undertakings to identify past rulings and all potential exchange jurisdictions were sufficient to meet the minimum standard in the absence of rulings being issued in practice. Brunei Darussalam's implementation in this regard remains unchanged, and therefore continues to meet the minimum standard.

Future rulings (ToR I.4.1.1, I.4.1.2, I.4.2.1)

For Brunei Darussalam, future rulings are any tax rulings within scope that are issued on or after 1 September 2017.

In the prior year peer review report, it was determined that Brunei Darussalam's implementation of a system to identify future rulings and all potential exchange jurisdictions was sufficient to meet the minimum standard in the absence of rulings being issued in practice. Brunei Darussalam's implementation in this regard remains unchanged, and therefore continues to meet the minimum standard.

Review and supervision (ToR I.4.3)

In the prior year peer review report, it was determined that Brunei Darussalam's review and supervision mechanism was sufficient to meet the minimum standard. Brunei Darussalam's implementation in this regard remains unchanged, and therefore continues to meet the minimum standard.

Conclusion on section A

Brunei Darussalam has met all of the ToR for the information gathering process and no recommendations are made.

B. The exchange of information

Legal basis for spontaneous exchange of information (ToR II.5.1, II.5.2)

Brunei Darussalam has the necessary domestic legal basis to exchange information spontaneously. Brunei Darussalam notes that there are no legal or practical impediments that prevent the spontaneous exchange of information on rulings as contemplated in the Action 5 minimum standard.

Brunei Darussalam is a party to international agreements permitting spontaneous exchange of information, including (i) double tax agreements in force with 17 jurisdictions.[2] Brunei Darussalam signed the *Multilateral Convention on Mutual Administrative Assistance in Tax Matters: Amended by the 2010 Protocol* (OECD/Council of Europe, 2011) ("the Convention") on 12 September 2017 and was in the process of ratifying the Convention during the year in review. The Convention was ratified in March 2019 and entered into force on 1 July 2019.

Completion and exchange of templates (ToR II.5.3, II.5.4, II.5.5, II.5.6, II.5.7)

In the prior year peer review report, it was determined that Brunei Darussalam's process for the completion and exchange of templates were sufficient to meet the minimum standard. Brunei Darussalam's implementation in this regard remains unchanged and therefore continues to meet the minimum standard.

As Brunei Darussalam did not issue any rulings in scope of the transparency framework in the relevant period, Brunei Darussalam was not required to exchange any information on rulings in the year in review and no data on the timeliness of exchanges can be reported.

Conclusion on section B

Brunei Darussalam has the necessary legal basis to undertake spontaneous exchange of information. Brunei Darussalam has met all of the ToR for the exchange of information process that can be met in the absence of rulings being issued and exchanged in practice and no recommendations are made.

C. Statistics (ToR IV)

As no rulings are issued, no statistics can be reported.

D. Matters related to intellectual property regimes (ToR I.4.1.3)

Brunei Darussalam does not offer an intellectual property regime for which transparency requirements under the Action 5 Report (OECD, 2015[5]) were imposed.

Summary of recommendations on implementation of the transparency framework

Aspect of implementation of the transparency framework that should be improved	Recommendation for improvement
	No recommendations are made.

Bulgaria

Bulgaria has met all aspects of the terms of reference (OECD, 2017[3]) (ToR) for the calendar year 2018 (year in review) that can be met in the absence of rulings being issued.

In the prior year report, Bulgaria did not receive any recommendations.

Bulgaria cannot legally issue any type of ruling within the scope of the transparency framework.

As no exchanges were required to take place, no peer input was received in respect of the exchanges of information on rulings received from Bulgaria.

Introduction

This peer review covers Bulgaria's implementation of the BEPS Action 5 transparency framework for the year 2018. The report has four parts, each relating to a key part of the ToR. Each part is discussed in turn. A summary of recommendations is included at the end of this report.

A. The information gathering process

As no rulings are issued, this section is not assessed.

B. The exchange of information

As no rulings are issued, this section is not assessed.

C. Statistics (ToR IV)

As no rulings are issued, no statistics can be reported.

D. Matters related to intellectual property regimes (ToR I.4.1.3)

Bulgaria does not offer an intellectual property regime for which transparency requirements under the Action 5 Report (OECD, 2015[5]) were imposed.

Summary of recommendations on implementation of the transparency framework

Aspect of implementation of the transparency framework that should be improved	Recommendation for improvement
	No recommendations are made.

Notes

[1] With respect to the following preferential regime: Investment incentive order.

[2] Brunei has bilateral agreements in force with Bahrain, Cambodia, China (People's Republic of), Indonesia, Japan, Kuwait, Lao People's Democratic Republic, Luxembourg, Malaysia, Oman, Pakistan, Qatar, Singapore, Korea, United Arab Emirates, United Kingdom and Viet Nam.

Burkina Faso

Burkina Faso has met all aspects of the terms of reference (OECD, 2017[3]) (ToR) for the calendar year 2018 (year in review) that can be met in the absence of rulings being issued.

In the prior year report, Burkina Faso did not receive any recommendations.

Burkina Faso does not issue any type of ruling within the scope of the transparency framework. Burkina Faso only issues interpretative rulings. These tax rulings are not binding for the tax authorities and are therefore not considered rulings as defined in the Action 5 Report (OECD, 2015[5]). In the event that Burkina Faso puts in place the administrative process to issue rulings within the scope of the transparency framework, Burkina Faso notes that it would implement the transparency framework obligations.

As no exchanges were required to take place, no peer input was received in respect of the exchanges of information on rulings received from Burkina Faso.

Introduction

This peer review covers Burkina Faso's implementation of the BEPS Action 5 transparency framework for the year 2018. The report has four parts, each relating to a key part of the ToR. Each part is discussed in turn. A summary of recommendations is included at the end of this report.

A. The information gathering process

As no rulings are issued, this section is not assessed.

B. The exchange of information

As no rulings are issued, this section is not assessed.

C. Statistics (ToR IV)

As no rulings are issued, no statistics can be reported.

D. Matters related to intellectual property regimes (ToR I.4.1.3)

Burkina Faso does not offer an intellectual property regime for which transparency requirements under the Action 5 Report (OECD, 2015[5]) were imposed.

Summary of recommendations on implementation of the transparency framework

Aspect of implementation of the transparency framework that should be improved	Recommendation for improvement
	No recommendations are made.

Cameroon

Cameroon has met all aspects of the terms of reference (OECD, 2017[3]) (ToR) for the calendar year 2018 (year in review).

In the prior year review, Cameroon received two recommendations. These recommendations have been addressed and are removed, as noted below.

Cameroon does not issue any type of ruling within the scope of the transparency framework. Theoretically, there is no impediment for Cameroon to issue rulings, but in practice Cameroon does not issue any rulings. In the prior year peer review report, it was noted that it was not known whether Cameroon has implemented the transparency framework. However, it has since been confirmed that Cameroon does not issue in practice rulings to which the transparency framework applies. The two recommendations from the prior year report, relating to the identification and exchange of information on rulings, are no longer applicable. In the event that Cameroon put in place the administrative process or develop the administrative capacity to issue rulings, Cameroon notes that it would implement the transparency framework obligations.

As no exchanges were required to take place, no peer input was received in respect of the exchanges of information on rulings received from Cameroon.

Introduction

This peer review covers Cameroon's implementation of the BEPS Action 5 transparency framework for the year 2018. The report has four parts, each relating to a key part of the ToR. Each part is discussed in turn. A summary of recommendations is included at the end of this report.

A. The information gathering process

As no rulings are issued, this section is not assessed.

B. The exchange of information

As no rulings are issued, this section is not assessed.

C. Statistics (ToR IV)

As no rulings are issued, no statistics can be reported.

D. Matters related to intellectual property regimes (ToR I.4.1.3)

Cameroon does not offer an intellectual property regime for which transparency requirements under the Action 5 Report (OECD, 2015[5]) were imposed.

Summary of recommendations on implementation of the transparency framework

Aspect of implementation of the transparency framework that should be improved	Recommendation for improvement
	No recommendations are made.

Canada

Canada has met all aspects of the terms of reference (OECD, 2017[3]) (ToR) for the calendar year 2018 (year in review) and no recommendations are made.

In the prior year report, Canada did not receive any recommendations.

Canada can legally issue four types of rulings within the scope of the transparency framework. In practice, Canada issued rulings within the scope of the transparency framework as follows:

- 12 past rulings;
- For the period 1 April 2016 - 31 December 2016: two future rulings;
- For the calendar year 2017: two future rulings, and
- For the year in review: one future ruling.

With the exception of APAs, Canada's rulings are published in redacted form by third-party publishers who provide access to the documents to their subscribers and redacted rulings are available from the Canada Revenue Agency ("CRA") upon request.

Peer input was received from one jurisdiction in respect of the exchanges of information on rulings received from Canada. The input was generally positive, noting that information was complete, in correct format and received in a timely manner.

Introduction

This peer review covers Canada's implementation of the BEPS Action 5 transparency framework for the year 2018. The report has four parts, each relating to a key part of the ToR. Each part is discussed in turn. A summary of recommendations is included at the end of this report.

A. The information gathering process

Canada can legally issue the four following types of rulings within the scope of the transparency framework: (i) rulings related to a preferential regime;[1] (ii) cross-border unilateral advance pricing arrangements (APAs) and any other cross-border unilateral tax rulings (such as an advance tax ruling) covering transfer pricing or the application of transfer pricing principles; (iii) permanent establishment rulings; and (iv) related party conduit rulings.

Past rulings (ToR I.4.1.1, I.4.1.2, I.4.2.1, I.4.2.2)

For Canada, past rulings are any tax rulings within scope that are issued either: (i) on or after 1 January 2014 but before 1 April 2016; or (ii) on or after 1 January 2010 but before 1 January 2014, provided they were still in effect as at 1 January 2014.

In the prior year peer review reports, it was determined that Canada's undertakings to identify past rulings and all potential exchange jurisdictions were sufficient to meet the minimum standard. Canada's implementation in this regard remains unchanged, and therefore continues to meet the minimum standard.

Future rulings (ToR I.4.1.1, I.4.1.2, I.4.2.1)

For Canada, future rulings are any tax rulings within scope that are issued on or after 1 April 2016.

In the prior year peer review reports, it was determined that Canada's implementation of a new system to identify future rulings and all potential exchange jurisdictions was sufficient to meet the minimum standard. Canada's implementation in this regard remains unchanged, and therefore continues to meet the minimum standard.

Review and supervision (ToR I.4.3)

In the prior year peer review reports, it was determined that Canada's review and supervision mechanism was sufficient to meet the minimum standard. Canada's implementation in this regard remains unchanged, and therefore continues to meet the minimum standard.

Conclusion on section A

Canada has met all of the ToR for the information gathering process and no recommendations are made.

B. The exchange of information

Legal basis for spontaneous exchange of information (ToR II.5.1, II.5.2)

Canada has the necessary domestic legal basis to exchange information spontaneously. Canada notes that there are no legal or practical impediments that prevent the spontaneous exchange of information on rulings as contemplated in the Action 5 minimum standard.

Canada has international agreements permitting spontaneous exchange of information, including being a party to the (i) *Multilateral Convention on Mutual Administrative Assistance in Tax Matters: Amended by the 2010 Protocol* (OECD/Council of Europe, 2011[4]) ("the Convention"), (ii) double tax agreements in force with 94 jurisdictions[2], and (iii) tax information exchange agreements in force with 24 jurisdictions.

Completion and exchange of templates (ToR II.5.3, II.5.4, II.5.5, II.5.6, II.5.7)

In the prior year peer review report, it was determined that the Canada's completion and exchange of templates were sufficient to meet the minimum standard. The Canada's implementation in this regard remains unchanged, and therefore continues to meet the minimum standard.

For the year in review, the timeliness of exchanges is as follows:

Past rulings in the scope of the transparency framework	Number of exchanges transmitted by 31 December 2018	Delayed exchanges		
		Number of exchanges not transmitted by 31 December 2018	Reasons for the delays	Any other comments
	0	0	N/A	N/A
Future rulings in the scope of the transparency framework	Number of exchanges transmitted within three months of the information becoming available to the competent authority or immediately after legal impediments have been lifted	Delayed exchanges		
		Number of exchanges transmitted later than three months of the information on rulings becoming available to the competent authority	Reasons for the delays	Any other comments
	1	7	See below.	See below.
Total	1	7		

Follow up requests received for exchange of the ruling	Number	Average time to provide response	Number of requests not answered
	0	N/A	N/A

Canada noted that the delays were due to issues in the identification process caused by staff turnover, which has impacted in the exchange of information aspect. Canada clarified that these exchanges occurred between four months and up to six months from the moment the information became available to the competent authority, and within the year in review. Canada further noted that this was not a recurring issue and that during the year in review steps have been taken to ensure that such delays do not occur again.

Conclusion on section B

Canada has the necessary legal basis for spontaneous exchange of information, a process for completing the templates in a timely way and has completed all exchanges within a short time after the end of the year in review. Canada has met all of the ToR for the exchange of information process and no recommendations are made.

C. Statistics (ToR IV)

The statistics for the year in review are as follows:

Category of ruling	Number of exchanges	Jurisdictions exchanged with
Ruling related to a preferential regime	0	N/A

Cross-border unilateral advance pricing agreements (APAs) and any other cross-border unilateral tax rulings (such as an advance tax ruling) covering transfer pricing or the application of transfer pricing principles	7	China (People's Republic of), Germany, Hong Kong (China), Mexico, Netherlands, United States
Cross-border rulings providing for a unilateral downward adjustment to the taxpayer's taxable profits that is not directly reflected in the taxpayer's financial / commercial accounts	0	N/A
Permanent establishment rulings	1	*De minimis* rule applies
Related party conduit rulings	N/A	N/A
De minimis rule	N/A	N/A
IP regimes: total exchanges on taxpayers benefitting from the third category of IP assets, new entrants benefitting from grandfathered IP regimes; and taxpayers making use of the option to treat the nexus ratio as a rebuttable presumption	N/A	N/A
Total	8	

D. Matters related to intellectual property regimes (ToR I.4.1.3)

Canada does not offer an intellectual property regime for which transparency requirements under the Action 5 Report (OECD, 2015[5]) were imposed.

Summary of recommendations on implementation of the transparency framework

Aspect of implementation of the transparency framework that should be improved	Recommendation for improvement
Canada experienced some delays in exchanging information on future rulings.	No recommendation is made because Canada has since completed exchanges on the delayed future rulings in the year in review and this is not a recurring issue.

Notes

[1] With respect to the following preferential regimes: 1) Life insurance business and 2) International shipping.

[2] Parties to the Convention are available here: www.oecd.org/tax/exchange-of-tax-information/convention-on-mutual-administrative-assistance-in-tax-matters.htm. Canada also has double tax agreements with Algeria, Argentina, Armenia, Australia, Austria, Azerbaijan, Bangladesh, Barbados, Belgium, Brazil, Bulgaria, Cameroon, Chile, China (People's Republic of), Colombia, Cote d'Ivoire, Croatia, Cyprus, Czech Republic, Denmark, Dominican Republic, Ecuador, Egypt, Estonia, Finland, France, Gabon, Germany, Greece, Guyana, Hong Kong (China), Hungary, Iceland, India, Indonesia, Ireland, Israel, Italy, Jamaica, Japan, Jordan, Kazakhstan, Kenya, Korea, Kuwait, Kyrgyzstan, Latvia, Lithuania, Luxembourg, Malaysia, Malta, Mexico, Moldova, Mongolia, Morocco, Netherlands, New Zealand, Nigeria, Norway, Oman, Pakistan, Papua New Guinea, Peru, Philippines, Poland, Portugal, Romania, Russia, Senegal, Serbia, Singapore, Slovak Republic, Slovenia, South Africa, Spain, Sri Lanka, Sweden, Switzerland, Chinese Taipei, Tanzania, Thailand, Trinidad & Tobago, Tunisia, Turkey, Ukraine, United Arab Emirates, United

Kingdom, United States, Uzbekistan, Venezuela, Viet Nam, Zambia and Zimbabwe. The TIEA with Aruba also permits spontaneous exchange of information.

Note by Turkey: The information in this document with reference to “Cyprus” relates to the southern part of the Island. There is no single authority representing both Turkish and Greek Cypriot people on the Island. Turkey recognises the Turkish Republic of Northern Cyprus (TRNC). Until a lasting and equitable solution is found within the context of the United Nations, Turkey shall preserve its position concerning the “Cyprus issue”.

Note by all the European Union Member States of the OECD and the European Union. The Republic of Cyprus is recognised by all members of the United Nations with the exception of Turkey. The information in this document relates to the area under the effective control of the Government of the Republic of Cyprus.

Chile

Chile has met all aspects of the terms of reference (OECD, 2017[3]) (ToR) for the calendar year 2018 (year in review) that can be met in the absence of rulings being issued.

In the prior year report, Chile did not receive any recommendations.

Chile can legally issue two types of rulings within the scope of the transparency framework. In practice, Chile has issued no rulings within the scope of the transparency framework.

As no exchanges were required to take place, no peer input was received in respect of the exchanges of information on rulings received from Chile.

Introduction

This peer review covers Chile's implementation of the BEPS Action 5 transparency framework for the year 2018. The report has four parts, each relating to a key part of the ToR. Each part is discussed in turn. A summary of recommendations is included at the end of this report.

A. The information gathering process

Chile can legally issue the two following types of rulings within the scope of the transparency framework: (i) cross-border unilateral advance pricing arrangements (APAs) and any other cross-border unilateral tax rulings (such as an advance tax ruling) covering transfer pricing or the application of transfer pricing principles and (ii) related party conduit rulings.

Past rulings (ToR I.4.1.1, I.4.1.2, I.4.2.1, I.4.2.2)

For Chile, past rulings are any tax rulings within scope that are issued either: (i) on or after 1 January 2014 but before 1 April 2016; or (ii) on or after 1 January 2010 but before 1 January 2014, provided they were still in effect as at 1 January 2014.

In the prior years' peer review reports, it was determined that Chile's undertakings to identify past rulings and all potential exchange jurisdictions were sufficient to meet the minimum standard in the absence of rulings being issued in practice. Chile's implementation in this regard remains unchanged, and therefore continues to meet the minimum standard.

Future rulings (ToR I.4.1.1, I.4.1.2, I.4.2.1)

For Chile, future rulings are any tax rulings within scope that are issued on or after 1 April 2016.

In the prior years' peer review reports, it was determined that Chile's undertakings to identify future rulings and all potential exchange jurisdictions was sufficient to meet the minimum standard in the absence of rulings being issued in practice. Chile's implementation in this regard remains unchanged, and therefore continues to meet the minimum standard.

Review and supervision (ToR I.4.3)

In the prior years' peer review reports, it was determined that Chile's review and supervision mechanism currently in place and the procedure to be implemented once a larger number of rulings are issued were sufficient to meet the minimum standard. Chile's implementation in this regard remains unchanged, and therefore continues to meet the minimum standard.

Conclusion on section A

Chile has met all of the ToR for the information gathering process and no recommendations are made.

B. The exchange of information

Legal basis for spontaneous exchange of information (ToR II.5.1, II.5.2)

Chile has the necessary domestic legal basis to exchange information spontaneously. Chile notes that there are no legal or practical impediments that prevent the spontaneous exchange of information on rulings as contemplated in the Action 5 minimum standard.

Chile has international agreements permitting spontaneous exchange of information, including being a party to the (i) *Multilateral Convention on Mutual Administrative Assistance in Tax Matters: Amended by the 2010 Protocol* (OECD/Council of Europe, 2011[4]) ("the Convention") and (ii) bilateral agreements in force with 32 jurisdictions.[1]

Completion and exchange of templates (ToR II.5.3, II.5.4, II.5.5, II.5.6, II.5.7)

In the prior years' peer review reports, it was determined that Chile's process for the completion and exchange of templates that would be applicable if rulings were issued in practice was sufficient to meet the minimum standard. Chile's implementation in this regard remains unchanged and therefore continues to meet the minimum standard.

As Chile did not issue any rulings in scope of the transparency framework in the relevant period, Chile was not required to exchange any information on rulings in the year in review and no data on the timeliness of exchanges can be reported.

Conclusion on section B

Chile has the necessary legal basis for spontaneous exchange of information, a process for completing the templates in a timely way. Chile has met all of the ToR for the exchange of information process that can be met in the absence of rulings being issued and exchanged in practice and no recommendations are made.

C. Statistics (ToR IV)

As no information on rulings was exchanged for the year in review, no statistical data can be reported.

D. Matters related to intellectual property regimes (ToR I.4.1.3)

Chile does not offer an intellectual property regime for which transparency requirements under the Action 5 Report (OECD, 2015[5]) were imposed.

Summary of recommendations on implementation of the transparency framework

Aspect of implementation of the transparency framework that should be improved	Recommendation for improvement
	No recommendations are made.

Notes

[1] Parties to the Convention are available here: www.oecd.org/tax/exchange-of-tax-information/convention-on-mutual-administrative-assistance-in-tax-matters.htm. Chile also has bilateral agreements in force with Argentina, Australia, Austria, Belgium, Brazil, Canada, China (People's Republic of), Colombia, Croatia, Czech Republic, Denmark, Ecuador, France, Ireland, Italy, Japan, Korea, Malaysia, Mexico, Norway, New Zealand, Paraguay, Peru, Poland, Portugal, Russia, Spain, South Africa, Sweden, Switzerland, Thailand, United Kingdom and Uruguay.

China (People's Republic of)

The People's Republic of China ("China") has met all aspects of the terms of reference (OECD, 2017[3]) (ToR) for the calendar year 2018 (year in review) and no recommendations are made.

In the prior year report, China received one recommendation regarding the timely provision of information on rulings to the Competent Authority for exchange of information (ToR II.5.5). This recommendation has been addressed and is removed.

China can legally issue one type of rulings within the scope of the transparency framework. In practice, China issued rulings within the scope of the transparency framework as follows:

- 11 past rulings;
- For the period 1 April 2016 - 31 December 2016: six future rulings;
- For the calendar year 2017: three future rulings, and
- For the year in review: two future rulings.

Peer input was received from one jurisdiction in respect of the exchanges of information on rulings received from China. The input was generally positive, noting that information was complete, in a correct format and received in a timely manner.

Introduction

This peer review covers China's implementation of the BEPS Action 5 transparency framework for the year 2018. The report has four parts, each relating to a key part of the ToR. Each part is discussed in turn. A summary of recommendations is included at the end of this report.

A. The information gathering process

China can legally issue one type of ruling within the scope of the transparency framework: cross-border unilateral advance pricing agreements (APAs) covering transfer pricing or the application of transfer pricing principles.

Past rulings (ToR I.4.1.1, I.4.1.2, I.4.2.1, I.4.2.2)

There is a legal barrier to the exchange of information on rulings on China, which does not allow the exchange of past rulings. The legal framework in China was amended to allow exchanges on future rulings. As such, the balance of this report relates only to future rulings.

Future rulings (ToR I.4.1.1, I.4.1.2, I.4.2.1)

For China, future rulings are any tax rulings within scope that are issued on or after 1 April 2016.

In the prior year peer review report, it was determined that China's undertakings to identify future rulings and all potential exchange jurisdictions were sufficient to meet the minimum standard. China's implementation in this regard remains unchanged, and therefore continues to meet the minimum standard.

Review and supervision (ToR I.4.3)

In the prior year peer review report, it was determined that China's undertakings to identify future rulings and all potential exchange jurisdictions were sufficient to meet the minimum standard. China's implementation in this regard remains unchanged, and therefore continues to meet the minimum standard.

Conclusion on section A

For the year in review, China has met all of the ToR for the information gathering process and no recommendations are made.

B. The exchange of information

Legal basis for spontaneous exchange of information (ToR II.5.1, II.5.2)

China has implemented the necessary domestic legal basis to exchange information spontaneously in place. The legal framework in place does not allow the exchange of past rulings but does allow the exchange of information on future rulings, as from 1 April 2016.[1]

China is a party to international agreements permitting spontaneous exchange of information, including (i) the *Multilateral Convention on Mutual Administrative Assistance in Tax Matters: Amended by the 2010 Protocol* (OECD/Council of Europe, 2011) ("the Convention") and (ii) double tax agreements in force with 100 jurisdictions.[2]

Completion and exchange of templates (ToR II.5.3, II.5.4, II.5.5, II.5.6, II.5.7)

In the prior year peer review report, it was determined that China's process for the completion and exchange of templates was sufficient to meet the minimum standard, except for the timely provision of information on rulings to the Competent Authority for exchange of information (ToR II.5.5) which took place on a yearly basis. As noted in the prior year report, China took actions in March 2018 to remedy this issue and reduce the timelines for providing information on future rulings to the Competent Authority. The new information system allows the Chinese tax administration to identify and process information relating to unilateral APAs issued by the local tax administration officers within 10 days after an APA is issued. As such, this recommendation is removed.

For the year in review, the timeliness of exchanges is as follows:

Past rulings in the scope of the transparency framework	Number of exchanges transmitted by 31 December 2018	Delayed exchanges		
		Number of exchanges not transmitted by 31 December 2018	Reasons for the delays	Any other comments
	0	0	N/A	N/A
Future rulings in the scope of the transparency framework	Number of exchanges transmitted within three months of the information becoming available to the competent authority or immediately after legal impediments have been lifted	Delayed exchanges		
		Number of exchanges transmitted later than three months of the information on rulings becoming available to the competent authority	Reasons for the delays	Any other comments
	3	0	N/A	N/A
Total	3	0		

Follow up requests received for exchange of the ruling	Number	Average time to provide response	Number of requests not answered
	0	N/A	N/A

Conclusion on section B

China has the necessary legal basis for spontaneous exchange of information, a process for completing the templates in a timely way and has completed all exchanges. China has met all of the ToR for the exchange of information process and no recommendations are made.

C. Statistics (ToR IV)

The statistics for the year in review are as follows:

Category of ruling	Number of exchanges	Jurisdictions exchanged with
Ruling related to a preferential regime	N/A	N/A
Cross-border unilateral advance pricing agreements (APAs) and any other cross-border unilateral tax rulings (such as an advance tax ruling) covering transfer pricing or the application of transfer pricing principles	*De minimis* rule applies	N/A
Cross-border rulings providing for a unilateral downward adjustment to the	N/A	N/A

taxpayer's taxable profits that is not directly reflected in the taxpayer's financial / commercial accounts		
Permanent establishment rulings	N/A	N/A
Related party conduit rulings	N/A	N/A
De minimis rule	3	N/A
IP regimes: total exchanges on taxpayers benefitting from the third category of IP assets, new entrants benefitting from grandfathered IP regimes; and taxpayers making use of the option to treat the nexus ratio as a rebuttable presumption	N/A	N/A
Total	3	

D. Matters related to intellectual property regimes (ToR I.4.1.3)

In the prior years' peer review reports, it was determined that the transparency requirements were not relevant for China's intellectual property regime (Reduced rate for high & new tech enterprises).

Summary of recommendations on implementation of the transparency framework

Aspect of implementation of the transparency framework that should be improved	Recommendation for improvement
	No recommendations are made.

Notes

[1] Public Notice on Matters Regarding Enhancing the Administration of Advance Pricing Arrangements (SAT Public Notice [2016] No. 64).

[2] Parties to the Convention are available here: www.oecd.org/tax/exchange-of-tax-information/convention-on-mutual-administrative-assistance-in-tax-matters.htm. China also has bilateral agreements in force with Albania, Algeria, Armenia, Australia, Austria, Azerbaijan, Bahrein, Bangladesh, Barbados, Belarus, Belgium, Bosnia and Herzegovina, Brazil, Brunei Darussalam, Bulgaria, Cambodia, Canada, Chile, Croatia, Cuba, Cyprus, Czech Republic, Denmark, Ecuador, Egypt, Estonia, Ethiopia, Finland, France, Georgia, Germany, Greece, Hungary, Iceland, India, Indonesia, Iran, Ireland, Israel, Italy, Jamaica, Japan, Kazakhstan, Korea, Kuwait, Kyrgyzstan, Lao People's Democratic Republic, Latvia, Lithuania, Luxembourg, Malaysia, Malta, Mauritius, Mexico, Moldova, Mongolia, Montenegro, Morocco, Nepal, Netherlands, New Zealand, Nigeria, North Macedonia, Norway, Oman, Pakistan, Papua New Guinea, Philippines, Poland, Portugal, Qatar, Romania, Russia, Saudi Arabia, Serbia, Seychelles, Singapore, Slovenia, South Africa, Spain, Sri Lanka, Sudan, Sweden, Switzerland, Syria, Tajikistan, Thailand, Trinidad and Tobago, Tunisia, Turkey, Turkmenistan, Ukraine, United Arab Emirates, United Kingdom, United States, Uzbekistan, Venezuela, Viet Nam, Zambia and Zimbabwe.

Note by Turkey: The information in this document with reference to "Cyprus" relates to the southern part of the Island. There is no single authority representing both Turkish and Greek Cypriot people on the Island. Turkey recognises the Turkish Republic of Northern Cyprus (TRNC). Until a lasting and equitable solution is found within the context of the United Nations, Turkey shall preserve its position concerning the "Cyprus issue".

Note by all the European Union Member States of the OECD and the European Union. The Republic of Cyprus is recognised by all members of the United Nations with the exception of Turkey. The information in this document relates to the area under the effective control of the Government of the Republic of Cyprus.

Colombia

Colombia has met all aspects of the terms of reference (OECD, 2017[3]) (ToR) for the calendar year 2018 (year in review) and no recommendations are made.

In the prior year report, Colombia had received one recommendation, to ensure that all information on past rulings is exchanged as soon as possible (ToR II.5.6). This recommendation has been addressed and is removed.

Colombia can legally issue one type of ruling within the scope of the transparency framework. In practice, Colombia issued rulings within the scope of the transparency framework as follows:

- One past ruling;
- For the period 1 April 2016 - 31 December 2016: no future rulings;
- For the calendar year 2017: no future rulings, and
- For the year in review: no future rulings.

As no exchanges were required to take place, no peer input was received in respect of the exchanges of information on rulings received from Colombia.

Introduction

This peer review covers Colombia's implementation of the BEPS Action 5 transparency framework for the year 2018. The report has four parts, each relating to a key part of the ToR. Each part is discussed in turn. A summary of recommendations is included at the end of this report.

A. The information gathering process

Colombia can legally issue one type of rulings within the scope of the transparency framework: cross-border unilateral advance pricing agreements (APAs) and any other cross-border unilateral tax rulings (such as an advance tax ruling) covering transfer pricing or the application of transfer pricing principles.

Past rulings (ToR I.4.1.1, I.4.1.2, I.4.2.1, I.4.2.2)

For Colombia, past rulings are any tax rulings within scope that are issued either: (i) on or after 1 January 2014 but before 1 April 2016; or (ii) on or after 1 January 2010 but before 1 January 2014, provided they were still in effect as at 1 January 2016.

In the prior years' peer review reports, it was determined that Colombia's undertakings to identify past rulings and all potential exchange jurisdictions were sufficient to meet the minimum standard. Colombia's implementation in this regard remains unchanged, and therefore continues to meet the minimum standard.

Future rulings (ToR I.4.1.1, I.4.1.2, I.4.2.1)

For Colombia, future rulings are any tax rulings within scope that are issued on or after 1 April 2016.

In the prior year peer review report, it was determined that Colombia's implementation of a new system to identify future rulings and all potential exchange jurisdictions was sufficient to meet the minimum standard. Colombia's implementation in this regard remains unchanged, and therefore continues to meet the minimum standard.

Review and supervision (ToR I.4.3)

In the prior years' peer review reports, it was determined that Colombia's review and supervision mechanism was sufficient to meet the minimum standard. Colombia's implementation in this regard remains unchanged, and therefore continues to meet the minimum standard.

Conclusion on section A

Colombia has met all of the ToR for the information gathering process and no recommendations are made.

B. The exchange of information

Legal basis for spontaneous exchange of information (ToR II.5.1, II.5.2)

Colombia has the necessary domestic legal basis to exchange information spontaneously. Colombia notes that there are no legal or practical impediments that prevent the spontaneous exchange of information on rulings as contemplated in the Action 5 minimum standard.

Colombia has international agreements permitting spontaneous exchange of information, including being a party to the (i) *Multilateral Convention on Mutual Administrative Assistance in Tax Matters: Amended by the 2010 Protocol* (OECD/Council of Europe, 2011[4]) ("the Convention"), (ii) double tax agreements in force with 9 jurisdictions, (iii) multilateral tax agreements in force with three jurisdictions and (iv) tax information exchange agreements with one jurisdictions.[1]

Completion and exchange of templates (ToR II.5.3, II.5.4, II.5.5, II.5.6, II.5.7)

In the prior year peer review report, it was determined that Colombia's process for the completion and exchange of templates met all the ToR, except for completing exchanges of information on past rulings in accordance with the timelines (ToR II.5.6). Therefore, Colombia was recommended to ensure that all information on past rulings is exchanged as soon as possible.

During the year in review, Colombia exchanged information on past rulings with the relevant Competent Authorities. Therefore, the ToR is met and recommendation is removed.

For the year in review, the timeliness of exchanges is as follows:

Past rulings in the scope of the transparency framework	Number of exchanges transmitted by 31 December 2018	Delayed exchanges		
		Number of exchanges not transmitted by 31 December 2018	Reasons for the delays	Any other comments
	2	0	N/A	N/A
Future rulings in the scope of the transparency framework	Number of exchanges transmitted within three months of the information becoming available to the competent authority or immediately after legal impediments have been lifted	Delayed exchanges		
		Number of exchanges transmitted later than three months of the information on rulings becoming available to the competent authority	Reasons for the delays	Any other comments
	0	0	N/A	N/A
Total	2	0		

Follow up requests received for exchange of the ruling	Number	Average time to provide response	Number of requests not answered
	0	N/A	N/A

Conclusion on section B

Colombia has the necessary legal basis for spontaneous exchange of information, a process for completing the templates in a timely way and has completed all exchanges. Colombia has met all of the ToR for the exchange of information process and no recommendations are made.

C. Statistics (ToR IV)

The statistics for the year in review are as follows:

Category of ruling	Number of exchanges	Jurisdictions exchanged with
Ruling related to a preferential regime	N/A	N/A
Cross-border unilateral advance pricing agreements (APAs) and any other cross-border unilateral tax rulings (such as an advance tax ruling) covering transfer pricing or the application of	*De minimis rule* applies	N/A

transfer pricing principles		
Cross-border rulings providing for a unilateral downward adjustment to the taxpayer's taxable profits that is not directly reflected in the taxpayer's financial / commercial accounts	N/A	N/A
Permanent establishment rulings	N/A	N/A
Related party conduit rulings	N/A	N/A
De minimis rule	2	N/A
IP regimes: total exchanges on taxpayers benefitting from the third category of IP assets, new entrants benefitting from grandfathered IP regimes; and taxpayers making use of the option to treat the nexus ratio as a rebuttable presumption	N/A	N/A
Total	2	

D. Matters related to intellectual property regimes (ToR I.4.1.3)

Colombia does not offer an intellectual property regime for which transparency requirements under the Action 5 Report (OECD, 2015[5]) were imposed.

Summary of recommendations on implementation of the transparency framework

Aspect of implementation of the transparency framework that should be improved	Recommendation for improvement
	No recommendations are made.

Notes

[1] Parties to the Convention are available here: www.oecd.org/tax/exchange-of-tax-information/convention-on-mutual-administrative-assistance-in-tax-matters.htm. Colombia also has bilateral agreements in force with Canada, Chile, Czech Republic, India, Korea, Mexico, Portugal, Spain and Switzerland; multilateral tax agreements in force with Bolivia, Ecuador and Peru; and a tax information exchange agreement with the United States.

Congo

Congo is taking steps to implement the legal basis for the transparency framework and to commence administrative preparations to ensure that information on rulings will be exchanged in a timely manner, in line with the terms of reference (OECD, 2017[3]) (ToR). Congo is recommended to ensure that it has put in place an effective information gathering process and to implement a review and supervision mechanism, as soon as possible (ToR I.4). In addition, Congo is recommended to develop a process to complete the templates on relevant rulings, to ensure that the exchanges of information on rulings occur in accordance with the form and timelines under the transparency framework going forward (ToR II.5).

Congo can legally issue two types of rulings within the scope of the transparency framework. In the prior year peer review report, it was noted that it was not known whether Congo has implemented the transparency framework. However, it has since been confirmed that Congo can issue rulings to which the transparency framework applies.

In practice, Congo has issued no rulings in the year in review.

As no exchanges were required to take place, no peer input was received in respect of the exchanges of information on rulings received from Congo.

Introduction

This peer review covers Congo's implementation of the BEPS Action 5 transparency framework for the year 2018. The report has four parts, each relating to a key part of the ToR. Each part is discussed in turn. A summary of recommendations is included at the end of this report.

A. The information gathering process

Congo can legally issue two types of rulings within the scope of the transparency framework: i) cross-border unilateral advance pricing agreements (APAs) and any other cross-border unilateral tax rulings (such as an advance tax ruling) covering transfer pricing or the application of transfer pricing principles and ii) PE rulings.

For Congo, past rulings are any tax rulings within scope that are issued either (i) on or after 1 January 2015 but before 1 April 2017; and (ii) on or after 1 January 2012 but before 1 January 2015, provided still in effect as at 1 January 2015.

In Congo, rulings are issued by the directorate of Legislation, within the Tax Administration. This unit is responsible for storing and reviewing such rulings and has reviewed its files, being able to confirm that no past rulings have been issued. To date no rulings have been issued. As such there was no need to identify potential exchange jurisdictions.

Future rulings (ToR I.4.1.1, I.4.1.2, I.4.2.1)

For Congo, future rulings are any tax rulings within scope that are issued on or after 1 April 2017.

No rulings were issued by Congo during the future rulings period in the year of review. However, Congo indicates that there are no processes in place for the record keeping of rulings for the purposes of the transparency framework. It is noted that Congo intends to implement guidelines and practices to make sure the necessary information to meet the requirements of the transparency framework is required in all cases.

Review and supervision (ToR I.4.3)

Congo did not yet have a review and supervision mechanism under the transparency framework for the year in review. Congo is discussing the implementation of a revision and supervision mechanism for ensuring implementation of the transparency framework.

Conclusion on section A

Congo is recommended to finalise its information gathering, with a review and supervision mechanism, as soon as possible (ToR I.4).

B. The exchange of information

Legal basis for spontaneous exchange of information (ToR II.5.1, II.5.2)

Congo is currently in the process of putting in place the necessary domestic legal basis to exchange information spontaneously.

Congo currently has three agreements in effect which would allow for spontaneous exchange of information under the transparency framework.[1] Congo is not a Party to the *Multilateral Convention on Mutual Administrative Assistance in Tax Matters: Amended by the 2010 Protocol* (OECD/Council of Europe, 2011[4]) ("the Convention"). Congo is encouraged to continue its efforts to expand its international exchange of information instruments to be able to exchange rulings. It is however noted that jurisdictions are assessed on their compliance with the transparency framework in respect of the exchange of information network in effect for the year of the particular annual review.

Completion and exchange of templates (ToR II.5.3, II.5.4, II.5.5, II.5.6, II.5.7)

Congo is still developing a process to complete the templates on relevant rulings, to make them available to the Competent Authority for exchange of information, and to exchange them with relevant jurisdictions.

As no exchanges were required to take place in the year of review, no data on the timeliness of exchanges can be reported.

Conclusion on section B

Congo is recommended to put in place a domestic legal framework allowing spontaneous exchange of information on rulings and to continue its efforts to complete the templates for all relevant rulings and to ensure that the exchanges of information on rulings occur as soon as possible (ToR II.5).

C. Statistics (ToR IV)

As no rulings are issued, no statistics can be reported.

D. Matters related to intellectual property regimes (ToR I.4.1.3)

Congo does not offer an intellectual property regime for which transparency requirements under the Action 5 Report (OECD, 2015[5]) were imposed.

Summary of recommendations on implementation of the transparency framework

Aspect of implementation of the transparency framework that should be improved	Recommendation for improvement
Congo has not yet finalised the steps to have in place its necessary information and gathering process.	Congo is recommended to finalise its information gathering process, with a review and supervision mechanism, as soon as possible.
Congo has not yet finalised the steps to have effective compulsory spontaneous exchange of information on the tax rulings within the scope of the transparency framework.	Congo is recommended to continue to put in place a domestic legal framework allowing spontaneous exchange of information on rulings and to continue its efforts to complete the templates for all relevant rulings and to ensure the timely exchange of information on rulings in the form required by the transparency framework.

Notes

[1] Congo has bilateral agreements in force with France, Italy and Mauritius.

Costa Rica

Costa Rica has met all aspects of the terms of reference (OECD, 2017[3]) (ToR) for the calendar year 2018 (year in review) except for having in place an effective review and supervision mechanism to ensure that all relevant information is captured adequately (ToR I.4.3) and ensuring that information on rulings is transmitted to the Competent Authority responsible for international exchange of information without undue delay (ToR II.5.5). Costa Rica receives two recommendations on these points for the year in review.

In the prior year report, Costa Rica had received three recommendations. For the year in review, two recommendations made in the prior year peer review report have been addressed and are removed. The other recommendation has not been addressed and remains in place. A new recommendation has been added.

Costa Rica can legally issue two types of rulings within the scope of the transparency framework. In practice, Costa Rica issued rulings within the scope of the transparency framework as follows:

- Six past rulings;
- For the period 1 April 2017 - 31 December 2017: three future rulings, and
- For the year in review: four future rulings.

No peer input was received in respect of the exchanges of information on rulings received from Costa Rica.

Introduction

This peer review covers Costa Rica's implementation of the BEPS Action 5 transparency framework for the year 2018. The report has four parts, each relating to a key part of the ToR. Each part is discussed in turn. A summary of recommendations is included at the end of this report.

A. The information gathering process

Costa Rica can legally issue the following two types of rulings within the scope of the transparency framework: (i) cross-border unilateral advance pricing arrangements (APAs) and any other cross-border unilateral tax rulings (such as an advance tax ruling) covering transfer pricing or the application of transfer pricing principles; and (ii) permanent establishment (PE) rulings. To date, Costa Rica has issued only PE rulings given the resolution that establishes the requirements taxpayers must provide has not been issue yet.

Past rulings (ToR I.4.1.1, I.4.1.2, I.4.2.1, I.4.2.2)

For Costa Rica, past rulings are any tax rulings within scope that are issued either: (i) on or after 1 January 2015 but before 1 April 2017; or (ii) on or after 1 January 2012 but before 1 January 2015, provided they were still in effect as at 1 January 2015.

In the prior year peer review report, it was determined that Costa Rica's undertakings to identify past rulings and all potential exchange jurisdictions met all the ToR, except for identifying information on the jurisdiction of the ultimate parent company through the "best efforts approach" (ToR I.4.2.2). Therefore, Costa Rica was recommended to continue its work to complete its information-gathering process on past rulings as soon as possible. During the year in review, Costa Rica identified all potential exchange jurisdictions. In practice, the jurisdictions identified were the same as the jurisdiction of residence of immediate parent entity, ultimate parent entity, head office or jurisdiction of the PE that had been previously identified. Costa Rica has addressed this issue and therefore this recommendation is removed.

In the course of making efforts to identify the remaining potential exchange jurisdictions in the year of review, Costa Rica determined that the two past rulings identified in the prior year peer review report were in fact future rulings and identified a total of six past rulings not previously reported. All past rulings have now been identified. Costa Rica was also able to identify the potential exchange jurisdictions for these rulings.

Future rulings (ToR I.4.1.1, I.4.1.2, I.4.2.1)

For Costa Rica, future rulings are any tax rulings within scope that are issued on or after 1 April 2017.

In the prior year peer review report, it was determined that Costa Rica's undertakings to identify future rulings and all potential exchange jurisdictions met all the ToR, except for ensuring that information on all potential exchange jurisdictions is obtained for future rulings (ToR I.4.2.1). Therefore, Costa Rica was recommended to continue its efforts to ensure that all potential exchange jurisdictions are identified swiftly for all future rulings.

In order to identify potential exchange jurisdictions, information is first obtained from the rulings. In practice, in most cases information is also publicly available, given that usually taxpayers requiring PE rulings are permanent establishments of companies listed on the stock exchange and subject to a regulatory framework which includes disclosing their head office details. For the year in review, the process described above allowed Costa Rica to identify all potential exchange jurisdictions. However, if any information on potential exchange jurisdictions was missing, Costa Rica would require the taxpayer to provide the information or would conduct a search for the information in possession of the local tax administrations, meaning the information would always be obtained. Therefore this recommendation is removed.

It is noted that Costa Rica is working to further strengthen the information gathering process for rulings, including through access to a shareholder register and draft resolutions on the issuance of rulings. This will be reviewed in the subsequent peer review.

During the year in review, in the course of making efforts to identify the remaining potential exchange jurisdictions, Costa Rica identified a total of three future rulings issued in 2017 and four future rulings issued in 2018 not previously reported. For all those future rulings, Costa Rica identified all potential exchange jurisdictions. For the sake of completeness, it is noted that for each ruling the immediate parent entity, ultimate parent entity, head office or PE are all resident in the same jurisdiction.

Review and supervision (ToR I.4.3)

In the prior year peer review report, it was determined that Costa Rica's review and supervision mechanism was sufficient to meet the minimum standard. During the year in review, as noted above, additional rulings were found that had not previously been identified. Costa Rica remedied the issue after the year in review and completed the additional exchanges in 2019. Costa Rica is recommended to strengthen its review and supervision mechanism to ensure that the information gathering process is working effectively to ensure that similar issues are not encountered in future.

Conclusion on section A

For the year in review, Costa Rica has met the ToR for the information gathering process, except for having in place a review and supervision mechanism to ensure that all relevant information is captured adequately (ToR I.4.3). Costa Rica is recommended to strengthen its review and supervision mechanism to ensure that the information gathering process is working effectively.

B. The exchange of information

Legal basis for spontaneous exchange of information (ToR II.5.1, II.5.2)

Costa Rica has the necessary domestic legal basis to exchange information spontaneously. Costa Rica notes that there are no legal or practical impediments that prevent the spontaneous exchange of information on rulings as contemplated in the Action 5 minimum standard.

Costa Rica has international agreements permitting spontaneous exchange of information, including being a party to the (i) *Multilateral Convention on Mutual Administrative Assistance in Tax Matters: Amended by the 2010 Protocol* (OECD/Council of Europe, 2011[4]) ("the Convention"), (ii) double tax agreements in force with three jurisdictions, and iii) tax information exchange agreements in force with two jurisdictions.[1]

Completion and exchange of templates (ToR II.5.3, II.5.4, II.5.5, II.5.6, II.5.7)

In the prior year peer review report, it was determined that Costa Rica's process for the completion and exchange of templates met all the ToR, except for having in place a process to complete the templates in the form required by the transparency framework and submit them to the Competent Authority and completing exchanges of information on rulings in accordance with the timelines (ToR II.5). Therefore, Costa Rica was recommended to continue its efforts to complete the templates for all relevant rulings and to ensure that the exchanges of information on rulings occur as soon as possible.

For the year in review, Costa Rica sought to ensure that the information exchanged was in the form of the template contained in Annex C of the 2015 Action 5 Report (OECD, 2015[5]), however in practice this did not happen in all cases and for four future rulings, corrected templates were required to be sent in 2019.

In terms of process, Costa Rica clarified that the Transfer Pricing unit is responsible for completing the template for PE rulings. Several levels of review and supervision are performed by the deputy director of the Transfer Pricing unit and the director of International Taxation. Once the template is approved by the

General Tax Administration Director, it is transmitted to the EOI unit which will perform the exchanges via encrypted email with relevant jurisdictions.

During the year in review, Costa Rica experienced some delay in the process of completing and exchanging the templates mainly due to issues in the information gathering process identified in part A above and the lack of a procedure for the timely transmission of templates to the Competent Authority after a ruling is issued. Costa Rica is currently working on a procedure to ensure that templates for future rulings are transmitted to the Competent Authority within two months from the date of their issuance. However, once templates were received by the Competent Authority, they were exchanged with the relevant jurisdictions within the agreed three month period, and on average after two days of the Competent Authority having received them.

For the year in review, the timeliness of exchanges is as follows:

Past rulings in the scope of the transparency framework	Number of exchanges transmitted by 31 December 2018	Delayed exchanges		
		Number of exchanges not transmitted by 31 December 2018	Reasons for the delays	Any other comments
	0	6	See below.	Costa Rica exchanged all information on its past rulings in June 2019.
Future rulings in the scope of the transparency framework	Number of exchanges transmitted within three months of the information becoming available to the competent authority or immediately after legal impediments have been lifted	Delayed exchanges		
		Number of exchanges transmitted later than three months of the information on rulings becoming available to the competent authority	Reasons for the delays	Any other comments
	7	0	See below.	Costa Rica exchanged all information on its future rulings by June 2019.
Total	7	6		

Follow up requests received for exchange of the ruling	Number	Average time to provide response	Number of requests not answered
	N/A	N/A	N/A

Costa Rica explained that the transmission delay is due to the delayed identification of tax rulings in scope (as noted in section A above) and the absence of a procedure aimed at ensuring that that templates rulings were timely transmitted to the Competent Authority.

Conclusion on section B

Costa Rica has the necessary legal basis for spontaneous exchange of information. Costa Rica has met all of the ToR for the exchange of information except for ensuring that information on rulings is transmitted to the Competent Authority responsible for international exchange of information without undue delay.

Costa Rica is recommended to continue its efforts to ensure that information on rulings is transmitted to the Competent Authority without undue delay (ToR II.5.5).

C. Statistics (ToR IV)

The statistics for the year in review are as follows:

Category of ruling	Number of exchanges	Jurisdictions exchanged with
Ruling related to a preferential regime	N/A	N/A
Cross-border unilateral advance pricing agreements (APAs) and any other cross-border unilateral tax rulings (such as an advance tax ruling) covering transfer pricing or the application of transfer pricing principles	N/A	N/A
Cross-border rulings providing for a unilateral downward adjustment to the taxpayer's taxable profits that is not directly reflected in the taxpayer's financial / commercial accounts	N/A	N/A
Permanent establishment rulings	*De minimis* rule applies	N/A
Related party conduit rulings	N/A	N/A
De minimis rule	5	N/A
IP regimes: total exchanges on taxpayers benefitting from the third category of IP assets, new entrants benefitting from grandfathered IP regimes; and taxpayers making use of the option to treat the nexus ratio as a rebuttable presumption	N/A	N/A
Total	5	

D. Matters related to intellectual property regimes (ToR I.4.1.3)

Costa Rica does not offer an intellectual property regime for which transparency requirements under the Action 5 Report (OECD, 2015[5]) were imposed.

Summary of recommendations on implementation of the transparency framework

Aspect of implementation of the transparency framework that should be improved	Recommendation for improvement
Costa Rica experienced difficulties in ensuring that all relevant information is captured adequately and identified additional past and future rulings that were not previously captured.	Costa Rica is recommended to strengthen its review and supervision mechanism to ensure that the information gathering process is working effectively.
Costa Rica experienced difficulties in ensuring that information on rulings is transmitted to the Competent Authority responsible for international exchange of information without undue delay.	Costa Rica is recommended to continue its efforts to ensure that information on rulings is transmitted to the Competent Authority without undue delay. This recommendation remains unchanged since the prior year peer review report.

Notes

[1] Parties to the Convention are available here: www.oecd.org/tax/exchange-of-tax-information/convention-on-mutual-administrative-assistance-in-tax-matters.htm. Costa Rica also has double tax agreements with Germany, Mexico, and Spain and tax information exchange agreements with Argentina and the United States.

Côte d'Ivoire

Côte d'Ivoire has met all aspects of the terms of reference (OECD, 2017[3]) (ToR) for the calendar year 2018 (year in review) that can be met in the absence of rulings being issued.

In the prior year report, Côte d'Ivoire did not receive any recommendations.

Côte d'Ivoire does not issue any type of ruling within the scope of the transparency framework. Côte d'Ivoire only issues interpretative rulings. These tax rulings are not binding for the tax authorities and are therefore not considered rulings as defined in the Action 5 Report (OECD, 2015[5]). In the event that Côte d'Ivoire puts in place the administrative process to issue rulings within the scope of the transparency framework, Côte d'Ivoire notes that it would implement the transparency framework obligations.

As no exchanges were required to take place, no peer input was received in respect of the exchanges of information on rulings received from Côte d'Ivoire.

Introduction

This peer review covers Côte d'Ivoire's implementation of the BEPS Action 5 transparency framework for the year 2018. The report has four parts, each relating to a key part of the ToR. Each part is discussed in turn. A summary of recommendations is included at the end of this report.

A. The information gathering process

As no rulings are issued, this section is not assessed.

B. The exchange of information

As no rulings are issued, this section is not assessed.

C. Statistics (ToR IV)

As no rulings are issued, no statistics can be reported.

D. Matters related to intellectual property regimes (ToR I.4.1.3)

Côte d'Ivoire does not offer an intellectual property regime for which transparency requirements under the Action 5 Report (OECD, 2015[5]) were imposed.

Summary of recommendations on implementation of the transparency framework

Aspect of implementation of the transparency framework that should be improved	Recommendation for improvement
	No recommendations are made.

Croatia

Croatia has met all aspects of the terms of reference (OECD, 2017[3]) (ToR) for the calendar year 2018 (year in review) and no recommendations are made.

In the prior year report, Croatia did not receive any recommendations.

Croatia can legally issue four types of rulings within the scope of the transparency framework. In practice, Croatia issued rulings within the scope of the transparency framework as follows:

- No past rulings;
- For the period 1 April 2017 - 31 December 2017: no future rulings; and
- For the year in review: one future ruling.

As no exchanges took place during the year in review, no peer input was received in respect of the exchanges of information on rulings received from Croatia.

Introduction

This peer review covers Croatia's implementation of the BEPS Action 5 transparency framework for the year 2018. The report has four parts, each relating to a key part of the ToR. Each part is discussed in turn. A summary of recommendations is included at the end of this report.

A. The information gathering process

Croatia can legally issue the following four types of rulings within the scope of the transparency framework: (i) cross-border unilateral APAs and any other cross-border unilateral tax rulings (such as an advance tax ruling) covering transfer pricing or the application of transfer pricing principles; (ii) rulings providing for unilateral downward adjustments; (iii) permanent establishment rulings; and (iv) related party conduit rulings.

Past rulings (ToR I.4.1.1, I.4.1.2, I.4.2.1, I.4.2.2)

For Croatia, past rulings are any tax rulings within scope that are issued either (i) on or after 1 January 2015 but before 1 April 2017; and (ii) on or after 1 January 2012 but before 1 January 2015, provided they were still in effect as at 1 January 2015.

In the prior year peer review report, it was determined that Croatia's undertakings to identify past rulings and all potential exchange jurisdictions were sufficient to meet the minimum standard. Croatia's implementation in this regard remains unchanged, and therefore continues to meet the minimum standard.

Future rulings (ToR I.4.1.1, I.4.1.2, I.4.2.1)

For Croatia, future rulings are any tax rulings within scope that are issued on or after 1 April 2017.

In the prior year peer review report, it was determined that Croatia's implementation of a new system to identify future rulings and all potential exchange jurisdictions was sufficient to meet the minimum standard. Croatia's implementation in this regard remains unchanged, and therefore continues to meet the minimum standard.

Review and supervision (ToR I.4.3)

In the prior year peer review report, it was determined that Croatia's review and supervision mechanism was sufficient to meet the minimum standard. Croatia's implementation in this regard remains unchanged, and therefore continues to meet the minimum standard.

Conclusion on section A

Croatia has met all of the ToR for the information gathering process and no recommendations are made.

B. The exchange of information

Legal basis for spontaneous exchange of information (ToR II.5.1, II.5.2)

Croatia has the necessary domestic legal basis to exchange information spontaneously. Croatia notes that there are no legal or practical impediments that prevent the spontaneous exchange of information on rulings as contemplated in the Action 5 minimum standard.

Croatia has international agreements permitting spontaneous exchange of information, including being a party to the (i) *Multilateral Convention on Mutual Administrative Assistance in Tax Matters: Amended by the 2010 Protocol* (OECD/Council of Europe, 2011[4]) ("the Convention"), (ii) the Directive 2011/16/EU with all other European Union Member States and (iii) double tax agreements in force with 63 jurisdictions.[1]

Completion and exchange of templates (ToR II.5.3, II.5.4, II.5.5, II.5.6, II.5.7)

In the prior year peer review report, it was determined that Croatia's process for the completion and exchange of templates were sufficient to meet the minimum standard. Croatia's implementation in this regard remains unchanged and therefore continues to meet the minimum standard.

For the year in review, the timeliness of exchanges is as follows:

		Delayed exchanges		
Past rulings in the scope of the transparency framework	Number of exchanges transmitted by 31 December 2018	Number of exchanges not transmitted by 31 December 2018	Reasons for the delays	Any other comments
	0	0	N/A	N/A
Future rulings in the scope of the transparency framework	Number of exchanges transmitted within three months of the information becoming available to the competent authority or immediately after legal impediments have been lifted	Number of exchanges transmitted later than three months of the information on rulings becoming available to the competent authority	Reasons for the delays	Any other comments
	0	1	Application of the EU DAC 3 deadlines.	The exchange took place in April 2019 and thus this will be taken into account in next year's peer review.
Total	0	1		

Follow up requests received for exchange of the ruling	Number	Average time to provide response	Number of requests not answered
	0	N/A	N/A

Croatia issued one ruling in November 2018 (which is towards the end of the year in review), which was exchanged later than three months after becoming available to the competent authority, because Croatia used the EU DAC3 timelines. After discussion with the Secretariat, Croatia exchanged information on the ruling as soon as possible, in April 2019, and changed the timelines for rulings in scope of the transparency framework going forward in order to meet the expectations under the BEPS Action 5 transparency framework. The information on these rulings will now be exchanged within three months after becoming available to the Competent Authority. As the information on the ruling is exchanged with a relatively short delay of five months after issue, and this is not a recurring issue, no recommendation is made.

Conclusion on section B

Croatia has the necessary legal basis for spontaneous exchange of information, a process for completing the templates in a timely way and has completed all exchanges. Croatia has met all of the ToR for the exchange of information process and no recommendations are made.

C. Statistics (ToR IV)

As there was no information on rulings exchanged by Croatia for the year in review, no statistics can be reported.

D. Matters related to intellectual property regimes (ToR I.4.1.3)

Croatia does not offer an intellectual property regime for which transparency requirements under the Action 5 Report (OECD, 2015[5]) were imposed.

Summary of recommendations on implementation of the transparency framework

Aspect of implementation of the transparency framework that should be improved	Recommendation for improvement
Croatia experienced some delays in exchanging information on one future ruling.	No recommendation is made because Croatia has since completed exchanges on the delayed future ruling quickly after the issues were identified and resolved, and this is not a recurring issue.

Notes

[1] Parties to the Convention are available here: www.oecd.org/tax/exchange-of-tax-information/convention-on-mutual-administrative-assistance-in-tax-matters.htm. Croatia also has bilateral agreements with Albania, Armenia, Austria, Azerbaijan, Belarus, Belgium, Bosnia and Herzegovina, Bulgaria, Canada, Chile, China (People's Republic of), Czech Republic, Denmark, Estonia, Finland, France, Georgia, Germany, Greece, Hungary, Iceland, India, Indonesia, Iran, Ireland, Israel, Italy, Jordan, Korea, Kosovo, Kuwait, Latvia, Lithuania, Luxembourg, Malaysia, Malta, Mauritius, Morocco, Moldova, Montenegro, Netherlands, North Macedonia, Norway, Oman, Poland, Portugal, Qatar, Romania, Russia, San Marino, Serbia, Slovak Republic, Slovenia, South Africa, Spain, Syrian Arab Republic, Sweden, Switzerland, Turkey, Turkmenistan, Ukraine, United Arab Emirates and United Kingdom.

Curaçao

Curaçao has met all aspects of the terms of reference (OECD, 2017[3]) (ToR) for the calendar year 2018 (year in review) except for identifying tax rulings that are in the scope of the transparency framework and which category of rulings they fall under (ToR I.4.1.2) and completing exchanges of information on rulings in accordance with the timelines (ToR II.5.5 and II.5.6). Curaçao receives two recommendations on these points for the year in review.

In the prior year report, Curaçao received the same two recommendations. As they have not been addressed, the recommendations remain in place.

Curaçao can legally issue five types of rulings within the scope of the transparency framework. In practice, Curaçao issued rulings that are potentially within the scope of the transparency framework as follows:

- 3,630 past rulings;
- For the period 1 April 2017 - 31 December 2017: 320 future rulings; and
- For the year in review: 50 future rulings.

Peer input was received from four jurisdictions in respect of the exchanges of information on rulings received from Curaçao. The input was generally positive, noting that information was complete, in a correct format and received in a timely manner.

Introduction

This peer review covers Curaçao's implementation of the BEPS Action 5 transparency framework for the year 2018. The report has four parts, each relating to a key part of the ToR. Each part is discussed in turn. A summary of recommendations is included at the end of this report.

A. The information gathering process

Curaçao can legally issue the five following types of rulings within the scope of the transparency framework: (i) taxpayer specific rulings related to preferential regimes;[1] (ii) cross-border unilateral advance pricing arrangements (APAs) and any other cross-border unilateral tax rulings (such as an advance tax ruling) covering transfer pricing or the application of transfer pricing principles; (iii) rulings providing for unilateral downward adjustments; and (iv) related party conduit rulings.

Past rulings (ToR I.4.1.1, I.4.1.2, I.4.2.1, I.4.2.2)

For Curaçao, past rulings are any tax rulings within scope that are issued either: (i) on or after 1 January 2015 but before 1 April 2017; or (ii) on or after 1 January 2012 but before 1 January 2015, provided they were still in effect as at 1 January 2015.

In the prior year peer review report, it was determined that Curaçao's undertakings to identify past rulings and all potential exchange jurisdictions have met all the ToR, except for completing the process of reviewing the templates to confirm that all past rulings identified are cross-border rulings and therefore within the scope of the transparency framework, and to identify which category of rulings they fall under (ToR I.4.1.2). Therefore, Curaçao was recommended to continue its work to complete its information gathering process on past rulings as soon as possible.

During the year in review, Curaçao continued its work to accurately identify and categorise past rulings. This process is still ongoing given the large number of rulings, many of which fall into more than one category. As Curaçao completes the identification and categorisation process, they are also identifying the potential exchange jurisdictions. This process will be completed by the end of 2019. Therefore, the prior year recommendation remains.

Future rulings (ToR I.4.1.1, I.4.1.2, I.4.2.1)

For Curaçao, future rulings are any tax rulings within scope that are issued on or after 1 April 2017.

In the prior year peer review report, it was determined that Curaçao's undertakings to identify future rulings and all potential exchange jurisdictions have met all the ToR, except for completing the process of reviewing the templates to confirm that all future rulings identified are cross border rulings and therefore within the scope of the transparency framework, and to identify which category each ruling falls into (ToR I.4.1.2). Therefore, Curaçao was recommended to continue its work to complete its information-gathering process on future rulings as soon as possible.

During the year in review, Curaçao continued its work on reviewing future rulings in order to identify all rulings in scope and assess the definitive number of rulings per category. This process is still ongoing with respect to future rulings issued before July 2018. This process will be completed by the end of 2019. Therefore, the prior year recommendation remains.

In addition, Curaçao has made amendments to the ruling practice. The new prerequisites to obtain a ruling are that an updated structure chart and a completed template must be provided to the Curaçao Tax Authority with the request for a tax ruling. Information regarding the type of rulings and the potential exchange jurisdictions is captured in this template. These additional prerequisites were communicated to taxpayers and tax advisers and published in February 2018, and implementation was completed by July 2018. This amended ruling process means that from July 2018, future rulings and potential exchange jurisdictions are immediately identified at the point of issue.

Curaçao is also working on the development of an electronic online system to digitalise the ruling request process. This new electronic procedure will further affect the information gathering process and the exchanges activities performed and will be reviewed in the subsequent peer reviews as soon as the online system is in operation.

Review and supervision (ToR I.4.3)

In the prior year peer review report, it was determined that Curaçao's review and supervision mechanism was sufficient to meet the minimum standard. Curaçao's implementation in this regard remains unchanged, and therefore continues to meet the minimum standard.

Conclusion on section A

Curaçao has met all of the ToR for the information gathering process except for identifying tax rulings that are in the scope of the transparency framework and which category of rulings they fall under (ToR I.4.1.2). Curaçao is recommended to finalise its information gathering process for identifying all past and future rulings in scope of the transparency framework as soon as possible.

B. The exchange of information

Legal basis for spontaneous exchange of information (ToR II.5.1, II.5.2)

Curaçao has the necessary domestic legal basis to exchange information spontaneously. Curaçao notes that there are no legal or practical impediments that prevent the spontaneous exchange of information on rulings as contemplated in the Action 5 minimum standard.

Curaçao has international agreements permitting spontaneous exchange of information, including being a party to the (i) *Multilateral Convention on Mutual Administrative Assistance in Tax Matters: Amended by the 2010 Protocol* (OECD/Council of Europe, 2011[4]) ("the Convention"), and (ii) double tax agreements in force with two jurisdictions.[2]

Completion and exchange of templates (ToR II.5.3, II.5.4, II.5.5, II.5.6, II.5.7)

In the prior year peer review report, it was determined that Curaçao's process for the completion and exchange of templates met all the ToR, except for the timely exchange of information on past and future rulings (ToR II.5.6). Therefore, Curaçao was recommended to continue its work to continue its efforts to ensure all information on past and future rulings is exchanged as soon as possible.

During the year in review, Curaçao continued its work on exchanging information on past and future rulings. Curaçao was able to complete a further 163 exchanges in 2018, but still needs to identify which of the approximately 3 500 rulings issued from the previous years meet the conditions to be exchanged. This process is expected to be completed by the end of 2019. Therefore, the prior year recommendation remains.

For the year in review, the timeliness of exchanges is as follows:

Past rulings in the scope of the transparency framework	Number of exchanges transmitted by 31 December 2018	Delayed exchanges		
		Number of exchanges not transmitted by 31 December 2018	Reasons for the delays	Any other comments
	126	See preceding paragraph	Curaçao has a large amount of rulings. Curaçao is currently identifying the rulings to be able to exchange information on all the cross border rulings.	As at August 2019, Curaçao had completed an additional 79 exchanges.
Future rulings in the scope of the transparency framework	Number of exchanges transmitted within three months of the information becoming available to the competent authority or immediately after legal impediments have been lifted	Delayed exchanges		
		Number of exchanges transmitted later than three months of the information on rulings becoming available to the competent authority	Reasons for the delays	Any other comments
	37	See preceding paragraph	Curaçao is currently identifying the rulings to be able to exchange information on all the cross border rulings.	As at August 2019, Curaçao completed an additional 73 exchanges.
Total	163	See preceding paragraph		

Follow up requests received for exchange of the ruling	Number	Average time to provide response	Number of requests not answered
	N/A	N/A	N/A

Conclusion on section B

Curaçao has met all of the ToR for the information gathering process except for completing exchanges of information on rulings in accordance with the timelines (ToR II.5.5 and II.5.6) and Curaçao is recommended to continue its efforts to ensure that all information on past and future rulings is exchanged as soon as possible.

C. Statistics (ToR IV)

The statistics for the year in review are as follows: [3]

Category of ruling	Number of exchanges	Jurisdictions exchanged with
Ruling related to a preferential regime	158	Andorra, Belgium, Belize, Canada, China (People's Republic of), Colombia, Denmark, Germany, India, Ireland, Isle of Man, Israel, Italy, Jersey, Liechtenstein, Luxembourg, Malta,

		Mauritius, Mexico, Netherlands, Poland, Portugal, Singapore, Spain, Switzerland, United Kingdom, United States
Cross-border unilateral advance pricing agreements (APAs) and any other cross-border unilateral tax rulings (such as an advance tax ruling) covering transfer pricing or the application of transfer pricing principles	5	*De minimis rule* applies
Cross-border rulings providing for a unilateral downward adjustment to the taxpayer's taxable profits that is not directly reflected in the taxpayer's financial / commercial accounts	0	N/A
Permanent establishment rulings	0	N/A
Related party conduit rulings	0	N/A
De minimis rule	N/A	N/A
IP regimes: total exchanges on taxpayers benefitting from the third category of IP assets, new entrants benefitting from grandfathered IP regimes; and taxpayers making use of the option to treat the nexus ratio as a rebuttable presumption	0	0
Total	163	

D. Matters related to intellectual property regimes (ToR I.4.1.3)

Curaçao offered an intellectual property regime (IP regime)[4] that was abolished from 30 June 2018 and not subject to the transparency requirements under the Action 5 Report (OECD, 2015[5]), because:

- ***New entrants benefitting from the grandfathered IP regime***: the IP regimes has been abolished without grandfathering for taxpayers entering after the relevant date from which enhanced transparency obligations apply. As such, no enhanced transparency requirements apply.
- ***Third category of IP assets***: not applicable as the IP regime has been abolished.
- ***Taxpayers making use of the option to treat the nexus ratio as a rebuttable presumption***: not applicable as the IP regime has been abolished.

In the year in review, Curaçao offered two intellectual property regimes (IP regime)[5] that are subject to the transparency requirements under the Action 5 Report (OECD, 2015[5]). It states that the identification of the benefitting taxpayers will occur as follows:

Curaçao investment company (formerly Tax exempt entity)

- ***New entrants benefitting from the grandfathered IP regime***: the IP regimes have been amended as of 1 July 2018 without grandfathering for taxpayers after the relevant date from which enhanced transparency obligations apply. As such, no enhanced transparency requirements apply.
- ***Third category of IP assets***: the regime allows the third category of IP assets, as described in paragraph 37 of the Action 5 report (OECD, 2015[5]), to qualify for the benefits, therefore enhanced transparency requirements apply to taxpayers benefitting from these IP assets. In order to benefit from the third category of assets, a specific ruling is required. As such, the identification of taxpayers benefitting from the third category of IP assets occurs, when they apply for the IP regime and the process for identifying and exchanging information is as described above for future rulings. For the year in review, no taxpayers have applied to benefit from the third category of IP assets

under the Curaçao investment company, and therefore no information on these taxpayers needed to be exchanged.

- ***Taxpayers making use of the option to treat the nexus ratio as a rebuttable presumption***: not applicable as the regime does not allow the nexus ratio to be treated as a rebuttable presumption.

Innovation box

- ***New entrants benefitting from the grandfathered IP regime***: the regime is a new nexus-compliant regime that came into effect from 1 July 2018 and therefore there is no grandfathered IP regime for which enhanced transparency requirements will apply.
- ***Third category of IP assets***: the identification of taxpayers benefiting from the third category of assets is identical to the process described above for the Curaçao investment company. For the year in review, no taxpayers applying for the Innovation box benefitted from the third category of IP assets, therefore no information on these taxpayers needed to be exchanged.
- ***Taxpayers making use of the option to treat the nexus ratio as a rebuttable presumption***: not applicable as the regime does not allow the nexus ratio to be treated as a rebuttable presumption.

Summary of recommendations on implementation of the transparency framework

Aspect of implementation of the transparency framework that should be improved	Recommendation for improvement
The information gathering process is still underway in Curaçao with respect to past and future rulings in scope of the transparency framework and the classification of these rulings under each category.	Curaçao is recommended to finalise its information gathering process for identifying all past and future rulings in scope of the transparency framework as soon as possible. This recommendation remains unchanged since the prior year peer review report.
Curaçao experienced delays in exchanging information on past and future rulings.	Curaçao is recommended to continue its efforts to ensure that all information on past and future rulings is exchanged as soon as possible. This recommendation remains unchanged since the prior year peer review report.

Notes

[1] With respect to the following preferential regimes: 1) Export facility; 2) Tax exempt entity; 3) Free zone; and 4) Offshore regimes. The offshore regime has been abolished in 2001 and is grandfathered for fiscal years preceding 30 June 2019.

[2] Parties to the Convention are available here: www.oecd.org/tax/exchange-of-tax-information/convention-on-mutual-administrative-assistance-in-tax-matters.htm. Curaçao also has double tax agreements with Netherlands and Norway.

[3] Curaçao issues dual category which have as main element a preferential regime but can also contain one of the other four categories mentioned above. In terms of counting, these dual category ruling have been included into the "preferential regime" category. Only when a ruling relates exclusively to one of the categories mentioned above, it is counted in that category.

[4] This regime is the Export facility.

[5] These regimes are: 1) Curaçao investment company (formerly Tax exempt entity); and 2) Innovation box.

Czech Republic

The Czech Republic has met all aspects of the terms of reference (OECD, 2017[3]) (ToR) for the calendar year 2018 (year in review) except for the timely exchange of information on future rulings (ToR II.5.6.). The Czech Republic receives one recommendation on this point for the year in review.

In the prior year report, as well as in the 2016 peer review, the Czech Republic received the same recommendation. As it has not been addressed, the recommendation remains in place.

The Czech Republic can legally issue two types of rulings within the scope of the transparency framework. In practice, the Czech Republic issued rulings within the scope of the transparency framework as follows:

- 48 past rulings;
- For the period 1 April 2016 - 31 December 2016: five future rulings;
- For the calendar year 2017: 11 future rulings, and
- For the year in review: seven future rulings.

Peer input was received from one jurisdiction in respect of the exchanges of information on rulings received from the Czech Republic. The input was positive, noting that information was complete, in a correct format and received in a timely manner.

Introduction

This peer review covers the Czech Republic's implementation of the BEPS Action 5 transparency framework for the year 2018. The report has four parts, each relating to a key part of the ToR. Each part is discussed in turn. A summary of recommendations is included at the end of this report.

A. The information gathering process

The Czech Republic can legally issue the following two types of rulings within the scope of the transparency framework: (i) cross-border unilateral APAs and any other cross-border unilateral tax rulings (such as an advance tax ruling) covering transfer pricing or the application of transfer pricing principles, and (ii) permanent establishment rulings, which can be issued as of 1 January 2018.

Past rulings (ToR I.4.1.1, I.4.1.2, I.4.2.1, I.4.2.2)

For the Czech Republic, past rulings are any tax rulings within scope that are issued either: (i) on or after 1 January 2014 but before 1 April 2016; or (ii) on or after 1 January 2010 but before 1 January 2014, provided they were still in effect as at 1 January 2014.

In the prior years' peer review reports, it was determined that the Czech Republic's undertakings to identify past rulings and all potential exchange jurisdictions were sufficient to meet the minimum standard. The Czech Republic's implementation in this regard remains unchanged, and therefore continues to meet the minimum standard.

Future rulings (ToR I.4.1.1, I.4.1.2, I.4.2.1)

For the Czech Republic, future rulings are any tax rulings within scope that are issued on or after 1 April 2016.

In the prior year peer review report, it was determined that the Czech Republic's undertakings to identify future rulings and all potential exchange jurisdictions was sufficient to meet the minimum standard. The Czech Republic's implementation in this regard remains unchanged, and therefore continues to meet the minimum standard.

Review and supervision (ToR I.4.3)

In the prior years' peer review reports, it was determined that the Czech Republic's review and supervision mechanism was sufficient to meet the minimum standard. The Czech Republic's implementation in this regard remains unchanged, and therefore continues to meet the minimum standard.

Conclusion on section A

The Czech Republic has met all of the ToR for the information gathering process and no recommendations are made.

B. The exchange of information

Legal basis for spontaneous exchange of information (ToR II.5.1, II.5.2)

The Czech Republic has the necessary domestic legal basis to exchange information spontaneously. The Czech Republic notes that there are no legal or practical impediments that prevent the spontaneous exchange of information on rulings as contemplated in the Action 5 minimum standard.

The Czech Republic has international agreements permitting spontaneous exchange of information, including being a party to the (i) *Multilateral Convention on Mutual Administrative Assistance in Tax Matters: Amended by the 2010 Protocol* (OECD/Council of Europe, 2011[4]) ("the Convention"), (ii) the Directive 2011/16/EU with all other European Union Member States and (iii) double tax agreements in force with 89 jurisdictions.[1]

Completion and exchange of templates (ToR II.5.3, II.5.4, II.5.5, II.5.6, II.5.7)

In the prior year peer review report, it was determined that the Czech Republic's process for the completion and exchange of templates were sufficient to meet the minimum standard. The Czech Republic applies the timelines under the EU. As such, the Czech Republic was recommended to apply the timelines for future rulings as set out in the transparency framework for all exchanges.

It is noted that the Czech Republic continues to apply the EU timelines, i.e. the exchanges of information on future rulings are carried out within three months after the end of the calendar half-year in which these rulings were issued, regardless of whether the exchange is transmitted to EU Member States or other jurisdictions. The Czech Republic notes that it prefers to have a single timeline system in order to avoid delays.

For the year in review, the timeliness of exchanges is as follows:

Past rulings in the scope of the transparency framework	Number of exchanges transmitted by 31 December 2018	Delayed exchanges		
		Number of exchanges not transmitted by 31 December 2018	Reasons for the delays	Any other comments
	44	1	The exchange could not be transmitted due to legal impediments in the receiving jurisdiction.	The 44 exchanges related to information that was delayed in 2017 and exchanged in 2018.
Future rulings in the scope of the transparency framework	Number of exchanges transmitted within three months of the information becoming available to the competent authority or immediately after legal impediments have been lifted	Delayed exchanges		
		Number of exchanges transmitted later than three months of the information on rulings becoming available to the competent authority	Reasons for the delays	Any other comments
	0	45	The Czech Republic applied the EU timelines for the exchange of information with EU Member States.	All 45 exchanges are related to EU Member States and have been exchanged within in the EU timelines.
Total	44	45		

Follow up requests received for exchange of the ruling	Number	Average time to provide response	Number of requests not answered
	1	90 days	1

Conclusion on section B

The Czech Republic has the necessary legal basis for spontaneous exchange of information and a process for completing the templates in a timely way. The Czech Republic continues to apply the EU timelines for the exchange of information on future rulings with other EU Member States. This recommendation was included in the 2016 peer review report and the 2017 peer review report, and has not been acted upon, and the recommendation is therefore retained with respect to information on future rulings, and the Czech Republic is recommended to ensure that all information on future rulings is exchanged as soon as possible (ToR II.5.6).

C. Statistics (ToR IV)

The statistics for the year in review are as follows:

Category of ruling	Number of exchanges	Jurisdictions exchanged with
Ruling related to a preferential regime	N/A	N/A
Cross-border unilateral advance pricing agreements (APAs) and any other cross-border unilateral tax rulings (such as an advance tax ruling) covering transfer pricing or the application of transfer pricing principles	87	Belgium, Cyprus,[2] Denmark, Estonia, Finland, France, Germany, Hungary, Italy, Japan, Luxembourg, Mexico, Netherlands, Poland, Portugal, Romania, Russia, Slovak Republic, South Africa, Sweden, Switzerland, Turkey, United Kingdom, United States
Cross-border rulings providing for a unilateral downward adjustment to the taxpayer's taxable profits that is not directly reflected in the taxpayer's financial / commercial accounts	N/A	N/A
Permanent establishment rulings	2	*De minimis* rule applies
Related party conduit rulings	N/A	N/A
De minimis rule	N/A	N/A
IP regimes: total exchanges on taxpayers benefitting from the third category of IP assets, new entrants benefitting from grandfathered IP regimes; and taxpayers making use of the option to treat the nexus ratio as a rebuttable presumption	N/A	N/A
Total	89	

D. Matters related to intellectual property regimes (ToR I.4.1.3)

The Czech Republic does not offer an intellectual property regime for which transparency requirements under the Action 5 Report (OECD, 2015[5]) were imposed.

Summary of recommendations on implementation of the transparency framework

Aspect of implementation of the transparency framework that should be improved	Recommendation for improvement
The Czech Republic experienced delays in the exchange of information on future rulings due to the application of the timelines set out in the EU Directive 2011/16/EU.	The Czech Republic is recommended to ensure that all information on future rulings is exchanged as soon as possible. This recommendation remains unchanged since the 2016 peer review report and the 2017 peer review report.

Notes

[1] Parties to the Convention are available here: www.oecd.org/tax/exchange-of-tax-information/convention-on-mutual-administrative-assistance-in-tax-matters.htm. The Czech Republic also has double tax agreements with Albania, Azerbaijan, Armenia, Australia, Austria, Bahrain, Barbados, Belarus, Belgium, Bosnia and Herzegovina, Brazil, Bulgaria, Canada, Chile, China (People's Republic of), Colombia, Croatia, Cyprus, Democratic People's Republic of Korea, Denmark, Egypt, Estonia, Ethiopia, Finland, France, Georgia, Germany, Greece, Hong Kong (China), Hungary, Iceland, India, Indonesia, Iran, Ireland, Israel, Italy, Japan, Jordan, Kazakhstan, Korea, Kuwait, Latvia, Lebanon, Liechtenstein, Lithuania, Luxembourg, Malaysia, Malta, Mexico, Moldovia, Mongolia, Montenegro, Morocco, Netherlands, New Zealand, Nigeria, North Macedonia, Norway, Pakistan, Panama, Philippines, Poland, Portugal, Romania, Russia, Saudi Arabia, Serbia, Singapore, Slovak Republic, Slovenia, South Africa, Spain, Sri Lanka, Sweden, Switzerland, Syria, Tajikistan, Thailand, Tunisia, Turkey, Turkmenistan, Ukraine, United Arab Emirates, United Kingdom, United States, Uzbekistan, Venezuela and Viet Nam.

Note by Turkey: The information in this document with reference to "Cyprus" relates to the southern part of the Island. There is no single authority representing both Turkish and Greek Cypriot people on the Island. Turkey recognises the Turkish Republic of Northern Cyprus (TRNC). Until a lasting and equitable solution is found within the context of the United Nations, Turkey shall preserve its position concerning the "Cyprus issue".

Note by all the European Union Member States of the OECD and the European Union. The Republic of Cyprus is recognised by all members of the United Nations with the exception of Turkey. The information in this document relates to the area under the effective control of the Government of the Republic of Cyprus.

[2] Note by Turkey: The information in this document with reference to "Cyprus" relates to the southern part of the Island. There is no single authority representing both Turkish and Greek Cypriot people on the Island. Turkey recognises the Turkish Republic of Northern Cyprus (TRNC). Until a lasting and equitable solution is found within the context of the United Nations, Turkey shall preserve its position concerning the "Cyprus issue".

Note by all the European Union Member States of the OECD and the European Union. The Republic of Cyprus is recognised by all members of the United Nations with the exception of Turkey. The information in this document relates to the area under the effective control of the Government of the Republic of Cyprus.

Democratic Republic of Congo

Democratic Republic of Congo has met all aspects of the terms of reference (OECD, 2017[3]) (ToR) for the calendar year 2018 (year in review) that can be met in the absence of rulings being issued.

In the prior year report, Democratic Republic of Congo did not receive any recommendations.

Democratic Republic of Congo indicates that it does not issue any type of rulings within the scope of the transparency framework. Theoretically, there is no impediment for Democratic Republic of the Congo to issue rulings, but in practice Democratic Republic of the Congo does not issue any rulings. In the event that Democratic Republic of the Congo put in place the administrative process or develop the administrative capacity to issue rulings, Democratic Republic of the Congo would be asked to implement the transparency framework obligations.

As no exchanges were required to take place, no peer input was received in respect of the exchanges of information on rulings received from Democratic Republic of Congo.

Introduction

This peer review covers Democratic Republic of Congo's implementation of the BEPS Action 5 transparency framework for the year 2018. The report has four parts, each relating to a key part of the ToR. Each part is discussed in turn. A summary of recommendations is included at the end of this report.

A. The information gathering process

As no rulings are issued, this section is not assessed.

B. The exchange of information

As no rulings are issued, this section is not assessed.

C. Statistics (ToR IV)

As no rulings are issued, no statistics can be reported.

D. Matters related to intellectual property regimes (ToR I.4.1.3)

Democratic Republic of Congo does not offer an intellectual property regime for which transparency requirements under the Action 5 Report (OECD, 2015[5]) were imposed.

Summary of recommendations on implementation of the transparency framework

Aspect of implementation of the transparency framework that should be improved	Recommendation for improvement
	No recommendations are made.

Denmark

Denmark has met all aspects of the terms of reference (ToR) for the calendar year 2018 (year in review) and no recommendations are made.

In the prior year report, Denmark did not receive any recommendations.

Denmark can legally issue five types of rulings within the scope of the transparency framework. In practice, Denmark issued rulings within the scope of the transparency framework as follows:

- 43 past rulings;
- For the period 1 April 2016 - 31 December 2016: seven future rulings;
- For the calendar year 2017: 17 future rulings, and
- For the year in review: 13 future rulings.

These rulings are published in anonymised form on the tax administration's website when they are deemed of general public interest.[1]

Peer input was received from two jurisdictions in respect of the exchanges of information on rulings received from Denmark. The input was generally positive, noting that information was complete, in a correct format and received in a timely manner.

Introduction

This peer review covers Denmark's implementation of the BEPS Action 5 transparency framework for the year 2018. The report has four parts, each relating to a key part of the ToR. Each part is discussed in turn. A summary of recommendations is included at the end of this report.

A. The information gathering process

Denmark can legally issue the five following types of rulings within the scope of the transparency framework: (i) preferential regimes;[2] (ii) cross-border unilateral advance pricing agreements (APAs) and any other cross-border unilateral tax rulings (such as an advance tax ruling) covering transfer pricing or the application of transfer pricing principles; (iii) rulings providing for unilateral downward adjustments; (iv) permanent establishment rulings; and (v) related party conduit rulings.

Past rulings (ToR I.4.1.1, I.4.1.2, I.4.2.1, I.4.2.2)

For Denmark, past rulings are any tax rulings within scope that are issued either: (i) on or after 1 January 2014 but before 1 April 2016; or (ii) on or after 1 January 2010 but before 1 January 2014, provided they were still in effect as at 1 January 2014.

In the prior year peer review reports, it was determined that Denmark's undertakings to identify past rulings and all potential exchange jurisdictions were sufficient to meet the minimum standard. Denmark's implementation in this regard remains unchanged, and therefore continues to meet the minimum standard.

Future rulings (ToR I.4.1.1, I.4.1.2, I.4.2.1)

For Denmark, future rulings are any tax rulings within scope that are issued on or after 1 April 2016.

In the prior year peer review reports, it was determined that Denmark's implementation of a new system to identify future rulings and all potential exchange jurisdictions was sufficient to meet the minimum standard. Denmark's implementation in this regard remains unchanged, and therefore continues to meet the minimum standard.

Review and supervision (ToR I.4.3)

In the prior year peer review reports, it was determined that Denmark's review and supervision mechanism was sufficient to meet the minimum standard. Denmark's implementation in this regard remains unchanged, and therefore continues to meet the minimum standard.

Conclusion on section A

Denmark has met all of the ToR for the information gathering process and no recommendations are made.

B. The exchange of information

Legal basis for spontaneous exchange of information (ToR II.5.1, II.5.2)

Denmark has the necessary domestic legal basis to exchange information spontaneously. Denmark notes that there are no legal or practical impediments that prevent the spontaneous exchange of information on rulings as contemplated in the Action 5 minimum standard.

Denmark has international agreements permitting spontaneous exchange of information, including being a party to the (i) *Multilateral Convention on Mutual Administrative Assistance in Tax Matters: Amended by the 2010 Protocol* (OECD/Council of Europe, 2011[4]) ("the Convention"), (ii) the Directive 2011/16/EU with all other European Union Member States and (iii) double tax agreements in force with 70 jurisdictions.[3]

Completion and exchange of templates (ToR II.5.3, II.5.4, II.5.5, II.5.6, II.5.7)

In the prior year peer review report, it was determined that Denmark's process for the completion and exchange of templates were sufficient to meet the minimum standard. Denmark's implementation in this regard remains unchanged and therefore continues to meet the minimum standard.

For the year in review, the timeliness of exchanges is as follows:

Past rulings in the scope of the transparency framework	Number of exchanges transmitted by 31 December 2018	Delayed exchanges		
		Number of exchanges not transmitted by 31 December 2018	Reasons for the delays	Any other comments
	0	0	N/A	N/A
Future rulings in the scope of the transparency framework	Number of exchanges transmitted within three months of the information becoming available to the competent authority or immediately after legal impediments have been lifted	Delayed exchanges		
		Number of exchanges transmitted later than three months of the information on rulings becoming available to the competent authority	Reasons for the delays	Any other comments
	13	1	A change in the personnel responsible for the exchange resulted in the delay.	N/A
Total	13	1		

Follow up requests received for exchange of the ruling	Number	Average time to provide response	Number of requests not answered
	0	N/A	N/A

It is noted that Denmark experienced a delay with respect to one exchange, due to a change in personnel. The exchange was completed within the year in review, and by seven months of the ruling being made available to the Competent Authority. Denmark has taken action to ensure this problem does not occur in the future by way of a data sheet with an overview of all rulings and dates of exchange, to assist case workers in keeping track of deadlines. As such, no recommendation is made given it was a non-recurring issue that was swiftly remedied.

Conclusion on section B

Denmark has the necessary legal basis for spontaneous exchange of information, a process for completing the templates in a timely way and has completed all exchanges. Denmark has met all of the ToR for the exchange of information process and no recommendations are made.

C. Statistics (ToR IV)

The statistics for the year in review are as follows:

Category of ruling	Number of exchanges	Jurisdictions exchanged with
Ruling related to a preferential regime	0	N/A
Cross-border unilateral advance pricing agreements (APAs) and any other cross-border unilateral tax rulings (such as an advance tax ruling) covering transfer pricing or the application of transfer pricing principles	0	N/A
Cross-border rulings providing for a unilateral downward adjustment to the taxpayer's taxable profits that is not directly reflected in the taxpayer's financial / commercial accounts	0	N/A
Permanent establishment rulings	13	Austria, Finland, Germany, Luxembourg, Switzerland, United Kingdom
Related party conduit rulings	0	N/A
De minimis rule	N/A	N/A
IP regimes: total exchanges on taxpayers benefitting from the third category of IP assets, new entrants benefitting from grandfathered IP regimes; and taxpayers making use of the option to treat the nexus ratio as a rebuttable presumption	N/A	N/A
Total	13	

D. Matters related to intellectual property regimes (ToR I.4.1.3)

Denmark does not offer an intellectual property regime for which transparency requirements under the Action 5 Report (OECD, 2015[5]) were imposed.

Summary of recommendations on implementation of the transparency framework

Aspect of implementation of the transparency framework that should be improved	Recommendation for improvement
	No recommendations are made.

Notes

[1] Available at www.skat.dk/skat.aspx?oid=80859&ik_navn=transport

[2] With respect to the following preferential regime: tonnage tax.

[3] Parties to the Convention are available here: www.oecd.org/tax/exchange-of-tax-information/convention-on-mutual-administrative-assistance-in-tax-matters.htm. Denmark also has double tax agreements with Argentina, Armenia, Aruba, Australia, Austria, Azerbaijan, Bangladesh, Belarus, Belgium, Brazil, British Virgin Islands, Bulgaria, Canada, Chile, China (People's Republic of), Croatia, Cyprus, Czech Republic, Egypt, Estonia, Georgia, Germany, Ghana, Greece, Hungary, India, Indonesia, Ireland, Israel, Italy, Jamaica, Japan, Kenya, Korea, Kuwait, Latvia, Lithuania, Luxembourg, Malaysia, Malta, Mexico, Montenegro, Morocco, Netherlands, New Zealand, Pakistan, Philippines, Poland, Portugal, North Macedonia, Romania, Russia, Serbia, Singapore, Slovak Republic, Slovenia, South Africa, Sri Lanka,

Switzerland, Chinese Taipei, Tanzania, Thailand, Trinidad and Tobago, Tunisia, Turkey, Uganda, Ukraine, United Kingdom, United States, Venezuela, Viet Nam and Zambia.

Note by Turkey: The information in this document with reference to "Cyprus" relates to the southern part of the Island. There is no single authority representing both Turkish and Greek Cypriot people on the Island. Turkey recognises the Turkish Republic of Northern Cyprus (TRNC). Until a lasting and equitable solution is found within the context of the United Nations, Turkey shall preserve its position concerning the "Cyprus issue".

Note by all the European Union Member States of the OECD and the European Union. The Republic of Cyprus is recognised by all members of the United Nations with the exception of Turkey. The information in this document relates to the area under the effective control of the Government of the Republic of Cyprus.

Djibouti

Djibouti has met all aspects of the terms of reference (OECD, 2017[3]) (ToR) for the calendar year 2018 (year in review) that can be met in the absence of rulings being issued.

In the prior year report, Djibouti did not receive any recommendations.

Djibouti indicates that it cannot legally issue any type of rulings within the scope of the transparency framework.

As no exchanges were required to take place, no peer input was received in respect of the exchanges of information on rulings received from Djibouti.

Introduction

This peer review covers Djibouti's implementation of the BEPS Action 5 transparency framework for the year 2018. The report has four parts, each relating to a key part of the ToR. Each part is discussed in turn. A summary of recommendations is included at the end of this report.

A. The information gathering process

As no rulings are issued, this section is not assessed.

B. The exchange of information

As no rulings are issued, this section is not assessed.

C. Statistics (ToR IV)

As no rulings are issued, no statistics can be reported.

D. Matters related to intellectual property regimes (ToR I.4.1.3)

Djibouti does not offer an intellectual property regime for which transparency requirements under the Action 5 Report (OECD, 2015[5]) were imposed.

Summary of recommendations on implementation of the transparency framework

Aspect of implementation of the transparency framework that should be improved	Recommendation for improvement
	No recommendations are made.

Egypt

Egypt's implementation of the transparency framework is still in the early stages of development. Egypt is taking steps to implement the legal basis for the transparency framework and to commence administrative preparations in line with the terms of reference (OECD, 2017[3]) (ToR) to ensure that it finalises its information gathering process (ToR I.4) and information on rulings will be identified and exchanged in a timely manner (ToR II.5). Egypt receives two recommendations on these points for the year in review.

This is Egypt's first review of implementation of the transparency framework.

Egypt can legally issue four types of rulings within the scope of the transparency framework. In practice, Egypt issued rulings within the scope of the transparency framework as follows:

- 31 past rulings;
- For the period 1 April 2018 - 31 December 2018: three future rulings.

As no exchanges took place, no peer input was received in respect of the exchanges of information on rulings received from Egypt.

Introduction

This peer review covers Egypt's implementation of the BEPS Action 5 transparency framework for the year 2018. The report has four parts, each relating to a key part of the ToR. Each part is discussed in turn. A summary of recommendations is included at the end of this report.

A. The information gathering process

Egypt can legally issue the four following types of rulings within the scope of the transparency framework: (i) cross-border unilateral advance pricing agreements (APAs) and any other cross-border unilateral tax rulings (such as an advance tax ruling) covering transfer pricing or the application of transfer pricing principles; (ii) rulings providing a downward adjustment of taxable profits; (iii) permanent establishment rulings; and (iv) related party conduit rulings. Egypt has had in place a legislative framework to issue unilateral APAs since October 2018, but in practice has never issued any unilateral APAs.

For Egypt, past rulings are any tax rulings within scope that are issued either (i) on or after 1 January 2016 but before 1 April 2018; and (ii) on or after 1 January 2014 but before 1 January 2016, provided still in effect as at 1 January 2016.

For Egypt, future rulings are any tax rulings within scope that are issued on or after 1 April 2018.

Egypt acknowledges that it did not implement the information gathering process during the year in review. Egypt has since engaged with the Secretariat during the peer review process in 2019, and is in the process of putting in place the procedures required under the information gathering process. These processes will be assessed during the subsequent year peer review. As at August 2019, Egypt had identified 31 past rulings and three future rulings in scope of the transparency framework.

Conclusion on section A

Egypt is recommended to ensure that it has put in place an effective information gathering process to identify all relevant past and future rulings and all potential exchange jurisdictions and to implement a review and supervision mechanism, as soon as possible (ToR I.4).

B. The exchange of information

Legal basis for spontaneous exchange of information (ToR II.5.1, II.5.2)

Egypt has the necessary legal basis to exchange information spontaneously. Egypt notes that there are no practical impediments that prevent the spontaneous exchange of information on rulings as contemplated in the Action 5 minimum standard.

Egypt has international agreements permitting spontaneous exchange of information, including double tax agreements in force with 55 jurisdictions.[1]

Completion and exchange of templates (ToR II.5.3, II.5.4, II.5.5, II.5.6, II.5.7)

Egypt acknowledges that it did not implement processes for the completion and exchange of templates during the year in review. Egypt will be developing a process to complete the templates on relevant rulings, to make them available to the Competent Authority for exchange of information and to exchange them with relevant jurisdictions.

For the year in review, Egypt had not undertaken any exchanges of information and therefore no data on the timeliness of exchanges can be reported.

Conclusion on section B

Egypt is recommended to develop a process to complete the templates on relevant rulings and to ensure that the exchanges of information on rulings occur in accordance with the form and timelines under the transparency framework (ToR II.5).

C. Statistics (ToR IV)

As there was no information on rulings exchanged by Egypt for the year in review, no statistics can be reported.

D. Matters related to intellectual property regimes (ToR I.4.1.3)

Egypt does not offer an intellectual property regime for which transparency requirements under the Action 5 Report (OECD, 2015[5]) were imposed.

Summary of recommendations on implementation of the transparency framework

Aspect of implementation of the transparency framework that should be improved	Recommendation for improvement
Egypt does not have in place the information gathering process as required under the transparency framework.	Egypt is recommended to ensure that it has put in place an effective information gathering process to identify all relevant past and future rulings and all potential exchange jurisdictions and to implement a review and supervision mechanism, as soon as possible.
Egypt does not have in place a process to ensure the timely exchange of information on rulings in the form required by the transparency framework.	Egypt is recommended to develop a process to complete the templates on relevant rulings and to ensure that the exchanges of information on rulings occur in accordance with the form and timelines under the transparency framework.

Notes

[1] Albania, Algeria, Austria, Bahrain, Belarus, Belgium, Bulgaria, Canada, China (People's Republic of), Cyprus, Czech Republic, Denmark, Ethiopia, Finland, France, Georgia, Germany, Greece, Hungary, India, Indonesia, Iraq, Ireland, Italy, Japan, Jordan, Korea, Kuwait, Lebanon, Libya, Malaysia, Malta, Mauritius, Morocco, Netherlands, Norway, Pakistan, Poland, Romania, Russia, Saudi Arabia, Serbia, Singapore, Spain, South Africa, Sudan, Sweden, Syria, Tunisia, Turkey, Ukraine, United Arab Emirates, United Kingdom, United States, and Yemen.

Note by Turkey: The information in this document with reference to "Cyprus" relates to the southern part of the Island. There is no single authority representing both Turkish and Greek Cypriot people on the Island. Turkey recognises the Turkish Republic of Northern Cyprus (TRNC). Until a lasting and equitable solution is found within the context of the United Nations, Turkey shall preserve its position concerning the "Cyprus issue".

Note by all the European Union Member States of the OECD and the European Union. The Republic of Cyprus is recognised by all members of the United Nations with the exception of Turkey. The information in this document relates to the area under the effective control of the Government of the Republic of Cyprus.

Estonia

Estonia has met all aspects of the terms of reference (OECD, 2017[3]) (ToR) for the calendar year 2018 (year in review) and no recommendations are made.

In the prior year report, Estonia did not receive any recommendations.

Estonia can legally issue two types of rulings within the scope of the transparency framework. In practice, Estonia issued rulings within the scope of the transparency framework as follows:

- 20 past rulings;
- For the period 1 April 2016 - 31 December 2016: eight future rulings;
- For the calendar year 2017: 11 future rulings, and
- For the year in review: nine future rulings.

  Estonian Tax and Customs Board publishes summaries of tax rulings on their website.[1]

No peer input was received in respect of the exchanges of information on rulings received from Estonia.

Introduction

This peer review covers Estonia's implementation of the BEPS Action 5 transparency framework for the year 2018. The report has four parts, each relating to a key part of the ToR. Each part is discussed in turn. A summary of recommendations is included at the end of this report.

A. The information gathering process

Estonia can legally issue the following two types of rulings within the scope of the transparency framework: (i) permanent establishment rulings; and (ii) related party conduit rulings.

Past rulings (ToR I.4.1.1, I.4.1.2, I.4.2.1, I.4.2.2)

For Estonia, past rulings are any tax rulings within scope that are issued either: (i) on or after 1 January 2014 but before 1 April 2016; or (ii) on or after 1 January 2010 but before 1 January 2014, provided they were still in effect as at 1 January 2014.

In the prior years' peer review reports, it was determined that Estonia's undertakings to identify past rulings and all potential exchange jurisdictions were sufficient to meet the minimum standard. Estonia's implementation in this regard remains unchanged, and therefore continues to meet the minimum standard.

Future rulings (ToR I.4.1.1, I.4.1.2, I.4.2.1)

For Estonia, future rulings are any tax rulings within scope that are issued on or after 1 April 2016.

In the prior years' peer review reports, it was determined that Estonia's implementation of a new system to identify future rulings and all potential exchange jurisdictions was sufficient to meet the minimum standard. Estonia's implementation in this regard remains unchanged, and therefore continues to meet the minimum standard.

Review and supervision (ToR I.4.3)

In the prior years' peer review reports, it was determined that Estonia's review and supervision mechanism was sufficient to meet the minimum standard. Estonia's implementation in this regard remains unchanged, and therefore continues to meet the minimum standard.

Conclusion on section A

Estonia has met all of the ToR for the information gathering process and no recommendations are made.

B. The exchange of information

Legal basis for spontaneous exchange of information (ToR II.5.1, II.5.2)

Estonia has the necessary domestic legal basis to exchange information spontaneously. Estonia notes that there are no legal or practical impediments that prevent the spontaneous exchange of information on rulings as contemplated in the Action 5 minimum standard.

Estonia has international agreements permitting spontaneous exchange of information, including being a party to the (i) *Multilateral Convention on Mutual Administrative Assistance in Tax Matters: Amended by the 2010 Protocol* (OECD/Council of Europe, 2011[4]) ("the Convention"), (ii) the Directive 2011/16/EU with all other European Union Member States and (iii) double tax agreements in force with 57 jurisdictions.[2]

Completion and exchange of templates (ToR II.5.3, II.5.4, II.5.5, II.5.6, II.5.7)

In the prior year peer review report, it was determined that Estonia's process for the completion and exchange of templates were sufficient to meet the minimum standard. Estonia's implementation in this regard remains unchanged and therefore continues to meet the minimum standard.

For the year in review, the timeliness of exchanges is as follows:

Past rulings in the scope of the transparency framework	Number of exchanges transmitted by 31 December 2018	Delayed exchanges		
		Number of exchanges not transmitted by 31 December 2018	Reasons for the delays	Any other comments
	0	0	N/A	N/A
Future rulings in the scope of the transparency framework	Number of exchanges transmitted within three months of the information becoming available to the competent authority or immediately after legal impediments have been lifted	Delayed exchanges		
		Number of exchanges transmitted later than three months of the information on rulings becoming available to the competent authority	Reasons for the delays	Any other comments
	12	0	N/A	N/A
Total	12	0		

Follow up requests received for exchange of the ruling	Number	Average time to provide response	Number of requests not answered
	0	N/A	N/A

Conclusion on section B

Estonia has the necessary legal basis for spontaneous exchange of information, a process for completing the templates in a timely way and has completed all exchanges. Estonia has met all of the ToR for the exchange of information process and no recommendations are made.

C. Statistics (ToR IV)

The statistics for the year in review are as follows:

Category of ruling	Number of exchanges	Jurisdictions exchanged with
Ruling related to a preferential regime	N/A	N/A
Cross-border unilateral advance pricing agreements (APAs) and any other cross-border unilateral tax rulings (such as an advance tax ruling) covering transfer pricing or the application of transfer pricing principles	N/A	N/A
Cross-border rulings providing for a unilateral downward adjustment to the taxpayer's taxable profits that is not directly reflected in the taxpayer's financial / commercial accounts	N/A	N/A
Permanent establishment rulings	4	*De minimis* rule applies
Related party conduit rulings	8	Finland, Latvia, Luxembourg,

		Netherlands, Sweden, Switzerland
De minimis rule	N/A	N/A
IP regimes: total exchanges on taxpayers benefitting from the third category of IP assets, new entrants benefitting from grandfathered IP regimes; and taxpayers making use of the option to treat the nexus ratio as a rebuttable presumption	N/A	N/A
Total	12	

D. Matters related to intellectual property regimes (ToR I.4.1.3)

Estonia does not offer an intellectual property regime for which transparency requirements under the Action 5 Report (OECD, 2015[5]) were imposed.

Summary of recommendations on implementation of the transparency framework

Aspect of implementation of the transparency framework that should be improved	Recommendation for improvement
	No recommendations are made.

Notes

[1]Available at: https://www.emta.ee/et/ariklient/maksukorraldus-maksude-tasumine/siduvad-eelotsused/siduvate-eelotsuste-kokkuvotted.

[2] Parties to the Convention are available here: www.oecd.org/tax/exchange-of-tax-information/convention-on-mutual-administrative-assistance-in-tax-matters.htm. Estonia also has double tax agreements with Albania, Armenia, Azerbaijan, Austria, Bahrein, Belarus, Belgium, Bulgaria, Canada, China (People's Republic of), Croatia, Cyprus, Czech Republic, Denmark, Finland, France, Georgia, Germany, Greece, Hungary, Iceland, India, Ireland, Isle of Man, Israel, Italy, Jersey, Kazakhstan, Korea, Latvia, Lithuania, Luxembourg, Malta, Mexico, Moldova, Netherlands, North Macedonia, Norway, Poland, Portugal, Romania, Serbia, Singapore, Slovak Republic, Slovenia, Spain, Sweden, Switzerland, Thailand, Turkey, Turkmenistan, Ukraine, United Arab Emirates, United Kingdom, United States, Uzbekistan and Viet Nam.

Note by Turkey: The information in this document with reference to "Cyprus" relates to the southern part of the Island. There is no single authority representing both Turkish and Greek Cypriot people on the Island. Turkey recognises the Turkish Republic of Northern Cyprus (TRNC). Until a lasting and equitable solution is found within the context of the United Nations, Turkey shall preserve its position concerning the "Cyprus issue".

Note by all the European Union Member States of the OECD and the European Union. The Republic of Cyprus is recognised by all members of the United Nations with the exception of Turkey. The information in this document relates to the area under the effective control of the Government of the Republic of Cyprus.

Finland

Finland has met all aspects of the terms of reference (OECD, 2017[2]) (ToR) for the calendar year 2018 (year in review) and no recommendations are made.

In the prior year report, Finland did not receive any recommendations.

Finland can legally issue four types of rulings within the scope of the transparency framework. In practice, Finland issued rulings within the scope of the transparency framework as follows:

- 42 past rulings;
- For the period 1 April 2016 - 31 December 2016: 13 rulings;
- For the calendar year 2017: 19 future rulings, and
- For the year in review: eight future rulings.

Some rulings are published on the Finland Tax Administration's website, at the discretion of the Central Tax Board.[1]

No peer input was received in respect of the exchanges of information on rulings received from Finland.

Introduction

This peer review covers Finland's implementation of the BEPS Action 5 transparency framework for the year 2018. The report has four parts, each relating to a key part of the ToR. Each part is discussed in turn. A summary of recommendations is included at the end of this report.

A. The information gathering process

Finland can legally issue the four following types of rulings within the scope of the transparency framework: (i) preferential regimes;[2] (ii) cross-border unilateral advance pricing arrangements (APAs) and any other cross-border unilateral tax rulings (such as an advance tax ruling) covering transfer pricing or the application of transfer pricing principles; (iii) permanent establishment rulings; and (iv) related party conduit rulings.

Past rulings (ToR I.4.1.1, I.4.1.2, I.4.2.1, I.4.2.2)

For Finland, past rulings are any tax rulings within scope that are issued either: (i) on or after 1 January 2014 but before 1 April 2016; or (ii) on or after 1 January 2010 but before 1 January 2014, provided they were still in effect as at 1 January 2014.

In the prior years' peer review reports, it was determined that Finland's undertakings to identify past rulings and all potential exchange jurisdictions were sufficient to meet the minimum standard. Finland's implementation in this regard remains unchanged, and therefore continues to meet the minimum standard.

Future rulings (ToR I.4.1.1, I.4.1.2, I.4.2.1)

For Finland, future rulings are any tax rulings within scope that are issued on or after 1 April 2016.

In the prior years' peer review reports, it was determined that Finland's undertakings to identify future rulings and all potential exchange jurisdictions was sufficient to meet the minimum standard. Finland's implementation in this regard remains unchanged, and therefore continues to meet the minimum standard.

Review and supervision (ToR I.4.3)

In the prior years' peer review reports, it was determined that Finland's review and supervision mechanism was sufficient to meet the minimum standard. Finland's implementation in this regard remains unchanged, and therefore continues to meet the minimum standard.

Conclusion on section A

Finland has met all of the ToR for the information gathering process and no recommendations are made.

B. The exchange of information

Legal basis for spontaneous exchange of information (ToR II.5.1, II.5.2)

Finland has the necessary domestic legal basis to exchange information spontaneously. Slovenia notes that there are no legal or practical impediments that prevent the spontaneous exchange of information on rulings as contemplated in the Action 5 minimum standard.

Finland is a party to international agreements permitting spontaneous exchange of information, including (i) the *Multilateral Convention on Mutual Administrative Assistance in Tax Matters: Amended by the 2010 Protocol* (OECD/Council of Europe, 2011) ("the Convention"), (ii) the Directive 2011/16/EU with all other European Union Member States and (iii) double tax agreements in force with 89 jurisdictions.[3]

Completion and exchange of templates (ToR II.5.3, II.5.4, II.5.5, II.5.6, II.5.7)

In the prior year peer review report, it was determined that Finland's process for the completion and exchange of templates were sufficient to meet the minimum standard. Finland's implementation in this regard remains unchanged and therefore continues to meet the minimum standard.

For the year in review, the timeliness of exchanges is as follows:

Past rulings in the scope of the transparency framework	Number of exchanges transmitted by 31 December 2018	Delayed exchanges		
		Number of exchanges not transmitted by 31 December 2018	Reasons for the delays	Any other comments
	0	0	N/A	N/A
Future rulings in the scope of the transparency framework	Number of exchanges transmitted within three months of the information becoming available to the competent authority or immediately after legal impediments have been lifted	Delayed exchanges		
		Number of exchanges transmitted later than three months of the information on rulings becoming available to the competent authority	Reasons for the delays	Any other comments
	9	0	N/A	N/A
Total	9	0		

Follow up requests received for exchange of the ruling	Number	Average time to provide response	Number of requests not answered
	0	N/A	N/A

Conclusion on section B

Finland has the necessary legal basis for spontaneous exchange of information, a process for completing the templates in a timely way and has completed all exchanges. Finland has met all of the ToR for the exchange of information process and no recommendations are made.

C. Statistics (ToR IV)

The statistics for the year in review are as follows:

Category of ruling	Number of exchanges	Jurisdictions exchanged with
Ruling related to a preferential regime	0	N/A
Cross-border unilateral advance pricing agreements (APAs) and any other cross-border unilateral tax rulings (such as an advance tax ruling) covering transfer pricing or the application of transfer pricing principles	9	Belgium, Denmark, Germany, Luxembourg, Netherlands, Sweden
Cross-border rulings providing for a unilateral downward adjustment to the taxpayer's taxable profits that is not directly reflected in the taxpayer's	N/A	N/A

financial / commercial accounts		
Permanent establishment rulings	0	N/A
Related party conduit rulings	0	N/A
De minimis rule	N/A	N/A
IP regimes: total exchanges on taxpayers benefitting from the third category of IP assets, new entrants benefitting from grandfathered IP regimes; and taxpayers making use of the option to treat the nexus ratio as a rebuttable presumption	N/A	N/A
Total	9	

D. Matters related to intellectual property regimes (ToR I.4.1.3)

Finland does not offer an intellectual property regime for which transparency requirements under the Action 5 Report (OECD, 2015[5]) were imposed.

Summary of recommendations on implementation of the transparency framework

Aspect of implementation of the transparency framework that should be improved	Recommendation for improvement
	No recommendations are made.

Notes

[1] Available at: https://www.vero.fi/syventavat-vero-ohjeet/ennakkoratkaisut/.

[2] With respect to the following preferential regime: shipping regime.

[3] Parties to the Convention are available here: www.oecd.org/tax/exchange-of-tax-information/convention-on-mutual-administrative-assistance-in-tax-matters.htm. Finland also has double tax agreements with Argentina, Armenia, Aruba, Australia, Austria, Azerbaijan, Bailiwick of Jersey, Barbados, Belarus, Belgium, Bermuda, Bosnia and Herzegovina, Brazil, British Virgin Islands, Bulgaria, Canada, Cayman Islands, China (People's Republic of), Cook Islands, Croatia, Cyprus, Czech Republic, Denmark, Egypt, Estonia, Faroe Islands, France, Georgia, Germany, Greece, Guatemala, Guernsey, Hungary, India, Indonesia, Ireland, Isle of Man, Israel, Italy, Japan, Kazakhstan, Korea, Kosovo, Kyrgyzstan, Latvia, Lebanon, Lithuania, Luxembourg, Malaysia, Malta, Mexico, Moldova, Monaco, Montenegro, Morocco, Netherlands, Netherlands Antilles, New Zealand, North Macedonia, Norway, Pakistan, Panama, Philippines, Poland, Portugal, Romania, Russia, Serbia, Singapore, Slovak Republic, Slovenia, South Africa, Spain, Sri Lanka, Sweden, Switzerland, Tajikistan, Tanzania, Thailand, Turkey, Turkmenistan, Ukraine, United Arab Emirates, United Kingdom, United States, Uruguay, Uzbekistan, Viet Nam and Zambia.

Note by Turkey: The information in this document with reference to "Cyprus" relates to the southern part of the Island. There is no single authority representing both Turkish and Greek Cypriot people on the Island. Turkey recognises the Turkish Republic of Northern Cyprus (TRNC). Until a lasting and equitable solution is found within the context of the United Nations, Turkey shall preserve its position concerning the "Cyprus issue".

Note by all the European Union Member States of the OECD and the European Union. The Republic of Cyprus is recognised by all members of the United Nations with the exception of Turkey. The information in this document relates to the area under the effective control of the Government of the Republic of Cyprus.

France

France has met all aspects of the terms of reference (OECD, 2017[3]) (ToR) for the calendar year 2018 (year in review) except that France did not identify or exchange information on new entrants to the IP regime or taxpayers benefitting from the third category of IP assets (ToR I.4.1.3). France receives one recommendation on this point for the year in review.

In the prior year report, as well as in the 2016 peer review, France received the same recommendation. As it has not been addressed, the recommendation remains in place.

France can legally issue three types of rulings within the scope of the transparency framework. In practice, France issued rulings within the scope of the transparency framework as follows:

- 45 past rulings;
- For the period 1 April 2016 - 31 December 2016: four future rulings;
- For the calendar year 2017: six future rulings, and
- For the year in review: six future rulings.

No peer input was received in respect of the exchanges of information on rulings received from France.

Introduction

This peer review covers France's implementation of the BEPS Action 5 transparency framework for the year 2018. The report has four parts, each relating to a key part of the ToR. Each part is discussed in turn. A summary of recommendations is included at the end of this report.

A. The information gathering process

France can legally issue the following three types of rulings within the scope of the transparency framework: (i) preferential regimes;[1] (ii) cross-border unilateral APAs and any other cross-border unilateral tax rulings (such as an advance tax ruling) covering transfer pricing or the application of transfer pricing principles; and (iii) permanent establishment rulings.

Past rulings (ToR I.4.1.1, I.4.1.2, I.4.2.1, I.4.2.2)

For France, past rulings are any tax rulings within the scope that are issued either: (i) on or after 1 January 2014 but before 1 April 2016; or (ii) on or after 1 January 2010 but before 1 January 2014, provided they were still in effect as at 1 January 2014.

In the prior years' peer review reports, it was determined that France's undertakings to identify past rulings and all potential exchange jurisdictions were sufficient to meet the minimum standard. France's implementation in this regard remains unchanged, and therefore continues to meet the minimum standard.

Future rulings (ToR I.4.1.1, I.4.1.2, I.4.2.1)

For France, future rulings are any tax rulings within scope that are issued on or after 1 April 2016.

In the prior years' peer review reports, it was determined that France's undertakings to identify future rulings and all potential exchange jurisdictions were sufficient to meet the minimum standard. France's implementation in this regard remains unchanged, and therefore continues to meet the minimum standard.

Review and supervision (ToR I.4.3)

In the prior years' peer review reports, it was determined that France's review and supervision mechanism was sufficient to meet the minimum standard. France notes that in order to improve relations between services, the competent authority has organized meetings with the services that issue decisions covered by the transparency framework. France's implementation in this regard remains unchanged, and therefore continues to meet the minimum standard.

Conclusion on section A

France has met all of the ToR for the information gathering process and no recommendations are made.

B. The exchange of information

Legal basis for spontaneous exchange of information (ToR II.5.1, II.5.2)

France has the necessary domestic legal basis to exchange information spontaneously. France notes that there are no legal or practical impediments that prevent the spontaneous exchange of information on rulings as contemplated in the Action 5 minimum standard.

France has international agreements permitting spontaneous exchange of information, including being a party to the (i) *Multilateral Convention on Mutual Administrative Assistance in Tax Matters: Amended by the 2010 Protocol* (OECD/Council of Europe, 2011[4]) ("the Convention"), (ii) the Directive 2011/16/EU with all other European Union Member States and (iii) double tax agreements in force with 125 jurisdictions.[2]

Completion and exchange of templates (ToR II.5.3, II.5.4, II.5.5, II.5.6, II.5.7)

In the prior years' peer review reports, it was determined that France's process for the completion and exchange of templates met all the ToR except that France was not able to exchange all information on future rulings by the timelines set out in the transparency framework (ToR II.5.6). During the year in review, all the exchanges on future rulings met the timelines set out in the transparency framework, thus the recommendation is removed.

For the year in review, the timeliness of exchanges is as follows:

Past rulings in the scope of the transparency framework	Number of exchanges transmitted by 31 December 2018	Delayed exchanges		
		Number of exchanges not transmitted by 31 December 2018	Reasons for the delays	Any other comments
	0	0	N/A	N/A
Future rulings in the scope of the transparency framework	Number of exchanges transmitted within three months of the information becoming available to the competent authority or immediately after legal impediments have been lifted	Delayed exchanges		
		Number of exchanges transmitted later than three months of the information on rulings becoming available to the competent authority	Reasons for the delays	Any other comments
	10	0	N/A	N/A
Total	10	0		

Follow up requests received for exchange of the ruling	Number	Average time to provide response	Number of requests not answered
	N/A	N/A	N/A

Conclusion on section B

France has the necessary legal basis for spontaneous exchange of information, a process for completing the templates in a timely way and has completed all exchanges. France has met all of the ToR for the exchange of information process and no recommendations are made.

C. Statistics (ToR IV)

The statistics for the year in review are as follows:

Category of ruling	Number of exchanges	Jurisdictions exchanged with
Ruling related to a preferential regime	0	N/A
Cross-border unilateral advance pricing agreements (APAs) and any other cross-border unilateral tax rulings (such as an advance tax ruling) covering transfer pricing or the application of transfer pricing principles	6	Belgium, Germany, Switzerland, United Kingdom, United States
Cross-border rulings providing for a unilateral downward adjustment to the	N/A	N/A

taxpayer's taxable profits that is not directly reflected in the taxpayer's financial / commercial accounts		
Permanent establishment rulings	4	*De minimis* rule applies
Related party conduit rulings	N/A	N/A
De minimis rule	N/A	N/A
IP regimes: total exchanges on taxpayers benefitting from the third category of IP assets, new entrants benefitting from grandfathered IP regimes; and taxpayers making use of the option to treat the nexus ratio as a rebuttable presumption	0	N/A
Total	10	

D. Matters related to intellectual property regimes (ToR I.4.1.3)

France offers an intellectual property regime (IP regime)[3] that is subject to the transparency requirements under the Action 5 Report (OECD, 2015[5]). This regime was amended with effect from 1 January 2019 and is compliant with the nexus approach. It states that the identification of the benefitting taxpayers will occur as follows:

- ***New entrants benefitting from the grandfathered IP regime:*** With respect to the previous form of the regime that existed until 31 December 2018, France should have information available and exchanged on new entrants after the relevant date from which enhanced transparency obligations apply. France has not identified information on new entrants to the previous IP regime, and as such has not exchanged information on these taxpayers. Therefore, France is recommended to identify and exchange information on all new entrants to the IP regime. This recommendation was included in the 2016 peer review report and the 2017 peer review report, and has not yet been acted upon, and the recommendation is therefore retained.
- ***Third category of IP assets***: The previous form of the regime provided benefits to income from patentable inventions, which appear to be a type of the "third category of IP asset" described in paragraph 37 of the Action 5 report (OECD, 2015). France has not implemented all of the requirements associated with this category of IP assets, thus the transparency requirements described in paragraph 37 would still apply to this case. France did not identify taxpayers benefitting from the third category of IP asset, and as such has not exchanged information on these taxpayers. This recommendation was included in the 2016 peer review report and the 2017 peer review report, and has not been acted upon, and the recommendation is therefore retained.

    It is noted that the amended nexus compliant regime allows benefits for the third category of assets and therefore transparency requirements will apply. As the new regime was only in force from 1 January 2019, this will be assessed in next year's peer review.
- ***Taxpayers making use of the option to treat the nexus ratio as a rebuttable presumption***: The amended nexus compliant regime allows taxpayers to treat the nexus ratio as a rebuttable presumption and therefore transparency requirements apply. As the new regime was only in force from 1 January 2019, this will be assessed in next year's peer review.

Summary of recommendations on implementation of the transparency framework

Aspect of implementation of the transparency framework that should be improved	Recommendation for improvement
France did not identify or exchange information on new entrants to the IP regime or taxpayers benefitting from the third category of IP asset with respect to the former IP regime.	France is recommended to identify and exchange information on all new entrants to the IP regime, and to identify and exchange information on taxpayers benefitting from the third category of IP assets. This recommendation remains unchanged since the 2016 peer review report and the 2017 peer review report.

Notes

[1] With respect to the following preferential regime: shipping regime.

[2] Parties to the Convention are available here: http://www.oecd.org/tax/exchange-of-tax-information/convention-on-mutual-administrative-assistance-in-tax-matters.htm. France also has double tax agreements with Albania, Algeria, Andorra, Argentina, Armenia, Australia, Austria, Azerbaijan, Bahrain, Bangladesh, Belarus, Belgium, Benin, Bolivia, Bosnia and Herzegovina, Botswana, Brazil, Bulgaria, Burkina Faso, Cameroon, Canada, Central African Republic, Chile, China (People's Republic of), Chinese Taipei, Congo, Côte d'Ivoire, Croatia, Cyprus, Czech Republic, Ecuador, Egypt, Estonia, Ethiopia, Finland, French Polynesia, Gabon, Georgia, Germany, Ghana, Greece, Guinea, Hong Kong (China), Hungary, Iceland, India, Indonesia, Iran, Ireland, Israel, Italy, Jamaica, Japan, Jordan, Kazakhstan, Kenya, Korea, Kosovo, Kuwait, Kyrgyzstan, Latvia, Lebanon, Libya, Lithuania, Luxembourg, Madagascar, Malawi, Malaysia, Mali, Malta, Mauritania, Mauritius, Mexico, Monaco, Mongolia, Montenegro, Morocco, Namibia, Netherlands, New Caledonia, New Zealand, Niger, Nigeria, North Macedonia, Norway, Oman, Pakistan, Panama, Philippines, Poland, Portugal, Qatar, Romania, Russia, Saudi Arabia, Senegal, Serbia, Singapore, Slovak Republic, Slovenia, South Africa, Spain, Sri Lanka, Saint Martin, Saint Pierre and Miquelon, Sweden, Switzerland, Syrian Arab Republic, Thailand, Togo, Trinidad and Tobago, Tunisia, Turkey, Turkmenistan, Ukraine, United Arab Emirates, United Kingdom, United States, Uzbekistan, Venezuela, Viet Nam, Zambia and Zimbabwe.

Note by Turkey: The information in this document with reference to "Cyprus" relates to the southern part of the Island. There is no single authority representing both Turkish and Greek Cypriot people on the Island. Turkey recognises the Turkish Republic of Northern Cyprus (TRNC). Until a lasting and equitable solution is found within the context of the United Nations, Turkey shall preserve its position concerning the "Cyprus issue".

Note by all the European Union Member States of the OECD and the European Union. The Republic of Cyprus is recognised by all members of the United Nations with the exception of Turkey. The information in this document relates to the area under the effective control of the Government of the Republic of Cyprus.

[3] Reduced corporation tax rate on IP income, formerly known as Reduced rate for long term capital gains and profits from the licensing of IP rights.

Gabon

Gabon is taking steps to implement the legal basis for the transparency framework and to commence administrative preparations to ensure that information on rulings will be exchanged in a timely manner,in line with the terms of reference (OECD, 2017[3]). Gabon is recommended to ensure that it has put in place an effective information gathering process and to implement a review and supervision mechanism, as soon as possible (ToR I.4). In addition, Gabon is recommended to develop a process to complete the templates on relevant rulings, to ensure that the exchanges of information on rulings occur in accordance with the form and timelines under the transparency framework going forward (ToR II.5).

This is Gabon's first review of implementation of the transparency framework.

Gabon can legally issue two types of rulings within the scope of the transparency framework. In practice, Gabon has issued no rulings in the year in review.

As no exchanges were required to take place, no peer input was received in respect of the exchanges of information on rulings received from Gabon.

Introduction

This peer review covers Gabon's implementation of the BEPS Action 5 transparency framework for the year 2018. The report has four parts, each relating to a key part of the ToR. Each part is discussed in turn. A summary of recommendations is included at the end of this report.

A. The information gathering process

Gabon can legally issue two types of rulings within the scope of the transparency framework: i) rulings related to a preferential regime[1] and ii) cross-border unilateral advance pricing agreements (APAs) and any other cross-border unilateral tax rulings (such as an advance tax ruling) covering transfer pricing or the application of transfer pricing principles.

For Gabon, past rulings are any tax rulings within scope that are issued either (i) on or after 1 January 2016 but before 1 April 2018; and (ii) on or after 1 January 2014 but before 1 January 2016, provided still in effect as at 1 January 2016.

In Gabon, rulings are issued by the directorate of Legislation, within the Tax Administration. This unit is responsible for storing and reviewing such rulings and has reviewed its files, being able to confirm that no past rulings have been issued. To date no rulings have been issued. As such there was no need to identify potential exchange jurisdictions.

Future rulings (ToR I.4.1.1, I.4.1.2, I.4.2.1)

For Gabon, future rulings are any tax rulings within scope that are issued on or after 1 April 2018.

No rulings were issued by Gabon during the future rulings period in the year of review. However, Gabon indicates that there are no processes in place for the record keeping of rulings for the purposes of the transparency framework. It is noted that Gabon intends to implement guidelines and practices to make sure the necessary information to meet the requirements of the transparency framework is required in all cases.

Review and supervision (ToR I.4.3)

Gabon did not yet have a review and supervision mechanism under the transparency framework for the year in review. Gabon is discussing the implementation of a revision and supervision mechanism for ensuring implementation of the transparency framework.

Conclusion on section A

Gabon is recommended to finalise its information gathering process, with a review and supervision mechanism, as soon as possible (ToR I.4).

B. The exchange of information

Legal basis for spontaneous exchange of information (ToR II.5.1, II.5.2)

Gabon is currently working to have in place the necessary domestic legal basis to exchange information spontaneously.

Gabon has (i) signed the *Multilateral Convention on Mutual Administrative Assistance in Tax Matters: Amended by the 2010 Protocol* (OECD/Council of Europe, 2011[4]) ("the Convention"), which is pending ratification and has (ii) bilateral agreements in force with five jurisdictions.[2] Gabon is encouraged to continue its efforts to expand its international exchange of information instruments to be able to exchange rulings. It is however noted that jurisdictions are assessed on their compliance with the transparency framework in respect of the exchange of information network in effect for the year of the particular annual review.

Completion and exchange of templates (ToR II.5.3, II.5.4, II.5.5, II.5.6, II.5.7)

Gabon is still developing a process to complete the templates on relevant rulings, to make them available to the Competent Authority for exchange of information, and to exchange them with relevant jurisdictions.

.

As no exchanges were required to take place in the year of review, no data on the timeliness of exchanges can be reported.

Conclusion on section B

Gabon is recommended to develop a process to complete the templates on relevant rulings and to ensure that the exchanges of information on rulings occur in accordance with the form and timelines under the transparency framework going forward (ToR II.5).

C. Statistics (ToR IV)

As the Secretariat is not aware whether information on rulings was exchanged by Gabon for the year in review, no statistics can be reported here.

D. Matters related to intellectual property regimes (ToR I.4.1.3)

Gabon does not offer an intellectual property regime for which transparency requirements under the Action 5 Report (OECD, 2015[5]) were imposed.

Summary of recommendations on implementation of the transparency framework

Aspect of implementation of the transparency framework that should be improved	Recommendation for improvement
Gabon has not yet finalised the steps to have in place its necessary information and gathering process.	Gabon is recommended to finalise its information gathering process, with a review and supervision mechanism, as soon as possible.
Gabon has not yet finalised the steps to have effective compulsory spontaneous exchange of information on the tax rulings within the scope of the transparency framework.	Gabon is recommended to continue to put in place a domestic legal framework allowing spontaneous exchange of information on rulings and to ensure the timely exchange of information on rulings in the form required by the transparency framework.

Notes

[1] With respect to the following preferential regime: Special economic zone.

[2] Gabon has bilateral agreements in force with Belgium, Canada, France, Korea and Morocco.

Georgia

Georgia has met all aspects of the terms of reference (OECD, 2017[3]) (ToR) for the calendar year 2018 (year in review).

This is Georgia's first review of implementation of the transparency framework.

Georgia can legally issue four types of rulings within the scope of the transparency framework. In practice, Georgia has not issued any rulings within the scope of the transparency framework.

As no exchanges were required to take place, no peer input was received in respect of the exchanges of information on rulings received from Georgia.

Introduction

This peer review covers Georgia's implementation of the BEPS Action 5 transparency framework for the year 2018. The report has four parts, each relating to a key part of the ToR. Each part is discussed in turn. A summary of recommendations is included at the end of this report.

A. The information gathering process

Georgia can legally issue the following four types of rulings within the scope of the transparency framework: (i) preferential regimes;[1] (ii) cross-border unilateral APAs and any other cross-border unilateral tax rulings (such as an advance tax ruling) covering transfer pricing or the application of transfer pricing principles; (iii) permanent establishment rulings; and (iv) related party conduit rulings. The Legal department of the Revenue Service of the Ministry of Finance is in charge of issuing rulings.

Past rulings (ToR I.4.1.1, I.4.1.2, I.4.2.1, I.4.2.2)

For Georgia, past rulings are any tax rulings within scope that are issued either (i) on or after 1 January 2016 but before 1 April 2018; and (ii) on or after 1 January 2014 but before 1 January 2016, provided they are still in effect as at 1 January 2016.

Georgia has been able to issue rulings since 2010. The team responsible for issuing rulings is the Advance rulings division, which is a part of the Legal department within the Revenue Service. The team consists of seven members.

All rulings that were issued are stored in a special database. This database includes information with respect to the date of issuing the ruling, information on related parties and a short summary of the ruling. Based on this, the members of the Advance rulings division conducted a manual review of all of the rulings included in the database. The Advance rulings division did not identify any rulings in scope of the Action 5 transparency framework. As such, no steps were required to be taken to identify potential exchange jurisdictions.

Future rulings (ToR I.4.1.1, I.4.1.2, I.4.2.1)

For Georgia, future rulings are any tax rulings within scope that are issued on or after 1 April 2018.

When a ruling is issued, the Advance rulings division is in charge of identifying whether the ruling meets the criteria under the Action 5 transparency framework and whether it needs to be exchanged upon or not.

A Ministerial decree has been issued in December 2018 with the rules and procedures relating to the advanced tax rulings. Despite this being after the start of the period for which future rulings could be issued, there were no rulings issued in practice and therefore there is no impact on the implementation of the transparency framework. In order to identify the potential exchange jurisdictions, the taxpayer needs to provide the information with respect to the related parties it transacts with, the immediate parent company, the ultimate parent company and any other relevant information with the application for the ruling. If information is missing, the Advance rulings division has the power to ask the taxpayer for the additional information. If the necessary information is not provided, no ruling can be issued.

Review and supervision (ToR I.4.3)

The Ministry of Finance is in charge of the review and supervision of tax rulings. Before a ruling is issued, it needs to be approved by the Ministry of Finance. The Ministry also double checks all rulings issued to see whether a ruling is in scope of the Action 5 transparency framework.

Once a ruling is identified as being in scope of the Action 5 transparency framework, it would be sent to the Tax and Customs policy department, which double-check the categorisation of the ruling and the identification of the potential exchange jurisdictions. This department is also responsible for conducting the exchange.

Conclusion on section A

Georgia has met all of the ToR for the information gathering process and no recommendations are made.

B. The exchange of information

Legal basis for spontaneous exchange of information (ToR II.5.1, II.5.2)

Georgia has the necessary domestic legal basis to exchange information spontaneously. Georgia notes that there are no legal or practical impediments that prevent the spontaneous exchange of information on rulings as contemplated in the Action 5 minimum standard.

Georgia has international agreements permitting spontaneous exchange of information, including being a party to the (i) *Multilateral Convention on Mutual Administrative Assistance in Tax Matters: Amended by the 2010 Protocol* (OECD/Council of Europe, 2011[4]) ("the Convention") and (ii) double tax agreements in force with 57 jurisdictions.[2]

Completion and exchange of templates (ToR II.5.3, II.5.4, II.5.5, II.5.6, II.5.7)

The procedure and timelines for the completion and exchange of templates are set out under a new Ministerial order (number 480), titled "Implementation of the obligatory measures under the Base Erosion and Profit Shifting (BEPS) project".

When a ruling has been issued and identified as in scope for the Action 5 transparency framework, the Advance ruling division will send it within two months to the Tax and Customs policy department, who is the Competent Authority. The Competent Authority is responsible for completing the templates and this must be done in the form of Annex C of the 2015 Action 5 Report (OECD, 2015[5]). The summary section of the template has to be completed in line with the internal FHTP suggested guidance. The template must then be sent to the relevant jurisdictions within one month of receiving the information from the Advance ruling division.

As Georgia did not issue any rulings in scope of the transparency framework in the relevant period, Georgia was not required to exchange any information on rulings in the year in review and no data on the timeliness of exchanges can be reported.

Conclusion on section B

Georgia has the necessary legal basis for spontaneous exchange of information and has a process for completing the templates in a timely way. Georgia has met all of the ToR for the exchange of information process that can be met in the absence of rulings being issued and exchanged in practice and no recommendations are made.

C. Statistics (ToR IV)

As there was no information on rulings exchanged by Georgia for the year in review, no statistics can be reported.

D. Matters related to intellectual property regimes (ToR I.4.1.3)

Georgia does not offer an intellectual property regime for which transparency requirements under the Action 5 Report (OECD, 2015[5]) were imposed.

Summary of recommendations on implementation of the transparency framework

Aspect of implementation of the transparency framework that should be improved	Recommendation for improvement
	No recommendations are made.

Notes

[1] With respect to the following preferential regimes: 1) International financial company and 2) Virtual zone person.

[2] Parties to the Convention are available here: www.oecd.org/tax/exchange-of-tax-information/convention-on-mutual-administrative-assistance-in-tax-matters.htm. Georgia also has bilateral agreements with Armenia, Austria, Azerbaijan, Bahamas, Bahrain, Belarus, Belgium, Bulgaria, China (People's Republic of), Croatia, Cyprus, Czech Republic, Denmark, Egypt, Estonia, Finland, France, Germany, Greece, Hungary, Iceland, India, Iran, Ireland, Israel, Italy, Japan, Kazakhstan, Korea, Kuwait, Latvia, Liechtenstein, Lithuania, Luxembourg, Malta, Moldova, Netherlands, Norway, Poland, Portugal, Qatar, Romania, San Marino, Saudi Arabia, Serbia, Singapore, Slovak Republic, Slovenia, Spain, Sweden, Switzerland, Turkey, Turkmenistan, Ukraine, United Arab Emirates, United Kingdom and Uzbekistan.

Note by Turkey: The information in this document with reference to "Cyprus" relates to the southern part of the Island. There is no single authority representing both Turkish and Greek Cypriot people on the Island. Turkey recognises the Turkish Republic of Northern Cyprus (TRNC). Until a lasting and equitable solution is found within the context of the United Nations, Turkey shall preserve its position concerning the "Cyprus issue".

Note by all the European Union Member States of the OECD and the European Union. The Republic of Cyprus is recognised by all members of the United Nations with the exception of Turkey. The information in this document relates to the area under the effective control of the Government of the Republic of Cyprus.

Germany

Germany has met all aspects of the terms of reference (OECD, 2017[3]) (ToR) for the calendar year 2018 (year in review) and no recommendations are made.

In the prior year report, Germany did not receive any recommendations. Germany can legally issue five types of rulings within the scope of the transparency framework. In practice, Germany issued rulings within the scope of the transparency framework as follows:

- 30 past rulings;[1]
- For the period 1 April 2016 - 31 December 2016: seven future rulings;
- For the calendar year 2017: 10 future rulings, and
- For the year in review: 10 future rulings.

Peer input was received from two jurisdictions in respect of the exchanges of information on rulings received from Germany. The input was positive, noting that information was complete, in a correct format and received in a timely manner.

Introduction

This peer review covers Germany's implementation of the BEPS Action 5 transparency framework for the year 2018. The report has four parts, each relating to a key part of the ToR. Each part is discussed in turn. A summary of recommendations is included at the end of this report.

A. The information gathering process

Germany can legally issue the following five types of rulings within the scope of the transparency framework: i) preferential regimes;[2] (ii) cross-border unilateral advance pricing agreements (APAs) and any other cross-border unilateral tax rulings (such as an advance tax ruling) covering transfer pricing or the application of transfer pricing principles; (iii) rulings providing for unilateral downward adjustments; (iv) permanent establishment rulings; and (v) related party conduit rulings.

Past rulings (ToR I.4.1.1, I.4.1.2, I.4.2.1, I.4.2.2)

For Germany, past rulings are any tax rulings within scope that are issued either: (i) on or after 1 January 2014 but before 1 April 2016; or (ii) on or after 1 January 2010 but before 1 January 2014, provided they were still in effect as at 1 January 2014.

In the prior years' peer review reports, it was determined that Germany's undertakings to identify past rulings and all potential exchange jurisdictions were sufficient to meet the minimum standard. Germany's implementation in this regard remains unchanged, and therefore continues to meet the minimum standard.

Future rulings (ToR I.4.1.1, I.4.1.2, I.4.2.1)

For Germany, future rulings are any tax rulings within scope that are issued on or after 1 April 2016.

In the prior years' peer review reports, it was determined that Germany's undertakings to identify future rulings and all potential exchange jurisdictions was sufficient to meet the minimum standard. Germany's implementation in this regard remains unchanged, and therefore continues to meet the minimum standard.

Review and supervision (ToR I.4.3)

In the prior years' peer review reports, it was determined that Germany's review and supervision mechanism was sufficient to meet the minimum standard. Germany's implementation in this regard remains unchanged, and therefore continues to meet the minimum standard.

Conclusion on section A

Germany has met all of the ToR for the information gathering process and no recommendations are made.

B. The exchange of information

Legal basis for spontaneous exchange of information (ToR II.5.1, II.5.2)

Germany has the necessary domestic legal basis to exchange information spontaneously. Germany notes that there are no legal or practical impediments that prevent the spontaneous exchange of information on rulings as contemplated in the Action 5 minimum standard.

Germany has international agreements permitting spontaneous exchange of information, including being a party to the (i) the *Multilateral Convention on Mutual Administrative Assistance in Tax Matters: Amended by the 2010 Protocol* (OECD/Council of Europe, 2011) ("the Convention"), (ii) the Directive 2011/16/EU with all other European Union Member States and (iii) double tax agreements in force with 95 jurisdictions.[3]

Completion and exchange of templates (ToR II.5.3, II.5.4, II.5.5, II.5.6, II.5.7)

In the prior year peer review report, it was determined that Germany's process for the completion and exchange of templates were sufficient to meet the minimum standard. Germany's implementation in this regard remains unchanged and therefore continues to meet the minimum standard.

For the year in review, the timeliness of exchanges is as follows:

Past rulings in the scope of the transparency framework	Number of exchanges transmitted by 31 December 2018	Delayed exchanges		
		Number of exchanges not transmitted by 31 December 2018	Reasons for the delays	Any other comments
	0	0	N/A	N/A
Future rulings in the scope of the transparency framework	Number of exchanges transmitted within three months of the information becoming available to the competent authority or immediately after legal impediments have been lifted	Delayed exchanges		
		Number of exchanges transmitted later than three months of the information on rulings becoming available to the competent authority	Reasons for the delays	Any other comments
	10	0	N/A	N/A
Total	10	0		

Follow up requests received for exchange of the ruling	Number	Average time to provide response	Number of requests not answered
	0	N/A	N/A

Conclusion on section B

Germany has the necessary legal basis for spontaneous exchange of information, a process for completing the templates in a timely way and has completed all exchanges. Germany has met all of the ToR for the exchange of information process and no recommendations are made.

C. Statistics (ToR IV)

The statistics for the year in review are as follows:

Category of ruling	Number of exchanges	Jurisdictions exchanged with
Ruling related to a preferential regime	1	*De minimis* rule applies
Cross-border unilateral advance pricing agreements (APAs) and any other cross-border unilateral tax rulings (such as an advance tax ruling) covering transfer pricing or the application of transfer pricing principles	1	*De minimis* rule applies
Cross-border rulings providing for a unilateral downward adjustment to the taxpayer's taxable profits that is not directly reflected in the taxpayer's financial / commercial accounts	0	N/A

Permanent establishment rulings	8	France, Slovak Republic, Switzerland, United Kingdom, United States
Related party conduit rulings	0	N/A
De minimis rule	N/A	N/A
IP regimes: total exchanges on taxpayers benefitting from the third category of IP assets, new entrants benefitting from grandfathered IP regimes; and taxpayers making use of the option to treat the nexus ratio as a rebuttable presumption	N/A	N/A
Total	10	

D. Matters related to intellectual property regimes (ToR I.4.1.3)

Germany does not offer an intellectual property regime for which transparency requirements under the Action 5 Report (OECD, 2015[5]) were imposed.

Summary of recommendations on implementation of the transparency framework

Aspect of implementation of the transparency framework that should be improved	Recommendation for improvement
	No recommendations are made.

Notes

[1] Including one that fells into more than one category under the BEPS Action 5 report.

[2] With respect to the following preferential regime: tonnage tax regime.

[3] Parties to the Convention are available here: www.oecd.org/tax/exchange-of-tax-information/convention-on-mutual-administrative-assistance-in-tax-matters.htm. Germany also has bilateral agreements in force with Albania, Algeria, Argentina, Armenia, Australia, Austria, Bangladesh, Belarus, Belgium, Bolivia, Bosnia and Herzegovina, Bulgaria, Canada, China (People's Republic of), Costa Rica, Côte d'Ivoire, Croatia, Cyprus, Czech Republic, Denmark, Ecuador, Egypt, Estonia, Finland, France, Georgia, Ghana, Greece, Hungary, Iceland, India, Indonesia, Iran, Ireland, Israel, Italy, Jamaica, Japan, Jersey, Kazakhstan, Kenia, Korea, Kosovo, Kuwait, Kyrgyzstan, Latvia, Liberia, Liechtenstein, Lithuania, Luxembourg, Malaysia, Malta, Morocco, Mauritius, Mexico, Moldavia, Mongolia, Montenegro, Namibia, Netherlands, New Zealand, North Macedonia, Norway, Pakistan, Philippines, Poland, Portugal, Romania, Russia, Serbia, Singapore, Slovak Republic, Slovenia, South Africa, Spain, Sri Lanka, Sweden, Switzerland, Syria, Tajikistan, Thailand, Trinidad and Tobago, Tunisia, Turkey, Turkmenistan, Ukraine, United Arab Emirates, United Kingdom, United States, Uruguay, Uzbekistan, Venezuela, Viet Nam, Zambia, Zimbabwe.

Note by Turkey: The information in this document with reference to "Cyprus" relates to the southern part of the Island. There is no single authority representing both Turkish and Greek Cypriot people on the Island. Turkey recognises the Turkish Republic of Northern Cyprus (TRNC). Until a lasting and equitable solution is found within the context of the United Nations, Turkey shall preserve its position concerning the "Cyprus issue".

Note by all the European Union Member States of the OECD and the European Union. The Republic of Cyprus is recognised by all members of the United Nations with the exception of Turkey. The information in this document relates to the area under the effective control of the Government of the Republic of Cyprus.

Greece

Greece has met all aspects of the terms of reference (OECD, 2017[3]) (ToR) for the calendar year 2018 (year in review) and no recommendations are made.

In the prior year report, Greece did not receive any recommendations.

Greece can legally issue one type of ruling within the scope of the transparency framework. In practice, Greece issued rulings within the scope of the transparency framework as follows:

- One past ruling;
- For the period 1 April 2016 - 31 December 2016: no future rulings;
- For the calendar year 2017: no future rulings, and
- For the year in review: two future rulings.

No peer input was received in respect of the exchanges of information on rulings received from Greece.

Introduction

This peer review covers Greece's implementation of the BEPS Action 5 transparency framework for the year 2018. The report has four parts, each relating to a key part of the ToR. Each part is discussed in turn. A summary of recommendations is included at the end of this report.

A. The information gathering process

Greece can legally issue the following type of ruling within the scope of the transparency framework: cross-border unilateral APAs and any other cross-border unilateral tax rulings (such as an advance tax ruling) covering transfer pricing or the application of transfer pricing principles.

Past rulings (ToR I.4.1.1, I.4.1.2, I.4.2.1, I.4.2.2)

For Greece, past rulings are any tax rulings within scope that are issued either: (i) on or after 1 January 2014 but before 1 April 2016; or (ii) on or after 1 January 2010 but before 1 January 2014, provided they were still in effect as at 1 January 2014.

In the prior years' peer review reports, it was determined that Greece's undertakings to identify past rulings and all potential exchange jurisdictions were sufficient to meet the minimum standard. Greece's implementation in this regard remains unchanged, and therefore continues to meet the minimum standard.

Future rulings (ToR I.4.1.1, I.4.1.2, I.4.2.1)

For Greece, future rulings are any tax rulings within scope that are issued on or after 1 April 2016.

In the prior years' peer review reports, it was determined that Greece's undertakings to identify future rulings and all potential exchange jurisdictions were sufficient to meet the minimum standard. Greece's implementation in this regard remains unchanged, and therefore continues to meet the minimum standard.

Review and supervision (ToR I.4.3)

Conclusion on section A

Greece has met all of the ToR for the information gathering process and no recommendations are made.

B. The exchange of information

Legal basis for spontaneous exchange of information (ToR II.5.1, II.5.2)

Greece has the necessary domestic legal basis to exchange information spontaneously. Greece notes that there are no legal or practical impediments that prevent the spontaneous exchange of information on rulings as contemplated in the Action 5 minimum standard.

Greece has international agreements permitting spontaneous exchange of information, including being a party to the (i) *Multilateral Convention on Mutual Administrative Assistance in Tax Matters: Amended by the 2010 Protocol* (OECD/Council of Europe, 2011[4]) ("the Convention"), (ii) the Directive 2011/16/EU with all other European Union Member States and (iii) double tax agreements in force with 57 jurisdictions.[1]

Completion and exchange of templates (ToR II.5.3, II.5.4, II.5.5, II.5.6, II.5.7)

In the prior year peer review report, it was determined that Greece's process for the completion and exchange of templates were sufficient to meet the minimum standard. Greece's implementation in this regard remains unchanged and therefore continues to meet the minimum standard.

For the year in review, the timeliness of exchanges is as follows:

Past rulings in the scope of the transparency framework	Number of exchanges transmitted by 31 December 2018	Delayed exchanges		
		Number of exchanges not transmitted by 31 December 2018	Reasons for the delays	Any other comments
	0	0	N/A	N/A
Future rulings in the scope of the transparency framework	Number of exchanges transmitted within three months of the information becoming available to the competent authority or immediately after legal impediments have been lifted	Delayed exchanges		
		Number of exchanges transmitted later than three months of the information on rulings becoming available to the competent authority	Reasons for the delays	Any other comments
	5	0	N/A	N/A
Total	5	0		

Follow up requests received for exchange of the ruling	Number	Average time to provide response	Number of requests not answered
	0	N/A	0

Conclusion on section B

Greece has the necessary legal basis for spontaneous exchange of information, a process for completing the templates in a timely way and has completed all exchanges. Greece has met all of the ToR for the exchange of information process and no recommendations are made.

C. Statistics (ToR IV)

The statistics for the year in review are as follows:

Category of ruling	Number of exchanges	Jurisdictions exchanged with
Ruling related to a preferential regime	N/A	N/A
Cross-border unilateral advance pricing agreements (APAs) and any other cross-border unilateral tax rulings (such as an advance tax ruling) covering transfer pricing or the application of transfer pricing principles	*De minimis* rule applies	N/A
Cross-border rulings providing for a unilateral downward adjustment to the taxpayer's taxable profits that is not directly reflected in the taxpayer's financial / commercial accounts	N/A	N/A
Permanent establishment rulings	N/A	N/A
Related party conduit rulings	N/A	N/A
De minimis rule	5	N/A
IP regimes: total exchanges on taxpayers benefitting from the third	N/A	N/A

category of IP assets, new entrants benefitting from grandfathered IP regimes; and taxpayers making use of the option to treat the nexus ratio as a rebuttable presumption		
Total	**5**	

D. Matters related to intellectual property regimes (ToR I.4.1.3)

Greece offers an intellectual property regime (IP regime)[2] that is not subject to the transparency requirements under the Action 5 Report (OECD, 2015[5]), because:

- ***New entrants benefitting from the grandfathered IP regime***: the regime is currently under review by the FHTP.
- ***Third category of IP assets***: not applicable as the regime does not allow the third category of IP assets to qualify for the benefits.
- ***Taxpayers making the use of the option to treat the nexus ratio as a rebuttable presumption***: not applicable the regime does not allow the nexus ratio to be treated as a rebuttable presumption.

Summary of recommendations on implementation of the transparency framework

Aspect of implementation of the transparency framework that should be improved	Recommendation for improvement
	No recommendations are made.

Notes

[1] Parties to the Convention are available here: www.oecd.org/tax/exchange-of-tax-information/convention-on-mutual-administrative-assistance-in-tax-matters.htm. Greece also has bilateral agreements with Albania, Armenia, Austria, Azerbaijan, Belgium, Bosnia and Herzegovina, Bulgaria, Canada, China (People's Republic of), Qatar, Croatia, Cyprus, Czech Republic, Denmark, Egypt, Estonia, Finland, France, Germany, Georgia, Hungary, Iceland, India, Ireland, Israel, Italy, Korea, Kuwait, Latvia, Lithuania, Luxembourg, Malta, Mexico, Moldova, Morocco, Netherlands, Norway, Poland, Portugal, Romania, Russian Federation, San Marino, Saudi Arabia, Serbia, Slovak Republic, Slovenia, Spain, South Africa, Sweden, Swiss Federation, Tunisia, Turkey, Ukraine, United Arab Emirates, United Kingdom, Uzbekistan and United States.

Note by Turkey: The information in this document with reference to "Cyprus" relates to the southern part of the Island. There is no single authority representing both Turkish and Greek Cypriot people on the Island. Turkey recognises the Turkish Republic of Northern Cyprus (TRNC). Until a lasting and equitable solution is found within the context of the United Nations, Turkey shall preserve its position concerning the "Cyprus issue".

Note by all the European Union Member States of the OECD and the European Union. The Republic of Cyprus is recognised by all members of the United Nations with the exception of Turkey. The information in this document relates to the area under the effective control of the Government of the Republic of Cyprus.

[2] Tax patent incentives regime.

Guernsey

Guernsey has met all aspects of the terms of reference (OECD, 2017[3]) (ToR) for the calendar year 2018 (year in review) and no recommendations are made.

In the prior year report, Guernsey did not receive any recommendations.

Guernsey can legally issue four types of rulings within the scope of the transparency framework. In practice, Guernsey issued rulings within the scope of the transparency framework as follows:

- Five past rulings;
- For the period 1 April 2017 - 31 December 2017: three future rulings, and
- For the year in review: two future rulings.

No peer input was received in respect of the exchanges of information on rulings received from Guernsey.

Introduction

This peer review covers Guernsey's implementation of the BEPS Action 5 transparency framework for the year 2018. The report has four parts, each relating to a key part of the ToR. Each part is discussed in turn. A summary of recommendations is included at the end of this report.

A. The information gathering process

Guernsey can legally issue the following four types of rulings within the scope of the transparency framework: (i) cross-border unilateral APAs and any other cross-border unilateral tax rulings (such as an advance tax ruling) covering transfer pricing or the application of transfer pricing principles; (ii) rulings providing for unilateral downward adjustments; (iii) permanent establishment rulings; and (iv) related party conduit rulings.

Past rulings (ToR I.4.1.1, I.4.1.2, I.4.2.1, I.4.2.2)

For Guernsey, past rulings are any tax rulings within scope that are issued either: (i) on or after 1 January 2015 but before 1 April 2017; or (ii) on or after 1 January 2012 but before 1 January 2015, provided they were still in effect as at 1 January 2015.

In the prior year peer review report, it was determined that Guernsey's undertakings to identify past rulings and all potential exchange jurisdictions were sufficient to meet the minimum standard. Guernsey's implementation in this regard remains unchanged, and therefore continues to meet the minimum standard.

Future rulings (ToR I.4.1.1, I.4.1.2, I.4.2.1)

For Guernsey, future rulings are any tax rulings within scope that are issued on or after 1 April 2017.

In the prior year peer review report, it was determined that Guernsey's undertakings to identify future rulings and all potential exchange jurisdictions were sufficient to meet the minimum standard. Guernsey's implementation in this regard remains unchanged, and therefore continues to meet the minimum standard.

Review and supervision (ToR I.4.3)

In the prior year peer review report, it was determined that Guernsey's review and supervision mechanism was sufficient to meet the minimum standard. Guernsey's implementation in this regard remains unchanged, and therefore continues to meet the minimum standard.

Conclusion on section A

Guernsey has met all of the ToR for the information gathering process and no recommendations are made.

B. The exchange of information

Legal basis for spontaneous exchange of information (ToR II.5.1, II.5.2)

Guernsey has the necessary domestic legal basis to exchange information spontaneously. Guernsey notes that there are no legal or practical impediments that prevent the spontaneous exchange of information on rulings as contemplated in the Action 5 minimum standard.

Guernsey has international agreements permitting spontaneous exchange of information, including being a party to the (i) *Multilateral Convention on Mutual Administrative Assistance in Tax Matters: Amended by the 2010 Protocol* (OECD/Council of Europe, 2011[4]) ("the Convention") and (ii) double tax agreements in force with 70 jurisdictions.[1]

Completion and exchange of templates (ToR II.5.3, II.5.4, II.5.5, II.5.6, II.5.7)

In the prior year peer review report, it was determined that Guernsey's process for the completion and exchange of templates were sufficient to meet the minimum standard. Guernsey's implementation in this regard remains unchanged and therefore continues to meet the minimum standard.

For the year in review, the timeliness of exchanges is as follows:

Past rulings in the scope of the transparency framework	Number of exchanges transmitted by 31 December 2018	Delayed exchanges		
		Number of exchanges not transmitted by 31 December 2018	Reasons for the delays	Any other comments
	0	0	N/A	N/A
Future rulings in the scope of the transparency framework	Number of exchanges transmitted within three months of the information becoming available to the competent authority or immediately after legal impediments have been lifted	Delayed exchanges		
		Number of exchanges transmitted later than three months of the information on rulings becoming available to the competent authority	Reasons for the delays	Any other comments
	4	0	N/A	N/A
Total	4	0		

Follow up requests received for exchange of the ruling	Number	Average time to provide response	Number of requests not answered
	0	N/A	N/A

Conclusion on section B

Guernsey has the necessary legal basis for spontaneous exchange of information, a process for completing the templates in a timely way and has completed all exchanges. Guernsey has met all of the ToR for the exchange of information process and no recommendations are made.

C. Statistics (ToR IV)

The statistics for the year in review are as follows:

Category of ruling	Number of exchanges	Jurisdictions exchanged with
Ruling related to a preferential regime	0	N/A
Cross-border unilateral advance pricing agreements (APAs) and any other cross-border unilateral tax rulings (such as an advance tax ruling) covering transfer pricing or the application of transfer pricing principles	*De minimis* rule applies	N/A
Cross-border rulings providing for a unilateral downward adjustment to the taxpayer's taxable profits that is not directly reflected in the taxpayer's	0	N/A

financial / commercial accounts		
Permanent establishment rulings	*De minimis* rule applies	N/A
Related party conduit rulings	0	N/A
De minimis rule	4	N/A
IP regimes: total exchanges on taxpayers benefitting from the third category of IP assets, new entrants benefitting from grandfathered IP regimes; and taxpayers making use of the option to treat the nexus ratio as a rebuttable presumption	N/A	N/A
Total	4	

D. Matters related to intellectual property regimes (ToR I.4.1.3)

Guernsey does not offer an intellectual property regime for which transparency requirements under the Action 5 Report (OECD, 2015[5]) were imposed.

Summary of recommendations on implementation of the transparency framework

Aspect of implementation of the transparency framework that should be improved	Recommendation for improvement
	No recommendations are made.

Notes

[1] Parties to the Convention are available here: www.oecd.org/tax/exchange-of-tax-information/convention-on-mutual-administrative-assistance-in-tax-matters.htm. Guernsey also has bilateral agreements in force with Argentina, Australia, Austria, Bahamas, Belgium, Bermuda, Botswana, Brazil, British Virgin Islands, Bulgaria, Canada, Cayman Islands, Chile, China (People's Republic of), Costa Rica, Cyprus, Czech Republic, Denmark, Faroe Islands, Finland, France, Germany, Gibraltar, Greece, Greenland, Hong Kong (China), Hungary, Iceland, India, Indonesia, Ireland, Isle of Man, Italy, Japan, Jersey, Korea, Latvia, Lesotho, Liechtenstein, Lithuania, Luxembourg, Macao (China), Malta, Mauritius, Mexico, Monaco, Montserrat, Netherlands, New Zealand, Norway, Poland, Portugal, Qatar, Romania, Saint Kitts and Nevis, San Marino, Seychelles, Singapore, Slovak Republic, Slovenia, South Africa, Spain, Swaziland, Sweden, Switzerland, Turkey, Turks and Caicos Islands, United Kingdom, United States and Uruguay.

Note by Turkey: The information in this document with reference to "Cyprus" relates to the southern part of the Island. There is no single authority representing both Turkish and Greek Cypriot people on the Island. Turkey recognises the Turkish Republic of Northern Cyprus (TRNC). Until a lasting and equitable solution is found within the context of the United Nations, Turkey shall preserve its position concerning the "Cyprus issue".

Note by all the European Union Member States of the OECD and the European Union. The Republic of Cyprus is recognised by all members of the United Nations with the exception of Turkey. The information in this document relates to the area under the effective control of the Government of the Republic of Cyprus.

Haiti

Haiti has met all aspects of the terms of reference (OECD, 2017[3]) (ToR) for the calendar year 2018 (year in review) that can be met in the absence of rulings being issued.

In the prior year report, Haiti did not receive any recommendations.

Haiti indicates that it cannot legally issue any type of rulings within the scope of the transparency framework.

As no exchanges were required to take place, no peer input was received in respect of the exchanges of information on rulings received from Haiti.

Introduction

This peer review covers Haiti's implementation of the BEPS Action 5 transparency framework for the year 2018. The report has four parts, each relating to a key part of the ToR. Each part is discussed in turn. A summary of recommendations is included at the end of this report.

A. The information gathering process

As no rulings are issued, this section is not assessed.

B. The exchange of information

As no rulings are issued, this section is not assessed.

C. Statistics (ToR IV)

As no rulings are issued, no statistics can be reported.

D. Matters related to intellectual property regimes (ToR I.4.1.3)

Haiti does not offer an intellectual property regime for which transparency requirements under the Action 5 Report (OECD, 2015[5]) were imposed.

Summary of recommendations on implementation of the transparency framework

Aspect of implementation of the transparency framework that should be improved	Recommendation for improvement
	No recommendations are made.

Hong Kong (China)

Hong Kong (China) ("Hong Kong") has met all aspects of the terms of reference (OECD, 2017[3]) (ToR) for the calendar year 2018 (year in review) and no recommendations are made.

In the prior year report, Hong Kong did not receive any recommendations.

Hong Kong can legally issue four types of rulings within the scope of the transparency framework. In practice, Hong Kong issued rulings within the scope of the transparency framework as follows:

- One past ruling;
- For the calendar year 2017: no future rulings, and
- For the year in review: no future rulings.

The Inland Revenue Department of Hong Kong may publish some advance rulings on its website in redacted form.1

As no exchanges were required to take place, no peer input was received in respect of the exchanges of information on rulings received from Hong Kong.

Introduction

This peer review covers Hong Kong's implementation of the BEPS Action 5 transparency framework for the year 2018. The report has four parts, each relating to a key part of the ToR. Each part is discussed in turn. A summary of recommendations is included at the end of this report.

A. The information gathering process

Hong Kong can legally issue the following four types of rulings within the scope of the transparency framework: (i) preferential regimes;[2] (ii) cross-border unilateral APAs and any other cross-border unilateral tax rulings (such as an advance tax ruling) covering transfer pricing or the application of transfer pricing principles; (iii) permanent establishment rulings; and (iv) related party conduit rulings.

Past rulings (ToR I.4.1.1, I.4.1.2, I.4.2.1, I.4.2.2)

For Hong Kong, past rulings are any tax rulings within scope that are issued either: (i) on or after 1 January 2015 but before 1 April 2017; or (ii) on or after 1 January 2012 but before 1 January 2015, provided they were still in effect as at 1 January 2015.

In the prior year peer review report, it was determined that Hong Kong's undertakings to identify past rulings and all potential exchange jurisdictions were sufficient to meet the minimum standard. Hong Kong's implementation in this regard remains unchanged, and therefore continues to meet the minimum standard.

Future rulings (ToR I.4.1.1, I.4.1.2, I.4.2.1)

For Hong Kong, future rulings are any tax rulings within scope that are issued on or after 1 April 2017.

In the prior year peer review report, it was determined that Hong Kong's undertakings to identify future rulings and all potential exchange jurisdictions were sufficient to meet the minimum standard. Hong Kong's implementation in this regard remains unchanged, and therefore continues to meet the minimum standard. It is noted that during the year in review, on 13 July 2018, Hong Kong enacted the Inland Revenue (Amendment) (No. 6) Ordinance 2018, which codifies Hong Kong's APA regime. The information gathering process for APAs is described in the prior year review report and meets the ToR.

Review and supervision (ToR I.4.3)

In the prior year peer review report, it was determined that Hong Kong's review and supervision mechanism was sufficient to meet the minimum standard. Hong Kong's implementation in this regard remains unchanged, and therefore continues to meet the minimum standard.

Conclusion on section A

Hong Kong has met all of the ToR for the information gathering process and no recommendations are made.

B. The exchange of information

Legal basis for spontaneous exchange of information (ToR II.5.1, II.5.2)

Hong Kong has the necessary domestic legal basis to exchange information spontaneously. Hong Kong notes that there are no legal or practical impediments that prevent the spontaneous exchange of information on rulings as contemplated in the Action 5 minimum standard.

Hong Kong is party to international agreements permitting spontaneous exchange of information, including double tax agreements in force with 33 jurisdictions.[3] In addition, by a declaration deposited with the OECD on 29 May 2018, China (People's Republic of) extended the application of the *Multilateral Convention on Mutual Administrative Assistance in Tax Matters: Amended by the 2010 Protocol* (OECD/Council of Europe, 2011[4]) ("the Convention") to Hong Kong (China).[4] The Convention entered into force in Hong Kong on 1 September 2018. Pursuant to the Convention, Hong Kong is able to undertake spontaneous exchange of information on tax rulings which relate to taxable periods beginning or charges to tax arising on or after 1 January 2019 under the transparency framework.

Completion and exchange of templates (ToR II.5.3, II.5.4, II.5.5, II.5.6, II.5.7)

In the prior year peer review report, it was determined that Hong Kong's process for the completion and exchange of templates was sufficient to meet the minimum standard. Hong Kong's implementation in this regard remains unchanged and therefore continues to meet the minimum standard.

As Hong Kong did not issue any rulings in scope of the transparency framework in the relevant period, Hong Kong was not required to exchange any information on rulings in the year in review and no data on the timeliness of exchanges can be reported.

Conclusion on section B

Hong Kong has the necessary legal basis for spontaneous exchange of information and a process for completing the templates in a timely way. Hong Kong has met all of the ToR for the exchange of information process and no recommendations are made.

C. Statistics (ToR IV)

As there were no rulings required to be exchanged by Hong Kong for the year in review, no statistics can be reported.

D. Matters related to intellectual property regimes (ToR I.4.1.3)

Hong Kong does not offer an intellectual property regime for which transparency requirements under the Action 5 Report (OECD, 2015[5]) were imposed.

Summary of recommendations on implementation of the transparency framework

Aspect of implementation of the transparency framework that should be improved	Recommendation for improvement
	No recommendations are made.

Notes

[1] https://www.ird.gov.hk/eng/ppr/arc.htm.

[2] With respect to the following preferential regimes: 1) profits tax concession for corporate treasury centres; 2) profits tax concession for professional reinsurers; 3) profits tax concession for captive insurers; 4) profits tax exemptions for ship operators; and 5) profits tax concessions for aircraft lessors and aircraft leasing managers.

[3] Hong Kong has bilateral agreements with Austria, Bailiwick of Guernsey, Belarus, Belgium, Canada, China (People's Republic of), Finland, France, Hungary, India, Indonesia, Ireland, Italy, Japan, Jersey, Korea, Latvia, Malta, Mexico, Netherlands, New Zealand, Pakistan, Portugal, Qatar, Romania, Saudi Arabia, South Africa, Spain, Switzerland, Thailand, United Arab Emirates, United Kingdom and Viet Nam.

[4] Parties to the Convention are available here: www.oecd.org/tax/exchange-of-tax-information/convention-on-mutual-administrative-assistance-in-tax-matters.htm.

Hungary

Hungary has met all aspects of the terms of reference (OECD, 2017[3]) (ToR) for the calendar year 2018 (year in review) except that Hungary did not apply the best efforts approach for past rulings (ToR I.4.2.2) and did not identify or exchange information on new entrants to the IP regime or taxpayers benefitting from the third category of IP assets (ToR I.4.1.3). Hungary receives two recommendations on these points for the year in review.

In the prior year report, Hungary received three recommendations. One recommendation been addressed and is removed. The other two recommendations from the prior year report, as well as from the 2016 peer review, have not been addressed and remain in place.

Hungary can legally issue four types of rulings within the scope of the transparency framework. In practice, Hungary issued rulings within the scope of the transparency framework as follows:

- 77 past rulings;
- For the period 1 April 2016 - 31 December 2016: four future rulings;
- For the calendar year 2017: nine future rulings, and
- For the year in review: 11 future rulings.

Peer input was received from five jurisdictions in respect of the exchanges of information on rulings received from Hungary. The input was generally positive, noting that information was complete, in a correct format and almost all received in a timely manner.

Introduction

This peer review covers Hungary's implementation of the BEPS Action 5 transparency framework for the year 2018. The report has four parts, each relating to a key part of the ToR. Each part is discussed in turn. A summary of recommendations is included at the end of this report.

A. The information gathering process

Hungary can legally issue the following four types of rulings within the scope of the transparency framework: (i) preferential regimes;[1] (ii) cross-border unilateral APAs and any other cross-border unilateral tax rulings (such as an advance tax ruling) covering transfer pricing or the application of transfer pricing principles; (iii) permanent establishment rulings; and (iv) related party conduit rulings.

Past rulings (ToR I.4.1.1, I.4.1.2, I.4.2.1, I.4.2.2)

For Hungary, past rulings are any tax rulings within scope that are issued either: (i) on or after 1 January 2014 but before 1 April 2016; or (ii) on or after 1 January 2010 but before 1 January 2014, provided they were still in effect as at 1 January 2014.

In the prior year peer review report, it was determined that Hungary had not used the best efforts approach to identify potential exchange jurisdictions, meaning that Hungary had only identified potential exchange jurisdictions for around half of the past ATRs, although it had identified most potential exchange jurisdictions for APAs but not necessarily the ultimate parent company jurisdiction. Therefore, Hungary was recommended to continue to apply the "best efforts approach" to identify potential exchange jurisdictions for all past rulings.

Hungary has not been able to take additional steps during the year in review. As such the recommendation is retained.

Future rulings (ToR I.4.1.1, I.4.1.2, I.4.2.1)

For Hungary, future rulings are any tax rulings within scope that are issued on or after 1 April 2016.

In the prior year peer review report, it was determined that Hungary's undertakings to identify future rulings and all potential exchange jurisdictions have met all the ToR, except for requiring the taxpayers to provide information on potential exchange jurisdictions (ToR I.4.2.1). Therefore, Hungary was recommended to ensure that all potential exchange jurisdictions are identified swiftly for all future rulings.

With respect to ATRs, Hungary has amended its legislation and its ruling practice with effect of 1 January 2018, requiring the taxpayer to provide information on immediate and ultimate parent company when applying for a ruling. Information on other potential exchange jurisdictions was already captured by the ruling application itself.

With respect to APAs, the application form was amended in the year in review, to ensure that it also captures information on the ultimate parent company. Other information was already captured by the ruling application itself.

This ensures that all relevant information is obtained with respect to both ATRs and APAs. As such, the recommendation is now removed.

Review and supervision (ToR I.4.3)

In the prior years' peer review reports, it was determined that Hungary's review and supervision mechanism was sufficient to meet the minimum standard. Hungary's implementation in this regard remains unchanged, and therefore continues to meet the minimum standard.

Conclusion on section A

Hungary has met all of the ToR for the information gathering process, except for applying the "best efforts approach" to identify potential exchange jurisdictions for all past rulings.

B. The exchange of information

Legal basis for spontaneous exchange of information (ToR II.5.1, II.5.2)

In the prior year peer review report, Hungary identified that it only had the domestic legal basis to exchange information with EU Member States and was therefore not able to exchange information with all members of the Inclusive Framework, as required by the transparency framework. Hungary has now introduced the legal basis to exchange information on all relevant rulings issued after 1 January 2010 with all members of the Inclusive Framework, from 1 January 2018.

As such, Hungary has the necessary domestic legal basis to exchange information spontaneously. Hungary notes that there are no legal or practical impediments that prevent the spontaneous exchange of information on rulings as contemplated in the Action 5 minimum standard.

Hungary has international agreements permitting spontaneous exchange of information, including being a party to the (i) *Multilateral Convention on Mutual Administrative Assistance in Tax Matters: Amended by the 2010 Protocol* (OECD/Council of Europe, 2011[4]) ("the Convention"), (ii) the Directive 2011/16/EU with all other European Union Member States and (iii) double tax agreements in force with 80 jurisdictions.[2]

Completion and exchange of templates (ToR II.5.3, II.5.4, II.5.5, II.5.6, II.5.7)

In the prior year peer review report, it was determined that Hungary's process for the completion and exchange of temples met all the ToR, except for the timely submission of the information to the Competent Authority (ToR II.5.5) and the timely exchange of information on rulings (ToR II.5.6). Therefore, Hungary was recommended to ensure that all information on future rulings is exchanged as soon as possible. It was also determined that Hungary only exchanged information with EU member states under EU timelines.

During the year in review, Hungary transmitted the delayed exchanges from the prior years by July 2018. Hungary has also taken steps to meet the timelines for forwarding information to the Competent Authority, whereby rulings are provided within three months of issue of the ruling, and the Competent Authority send regular reminders to the relevant officials in the Ministry of Finance or the National Tax and Customs Administration ("NCTA").

For the year in review, the timeliness of exchanges is as follows:

Past rulings in the scope of the transparency framework	Number of exchanges transmitted by 31 December 2018	Delayed exchanges		
		Number of exchanges not transmitted by 31 December 2018	Reasons for the delays	Any other comments
	92	0	N/A	N/A
Future rulings in the scope of the	Number of exchanges transmitted within three	Delayed exchanges		
		Number of exchanges	Reasons for the	Any other

transparency framework	months of the information becoming available to the competent authority or immediately after legal impediments have been lifted	transmitted later than three months of the information on rulings becoming available to the competent authority	delays	comments
	26	0	N/A	N/A
Total	118	0		

Follow up requests received for exchange of the ruling	Number	Average time to provide response	Number of requests not answered
	0	N/A	N/A

Conclusion on section B

Hungary has the necessary legal basis for spontaneous exchange of information, a process for completing the templates in a timely way and has completed all exchanges. As the issues regarding the timely submission of the information to the Competent Authority (ToR II.5.5) and the timely exchange of information on rulings (ToR II.5.6) have been resolved, these recommendations are now removed. Hungary has met all of the ToR for the exchange of information process and no recommendations are made.

C. Statistics (ToR IV)

The statistics for the year in review are as follows:

Category of ruling	Number of exchanges	Jurisdictions exchanged with
Ruling related to a preferential regime	6	France, Luxembourg, Netherlands, Switzerland, United States
Cross-border unilateral advance pricing agreements (APAs) and any other cross-border unilateral tax rulings (such as an advance tax ruling) covering transfer pricing or the application of transfer pricing principles	80	Austria, Belgium, Brazil, Canada, Croatia, Cyprus,[3] France, Germany, Ireland, Japan, Korea, Malta, Mexico, Netherlands, Poland, Romania, Russia, Serbia, Slovak Republic, Slovenia, South Africa, Sweden, Ukraine, United Kingdom, United States
Cross-border rulings providing for a unilateral downward adjustment to the taxpayer's taxable profits that is not directly reflected in the taxpayer's financial / commercial accounts	N/A	N/A
Permanent establishment rulings	32	Canada, France, Ireland, Korea, Luxembourg, Mexico, Netherlands, Norway, Poland, Singapore, Switzerland, Uruguay, United States
Related party conduit rulings	0	N/A
De minimis rule	N/A	N/A
IP regimes: total exchanges on taxpayers benefitting from the third category of IP assets, new entrants benefitting from grandfathered IP regimes; and taxpayers making use of the option to treat the nexus ratio as a rebuttable presumption	0	x
Total	118	

D. Matters related to intellectual property regimes (ToR I.4.1.3)

Hungary offers an intellectual property regime (IP regime)[4] that is subject to the transparency requirements under the Action 5 Report (OECD, 2015[5]) (IP Regime for royalties and capital gains). It states that the identification of the benefitting taxpayers will occur as follows:

- ***New entrants benefitting from the grandfathered IP regime***: Taxpayers that are new entrants to the IP regime can be identified in the tax return. The first tax returns containing information on new entrants have been filed after the relevant date from which enhanced transparency obligations apply. Hungary is currently trying to identify new taxpayers by analysing previous tax returns of taxpayers who have opted into the grandfathered regime. However, new IP assets cannot be identified in the absence of the relevant data in the tax returns and the identification of the new IP assets requires detailed inspection of each taxpayer benefitting from the IP regime. Therefore, Hungary has not exchanged information on new entrants to the grandfathered regime yet. Hungary intends to exchange the information on a retroactive basis as soon as it has identified the new entrants (i.e. both new taxpayers and new IP assets).
- ***Third category of IP assets***: not applicable as the regime does not allow the third category of IP assets to qualify for the benefits.
- ***Taxpayers making use of the option to treat the nexus ratio as a rebuttable presumption***: not applicable the regime does not allow the nexus ratio to be treated as a rebuttable presumption.

Hungary is recommended to continue its efforts to identify and exchange information on all new entrants to the IP regime as soon as possible (ToR I.4.1.3)

Summary of recommendations on implementation of the transparency framework

Aspect of implementation of the transparency framework that should be improved	Recommendation for improvement
Hungary did not yet apply the "best efforts approach" to indemnify potential exchange jurisdictions for all past rulings.	Hungary is recommended to continue to apply the "best efforts approach" to identify potential exchange jurisdictions for all past rulings. This recommendation remains unchanged since the 2016 peer review report and the 2017 peer review report.
Hungary did not identify or exchange information on new entrants to the grandfathered IP regime.	Hungary is recommended to continue its efforts to identify and exchange information on all new entrants to the grandfathered IP regime. This recommendation remains unchanged since the 2016 peer review report and the 2017 peer review report.

Notes

[1] With respect to the following preferential regime: IP regime for royalties and capital gains.

[2] Parties to the Convention are available here: www.oecd.org/tax/exchange-of-tax-information/convention-on-mutual-administrative-assistance-in-tax-matters.htm. Hungary also has double tax agreements with Albania, Armenia, Australia, Austria, Azerbaijan, Bahrain, Belarus, Belgium, Bosnia and Herzegovina, Brazil, Bulgaria, Canada, China (People's Republic of), Chinese Taipei, Croatia, Cyprus, Czech Republic, Denmark, Egypt, Estonia, Finland, France, Georgia, Germany, Greece, Hong Kong (China), Iceland, India, Indonesia, Iran, Ireland, Israel, Italy, Japan, Kazakhstan, Korea, Kosovo, Kuwait, Latvia, Liechtenstein, Lithuania, Luxembourg, Malaysia, Malta, Mexico, Moldova, Mongolia, Montenegro, Morocco, Netherlands, North Macedonia, Norway, Oman, Pakistan, Philippines, Poland, Portugal, Qatar, Romania, Russia, San Marino, Saudi Arabia, Serbia, Singapore, Slovak Republic, Slovenia, South Africa, Spain, Sweden,

Switzerland, Thailand, Tunisia, Turkey, Turkmenistan, Ukraine, United Arab Emirates, United Kingdom, United States, Uruguay, Uzbekistan and Viet Nam.

Note by Turkey: The information in this document with reference to “Cyprus” relates to the southern part of the Island. There is no single authority representing both Turkish and Greek Cypriot people on the Island. Turkey recognises the Turkish Republic of Northern Cyprus (TRNC). Until a lasting and equitable solution is found within the context of the United Nations, Turkey shall preserve its position concerning the “Cyprus issue”.

Note by all the European Union Member States of the OECD and the European Union. The Republic of Cyprus is recognised by all members of the United Nations with the exception of Turkey. The information in this document relates to the area under the effective control of the Government of the Republic of Cyprus.

[3] Note by Turkey: The information in this document with reference to “Cyprus” relates to the southern part of the Island. There is no single authority representing both Turkish and Greek Cypriot people on the Island. Turkey recognises the Turkish Republic of Northern Cyprus (TRNC). Until a lasting and equitable solution is found within the context of the United Nations, Turkey shall preserve its position concerning the “Cyprus issue”.

Note by all the European Union Member States of the OECD and the European Union. The Republic of Cyprus is recognised by all members of the United Nations with the exception of Turkey. The information in this document relates to the area under the effective control of the Government of the Republic of Cyprus.

[4] IP Regime for royalties and capital gains.

Iceland

Iceland has met all aspects of the terms of reference (OECD, 2017[3]) (ToR) for the calendar year 2018 (year in review) and no recommendations are made.

In the prior year report, Iceland did not receive any recommendations.

Iceland can legally issue two types of rulings within the scope of the transparency framework. In practice, Iceland issued rulings within the scope of the transparency framework as follows:

- One past ruling;
- For the period 1 April 2016 - 31 December 201: no future rulings;
- For the calendar year 2017: no future rulings, and
- For the year in review: no future rulings.

Rulings are published on the tax administration website in anonymised form.

As no exchanges took place, no peer input was received in respect of the exchanges of information on rulings received from Iceland.

Introduction

This peer review covers Iceland's implementation of the BEPS Action 5 transparency framework for the year 2018. The report has four parts, each relating to a key part of the ToR. Each part is discussed in turn. A summary of recommendations is included at the end of this report.

A. The information gathering process

Iceland can legally issue the following two types of rulings within the scope of the transparency framework: (i) permanent establishment rulings and (ii) related party conduit rulings.

Past rulings (ToR I.4.1.1, I.4.1.2, I.4.2.1, I.4.2.2)

For Iceland, past rulings are any tax rulings within scope that are issued either: (i) on or after 1 January 2014 but before 1 April 2016; or (ii) on or after 1 January 2010 but before 1 January 2014, provided they were still in effect as at 1 January 2014.

In the prior years' peer review reports, it was determined that Iceland's undertakings to identify past rulings and all potential exchange jurisdictions were sufficient to meet the minimum standard. Iceland's implementation in this regard remains unchanged, and therefore continues to meet the minimum standard.

Future rulings (ToR I.4.1.1, I.4.1.2, I.4.2.1)

For Iceland, future rulings are any tax rulings within scope that are issued on or after 1 April 2016.

In the prior years' peer review reports, it was determined that Iceland's undertakings to identify future rulings and all potential exchange jurisdictions were sufficient to meet the minimum standard. In the prior year, the individual department Directors were responsible for the identification of rulings in scope. In the year of review, Iceland assigned the competent authority to undertake the role of identifying and exchanging information on rulings in order to centralise and streamline the process. The competent authority will apply the same information gathering process as previously in place and will identify all relevant rulings and potential exchange jurisdictions at the point of issue of the ruling. The implementation of the new system to identify future rulings and all potential exchange jurisdictions is sufficient to meet the minimum standard.

Review and supervision (ToR I.4.3)

In the prior years' peer review reports, it was determined that Iceland's review and supervision mechanism was sufficient to meet the minimum standard. Iceland's implementation in this regard remains unchanged, whereby the Tax Commissioner and Deputy Tax Commissioner are responsible for supervision, and therefore continues to meet the minimum standard.

Conclusion on section A

Iceland has met all of the ToR for the information gathering process and no recommendations are made.

B. The exchange of information

Legal basis for spontaneous exchange of information (ToR II.5.1, II.5.2)

Iceland has the necessary domestic legal basis to exchange information spontaneously. Iceland notes that there are no legal or practical impediments that prevent the spontaneous exchange of information on rulings as contemplated in the Action 5 minimum standard.

Iceland has international agreements permitting spontaneous exchange of information, including being a party to the (i) *Multilateral Convention on Mutual Administrative Assistance in Tax Matters: Amended by the 2010 Protocol* (OECD/Council of Europe, 2011[4]) ("the Convention"), (ii) the Nordic Convention with Denmark, Faroe Islands, Finland, Greenland, Norway and Sweden and (iii) double tax agreements in force with 40 jurisdictions.[1]

Completion and exchange of templates (ToR II.5.3, II.5.4, II.5.5, II.5.6, II.5.7)

In the prior year peer review report, it was determined that Iceland's process for the completion and exchange of templates were sufficient to meet the minimum standard. Iceland's implementation in this regard remains unchanged and therefore continues to meet the minimum standard.

As no future rulings have been issued during the year in review, Iceland was not required to complete any exchanges of information and there is no data to report on timeliness of exchanges.

Conclusion on section B

Iceland has the necessary legal basis for spontaneous exchange of information, a process for completing the templates in a timely way. Iceland has met all of the ToR for the exchange of information process and no recommendations are made.

C. Statistics (ToR IV)

As no exchanges were required to occur in the year of review, no statistics can be reported.

D. Matters related to intellectual property regimes (ToR I.4.1.3)

Iceland does not offer an intellectual property regime for which transparency requirements under the Action 5 Report (OECD, 2015[5]) were imposed.

Summary of recommendations on implementation of the transparency framework

Aspect of implementation of the transparency framework that should be improved	Recommendation for improvement
	No recommendations are made.

Notes

[1] Parties to the Convention are available here: www.oecd.org/tax/exchange-of-tax-information/convention-on-mutual-administrative-assistance-in-tax-matters.htm. Iceland also has bilateral agreements in force with Albania, Austria, Barbados, Belgium, Canada, China (People's Republic of), Croatia, Cyprus, Czech Republic, Estonia, France, Georgia, Greece, Greenland, Germany, Hungary, India, Ireland, Italy, Japan, Korea, Latvia, Liechtenstein, Lithuania, Luxembourg, Malta, Mexico, Netherlands, Poland, Portugal, Romania, Russia, Slovak Republic, Slovenia, Spain, Switzerland, Ukraine, United Kingdom, United States, Viet Nam.

Note by Turkey: The information in this document with reference to "Cyprus" relates to the southern part of the Island. There is no single authority representing both Turkish and Greek Cypriot people on the Island. Turkey recognises the Turkish Republic of Northern Cyprus (TRNC). Until a lasting and equitable solution is found within the context of the United Nations, Turkey shall preserve its position concerning the "Cyprus issue".

Note by all the European Union Member States of the OECD and the European Union. The Republic of Cyprus is recognised by all members of the United Nations with the exception of Turkey. The information in this document relates to the area under the effective control of the Government of the Republic of Cyprus.

India

India has met all aspects of the terms of reference (ToR) for the calendar year 2018 (year in review) except for the timely exchange of information on future APAs (ToR II.5.6). India receives one recommendation on this issue for the year in review.

In the prior year report, India received three recommendations. Two recommendations have been addressed and are removed. The other recommendation has not been addressed and remains in place.

India can legally issue two types of rulings within the scope of the transparency framework. In practice, India issued rulings within the scope of the transparency framework as follows:

- 69 past rulings;
- For the period 1 April 2016 - 31 December 2016: 55 future rulings;
- For the calendar year 2017: 73 future rulings, and
- For the year in review: 44 future rulings.

PE rulings are published unless it is stated to be confidential by the Authority issuing the ruling, whereas unilateral APAs are not.[1]

Peer input was received from seven jurisdictions in respect of the exchanges of information on rulings received from India. The input was generally positive, noting that information was complete, in a correct format and almost all received in a timely manner.

Introduction

This peer review covers India's implementation of the BEPS Action 5 transparency framework for the year 2018. The report has four parts, each relating to a key part of the ToR. Each part is discussed in turn. A summary of recommendations is included at the end of this report.

A. The information gathering process

India can legally issue the following two types of rulings within the scope of the transparency framework: (i) cross-border unilateral APAs and (ii) permanent establishment rulings.

Past rulings (ToR I.4.1.1, I.4.1.2, I.4.2.1, I.4.2.2)

For India, past rulings are any tax rulings within scope that are issued either: (i) on or after 1 January 2014 but before 1 April 2016; or (ii) on or after 1 January 2010 but before 1 January 2014, provided they were still in effect as at 1 January 2014.

In the prior years' peer review reports, it was determined that India's undertakings to identify past rulings have met the ToR, except that India was recommended to apply the "best efforts approach" to identify the immediate parent and ultimate parent companies for all relevant past PE rulings and past APAs. India obtained additional information by reviewing tax filings and in cases where information could be obtained, further exchanges have been made.

During the year in review, it is determined that India's best effort approach is sufficient to identify past rulings and all potential exchange jurisdictions and meets the minimum standard and the recommendation is now removed.

Future rulings (ToR I.4.1.1, I.4.1.2, I.4.2.1)

For India, future rulings are any tax rulings within scope that are issued on or after 1 April 2016.

In the prior years' peer review reports, India was recommended to ensure that all potential exchange jurisdictions are identified swiftly for all future rulings (ToR I 4.2.1). India has amended its application forms for rulings, which now include details of the immediate parent and ultimate parent company in the application with effect from 16 June 2017 for APAs and from 13 July 2018 for PE rulings. Where future rulings have been issued prior to the amendment to the application forms, additional guidance has been issued to all officers who are responsible for completing these templates, including identification of potential exchange jurisdictions using the "best efforts approach."

As such, India's procedures to identify future rulings and all potential exchange jurisdictions are sufficient to meet the minimum standard and therefore the recommendation is removed.

Review and supervision (ToR I.4.3)

In the prior years' peer review reports, it was determined that India's review and supervision mechanism was sufficient to meet the minimum standard. India's implementation in this regard remains unchanged, and therefore continues to meet the minimum standard.

Conclusion on section A

India has met all of the ToR for the information gathering process and no recommendations are made.

B. The exchange of information

Legal basis for spontaneous exchange of information (ToR II.5.1, II.5.2)

India has the necessary domestic legal basis to exchange information spontaneously. India notes that there are no legal or practical impediments that prevent the spontaneous exchange of information on rulings as contemplated in the Action 5 minimum standard.

India has international agreements permitting spontaneous exchange of information, including being a party to the (i) *Multilateral Convention on Mutual Administrative Assistance in Tax Matters: Amended by the 2010 Protocol* (OECD/Council of Europe, 2011[4]) ("the Convention"), (ii) double tax agreements and (iii) the South Asian Association for Regional Cooperation (SAARC) Agreement.[2]

Completion and exchange of templates (ToR II.5.3, II.5.4, II.5.5, II.5.6, II.5.7)

In the prior year peer review report, it was determined that India's process for the completion and exchange of templates met all the ToR, except for ensuring that information on rulings is transmitted to the competent authority without undue delay and that information is transmitted to the relevant jurisdictions in accordance with the applicable timelines (ToR II 5.5 and ToR II. 5.6). India was recommended to ensure that all information on past and future APAs is exchanged as soon as possible.

To some extent, the delay was caused by the delay in identifying potential exchange jurisdictions, which is noted above in Part A. Furthermore, there were delays in the centralised office in the Competent Authority due to the volume of past and future rulings. As mentioned in the prior year's report, India exchanged information pertaining to the remaining 51 past rulings by June 2018 and experienced continuing delays in the exchange of all future APAs. This was mostly due to the timely completion of the exchange templates. India has issued additional guidance to the responsible officers on the completion of exchange templates to ensure that the timelines are met for the exchange of information on future rulings. India expects no further delays in the exchange of future rulings.

For the year in review, the timeliness of exchanges is as follows:

Past rulings in the scope of the transparency framework	Number of exchanges transmitted by 31 December 2018	Delayed exchanges		
		Number of exchanges not transmitted by 31 December 2018	Reasons for the delays	Any other comments
	135	0	N/A	These exchanges relate to past rulings where the ultimate and immediate parent company has been identified during the year of review enhancing India's best effort approach.
Future rulings in the scope of the transparency framework	Number of exchanges transmitted within three months of the information becoming available to the competent authority or immediately after legal impediments have been lifted	Delayed exchanges		
		Number of exchanges transmitted later than three months of the information on rulings becoming available to the competent authority	Reasons for the delays	Any other comments
	132	208	N/A	The delays relate to future rulings

				that have been issued before the application process was amended and time taken for the identification of ultimate and immediate parent companies using the best effort approach.
Total	267	208		

Follow up requests received for exchange of the ruling	Number	Average time to provide response	Number of requests not answered
	8	90 days	0

With respect to follow up requests, India took on average 90 days to respond or to provide a status update. For one follow up request, India sought clarification from the FHTP Secretariat pertaining to foreseeable relevance, leading to a slightly longer time to provide a response to the requesting treaty partner.

Conclusion on section B

India has the necessary legal basis for spontaneous exchange of information, a process for completing the templates in a timely way and has completed all exchanges. As India continued to experience delays it is determined that India has met all of the ToR for the exchange of information process except for ensuring that information on future APA rulings is exchanged as soon as possible (ToR II.5.6). India is recommended to ensure the timely exchange of information on future APA rulings.

C. Statistics (ToR IV)

The statistics for the year in review are as follows:

Category of ruling	Number of exchanges	Jurisdictions exchanged with
Ruling related to a preferential regime	N/A	N/A
Cross-border unilateral advance pricing agreements (APAs) and any other cross-border unilateral tax rulings (such as an advance tax ruling) covering transfer pricing or the application of transfer pricing principles	454	Argentina, Australia, Austria, Bangladesh, Barbados, Belgium, Botswana, Brazil, Bulgaria, Cameroon, Canada, Chile, Colombia, Costa Rica, Croatia, Czech Republic, Denmark, Dominican Republic, Egypt, Estonia, Finland, France, Germany, Ghana, Greece, Guatemala, Hong Kong (China), Hungary, Iceland, Indonesia, Ireland, Israel, Italy, Japan, Jordan, Kenya, Korea, Lebanon, Lithuania, Luxembourg, Malaysia, Malta, Mauritius, Mexico, Morocco, Mozambique, Netherlands, New Zealand, Nigeria, North Macedonia, Norway, Oman, Philippines, Poland, Portugal, Qatar, Russia, Saudi Arabia, Senegal, Singapore, Slovak Republic, Slovenia, South Africa, Spain, Sri Lanka, Sweden, Switzerland, Taiwan, Tanzania, Thailand, Tunisia, Turkey, Uganda, United Kingdom, United States, Uruguay, Viet Nam, Zambia

Cross-border rulings providing for a unilateral downward adjustment to the taxpayer's taxable profits that is not directly reflected in the taxpayer's financial / commercial accounts	N/A	N/A
Permanent establishment rulings	21	Belgium, France, Germany, Saudi Arabia, Switzerland, United Kingdom, United States
Related party conduit rulings	N/A	N/A
De minimis rule	N/A	N/A
IP regimes: total exchanges on taxpayers benefitting from the third category of IP assets, new entrants benefitting from grandfathered IP regimes; and taxpayers making use of the option to treat the nexus ratio as a rebuttable presumption	N/A	N/A
Total	475	

D. Matters related to intellectual property regimes (ToR I.4.1.3)

India offers an intellectual property regime (IP regime)[3] that is not subject to the transparency requirements under the Action 5 Report (OECD, 2015[5]), because:

- ***New entrants benefitting from the grandfathered IP regime***: the regime is a new nexus-compliant regime and therefore there is no grandfathered IP regime for which enhanced transparency requirements will apply.
- ***Third category of IP assets***: not applicable as the regime does not allow the third category of IP assets to qualify for the benefits.
- ***Taxpayers making the use of the option to treat the nexus ratio as a rebuttable presumption***: not applicable the regime does not allow the nexus ratio to be treated as a rebuttable presumption.

Summary of recommendations on implementation of the transparency framework

Aspect of implementation of the transparency framework that should be improved	Recommendation for improvement
India experienced delays in the exchange of information on future APAs.	India is recommended to continue its efforts to ensure that all information on future APAs is exchanged as soon as possible. This recommendation remains unchanged since the prior year peer review report.

Notes

[1] Available at: www.aarrulings.in.

[2] Parties to the Convention are available here: www.oecd.org/tax/exchange-of-tax-information/convention-on-mutual-administrative-assistance-in-tax-matters.htm. India also has bilateral agreements with Albania, Armenia, Australia, Austria, Azerbaijan, Bangladesh, Belarus, Belgium, Bhutan, Botswana, Brazil, Bulgaria, Canada, China (People's Republic of), Colombia, Croatia, Cyprus, Czech Republic, Denmark, Egypt, Estonia, Ethiopia, Faroe Islands, Fiji, Finland, France, Georgia, Germany, Greece, Hungary, Iceland, Indonesia, Ireland, Israel, Italy, Japan, Jordan, Kazakhstan, Kenya, Korea, Kuwait, Kyrgyzstan, Latvia, Libya, Lithuania, Luxembourg, Malaysia, Malta, Mauritius, Mexico, Moldova, Mongolia, Morocco, Montenegro, Mozambique, Myanmar, Namibia, Nepal, Netherlands, New Zealand, North Macedonia, Norway, Oman, Philippines, Poland, Portugal, Qatar, Romania, Russia, Saudi Arabia, Serbia, , Singapore, Slovak Republic, Slovenia, South Africa, Spain, Sri Lanka, Sudan, Sweden, Switzerland, Syria, Chinese Taipei, Tajikistan, Tanzania, Thailand, Trinidad and Tobago, Turkey, Turkmenistan, Uganda, Ukraine, United Arab Emirates, United Kingdom, United States, Uruguay, Uzbekistan, and Zambia. The SAARC was entered into force on 19 May 2010 and provides for exchanges with Bangladesh, Bhutan, Maldives, Nepal, Pakistan and Sri Lanka.

Note by Turkey: The information in this document with reference to "Cyprus" relates to the southern part of the Island. There is no single authority representing both Turkish and Greek Cypriot people on the Island. Turkey recognises the Turkish Republic of Northern Cyprus (TRNC). Until a lasting and equitable solution is found within the context of the United Nations, Turkey shall preserve its position concerning the "Cyprus issue".

Note by all the European Union Member States of the OECD and the European Union. The Republic of Cyprus is recognised by all members of the United Nations with the exception of Turkey. The information in this document relates to the area under the effective control of the Government of the Republic of Cyprus.

[3] Tax on income from patent.

Indonesia

Indonesia has met all aspects of the terms of reference (OECD, 2017[3]) (ToR) for the calendar year 2018 (year in review) that can be met in the absence of rulings being issued and no recommendations are made.

In the prior year report, Indonesia did not receive any recommendations.

Indonesia can legally issue one type of rulings within the scope of the transparency framework. In practice, Indonesia issued no rulings within the scope of the transparency framework. 16 requests for unilateral APAs, including 15 requests mentioned in the prior year report, have been received from taxpayers until 31 December 2018. Five of the requests are still under consideration by Directorate General of Taxes, and 11 requests have been withdrawn by the taxpayers.

As no exchanges were required to take place, no peer input was received in respect of the exchanges of information on rulings received from Indonesia.

Introduction

This peer review covers Indonesia's implementation of the BEPS Action 5 transparency framework for the year 2018. The report has four parts, each relating to a key part of the ToR. Each part is discussed in turn. A summary of recommendations is included at the end of this report.

A. The information gathering process

Indonesia can legally issue the following type of ruling within the scope of the transparency framework: cross-border unilateral APAs and any other cross-border unilateral tax rulings (such as an advance tax ruling) covering transfer pricing or the application of transfer pricing principles.

Past rulings (ToR I.4.1.1, I.4.1.2, I.4.2.1, I.4.2.2)

For Indonesia, past rulings are any tax rulings within scope that are issued either: (i) on or after 1 January 2014 but before 1 April 2016; or (ii) on or after 1 January 2010 but before 1 January 2014, provided they were still in effect as at 1 January 2014.

In the prior years' peer review reports, it was determined that Indonesia's undertakings to identify past rulings and all potential exchange jurisdictions were sufficient to meet the minimum standard in the absence of rulings being issued in practice. Indonesia's implementation in this regard remains unchanged, and therefore continues to meet the minimum standard.

Future rulings (ToR I.4.1.1, I.4.1.2, I.4.2.1)

For Indonesia, future rulings are any tax rulings within scope that are issued on or after 1 April 2016.

In the prior years' peer review reports, it was determined that Indonesia's undertakings to identify future rulings and all potential exchange jurisdictions were sufficient to meet the minimum standard in the absence of rulings being issued in practice. Indonesia's implementation in this regard remains unchanged, and therefore continues to meet the minimum standard.

Review and supervision (ToR I.4.3)

In the prior years' peer review reports, it was determined that Indonesia's review and supervision mechanism was sufficient to meet the minimum standard in the absence of rulings being issued in practice. Indonesia's implementation in this regard remains unchanged, and therefore continues to meet the minimum standard.

Conclusion on section A

Indonesia has met all of the ToR for the information gathering process and no recommendations are made.

B. The exchange of information

Legal basis for spontaneous exchange of information (ToR II.5.1, II.5.2)

Indonesia has the necessary domestic legal basis to exchange information spontaneously. Indonesia notes that there are no legal or practical impediments that prevent the spontaneous exchange of information on rulings as contemplated in the Action 5 minimum standard.

Indonesia has international agreements permitting spontaneous exchange of information, including being a party to the (i) *Multilateral Convention on Mutual Administrative Assistance in Tax Matters: Amended by the 2010 Protocol* (OECD/Council of Europe, 2011[4]) ("the Convention"), and (ii) double tax agreements in force with 67 jurisdictions.[1]

Completion and exchange of templates (ToR II.5.3, II.5.4, II.5.5, II.5.6, II.5.7)

In the prior year peer review report, it was determined that Indonesia's process for the completion and exchange of templates were sufficient to meet the minimum standard in the absence of any rulings being issue. Indonesia's implementation in this regard remains unchanged and therefore continues to meet the minimum standard.

As no future rulings have been issued during the year in review, Indonesia was not required to complete any exchanges of information and there is no data to report on timeliness of exchanges.

Conclusion on section B

Indonesia has the necessary legal basis for spontaneous exchange of information, a process for completing the templates in a timely way and has completed all exchanges. Indonesia has met all of the ToR for the exchange of information process that can be met in the absence of rulings being issued in practice and no recommendations are made.

C. Statistics (ToR IV)

As there was no information on rulings exchanged by Indonesia for the year in review, no statistics can be reported.

D. Matters related to intellectual property regimes (ToR I.4.1.3)

Indonesia does not offer an intellectual property regime for which transparency requirements under the Action 5 Report (OECD, 2015[5]) were imposed.

Summary of recommendations on implementation of the transparency framework

Aspect of implementation of the transparency framework that should be improved	Recommendation for improvement
	No recommendations are made.

Notes

[1] Parties to the Convention are available here: www.oecd.org/tax/exchange-of-tax-information/convention-on-mutual-administrative-assistance-in-tax-matters.htm. Indonesia also has bilateral agreements with Algeria, Armenia, Australia, Austria, Bangladesh, Belgium, Brunei Darussalam, Bulgaria, Canada, China (People's Republic of), Croatia, Czech Republic, Democratic People's Republic of Korea, Denmark, Egypt, Finland, France, Germany, Hong Kong (China), Hungary, India, Iran, Italy, Japan, Jordan, Korea, Kuwait, Lao People's Democratic Republic, Luxembourg, Malaysia, Mexico, Mongolia, Morocco, Netherlands, New Zealand, Norway, Pakistan, Papua New Guinea, Philippines, Poland, Portugal, Qatar, Romania, Russia, Seychelles, Singapore, Slovak Republic, South Africa, Spain, Sri Lanka, Sudan, Suriname, Sweden, Syria, Chinese Taipei, Thailand, Tunisia, Turkey, Ukraine, United Arab Emirates, United Kingdom, United States, Uzbekistan, Venezuela, Viet Nam.

Ireland

Ireland has met all aspects of the terms of reference (OECD, 2017[3]) (ToR) for the calendar year 2018 (year in review) and no recommendations are made.

In the prior year report, Ireland did not receive any recommendations.

Ireland can legally issue three types of rulings within the scope of the transparency framework. In practice, Ireland issued rulings within the scope of the transparency framework as follows:

- 29 past rulings;[1]
- For the period 1 April 2016 - 31 December 2016: no future rulings;
- For the calendar year 2017: two future rulings, and
- For the year in review: 39 future rulings.

These rulings are not published; however, the Irish tax administration publishes a briefing or guidance note on noticeable issues raised by specific cases.

Peer input was received from two jurisdictions in respect of the exchanges of information on rulings received from Ireland. The input was generally positive, noting that information was complete, in a correct format and received in a timely manner.

Introduction

This peer review covers Ireland's implementation of the BEPS Action 5 transparency framework for the year 2018. The report has four parts, each relating to a key part of the ToR. Each part is discussed in turn. A summary of recommendations is included at the end of this report.

A. The information gathering process

Ireland can legally issue the three following types of rulings within the scope of the transparency framework: (i) preferential regimes;[2] (ii) cross-border unilateral advance pricing agreements (APAs) and any other cross-border unilateral tax rulings (such as an advance tax ruling) covering transfer pricing or the application of transfer pricing principles; and (iii) permanent establishment rulings.

Past rulings (ToR I.4.1.1, I.4.1.2, I.4.2.1, I.4.2.2)

For Ireland, past rulings are any tax rulings within scope that are issued either: (i) on or after 1 January 2014 but before 1 April 2016; or (ii) on or after 1 January 2010 but before 1 January 2014, provided they were still in effect as at 1 January 2014.

In the prior years' peer review reports, it was determined that Ireland's undertakings to identify past rulings and all potential exchange jurisdictions were sufficient to meet the minimum standard. Ireland's implementation in this regard remains unchanged, and therefore continues to meet the minimum standard.

Future rulings (ToR I.4.1.1, I.4.1.2, I.4.2.1)

For Ireland, future rulings are any tax rulings within scope that are issued on or after 1 April 2016.

In the prior years' peer review reports, it was determined that Ireland's undertakings to identify future rulings and all potential exchange jurisdictions was sufficient to meet the minimum standard. Ireland's implementation in this regard remains unchanged, and therefore continues to meet the minimum standard.

Review and supervision (ToR I.4.3)

In the prior years' peer review report, it was determined that Ireland's review and supervision mechanism was sufficient to meet the minimum standard. Ireland's implementation in this regard remains unchanged, and therefore continues to meet the minimum standard.

Conclusion on section A

Ireland has met all of the ToR for the information gathering process and no recommendations are made.

B. The exchange of information

Legal basis for spontaneous exchange of information (ToR II.5.1, II.5.2)

Ireland has the necessary domestic legal basis to exchange information spontaneously. Ireland notes that there are no legal or practical impediments that prevent the spontaneous exchange of information on rulings as contemplated in the Action 5 minimum standard.

Ireland has international agreements permitting spontaneous exchange of information, including being a party to the (i) *Multilateral Convention on Mutual Administrative Assistance in Tax Matters: Amended by the 2010 Protocol* (OECD/Council of Europe, 2011[4]) ("the Convention"), (ii) the Directive 2011/16/EU with all other European Union Member States and (iii) double tax agreements in force with 73 jurisdictions, 69 of which allow for spontaneous exchange of information.[3]

Completion and exchange of templates (ToR II.5.3, II.5.4, II.5.5, II.5.6, II.5.7)

In the prior year peer review report, it was determined that Ireland's process for the completion and exchange of templates were sufficient to meet the minimum standard. Ireland's implementation in this regard remains unchanged and therefore continues to meet the minimum standard.

In addition, it is noted that Ireland took steps to formalise and strengthen its process. This included additional efforts to ensure the quality of the summary of the ruling by providing staff with a template for certain rulings, ensuring additional quality reviews, and formalising processes in an updated internal manual.

For the year in review, the timeliness of exchanges is as follows:

Past rulings in the scope of the transparency framework	Number of exchanges transmitted by 31 December 2018	Delayed exchanges		
		Number of exchanges not transmitted by 31 December 2018	Reasons for the delays	Any other comments
	1	0	This delay occurred due to the late identification of this opinion by the caseworker.	See below
Future rulings in the scope of the transparency framework	Number of exchanges transmitted within three months of the information becoming available to the competent authority or immediately after legal impediments have been lifted	Delayed exchanges		
		Number of exchanges transmitted later than three months of the information on rulings becoming available to the competent authority	Reasons for the delays	Any other comments
	33	6	The delays occurred due to issues around the quality of the summary information provided to the Competent Authority.	See below.
Total	34	6		

Follow up requests received for exchange of the ruling	Number	Average time to provide response	Number of requests not answered
	0	N/A	0

Some delays were encountered during the year in review, in all cases which only affected the permanent establishment category of rulings and related to opinions issued in respect of construction projects in Ireland. To prevent the recurrence of the delays encountered in 2018, Ireland has since undertaken the following measures: (i) engaged with the caseworkers in the relevant Division dealing with construction companies, to highlight Ireland's obligations with respect to the exchange framework and the timelines involved; (ii) provided a template for completion in respect of the type of rulings issued, which related to construction project PE's to ensure the summaries provided were of a high standard and contained all of the relevant information and; (iii) engaged with senior management within the Division to ensure the issue was addressed. As Ireland took steps to identify and remedy the issue within the year in review, all exchanges were completed in the year in review, and this is not expected to be a recurring issue, no recommendations are made.

Conclusion on section B

Ireland has the necessary legal basis for spontaneous exchange of information, a process for completing the templates in a timely way and has completed all exchanges. Ireland has met all of the ToR for the exchange of information process and no recommendations are made.

C. Statistics (ToR IV)

The statistics for the year in review are as follows:

Category of ruling	Number of exchanges	Jurisdictions exchanged with
Ruling related to a preferential regime	1	*De minimis* rule applies
Cross-border unilateral advance pricing agreements (APAs) and any other cross-border unilateral tax rulings (such as an advance tax ruling) covering transfer pricing or the application of transfer pricing principles	0	N/A
Cross-border rulings providing for a unilateral downward adjustment to the taxpayer's taxable profits that is not directly reflected in the taxpayer's financial / commercial accounts	N/A	N/A
Permanent establishment rulings	39	Austria, Denmark, Germany, Norway, Poland, Romania, Spain, Switzerland, United Kingdom
Related party conduit rulings	N/A	N/A
De minimis rule	N/A	N/A
IP regimes: total exchanges on taxpayers benefitting from the third category of IP assets, new entrants benefitting from grandfathered IP regimes; and taxpayers making use of the option to treat the nexus ratio as a rebuttable presumption	0	N/A
Total	40	

D. Matters related to intellectual property regimes (ToR I.4.1.3)

Ireland offers an intellectual property regime (IP regime)[4] that is subject to the transparency requirements under the Action 5 Report (OECD, 2015[5]). It states that the identification of the benefitting taxpayers will occur as follows:

- ***New entrants benefitting from the grandfathered IP regime***: as this is a new IP regime rather than a grandfathered IP regime, transparency on new entrants is not relevant.
- ***Third category of IP assets***: The relevant portion of the annual corporation tax return has been designed to capture the data that Ireland will require for its reporting and exchange of information obligations under the framework. The first returns were filed in mid-to-late 2018 and to date, the required information was submitted to the FHTP and will be exchanged with other jurisdictions as

required, and in all cases within 12 months of receipt of the return as required by the transparency framework.

- ***Taxpayers making use of the option to treat the nexus ratio as a rebuttable presumption***: not applicable as the regime does not allow the nexus ratio to be treated as a rebuttable presumption.

Summary of recommendations on implementation of the transparency framework

Aspect of implementation of the transparency framework that should be improved	Recommendation for improvement
Ireland experienced some delays in exchanging information on future rulings.	No recommendation is made because Ireland has quickly remedied the issue, completed exchanges on the delayed future rulings in the year in review and is not a recurring issue.

Notes

[1] Including five that fell into more than one category under the BEPS Action 5 report.

[2] With respect to the following preferential regimes: 1) Shipping regime and 2) Knowledge development box.

[3] Parties to the Convention are available here: www.oecd.org/tax/exchange-of-tax-information/convention-on-mutual-administrative-assistance-in-tax-matters.htm. Ireland also has double tax agreements that allow for spontaneous exchange of information with Albania, Armenia, Australia, Bahrain, Belarus, Belgium, Bosnia and Herzegovina, Botswana, Bulgaria, Canada, Chile, China (People's Republic of), Croatia, Cyprus, Czech Republic, Denmark, Egypt, Estonia, Ethiopia, Finland, France, Georgia, Germany, Greece, Hungary, Iceland, India, Israel, Italy, Japan, Kazakhstan, Korea, Kuwait, Latvia, Lithuania, Luxembourg, Malaysia, Malta, Mexico, Moldova, Montenegro, Morocco, Netherlands, New Zealand, North Macedonia, Norway, Pakistan, Poland, Portugal, Qatar, Romania, Russia, Saudi Arabia, Servia, Singapore, Slovak Republic, Slovenia, South Africa, Spain, Sweden, Thailand, Turkey, United Arab Emirates, Ukraine, United Kingdom, United States, Uzbekistan, Viet Nam, and Zambia.

Note by Turkey: The information in this document with reference to "Cyprus" relates to the southern part of the Island. There is no single authority representing both Turkish and Greek Cypriot people on the Island. Turkey recognises the Turkish Republic of Northern Cyprus (TRNC). Until a lasting and equitable solution is found within the context of the United Nations, Turkey shall preserve its position concerning the "Cyprus issue".

Note by all the European Union Member States of the OECD and the European Union. The Republic of Cyprus is recognised by all members of the United Nations with the exception of Turkey. The information in this document relates to the area under the effective control of the Government of the Republic of Cyprus.

[4] Knowledge Development Box.

Isle of Man

The Isle of Man has met all aspects of the terms of reference (ToR) for the calendar year 2017 (year in review) and no recommendations are made.

In the prior year report, the Isle of Man did not receive any recommendations.

The Isle of Man can legally issue two types of rulings within the scope of the transparency framework. In practice, the Isle of Man has issued rulings within the scope of the transparency framework as follows:

- Two past rulings;
- For the calendar year 2017: no future rulings, and
- For the year in review: no future rulings.

As no exchanges were required to take place, no peer input was received in respect of the exchanges of information on rulings received from the Isle of Man.

Introduction

This peer review covers the Isle of Man's implementation of the BEPS Action 5 transparency framework for the year 2018. The report has four parts, each relating to a key part of the ToR. Each part is discussed in turn. A summary of recommendations is included at the end of this report.

A. The information gathering process

The Isle of Man can legally issue the following two types of rulings within the scope of the transparency framework: (i) cross-border giving a unilateral downward adjustment to the taxpayer's taxable profits in the country giving the ruling; and (ii) permanent establishment rulings.

Past rulings (ToR I.4.1.1, I.4.1.2, I.4.2.1, I.4.2.2)

For the Isle of Man, past rulings are any tax rulings within scope that are issued either: (i) on or after 1 January 2015 but before 1 April 2017; or (ii) on or after 1 January 2012 but before 1 January 2015, provided they were still in effect as at 1 January 2015.

In the prior year peer review report, it was determined that the Isle of Man's undertakings to identify past rulings and all potential exchange jurisdictions were sufficient to meet the minimum standard. The Isle of Man's implementation in this regard remains unchanged, and therefore continues to meet the minimum standard.

Future rulings (ToR I.4.1.1, I.4.1.2, I.4.2.1)

For the Isle of Man, future rulings are any tax rulings within scope that are issued on or after 1 April 2017.

In the prior year peer review report, it was determined that the Isle of Man's undertakings to identify future rulings and all potential exchange jurisdictions were sufficient to meet the minimum standard. The Isle of Man's implementation in this regard remains unchanged, and therefore continues to meet the minimum standard.

Review and supervision (ToR I.4.3)

In the prior year peer review report, it was determined that the Isle of Man's review and supervision mechanism was sufficient to meet the minimum standard. The Isle of Man's implementation in this regard remains unchanged, and therefore continues to meet the minimum standard.

Conclusion on section A

The Isle of Man has met all of the ToR for the information gathering process and no recommendations are made.

B. The exchange of information

Legal basis for spontaneous exchange of information (ToR II.5.1, II.5.2)

The Isle of Man has the necessary domestic legal basis to exchange information spontaneously. The Isle of Man notes that there are no legal or practical impediments that prevent the spontaneous exchange of information on rulings as contemplated in the Action 5 minimum standard.

The Isle of Man is a party to international agreements permitting spontaneous exchange of information, including (i) the *Multilateral Convention on Mutual Administrative Assistance in Tax Matters: Amended by the 2010 Protocol* (OECD/Council of Europe, 2011) ("the Convention"), (ii) double tax agreements in force with 10 jurisdictions, all of which allow for spontaneous exchange of information and (iii) more than 30 tax information exchange agreements, of which four permit spontaneous exchange of information.[1]

Completion and exchange of templates (ToR II.5.3, II.5.4, II.5.5, II.5.6, II.5.7)

In the prior year peer review report, it was determined that the Isle of Man's process for the completion and exchange of templates were sufficient to meet the minimum standard. The Isle of Man's implementation in this regard remains unchanged and therefore continues to meet the minimum standard.

As the Isle of Man did not issue any future rulings in scope of the transparency framework in the relevant period, the Isle of Man was not required to exchange any information on rulings in the year in review and no data on the timeliness of exchanges can be reported.

Conclusion on section B

The Isle of Man has the necessary legal basis for spontaneous exchange of information and a process for completing the templates and exchanges in a timely way. The Isle of Man has met all of the ToR for the exchange of information process and no recommendations are made.

C. Statistics (ToR IV)

As there was no information on rulings exchanged by Isle of Man for the year in review, no statistics can be reported.

D. Matters related to intellectual property regimes (ToR I.4.1.3)

The Isle of Man does not offer an intellectual property regime for which transparency requirements under the Action 5 Report (OECD, 2015[5]) were imposed.

Summary of recommendations on implementation of the transparency framework

Aspect of implementation of the transparency framework that should be improved	Recommendation for improvement
	No recommendations are made.

Notes

[1] Parties to the Convention are available here: www.oecd.org/tax/exchange-of-tax-information/convention-on-mutual-administrative-assistance-in-tax-matters.htm. The Isle of Man has bilateral agreements in force with Bahrain, British Virgin Islands, Cayman Islands, Estonia, Guernsey, Jersey, Luxembourg, Malta, Qatar, Seychelles, Singapore, Turks & Caicos Islands, United Kingdom and United States.

Israel

Israel has met all aspects of the terms of reference (OECD, 2017[3]) (ToR) for the calendar year 2018 (year in review) except the timely provision of information on rulings to the Competent Authority for exchange of information (ToR II.5.5), and the timely exchange of information on future rulings (ToR II.5.6). Israel receives two recommendations on these points.

In the prior year report, Israel received the same two recommendations. As they have not been addressed, the recommendations remain in place.

Israel can legally issue five types of rulings within the scope of the transparency framework. In practice, Israel issued rulings within the scope of the transparency framework as follows:[1]

- 79 past rulings;
- For the period 1 April 2016 - 31 December 2016: 5 future rulings;
- For the calendar year 2017: 16 future rulings, and
- For the year in review: 15 future rulings.

No peer input was received in respect of the exchanges of information on rulings received from Israel.

Introduction

This peer review covers Israel's implementation of the BEPS Action 5 transparency framework for the year 2018. The report has four parts, each relating to a key part of the ToR. Each part is discussed in turn. A summary of recommendations is included at the end of this report.

A. The information gathering process

Israel can legally issue the following five types of rulings within the scope of the transparency framework: (i) preferential regimes;[2] (ii) cross-border unilateral APAs and any other cross-border unilateral tax rulings (such as an advance tax ruling) covering transfer pricing or the application of transfer pricing principles; (iii) rulings providing for unilateral downward adjustments, (iv) permanent establishment rulings; and (v) related party conduit rulings.

Past rulings (ToR I.4.1.1, I.4.1.2, I.4.2.1, I.4.2.2)

For Israel, past rulings are any tax rulings within scope that are issued either: (i) on or after 1 January 2014 but before 1 April 2016; or (ii) on or after 1 January 2010 but before 1 January 2014, provided they were still in effect as at 1 January 2014.

In the prior year peer review report, it was determined that Israel's undertakings to identify past rulings and all potential exchange jurisdictions were sufficient to meet the minimum standard. Israel's implementation in this regard remains unchanged, and therefore continues to meet the minimum standard.

Future rulings (ToR I.4.1.1, I.4.1.2, I.4.2.1)

For Israel, future rulings are any tax rulings within scope that are issued on or after 1 April 2016.

In the prior years' peer review reports, it was determined that Israel's implementation of a new system to identify future rulings and all potential exchange jurisdictions was sufficient to meet the minimum standard. Israel's implementation in this regard remains unchanged, and therefore continues to meet the minimum standard.

Review and supervision (ToR I.4.3)

In the prior years' peer review reports, it was determined that Israel's review and supervision mechanism was sufficient to meet the minimum standard. Israel's implementation in this regard remains unchanged, and therefore continues to meet the minimum standard.

Conclusion on section A

Israel continues to meet all of the ToR for the information gathering process and no recommendations are made.

B. The exchange of information

Legal basis for spontaneous exchange of information (ToR II.5.1, II.5.2)

Israel has the necessary domestic legal basis to exchange information spontaneously. Israel notes that there are no legal or practical impediments that prevent the spontaneous exchange of information on rulings as contemplated in the Action 5 minimum standard.

Israel has international agreements permitting spontaneous exchange of information, including being a party to the (i) *Multilateral Convention on Mutual Administrative Assistance in Tax Matters: Amended by the 2010 Protocol* (OECD/Council of Europe, 2011[4]) ("the Convention") and (ii) double tax agreements in force with 54 jurisdictions.[3]

Completion and exchange of templates (ToR II.5.3, II.5.4, II.5.5, II.5.6, II.5.7)

In the prior year peer review report, it was determined that Israel's process for the completion and exchange of templates met all the ToR, except for the timely provision of information on rulings to the Competent Authority (ToR II.5.5) and for the timely exchange of information on past and future rulings (ToR II.5.6). Therefore, Israel was recommended to reduce the timelines for providing the information on future rulings to the Competent Authority and to ensure that all information on future rulings is exchanged as soon as possible.

In late 2018, the internal computer system which is used by the departments to issue rulings was amended, to add a feature which marks rulings as being relevant for exchange. When this is marked as such, the ruling is automatically transmitted and available to the EOI department. This system became operational in 2019, and will be taken into account in the subsequent peer review. Israel notes that the 16 rulings issued in 2017 and the 15 rulings issued in 2018 were exchanged during 2019. These exchanges will be included in the next year's peer review report.

As there were no exchanges for the year in review, no data on the timeliness of exchanges can be reported.

Conclusion on section B

Israel is recommended to continue its efforts to reduce the timelines for providing the information on future rulings to the Competent Authority, and to ensure that all information on future rulings is exchanged as soon as possible.

C. Statistics (ToR IV)

As there were no rulings exchanged by Israel for the year in review, no statistics can be reported.

D. Matters related to intellectual property regimes (ToR I.4.1.3)

Israel offers two intellectual property regimes (IP regime)[4] that is subject to the transparency requirements under the Action 5 Report (OECD, 2015[5]). It states that the identification of the benefitting taxpayers will occur as follows:

- ***New entrants benefitting from the grandfathered IP regime***: the process on the collection of information regarding new entrants in the grandfathered IP regime is described in the previous year peer review report, and the process was completed in a manner that met the ToR.
- ***Third category of IP assets***: the regimes provide benefits to the third category of IP assets. The process on the collection of information is described in the previous year peer review report and

meets the ToR. In the absence of information to the contrary, it is assumed that Israel's implementation of this aspect remains unchanged and continues to meet the ToR.

- ***Taxpayers making use of the option to treat the nexus ratio as a rebuttable presumption***: not applicable as the regime does not allow the nexus ratio to be treated as a rebuttable presumption.

Summary of recommendations on implementation of the transparency framework

Aspect of implementation of the transparency framework that should be improved	Recommendation for improvement
During the year in review, Israel continued to experience delays in the provision of rulings to the Competent Authority.	Israel is recommended to continue its efforts to reduce the timelines for providing the information on future rulings to the Competent Authority. This recommendation remains unchanged since the prior year peer review report.
Israel continued to encounter delays in the exchange of information for all future rulings within the scope of the transparency framework.	Israel is recommended to ensure that all information on future rulings is exchanged as soon as possible. This recommendation remains unchanged since the 2016 peer review report and the 2017 peer review report.

Notes

[1] Note: The statistical data for Israel are supplied by and under the responsibility of the relevant Israeli authorities. The use of such data by the OECD is without prejudice to the status of the Golan Heights, East Jerusalem and Israeli settlements in the West Bank under the terms of international law.

[2] With respect to the following preferential regimes: Preferred company regime and Preferred technological enterprise regime

[3] Parties to the Convention are available here: www.oecd.org/tax/exchange-of-tax-information/convention-on-mutual-administrative-assistance-in-tax-matters.htm. Israel also has double tax agreements with Austria, Belarus, Belgium, Brazil, Bulgaria, Canada, China (People's Republic of), Chinese Taipei, Croatia, Czech Republic, Denmark, Estonia, Ethiopia, Finland, France, Georgia, Germany, Greece, Hungary, India, Ireland, Italy, Jamaica, Japan, Korea, Latvia, Lithuania, Luxembourg, Malta, Mexico, Moldova, Netherlands, Norway, Panama, Philippines, Poland, Portugal, Romania, Russia, Singapore, Slovak Republic, Slovenia, South Africa, Spain, Sweden, Switzerland, Thailand, Turkey, Ukraine, United Kingdom, United States, Uzbekistan and Viet Nam.

[4] The Preferred company regime which is the grandfathered regime, and the Preferred technological enterprise regime which is the amended regime.

Italy

Italy has met all aspects of the terms of reference (OECD, 2017[3]) (ToR) for the calendar year 2018 (year in review) except providing information to the Competent Authority without undue delay (ToR II.5.5)and exchanging information during the year of review on new entrants to the IP regime that obtained benefits with respect to trademarks (ToR I.4.1.3). Italy receives two recommendations on these points for the year in review.

In the prior year report, as well as in the 2016 peer review, Italy received two recommendations in connection with the same issues. The recommendation with respect to the IP regime has been fully addressed in mid-2019 by the completion of the exchange on new entrants, however the relevant recommendation remains in place for the 2018 year in review. As regards the recommendation providing information to the Competent Authority without undue delay, Italy has introduced measures that are expected to take effect as of next year's review.

Italy can legally issue three types of rulings within the scope of the transparency framework. In practice, Italy issued rulings within the scope of the transparency framework as follows:

- 58 past rulings;
- For the period 1 April 2016 - 31 December 2016: 39 future rulings;
- For the calendar year 2017: 123 future rulings, and
- For the year in review: 308 future rulings.

Rulings other than APAs and ad hoc Patent Box may be published, in an anonymised form, as a general ruling (Resolutions)[1] when the underlying issue is new and relevant, or the response to the query may apply to groups or types of taxpayers in the same situation, providing guidance on the position of the Italian tax administration on the matters of the query. Moreover, as of August 2018 the basic principles underpinning the replies given to a single taxpayer by the Central Directorates to the so called "ordinary rulings" ("interpelli") are published on the Revenue Agency website.[2]

Peer input was received from nine jurisdictions in respect of the exchanges of information on rulings received from Italy. The input was generally positive, noting that information was mostly complete and in in a correct format.

Introduction

This peer review covers Italy's implementation of the BEPS Action 5 transparency framework for the year 2018. The report has four parts, each relating to a key part of the ToR. Each part is discussed in turn. A summary of recommendations is included at the end of this report.

A. The information gathering process

Italy can legally issue the following three types of rulings within the scope of the transparency framework: (i) rulings related to preferential regimes;[3] (ii) cross-border unilateral advance pricing arrangements (APAs) and any other cross-border unilateral tax rulings (such as an advance tax ruling) covering transfer pricing or the application of transfer pricing principles; and (iii) as of May 2016, permanent establishment rulings.

Past rulings (ToR I.4.1.1, I.4.1.2, I.4.2.1, I.4.2.2)

For Italy, past rulings are any tax rulings within scope that are issued either: (i) on or after 1 January 2014 but before 1 April 2016; or (ii) on or after 1 January 2010 but before 1 January 2014, provided they were still in effect as at 1 January 2014.

In the prior year peer review report, it was determined that Italy's undertakings to identify past rulings and all potential exchange jurisdictions were sufficient to meet the minimum standard. Italy's implementation in this regard remains unchanged, and therefore continues to meet the minimum standard.

Future rulings (ToR I.4.1.1, I.4.1.2, I.4.2.1)

For Italy, future rulings are any tax rulings within scope that are issued on or after 1 April 2016.

In the prior year peer review report, it was determined that Italy's implementation undertakings to identify future rulings and all potential exchange jurisdictions were sufficient to meet the minimum standard. Italy's implementation in this regard remains unchanged, and therefore continues to meet the minimum standard.

Review and supervision (ToR I.4.3)

In the prior years' peer review reports, it was determined that Italy's review and supervision mechanism was sufficient to meet the minimum standard. Italy's implementation in this regard remains unchanged, and therefore continues to meet the minimum standard.

Conclusion on section A

Italy has met all of the ToR for the information gathering process and no recommendations are made.

B. The exchange of information

Legal basis for spontaneous exchange of information (ToR II.5.1, II.5.2)

Italy has the necessary domestic legal basis to exchange information spontaneously. Italy notes that there are no legal or practical impediments that prevent the spontaneous exchange of information on rulings as contemplated in the Action 5 minimum standard.

Italy has international agreements permitting spontaneous exchange of information, including being a party to the (i) *Multilateral Convention on Mutual Administrative Assistance in Tax Matters: Amended by the*

2010 Protocol (OECD/Council of Europe, 2011[4]) ("the Convention"), (ii) the Directive 2011/16/EU with all other European Union Member States and (iii) double tax agreements in force with 99 jurisdictions.[4]

Completion and exchange of templates (ToR II.5.3, II.5.4, II.5.5, II.5.6, II.5.7)

In the prior year peer review report, it was determined that Italy's process for the completion and exchange of temples met all the ToR, except for providing the information on future rulings to the Competent Authority in a timely manner (ToR II.5.5). Therefore, Italy was recommended to continue its efforts to reduce the timelines.

During the year in review, Italy still experienced delays when forwarding information on rulings to the Competent Authority and information has been forwarded to the Competent Authority at six monthly intervals. Italy issued new internal guidelines in February 2019 to make information on rulings available on a quarterly basis to the Competent Authority, so that exchange of information on is conducted in a timely manner as required under the transparency framework. In addition, the Revenue Agency, in collaboration with its IT partner, is implementing an IT application intended to allow an automatic download of the rulings contained in the relevant databases and their subsequent transmission to the Competent Authority. This will be assessed in the subsequent peer review report.

For the year in review, the timeliness of exchanges is as follows:

Past rulings in the scope of the transparency framework	Number of exchanges transmitted by 31 December 2018	Delayed exchanges		
		Number of exchanges not transmitted by 31 December 2018	Reasons for the delays	Any other comments
	0	0	N/A	N/A
Future rulings in the scope of the transparency framework	Number of exchanges transmitted within three months of the information becoming available to the competent authority or immediately after legal impediments have been lifted	Delayed exchanges		
		Number of exchanges transmitted later than three months of the information on rulings becoming available to the competent authority	Reasons for the delays	Any other comments
	1 155	0	N/A	N/A
Total	1 155	0		

Follow up requests received for exchange of the ruling	Number	Average time to provide response	Number of requests not answered
	1	1 week	1

Italy has the necessary legal basis for spontaneous exchange of information, a process for completing the templates in a timely way and has completed all exchanges. As Italy continued to experience delays when forwarding information on rulings to the Competent Authority during the year of review, the recommendation is retained and Italy is recommended to continue its efforts to ensure that information is made available to the Competent Authority without undue delay (ToR II. 5.5).

C. Statistics (ToR IV)

The statistics for the year in review are as follows:

Category of ruling	Number of exchanges	Jurisdictions exchanged with
Ruling related to a preferential regime	1 063	Andorra, Argentina, Australia, Austria, Belgium, Botswana, Brazil, Bulgaria, Canada, Chile, China (People's Republic of), Colombia, , Costa Rica, Croatia, Czech Republic, Denmark, Estonia, Finland, France, Germany, Greece, Hong Kong (China), Hungary, India, Indonesia, Ireland, Israel, Jamaica, Japan, Jersey, Kazakhstan, Korea, Luxembourg, Macao (China), Malaysia, Mauritius, Mexico, Monaco, Netherlands, New Zealand, Norway, Panama, Peru, Poland, Portugal, Qatar, Romania, Russia, San Marino, Saudi Arabia, Serbia, Singapore, Slovak Republic, Slovenia, South Africa, Spain, Sweden, Switzerland, Thailand, Tunisia, Turkey, Ukraine, United Kingdom, United States, Zambia
Cross-border unilateral advance pricing agreements (APAs) and any other cross-border unilateral tax rulings (such as an advance tax ruling) covering transfer pricing or the application of transfer pricing principles	87	Australia, Austria, Belgium, Brazil, China (People's Republic of), Denmark, Finland, France, Germany, Hong Kong (China), Hungary, Ireland, Japan, Korea, Luxembourg, Malaysia, Netherlands, Norway, Poland, Portugal, Russia, Slovak Republic, Singapore, Spain, Sweden, Switzerland, Turkey, Ukraine, United Kingdom, United States
Cross-border rulings providing for a unilateral downward adjustment to the taxpayer's taxable profits that is not directly reflected in the taxpayer's financial / commercial accounts	N/A	N/A
Permanent establishment rulings	5	France, Hungary, Ireland, Luxembourg United Kingdom
Related party conduit rulings	N/A	N/A
De minimis rule	N/A	N/A
IP regimes: total exchanges on taxpayers benefitting from the third category of IP assets, new entrants benefitting from grandfathered IP regimes; and taxpayers making use of the option to treat the nexus ratio as a rebuttable presumption	0	N/A
Total	1 155	

D. Matters related to intellectual property regimes (ToR I.4.1.3)

Italy offered an intellectual property regime ("IP regime")[5] that was amended with effect as of 1 January 2017 to the extent it was not nexus compliant (i.e. for benefits for trademarks) and is subject to transparency requirements under the Action 5 Report (OECD, 2015[5]). It states that the identification of the benefitting taxpayers will occur as follows:

- ***New entrants benefitting from the grandfathered IP regime***:

In the prior year peer review report, Italy was recommended to continue its efforts to identify and exchange information on new entrants to the grandfathered IP regime. Italy issued an Inter-Ministerial Decree which came into force on 6 February 2018 and stipulates that every taxpayer who has benefitted as a new entrant from the grandfathered Italian Patent Box regime shall indicate this in the annual tax return. In addition, the taxpayer shall provide the following information to the *Agenzia delle Entrate*, which is the competent body to issue ad hoc rulings and regime rulings relating to the Patent Box regime:

- the type and the number of eligible assets (patent, trademarks, etc.) to which the benefit applies;
- the amount of the eligible income resulting from the use of the assets; and
- as regards benefits for trademarks, information on relevant jurisdictions where related parties are fiscally resident

- The first tax return containing this information was filed at the end of 2018. The information was gathered in early 2019. As such, the part of the recommendation relating to the identification of the relevant new entrants is removed. On the basis of 2018 tax returns, the following information on new entrants has been gathered: 512 taxpayers have opted for the Italian IP regime for 6 116 trademarks. Of these taxpayers, 391 are purely domestic taxpayers while 121 have related parties in other jurisdictions. Italy has fully exchanged this information by July 2019. This will be taken into account in the subsequent peer review, and this is not a recurring issue.

Third category of IP assets: not applicable as the regime does not allow the third category of IP assets to qualify for the benefits.

- ***Taxpayers making use of the option to treat the nexus ratio as a rebuttable presumption***: not applicable as the regime does not allow the nexus ratio to be treated as a rebuttable presumption.

Summary of recommendations on implementation of the transparency framework

Aspect of implementation of the transparency framework that should be improved	Recommendation for improvement
During the year of review Italy continued to experience delays when forwarding information to the Competent Authority.	Italy is recommended to continue its efforts to continue its efforts to apply reduced timelines for providing the information on future rulings to the Competent Authority. This recommendation remains unchanged since the 2016 peer review report and the 2017 peer review report.
Italy has completed the exchange of information on new entrants to the grandfathered IP regime that obtained benefits with respect to trademarks in mid-2019.	As the exchange was done by mid-2019 (after the year in review), the recommendation to complete the exchanges on the new entrants is retained, though this is not a recurring issue. A recommendation on this issue remains since the 2016 peer review report and the 2017 peer review report.

Notes

[1] Available here:
https://www.agenziaentrate.gov.it/wps/content/Nsilib/Nsi/Normativa+e+Prassi/Risoluzioni.

[2] Available here:
https://www.agenziaentrate.gov.it/wps/content/nsilib/nsi/normativa+e+prassi/risposte+agli+interpelli.

[3] With respect to the following preferential regimes: 1) International shipping and 2) Patent Box.

[4] Parties to the Convention are available here: www.oecd.org/tax/exchange-of-tax-information/convention-on-mutual-administrative-assistance-in-tax-matters.htm. Italy also has bilateral agreements with Albania, Algeria, Argentina, Armenia, Australia, Austria, Azerbaijan, Bangladesh, Barbados, Belarus, Belgium, Bosnia and Herzegovina, Brazil, Bulgaria, Canada, Chile, China (People's Republic of), Congo, Côte d'Ivoire, Croatia, Cyprus, Czech Republic, Denmark, Ecuador, Egypt, Estonia, Ethiopia, Finland, Former Yugoslav Republic of Macedonia, France, Georgia, Germany, Ghana, Greece, Hong Kong (China), Hungary, Iceland, India, Indonesia, Ireland, Israel, Japan, Jordan, Kazakhstan, Korea, Kuwait, Kyrgyzstan, Latvia, Lebanon, Lithuania, Luxembourg, Malaysia, Malta, Mauritius, Mexico, Moldova, Montenegro, Morocco, Mozambique, Netherlands, New Zealand, Norway, Oman, Pakistan, Philippines, Poland, Portugal, Qatar, Romania, Russia, San Marino, Saudi Arabia, Senegal, Serbia, Singapore, Slovak Republic, Slovenia, South Africa, Spain, Sri Lanka, Sweden, Switzerland, Syrian Arab Republic, Chinese Taipei, Tajikistan, Tanzania, Thailand, Trinidad and Tobago, Tunisia, Turkey, Uganda, Ukraine, United Arab Emirates, United Kingdom, United States, Uzbekistan, Venezuela, Viet Nam and Zambia.

Note by Turkey: The information in this document with reference to "Cyprus" relates to the southern part of the Island. There is no single authority representing both Turkish and Greek Cypriot people on the Island. Turkey recognises the Turkish Republic of Northern Cyprus (TRNC). Until a lasting and equitable solution is found within the context of the United Nations, Turkey shall preserve its position concerning the "Cyprus issue".

Note by all the European Union Member States of the OECD and the European Union. The Republic of Cyprus is recognised by all members of the United Nations with the exception of Turkey. The information in this document relates to the area under the effective control of the Government of the Republic of Cyprus.

[5] Partial exemption for income/gains derived from certain IP rights.

Jamaica

Jamaica has met all aspects of the terms of reference (OECD, 2017[3]) (ToR) for the calendar year 2018 (year in review) that can be met in the absence of rulings being issued in practice.

In the prior year report, Jamaica received two recommendations. Jamaica did not provide a completed peer review questionnaire to the Secretariat, and therefore it was not known whether Jamaica had implemented the transparency framework. These recommendations made in the prior year peer review report have been addressed and are removed.

Jamaica can legally issue five types of rulings within the scope of the transparency framework. In practice, Jamaica has not issued any rulings within the scope of the transparency framework.

As no exchanges were required to take place, no peer input was received in respect of the exchanges of information on rulings received from Jamaica.

Introduction

This peer review covers Jamaica's implementation of the BEPS Action 5 transparency framework for the year 2018. The report has four parts, each relating to a key part of the ToR. Each part is discussed in turn. A summary of recommendations is included at the end of this report.

A. The information gathering process

Jamaica can legally issue the following four types of rulings within the scope of the transparency framework: (i) preferential regimes;[1] (ii) cross-border unilateral APAs and any other cross-border unilateral tax rulings (such as an advance tax ruling) covering transfer pricing or the application of transfer pricing principles; (iii) rulings providing for unilateral downward adjustments; and (iv) permanent establishment rulings; and (v) related party conduit rulings. Rulings are issued under the Commissioner General's powers and processed by the Interpretations, Rulings and Opinions Committee (IROC), a committee created under the auspices of the Commissioner General's Executive Office of Tax Administration Jamaica (TAJ).

Past rulings (ToR I.4.1.1, I.4.1.2, I.4.2.1, I.4.2.2)

For Jamaica, past rulings are any tax rulings within scope that are issued either: (i) on or after 1 January 2015 but before 1 April 2017; or (ii) on or after 1 January 2012 but before 1 January 2015, provided they were still in effect as at 1 January 2015.

Since the introduction of legislation in 2014 and 2015 empowering the Commissioner General to issue taxpayer-specific tax rulings, Jamaica has not issued any rulings within scope of the transparency framework. Therefore, Jamaica has not issued any rulings during the past rulings period. As no rulings were issued, it was not relevant to identify any exchange jurisdictions for past rulings.

Future rulings (ToR I.4.1.1, I.4.1.2, I.4.2.1)

For Jamaica, future rulings are any tax rulings within scope that are issued on or after 1 April 2017.

No rulings were issued by Jamaica during the future rulings period in the year of review. However, Jamaica indicates that there are processes being put in place for the issuance and review of rulings for the purposes of the transparency framework.

The IROC is the committee tasked with reviewing and establishing whether any rulings issued fall in scope of the transparency framework. As the IROC is also the committee that processes the issuance of rulings, it is able to concurrently manually review all rulings issued to establish whether they are in scope of the transparency framework. Information on relevant exchange jurisdictions will be sought from the taxpayers during the ruling application process prior to the issuance of the ruling. Jamaica is currently developing guidelines to be published, which will specify the information that must be included in rulings applications such as organisational charts with all relevant parties' jurisdiction of relevance. TAJ can also consult existing taxpayer records to verify the information provided.

Review and supervision (ToR I.4.3)

The accuracy of the information gathering process and the identification of rulings in scope of the transparency framework is overseen by the Commissioner General Executive office, in conjunction with the IROC and the Legislation, Treaties and International Tax Matters Unit.

Conclusion on section A

Jamaica has met all of the ToR for the information gathering process that can be met in the absence of rulings being issued in practice and no recommendations are made.

B. The exchange of information

Legal basis for spontaneous exchange of information (ToR II.5.1, II.5.2)

Jamaica has the necessary domestic legal basis to exchange information spontaneously. Jamaica notes that there are no legal or practical impediments that prevent the spontaneous exchange of information on rulings as contemplated in the Action 5 minimum standard.

Jamaica is a party to international agreements permitting spontaneous exchange of information, including (i) the *Multilateral Convention on Mutual Administrative Assistance in Tax Matters: Amended by the 2010 Protocol* (OECD/Council of Europe, 2011) ("the Convention"), and (ii) double tax agreements and tax information exchange agreements in force with 26 jurisdictions.[2]

Completion and exchange of templates (ToR II.5.3, II.5.4, II.5.5, II.5.6, II.5.7)

Jamaica notes that the Legislation, Treaties and International Tax Matters Unit would be responsible for the completion and quality check of the information required in the template contained in Annex C of the Action 5 Report (OECD, 2015). This would include providing a detailed summary of the ruling following the instructions in Annex C. Final review of the template would be conducted by the Chief Tax Counsel of the Legislation, Treaties and International Tax Matters Unit. The Legislation, Treaties and International Tax Matters Unit is involved in the oversight of the issuing of rulings, and all tax rulings will be readily available to the Commissioner General as Competent Authority for exchange of information, and no delays are expected.

As Jamaica did not issue any rulings in scope of the transparency framework in the relevant period, Jamaica was not required to exchange any information on rulings in the year in review and no data on the timeliness of exchanges can be reported.

Conclusion on section B

Jamaica has the necessary legal basis to undertake spontaneous exchange of information. Jamaica has met all of the ToR for the exchange of information process that can be met in the absence of rulings being issued and exchanged in practice and no recommendations are made.

C. Statistics (ToR IV)

As there was no information on rulings exchanged by Jamaica for the year in review, no statistics can be reported.

D. Matters related to intellectual property regimes (ToR I.4.1.3)

Jamaica does not offer an intellectual property regime for which transparency requirements under the Action 5 Report (OECD, 2015[5]) were imposed.

Summary of recommendations on implementation of the transparency framework

Aspect of implementation of the transparency framework that should be improved	Recommendation for improvement
	No recommendations are made.

Notes

[1] With respect to the following preferential regimes: Special economic zones.

[2] Parties to the Convention are available here: www.oecd.org/tax/exchange-of-tax-information/convention-on-mutual-administrative-assistance-in-tax-matters.htm. Jamaica also has bilateral agreements with Antigua and Barbuda, Barbados, Belize, Canada, China (People's Republic of), Denmark, Dominica, Faroe Islands, Finland, France, Germany, Greenland, Grenada, Guyana, Iceland, Israel, Mexico, Norway, Saint Kitts and Nevis, Saint Lucia, Saint Vincent and the Grenadines, Spain, Sweden, Trinidad and Tobago, United Kingdom and United States.

Japan

Japan has met all aspects of the terms of reference (ToR) for the calendar year 2018 (year in review) and no recommendations are made.

In the prior year report, Japan did not receive any recommendations.

Japan can legally issue three types of rulings within the scope of the transparency framework. In practice, Japan has issued rulings within the scope of the transparency framework as follows:

- 51 past rulings;
- For the period 1 April 2016 - 31 December 2016: 12 future rulings;
- For the calendar year 2017: 14 future rulings, and
- For the year in review: 16 future rulings.

Unilateral APAs are not published, whereas written answers under the Written Reply Procedure are published on the National Tax Agency ("NTA") website.

Peer input was received from two jurisdictions in respect of the exchanges of information on rulings received from Japan. The input was generally positive, noting that information was complete, in a correct format and received in a timely manner.

Introduction

This peer review covers Japan's implementation of the BEPS Action 5 transparency framework for the year 2018. The report has four parts, each relating to a key part of the ToR. Each part is discussed in turn. A summary of recommendations is included at the end of this report.

A. The information gathering process

Japan can legally issue the three following types of rulings within the scope of the transparency framework: (i) cross-border unilateral advance pricing arrangements (APAs) and any other cross-border unilateral tax rulings (such as an advance tax ruling) covering transfer pricing or the application of transfer pricing principles; (ii) permanent establishment rulings; and (iii) related party conduit rulings.

Past rulings (ToR I.4.1.1, I.4.1.2, I.4.2.1, I.4.2.2)

For Japan, past rulings are any tax rulings within scope that are issued either: (i) on or after 1 January 2014 but before 1 April 2016; or (ii) on or after 1 January 2010 but before 1 January 2014, provided they were still in effect as at 1 January 2014.

In the prior years' peer review reports, it was determined that Japan's undertakings to identify past rulings and all potential exchange jurisdictions were sufficient to meet the minimum standard. Japan's implementation in this regard remains unchanged, and therefore continues to meet the minimum standard.

Future rulings (ToR I.4.1.1, I.4.1.2, I.4.2.1)

For Japan, future rulings are any tax rulings within scope that are issued on or after 1 April 2016.

In the prior years' peer review reports, it was determined that Japan's undertakings to identify future rulings and all potential exchange jurisdictions was sufficient to meet the minimum standard. Japan's implementation in this regard remains unchanged, and therefore continues to meet the minimum standard.

Review and supervision (ToR I.4.3)

In the prior years' peer review reports, it was determined that Japan's review and supervision mechanism was sufficient to meet the minimum standard. Japan's implementation in this regard remains unchanged, and therefore continues to meet the minimum standard.

Conclusion on section A

Japan has met all of the ToR for the information gathering process and no recommendations are made.

B. The exchange of information

Legal basis for spontaneous exchange of information (ToR II.5.1, II.5.2)

Japan has the necessary domestic legal basis to exchange information spontaneously. Japan notes that there are no legal or practical impediments that prevent the spontaneous exchange of information on rulings as contemplated in the Action 5 minimum standard.

Japan is a party to international agreements permitting spontaneous exchange of information, including (i) the *Multilateral Convention on Mutual Administrative Assistance in Tax Matters: Amended by the 2010*

Protocol (OECD/Council of Europe, 2011) ("the Convention") and (ii) double tax agreements in force with 71 jurisdictions.[1]

Completion and exchange of templates (ToR II.5.3, II.5.4, II.5.5, II.5.6, II.5.7)

In the prior year peer review report, it was determined that Japan's completion and exchange of templates were sufficient to meet the minimum standard. Japan's implementation in this regard remains unchanged, and therefore continues to meet the minimum standard.

For the year in review, the timeliness of exchanges is as follows:

Past rulings in the scope of the transparency framework	Number of exchanges transmitted by 31 December 2018	Delayed exchanges		
		Number of exchanges not transmitted by 31 December 2018	Reasons for the delays	Any other comments
	0	0	N/A	N/A
Future rulings in the scope of the transparency framework	Number of exchanges transmitted within three months of the information becoming available to the competent authority or immediately after legal impediments have been lifted	Delayed exchanges		
		Number of exchanges transmitted later than three months of the information on rulings becoming available to the competent authority	Reasons for the delays	Any other comments
	38	0	N/A	N/A
Total	38	0		

Follow up requests received for exchange of the ruling	Number	Average time to provide response	Number of requests not answered
	0	N/A	N/A

Conclusion on section B

Japan has the necessary legal basis for spontaneous exchange of information and a process for completing the templates in a timely way. Japan has met all of the ToR for the exchange of information process and no recommendations are made.

C. Statistics (ToR IV)

The statistics for the year in review are as follows:

Category of ruling	Number of exchanges	Jurisdictions exchanged with
Ruling related to a preferential regime	N/A	N/A
Cross-border unilateral advance pricing agreements (APAs) and any other cross-border unilateral tax rulings (such as an advance tax ruling) covering transfer pricing or the application of transfer pricing principles	38	Australia, Belgium, China (People's Republic of), Hong Kong (China), India, Indonesia, Ireland, Korea, Malaysia, Netherlands, Philippines, Singapore, Switzerland, Thailand, United Kingdom, United States
Cross-border rulings providing for a unilateral downward adjustment to the taxpayer's taxable profits that is not directly reflected in the taxpayer's financial / commercial accounts	N/A	N/A
Permanent establishment rulings	0	N/A

Related party conduit rulings	0	N/A
De minimis rule	N/A	N/A
IP regimes: total exchanges on taxpayers benefitting from the third category of IP assets, new entrants benefitting from grandfathered IP regimes; and taxpayers making use of the option to treat the nexus ratio as a rebuttable presumption	N/A	N/A
Total	38	

D. Matters related to intellectual property regimes (ToR I.4.1.3)

Japan does not offer an intellectual property regime for which transparency requirements under the Action 5 Report (OECD, 2015[5]) were imposed.

Summary of recommendations on implementation of the transparency framework

Aspect of implementation of the transparency framework that should be improved	Recommendation for improvement
	No recommendations are made.

Notes

[1] Parties to the Convention are available here: www.oecd.org/tax/exchange-of-tax-information/convention-on-mutual-administrative-assistance-in-tax-matters.htm. Japan also has bilateral agreements in force with Armenia, Bangladesh, Belarus, Brunei Darussalam, Egypt, Fiji, Hong Kong (China), Kuwait, Kyrgyzstan, Oman, Philippines, Qatar, Sri Lanka, Chinese Taipei, Tajikistan, Thailand, Turkey, Turkmenistan, United States, Uzbekistan, Viet Nam and Zambia.

Jersey

Jersey has met all aspects of the terms of reference (OECD, 2017[3]) (ToR) for the calendar year 2018 (year in review) and no recommendations are made.

In the prior year report, Jersey did not receive any recommendations.

Jersey can legally issue four types of rulings within the scope of the transparency framework. In practice, Jersey issued rulings within the scope of the transparency framework as follows:

- 16 past rulings;
- For the period 1 April 2017 - 31 December 2017: one future ruling, and
- For the year in review: no future rulings.

As no exchanges were required to take place during the year in review, no peer input was received in respect of the exchanges of information on rulings received from Jersey.

Introduction

This peer review covers Jersey's implementation of the BEPS Action 5 transparency framework for the year 2018. The report has four parts, each relating to a key part of the ToR. Each part is discussed in turn. A summary of recommendations is included at the end of this report.

A. The information gathering process

Jersey can legally issue the following four types of rulings within the scope of the transparency framework: (i) cross-border unilateral APAs and any other cross-border unilateral tax rulings (such as an advance tax ruling) covering transfer pricing or the application of transfer pricing principles; (ii) rulings providing for unilateral downward adjustments, (iii) permanent establishment rulings; and (iv) related party conduit rulings.

Past rulings (ToR I.4.1.1, I.4.1.2, I.4.2.1, I.4.2.2)

For Jersey, past rulings are any tax rulings within scope that are issued either (i) on or after 1 January 2015 but before 1 April 2017; and (ii) on or after 1 January 2012 but before 1 January 2015, provided they were still in effect as at 1 January 2015.

In the prior year peer review report, it was determined that Jersey's undertakings to identify past rulings and all potential exchange jurisdictions were sufficient to meet the minimum standard. Jersey's implementation in this regard remains unchanged, and therefore continues to meet the minimum standard.

Future rulings (ToR I.4.1.1, I.4.1.2, I.4.2.1)

For Jersey, future rulings are any tax rulings within scope that are issued on or after 1 April 2017.

In the prior year peer review report, it was determined that Jersey's implementation of a new system to identify future rulings and all potential exchange jurisdictions was sufficient to meet the minimum standard. Jersey's implementation in this regard remains unchanged, and therefore continues to meet the minimum standard.

Review and supervision (ToR I.4.3)

In the prior year peer review report, it was determined that Jersey's review and supervision mechanism was sufficient to meet the minimum standard. Jersey's implementation in this regard remains unchanged, and therefore continues to meet the minimum standard.

Conclusion on section A

Jersey has met all of the ToR for the information gathering process and no recommendations are made.

B. The exchange of information

Legal basis for spontaneous exchange of information (ToR II.5.1, II.5.2)

Jersey has the necessary domestic legal basis to exchange information spontaneously. Jersey notes that there are no legal or practical impediments that prevent the spontaneous exchange of information on rulings as contemplated in the Action 5 minimum standard.

Jersey has international agreements permitting spontaneous exchange of information, including being a party to the (i) *Multilateral Convention on Mutual Administrative Assistance in Tax Matters: Amended by the 2010 Protocol* (OECD/Council of Europe, 2011[4]) ("the Convention") and (ii) double tax agreements in force with 16 jurisdictions.[1]

Completion and exchange of templates (ToR II.5.3, II.5.4, II.5.5, II.5.6, II.5.7)

In the prior year peer review report, it was determined that Jersey's process for the completion and exchange of templates were sufficient to meet the minimum standard. Jersey's implementation in this regard remains unchanged and therefore continues to meet the minimum standard.

For the year in review, the timeliness of exchanges is as follows:

Past rulings in the scope of the transparency framework	Number of exchanges transmitted by 31 December 2018	Delayed exchanges		
		Number of exchanges not transmitted by 31 December 2018	Reasons for the delays	Any other comments
	2	0	A minor error occurred in the identification of immediate and ultimate parent companies in the case of PE rulings.	This was a one-time issue and solved by completing the exchanges on 2 March 2018.
Future rulings in the scope of the transparency framework	Number of exchanges transmitted within three months of the information becoming available to the competent authority or immediately after legal impediments have been lifted	Delayed exchanges		
		Number of exchanges transmitted later than three months of the information on rulings becoming available to the competent authority	Reasons for the delays	Any other comments
	0	0	N/A	N/A
Total	2	0		

Follow up requests received for exchange of the ruling	Number	Average time to provide response	Number of requests not answered
	0	N/A	N/A

A minor error was detected in connection with past rulings, relating to the incorrect identification of exchange jurisdictions. The additional required exchanges were completed as soon as possible after the error was identified, and within the year in review. To ensure no additional errors had occurred, Jersey reviewed all of the rulings identified for exchange. This review also identified an error in the layout of Jersey's template for exchange of rulings, which was the cause of the incorrect identification of exchange jurisdictions noted above. As this appears to be a one-off error that was quickly remedied, no recommendation is made.

Conclusion on section B

Jersey has the necessary legal basis for spontaneous exchange of information, a process for completing the templates in a timely way and has completed all exchanges. Jersey has met all of the ToR for the exchange of information process and no recommendations are made.

C. Statistics (ToR IV)

The statistics for the year in review are as follows:

Category of ruling	Number of exchanges	Jurisdictions exchanged with
Ruling related to a preferential regime	N/A	N/A
Cross-border unilateral advance pricing agreements (APAs) and any other cross-border unilateral tax rulings (such as an advance tax ruling) covering transfer pricing or the application of transfer pricing principles	0	N/A
Cross-border rulings providing for a unilateral downward adjustment to the taxpayer's taxable profits that is not directly reflected in the taxpayer's financial / commercial accounts	0	N/A
Permanent establishment rulings	*De minimis* rule applies	N/A
Related party conduit rulings	0	N/A
De minimis rule	2	N/A
IP regimes: total exchanges on taxpayers benefitting from the third category of IP assets, new entrants benefitting from grandfathered IP regimes; and taxpayers making use of the option to treat the nexus ratio as a rebuttable presumption	N/A	N/A
Total	2	

D. Matters related to intellectual property regimes (ToR I.4.1.3)

Jersey does not offer an intellectual property regime for which transparency requirements under the Action 5 Report (OECD, 2015[5]) were imposed.

Summary of recommendations on implementation of the transparency framework

Aspect of implementation of the transparency framework that should be improved	Recommendation for improvement
	No recommendations are made.

Notes

[1] Parties to the Convention are available here: www.oecd.org/tax/exchange-of-tax-information/convention-on-mutual-administrative-assistance-in-tax-matters.htm. Jersey also has bilateral agreements with Cyprus, Estonia, Guernsey, Hong Kong (China), Isle of Man, Liechtenstein, Luxembourg, Malta, Mauritius, Qatar, Rwanda, Seychelles, Singapore, United Arab Emirates, United Kingdom and United States.

Note by Turkey: The information in this document with reference to "Cyprus" relates to the southern part of the Island. There is no single authority representing both Turkish and Greek Cypriot people on the Island. Turkey recognises the Turkish Republic of Northern Cyprus (TRNC). Until a lasting and equitable solution is found within the context of the United Nations, Turkey shall preserve its position concerning the "Cyprus issue".

Note by all the European Union Member States of the OECD and the European Union. The Republic of Cyprus is recognised by all members of the United Nations with the exception of Turkey. The information in this document relates to the area under the effective control of the Government of the Republic of Cyprus.

Jordan

Jordan has met all aspects of the terms of reference (OECD, 2017[3]) (ToR) for the calendar year 2018 (year in review) that can be met in the absence of rulings being issued.

In the prior year report, Jordan did not receive any recommendations.

Jordan does not issue any type of rulings within the scope of the transparency framework. Jordan issues "circulars" and "opinion statements" which give a general clarification with respect the interpretation and application of the tax legislation per specific taxpayer. Since these documents are very general and not legally binding on the tax administration, these tax opinions are not rulings as defined in the Action 5 report (OECD, 2015). During the year in review, Jordan clarified that theoretically, there is no legal impediment for Jordan to issue rulings, but in practice Jordan does not issue any rulings. In the event that Jordan put in place the administrative process to issue rulings, Jordan would be asked to implement the transparency framework obligations.

As no exchanges were required to take place, no peer input was received in respect of the exchanges of information on rulings received from Jordan.

Introduction

This peer review covers Jordan's implementation of the BEPS Action 5 transparency framework for the year 2018. The report has four parts, each relating to a key part of the ToR. Each part is discussed in turn. A summary of recommendations is included at the end of this report.

A. The information gathering process

As no rulings are issued, this section is not assessed.

B. The exchange of information

As no rulings are issued, this section is not assessed.

D. Statistics (ToR IV)

As no rulings are issued, no statistics can be reported.

E. Matters related to intellectual property regimes (ToR I.4.1.3)

Jordan offers two intellectual property regimes (IP regime)[1] that are not subject to the transparency requirements under the Action 5 Report (OECD, 2015[5]), because:

- ***New entrants benefitting from the grandfathered IP regime***: not applicable for the year in review, because the Development zone was reported in the year 2018 as potentially harmful (and in July 2019 reported as actually harmful) and the Aqaba special economic zone as under review. Jordan is expected to amend or abolish these regimes and has not taken a decision yet on whether it will provide grandfathering to existing taxpayers. Should Jordan provide grandfathering to taxpayers for IP income benefits and that entered the regimes after the relevant date from which enhanced transparency obligations apply, transparency requirements will apply and this will be taken into account during the subsequent peer review.
- ***Third category of IP assets***: not applicable to these regimes.
- ***Taxpayers making the use of the option to treat the nexus ratio as a rebuttable presumption***: not applicable to these regimes.

Summary of recommendations on implementation of the transparency framework

Aspect of implementation of the transparency framework that should be improved	Recommendation for improvement
	No recommendations are made.

Kazakhstan

Kazakhstan is taking steps to implement the legal basis for the transparency framework and to commence administrative preparations (in line with the terms of reference (OECD, 2017[3]) (ToR)) to ensure that it finalises its information gathering process (ToR I.4), information on rulings will be identified and exchanged in a timely manner (ToR II.5). Kazakhstan receives two recommendations on these points for the year in review.

This is Kazakhstan's first review of implementation of the transparency framework.

Kazakhstan can legally issue one type of ruling within the scope of the transparency framework. These rulings are not published.

In practice, Kazakhstan issued rulings within the scope of the transparency framework as follows:

- One past ruling;
- For the period 1 April 2016 - 31 December 2016: no future rulings;
- For the calendar year 2017: no future rulings, and
- For the year in review: no future rulings.

Kazakhstan publishes its tax rulings on a website.[2]

As no exchanges took place, no peer input was received in respect of the exchanges of information on rulings received from Kazakhstan.

Introduction

This peer review covers Kazakhstan's implementation of the BEPS Action 5 transparency framework for the year 2018. The report has four parts, each relating to a key part of the ToR. Each part is discussed in turn. A summary of recommendations is included at the end of this report.

A. The information gathering process

Kazakhstan can legally issue the following type of rulings within the scope of the transparency framework: cross-border unilateral APAs and any other cross-border unilateral tax rulings (such as an advance tax ruling) covering transfer pricing or the application of transfer pricing principles. The transfer pricing division within the state revenue committee is responsible for issuing rulings in Kazakhstan.

Past rulings (ToR I.4.1.1, I.4.1.2, I.4.2.1, I.4.2.2)

For Kazakhstan, past rulings are any tax rulings within scope that are issued either (i) on or after 1 January 2016 but before 1 April 2018; and (ii) on or after 1 January 2014 but before 1 January 2016, provided still in effect as at 1 January 2016.

One past ruling was issued. It is noted that the responsible team is currently elaborating guidelines and practices to collect and record the relevant information for the purposes of the transparency framework.

Future rulings (ToR I.4.1.1, I.4.1.2, I.4.2.1)

For Kazakhstan, future rulings are any tax rulings within scope that are issued on or after 1 April 2018.

Kazakhstan notes that that when requesting an APA, the taxpayer must identify all transactions that will be covered by the agreement and provide all necessary information about these related parties. However, it is not clear that information on the immediate parent and ultimate parent is collected. It is noted that guidelines and practices are being implemented to make sure that the relevant information is adequately processed for the purposes of the transparency framework.

Review and supervision (ToR I.4.3)

Kazakhstan is in the process of implementing a review and supervision mechanism. Once issued by the transfer pricing division, rulings should be reviewed by the non-residents taxation division, which will be responsible to collect the relevant information and to make sure that all relevant information is captured adequately and submitted to all relevant jurisdictions without delay.

Conclusion on section A

Kazakhstan is recommended to finalise its information gathering process for identifying all relevant past and future rulings and all potential exchange jurisdictions and to implement a review and supervision mechanism, as soon as possible (ToR I.4).

B. The exchange of information

Legal basis for spontaneous exchange of information (ToR II.5.1, II.5.2)

Kazakhstan does not have the necessary domestic legal basis to exchange information on rulings spontaneously. Kazakhstan is recommended to put in place a domestic legal framework allowing spontaneous exchange of information on rulings if needed (ToR II.5.1). It is noted that Kazakhstan expects to conclude its exchange of information regulation in 2019. This will be taken into account in the next year's peer review.

Kazakhstan has international agreements permitting spontaneous exchange of information, including being a party to the (i) *Multilateral Convention on Mutual Administrative Assistance in Tax Matters: Amended by the 2010 Protocol* (OECD/Council of Europe, 2011[4]) ("the Convention") and (ii) double tax agreements in force with 59 jurisdictions.[3]

Completion and exchange of templates (ToR II.5.3, II.5.4, II.5.5, II.5.6, II.5.7)

Kazakhstan is still developing a process to complete the templates on relevant rulings, to make them available to the Competent Authority for exchange of information, and to exchange them with relevant jurisdictions.

At this stage, timelines for the transmission of the template to the Competent Authority and for the completion of exchanges have not been established. Kazakhstan is planning to issue internal guidance on this. Kazakhstan intends to complete the templates in the form of Annex C of the BEPS Action 5 Final Report (OECD, 2015[5]) and to complete the summary section of the template in line with the internal FHTP suggested guidance.

As no exchanges of information on rulings took place during the year in review, there is no data to report on timeliness of exchanges.

Conclusion on section B

Kazakhstan is recommended to put in place a domestic legal framework allowing spontaneous exchange of information on rulings and to ensure the timely exchange of information on rulings in the form required by the transparency framework (ToR II.5).

C. Statistics (ToR IV)

As there was no information on rulings exchanged by Kazakhstan for the year in review, no statistics can be reported.

D. Matters related to intellectual property regimes (ToR I.4.1.3)

Kazakhstan does not offer an intellectual property regime for which transparency requirements under the Action 5 Report (OECD, 2015[5]) were imposed.

Summary of recommendations on implementation of the transparency framework

Aspect of implementation of the transparency framework that should be improved	Recommendation for improvement
Kazakhstan does not have information gathering process in place.	Kazakhstan is recommended to finalise its information gathering process for identifying all relevant past and future rulings and all potential exchange jurisdictions and to implement a review and supervision mechanism, as soon as possible.
Kazakhstan does not have a domestic legal framework allowing spontaneous exchange of information on rulings and has in place a process for completion of templates and exchange of information on rulings.	Kazakhstan is recommended to put in place a domestic legal framework allowing spontaneous exchange of information on rulings and to ensure the timely exchange of information on rulings in the form required by the transparency framework.

Notes

[1] These regimes are the Development zone and the Aqaba special economic zone.

[2] Available at: online.zakon.kz.

[3] Parties to the Convention are available here: www.oecd.org/tax/exchange-of-tax-information/convention-on-mutual-administrative-assistance-in-tax-matters.htm. Kazakhstan also has double tax agreements with Albania, Armenia, Austria, Azerbaijan, Belarus, Belgium, Bulgaria, Canada, China (People's Republic of), Croatia, Czech Republic, Denmark, Estonia, Finland, France, Georgia, Germany, Hungary, Iceland, India, Iran, Ireland, Italy, Japan, Korea, Kyrgyzstan, Latvia, Lithuania, Luxembourg, Malaysia, Moldova, Mongolia, Montenegro, Morocco, Netherlands, North Macedonia, Norway, Pakistan, Poland, Portugal, Qatar, Romania, Russian Federation, Saudi Arabia, Serbia, Singapore, Slovak Republic, Slovenia, Spain, Sweden, Switzerland, Tajikistan, Turkey, Turkmenistan, Ukraine, United Arab Emirates, United Kingdom, United States and Uzbekistan.

Kenya

Kenya has met all aspects of the terms of reference (ToR) for the calendar year 2018 (year in review) that can be met in the absence of rulings being issued.

This is Kenya's first review of implementation of the transparency framework.

Kenya can legally issue four types of rulings within the scope of the transparency framework. In practice, Kenya has issued no rulings within the scope of the transparency framework.

As no exchanges were required to take place, no peer input was received in respect of the exchanges of information on rulings received from Kenya.

Introduction

This peer review covers Kenya's implementation of the BEPS Action 5 transparency framework for the year 2018. The report has four parts, each relating to a key part of the ToR. Each part is discussed in turn. A summary of recommendations is included at the end of this report.

A. The information gathering process

Kenya can legally issue the following four types of rulings within the scope of the transparency framework: (i) preferential regimes[1]; (ii) rulings providing for unilateral downward adjustments; (iii) permanent establishment rulings; and (iv) related party conduit rulings.

Past rulings (ToR I.4.1.1, I.4.1.2, I.4.2.1, I.4.2.2)

For Kenya, past rulings are any tax rulings within scope that are issued either (i) on or after 1 January 2016 but before 1 April 2018; and (ii) on or after 1 January 2014 but before 1 January 2016, provided still in effect as at 1 January 2016.

In Kenya, rulings are issued by the centralised policy and tax advisory division. The International Tax Office policy unit (ITO) is then responsible for identifying the rulings in order to establish whether they are in scope of the transparency framework. The ITO has performed a manual review of individual files, which were referenced according to the topic and relevant section of the tax legislation (such as transfer pricing or permanent establishment), which facilitated this manual search. The ITO is currently in the process of developing an electronic register with specific files for each ruling issued.

All rulings are further organised according to date of issue. This allowed the ITO to identify whether a certain ruling would fall within the past or future rulings categories. To date no rulings have been issued. As such there was no need to identify potential exchange jurisdictions.

Future rulings (ToR I.4.1.1, I.4.1.2, I.4.2.1)

For Kenya, future rulings are any tax rulings within scope that are issued on or after 1 April 2018.

The process for identifying future rulings and potential exchange jurisdictions is similar to the process regarding the past rulings. The ITO is planning to introduce an electronic repository with search filters, which will help in increasing efficiency in terms of identifying relevant rulings. In order to identify potential exchange jurisdictions, Kenya would manually review the ruling and the taxpayer file, if necessary. Kenya confirms that if information on any potential exchange jurisdiction was not contained in the file, it would exercise its information gathering powers to require this information to be provided by the taxpayer.

Review and supervision (ToR I.4.3)

The review and supervision mechanism in Kenya is handled by an officer working on the specific file who then forwards it to the manager for review. The centralised policy and tax advisory department also reviews the rulings. There is continuous training of staff on the subject area, including a technical forum established by the Commissioner of domestic taxes to discuss ruling matters. In addition, a user manual is in the process of being developed and which would document the required steps for the transparency framework.

Conclusion on section A

Kenya has met all of the ToR for the information gathering process and no recommendations are made.

B. The exchange of information

Legal basis for spontaneous exchange of information (ToR II.5.1, II.5.2)

Kenya has the necessary domestic legal basis to exchange information spontaneously. Kenya notes that there are no legal or practical impediments that prevent the spontaneous exchange of information on rulings as contemplated in the Action 5 minimum standard.

Kenya (i) has signed the *Multilateral Convention on Mutual Administrative Assistance in Tax Matters: Amended by the 2010 Protocol* (OECD/Council of Europe, 2011[4]) (the "Convention") which is currently in undergoing internal process before being sent for ratification and (ii) has international agreements permitting spontaneous exchange of information, including double tax agreements in force with 15 jurisdictions.[2] Kenya is encouraged to continue its efforts to expand its international exchange of information instruments to be able to exchange rulings. It is however noted that jurisdictions are assessed on their compliance with the transparency framework in respect of the exchange of information network in effect for the year of the particular annual review.

Completion and exchange of templates (ToR II.5.3, II.5.4, II.5.5, II.5.6, II.5.7)

A ruling subject to exchange is identified by ITO from the list of rulings issued by the policy tax and advisory division. The ruling is then forwarded to the Competent Authority for onward exchange to the relevant jurisdiction. This process is envisaged to be completed within seven days after issue of the ruling. Kenya affirms it would complete the template (Annex C of the Action 5 Report (OECD, 2015[5])), with the summary section of the template completed in line with the internal FHTP suggested guidance. The competent authority function has been delegated to an officer within the Intelligence and Strategic Operation unit who ensures that there is no delay in exchanging the rulings, taking place no later than three months after receipt from the ITO.

As no rulings within the scope of the transparency framework have been issued in practice, Kenya was not required to complete any exchanges of information and there is no data to report on the timeliness of exchanges.

Conclusion on section B

Kenya has the necessary legal basis for spontaneous exchange of information, a process for completing the templates in a timely way. Kenya has met all of the ToR for the exchange of information process that can be met in the absence of rulings being issued and exchanged in practice and no recommendations are made.

C. Statistics (ToR IV)

As there was no information on rulings exchanged by Kenya for the year in review, no statistics can be reported.

D. Matters related to intellectual property regimes (ToR I.4.1.3)

Kenya does not offer an intellectual property regime for which transparency requirements under the Action 5 Report (OECD, 2015[5]) were imposed.

Summary of recommendations on implementation of the transparency framework

Aspect of implementation of the transparency framework that should be improved	Recommendation for improvement
	No recommendations are made.

Notes

[1] With respect to the following preferential regimes: 1) Export processing zone and 2) Special economic zone.

[2] Kenya has bilateral agreements with: Canada, Denmark, France, Germany, India, Iran, Korea, Norway, Qatar, Seychelles, South Africa, Sweden, United Arab Emirates, United Kingdom and Zambia.

Korea

Korea has met all aspects of the terms of reference (OECD, 2017[3]) (ToR) for the calendar year 2018 (year in review) and no recommendations are made.

In the prior year report, Korea did not receive any recommendations.

Korea can legally issue one type of rulings within the scope of the transparency framework. In practice, Korea issued rulings within the scope of the transparency framework as follows:

- 45 past rulings;
- For the period 1 April 2016 - 31 December 2016: one future ruling;
- For the calendar year 2017: four future rulings, and
- For the year in review: five future rulings.

Peer input was received from five jurisdictions in respect of the exchanges of information on rulings received from Korea. The input was generally positive, noting that information was complete, in a correct format and received in a timely manner. One peer noted that the information provided in the summary section was too brief. Korea is reviewing the particular case to consider whether further changes to its practice should be made.

Introduction

This peer review covers Korea's implementation of the BEPS Action 5 transparency framework for the year 2018. The report has four parts, each relating to a key part of the ToR. Each part is discussed in turn. A summary of recommendations is included at the end of this report.

A. The information gathering process

Korea can legally issue the following type of rulings within the scope of the transparency framework: cross-border unilateral APAs and any other cross-border unilateral tax rulings (such as an advance tax ruling) covering transfer pricing or the application of transfer pricing principles.

Past rulings (ToR I.4.1.1, I.4.1.2, I.4.2.1, I.4.2.2)

For Korea, past rulings are any tax rulings within scope that are issued either: (i) on or after 1 January 2014 but before 1 April 2016; or (ii) on or after 1 January 2010 but before 1 January 2014, provided they were still in effect as at 1 January 2014.

In the prior years' peer review reports, it was determined that Korea's undertakings to identify past rulings and all potential exchange jurisdictions have met all the ToR.

Future rulings (ToR I.4.1.1, I.4.1.2, I.4.2.1)

For Korea, future rulings are any tax rulings within scope that are issued on or after 1 April 2016.

In the prior years' peer review reports, it was determined that Korea's undertakings to identify future rulings and all potential exchange jurisdictions have met all the ToR.

Review and supervision (ToR I.4.3)

In the prior years' peer review reports, it was determined that Korea's review and supervision mechanism was sufficient to meet the minimum standard. Korea's implementation in this regard remains unchanged, and therefore continues to meet the minimum standard.

Conclusion on section A

Korea has met all of the ToR for the information gathering process and no recommendations are made.

B. The exchange of information

Legal basis for spontaneous exchange of information (ToR II.5.1, II.5.2)

As of 13 February 2018, Korea has the necessary domestic legal basis to exchange information spontaneously. Korea notes that there are no legal or practical impediments that prevent the spontaneous exchange of information on rulings as contemplated in the Action 5 minimum standard.

Korea has international agreements permitting spontaneous exchange of information, including being a party to the (i) *Multilateral Convention on Mutual Administrative Assistance in Tax Matters: Amended by the 2010 Protocol* (OECD/Council of Europe, 2011) ("the Convention") and (ii) double tax agreements in force with 93 jurisdictions.[1]

Completion and exchange of templates (ToR II.5.3, II.5.4, II.5.5, II.5.6, II.5.7)

In the prior year peer review report, it was determined that Korea's process for the completion and exchange of templates were sufficient to meet the minimum standard. Korea's implementation in this regard remains unchanged and therefore continues to meet the minimum standard.

The year in review was the first time exchanges were able to take place. The National Tax Service ("NTS") is still in contact with other jurisdictions in order to test the exchange through the OECD Common Transition System. Until that is confirmed, information on rulings is exchanged in the form of Annex C of the 2015 Action 5 Report (OECD, 2015[5]) and sent via electronic and postal mail.

For the year in review, the timeliness of exchanges is as follows:

Past rulings in the scope of the transparency framework	Number of exchanges transmitted by 31 December 2018	Delayed exchanges		
		Number of exchanges not transmitted by 31 December 2018	Reasons for the delays	Any other comments
	135	0	No domestic basis in previous years for the exchange of information.	As of 13 February 2018, the domestic basis for the exchange of information is in place and Korea exchanged the information within two months after this.
Future rulings in the scope of the transparency framework	Number of exchanges transmitted within three months of the information becoming available to the competent authority or immediately after legal impediments have been lifted	Delayed exchanges		
		Number of exchanges transmitted later than three months of the information on rulings becoming available to the competent authority	Reasons for the delays	Any other comments
	45	0	N/A	N/A
Total	180	0		

Follow up requests received for exchange of the ruling	Number	Average time to provide response	Number of requests not answered
	0	N/A	N/A

Conclusion on section B

Korea has the necessary legal basis for spontaneous exchange of information, a process for completing the templates in a timely way and has completed all exchanges. Korea has met all of the ToR for the exchange of information process and no recommendations are made.

C. Statistics (ToR IV)

The statistics for the year in review are as follows:

Category of ruling	Number of exchanges	Jurisdictions exchanged with
Ruling related to a preferential regime	N/A	N/A
Cross-border unilateral advance pricing	180	Argentina, Australia, Belgium, Brazil,

agreements (APAs) and any other cross-border unilateral tax rulings (such as an advance tax ruling) covering transfer pricing or the application of transfer pricing principles		Canada, China (People's Republic of), Czech Republic, Denmark, France, Germany, Hong Kong (China), India, Indonesia, Ireland, Italy, Japan, Luxembourg, Malaysia, Mauritius, Mexico, Netherlands, New Zealand, Philippines, Saudi Arabia, Singapore, Spain, Sweden, Switzerland, Thailand, Turkey, United Kingdom, United States, Viet Nam
Cross-border rulings providing for a unilateral downward adjustment to the taxpayer's taxable profits that is not directly reflected in the taxpayer's financial / commercial accounts	N/A	N/A
Permanent establishment rulings	N/A	N/A
Related party conduit rulings	N/A	N/A
De minimis rule	N/A	N/A
IP regimes: total exchanges on taxpayers benefitting from the third category of IP assets, new entrants benefitting from grandfathered IP regimes; and taxpayers making use of the option to treat the nexus ratio as a rebuttable presumption	0	N/A
Total	180	

D. Matters related to intellectual property regimes (ToR I.4.1.3)

Korea offers an intellectual property regime (IP regime)[2] that is subject to the transparency requirements under the Action 5 Report (OECD, 2015[5]). It states that the identification of the benefitting taxpayers will occur as follows:

- ***New entrants benefitting from the grandfathered IP regime***: as this is a new IP regime rather than a grandfathered IP regime, transparency on new entrants is not relevant.
- ***Third category of IP assets***: the regime provides benefits to the third category of IP assets. The process on the collection of information is described in the previous year peer review report and meets the ToR. In practice, no taxpayers have applied for the corporate income tax benefits for the third category of IP assets, and as such no exchanges were required to take place.
- ***Taxpayers making use of the option to treat the nexus ratio as a rebuttable presumption***: not applicable as the regime does not allow the nexus ratio to be treated as a rebuttable presumption.

Summary of recommendations on implementation of the transparency framework

Aspect of implementation of the transparency framework that should be improved	Recommendation for improvement
	No recommendations are made.

Notes

[1] Parties to the Convention are available here: http://www.oecd.org/tax/exchange-of-tax-information/convention-on-mutual-administrative-assistance-in-tax-matters.htm. Korea also has double tax agreements with Albania, Algeria, Australia, Austria, Azerbaijan, Bahrain, Bangladesh, Belarus, Belgium, Brazil, Brunei Darussalam, Bulgaria, Canada, Chile, China (People's Republic of), Colombia, Croatia, Czech Republic, Denmark, Ecuador, Egypt, Estonia, Ethiopia, Fiji, Finland, France, Gabon, Georgia, Germany, Greece, Hong Kong (China), Hungary, Iceland, India, Indonesia, Iran, Ireland, Israel, Italy, Japan, Jordan, Kazakhstan, Kenya, Kuwait, Kyrgyzstan, Laos, Latvia, Lithuania, Luxembourg, Malaysia, Malta, Mexico, Mongolia, Morocco, Myanmar, Nepal, Netherlands, New Zealand, Norway, Oman, Pakistan, Panama, Papua New Guinea, Peru, Philippines, Poland, Portugal, Qatar, Romania, Russia, Saudi Arabia, Serbia, Singapore, Slovak Republic, Slovenia, South Africa, Spain, Sri Lanka, Sweden, Switzerland, Tajikistan, Thailand, Tunisia, Turkey, Turkmenistan, Ukraine, United Arab Emirates, United Kingdom, United States, Uruguay, Uzbekistan, Venezuela and Viet Nam.

[2] Special taxation for transfer, acquisition, etc. of technology.

Latvia

Latvia has met all aspects of the terms of reference (OECD, 2017[3]) (ToR) for the calendar year 2018 (year in review) and no recommendations are made.

In the prior year report, Latvia received two recommendations. These recommendations have been addressed and are removed.

Latvia can legally issue three types of rulings within the scope of the transparency framework. In practice, Latvia issued rulings within the scope of the transparency framework as follows:

- One past ruling;
- For the period 1 April 2016 - 31 December 2016: one future ruling;
- For the calendar year 2017: two future rulings, and
- For the year in review: three future rulings.

Summaries of rulings are published in an anonymised way.[1]

No peer input was received in respect of the exchanges of information on rulings received from Latvia.

Introduction

This peer review covers Latvia's implementation of the BEPS Action 5 transparency framework for the year 2018. The report has four parts, each relating to a key part of the ToR. Each part is discussed in turn. A summary of recommendations is included at the end of this report.

A. The information gathering process

Latvia can legally issue the following three types of rulings within the scope of the transparency framework: (i) preferential regimes;[2] (ii) cross-border unilateral APAs and any other cross-border unilateral tax rulings (such as an advance tax ruling) covering transfer pricing or the application of transfer pricing principles; and (iii) permanent establishment rulings.

Past rulings (ToR I.4.1.1, I.4.1.2, I.4.2.1, I.4.2.2)

For Latvia, past rulings are any tax rulings within scope that are issued either: (i) on or after 1 January 2014 but before 1 April 2016; or (ii) on or after 1 January 2010 but before 1 January 2014, provided they were still in effect as at 1 January 2014.

In the prior year peer review report, it was determined that Latvia's undertakings to identify past rulings and all potential exchange jurisdictions have met all the ToR. Latvia's implementation in this regard remains unchanged, and therefore continues to meet the minimum standard.

Future rulings (ToR I.4.1.1, I.4.1.2, I.4.2.1)

For Latvia, future rulings are any tax rulings within scope that are issued on or after 1 April 2016.

In the prior year peer review report, it was determined that Latvia's undertakings to identify future rulings and all potential exchange jurisdictions have met all the ToR. Latvia's implementation in this regard remains unchanged, and therefore continues to meet the minimum standard.

Review and supervision (ToR I.4.3)

In the prior year peer review report, it was determined that Latvia's review and supervision mechanism was sufficient to meet the minimum standard. Latvia's implementation in this regard remains unchanged, and therefore continues to meet the minimum standard.

Conclusion on section A

Latvia has met all of the ToR for the information gathering process and no recommendations are made.

B. The exchange of information

Legal basis for spontaneous exchange of information (ToR II.5.1, II.5.2)

Latvia has the necessary domestic legal basis to exchange information spontaneously. Latvia notes that there are no legal or practical impediments that prevent the spontaneous exchange of information on rulings as contemplated in the Action 5 minimum standard.

Latvia has international agreements permitting spontaneous exchange of information, including being a party to the (i) *Multilateral Convention on Mutual Administrative Assistance in Tax Matters: Amended by the 2010 Protocol* (OECD/Council of Europe, 2011[4]) ("the Convention"), (ii) the Directive 2011/16/EU with all other European Union Member States and (iii) double tax agreements in force with 62 jurisdictions.[3]

Completion and exchange of templates (ToR II.5.3, II.5.4, II.5.5, II.5.6, II.5.7)

In the prior year peer review report, it was determined that Latvia's process for the completion and exchange of temples met all the ToR, except for having in place the necessary regulatory framework to exchange information on rulings with jurisdictions other than EU Member States (ToR II.5.1) and the timelines by which information on rulings is provided to the Competent Authority for exchange of information (ToR II.5.5). Therefore, Latvia was recommended to finalise the amendments to their regulatory framework to allow exchange of information on rulings with non-EU Member States under the transparency framework as soon as possible and to reduce the timelines for providing the information to the Competent Authority.

During the year in review, Latvia finalised the amendments to the regulatory framework. The amended internal regulations stipulate that in respect of all rulings, regardless of the recipient jurisdiction, information will be sent within three months after the date on which the ruling was issued. Therefore, both of the prior year recommendations can be removed.

For the year in review, the timeliness of exchanges is as follows:

Past rulings in the scope of the transparency framework	Number of exchanges transmitted by 31 December 2018	Delayed exchanges		
		Number of exchanges not transmitted by 31 December 2018	Reasons for the delays	Any other comments
	0	0	N/A	No additional exchanges on past rulings were required, as notwithstanding the legal impediment noted above, in practice all past rulings were relevant for exchange with EU Member States.
Future rulings in the scope of the transparency framework	Number of exchanges transmitted within three months of the information becoming available to the competent authority or immediately after legal impediments have been lifted	Delayed exchanges		
		Number of exchanges transmitted later than three months of the information on rulings becoming available to the competent authority	Reasons for the delays	Any other comments
	3	0	N/A	N/A
Total	3	0		

Follow up requests received for exchange of the ruling	Number	Average time to provide response	Number of requests not answered
	0	N/A	N/A

Conclusion on section B

Latvia has the necessary legal basis for spontaneous exchange of information, a process for completing the templates in a timely way and has completed all exchanges. Latvia has met all of the ToR for the exchange of information process and no recommendations are made.

C. Statistics (ToR IV)

The statistics for the year in review are as follows:

Category of ruling	Number of exchanges	Jurisdictions exchanged with
Ruling related to a preferential regime	0	N/A
Cross-border unilateral advance pricing agreements (APAs) and any other cross-border unilateral tax rulings (such as an advance tax ruling) covering transfer pricing or the application of transfer pricing principles	*De minimis* rule applies	N/A
Cross-border rulings providing for a unilateral downward adjustment to the taxpayer's taxable profits that is not directly reflected in the taxpayer's financial / commercial accounts	N/A	N/A
Permanent establishment rulings	0	N/A
Related party conduit rulings	N/A	N/A
De minimis rule	3	N/A
IP regimes: total exchanges on taxpayers benefitting from the third category of IP assets, new entrants benefitting from grandfathered IP regimes; and taxpayers making use of the option to treat the nexus ratio as a rebuttable presumption	N/A	N/A
Total	3	

D. Matters related to intellectual property regimes (ToR I.4.1.3)

Latvia does not offer an intellectual property regime for which transparency requirements under the Action 5 Report (OECD, 2015[5]) were imposed.

Summary of recommendations on implementation of the transparency framework

Aspect of implementation of the transparency framework that should be improved	Recommendation for improvement
	No recommendations are made.

Notes

[1] Available at: www.vid.gov.lv.

[2] With respect to the following preferential regimes: 1) Shipping tax regime and 2) Special economic zones.

[3] Parties to the Convention are available here: www.oecd.org/tax/exchange-of-tax-information/convention-on-mutual-administrative-assistance-in-tax-matters.htm. Latvia also has bilateral agreements with Albania, Armenia, Austria, Azerbaijan, Belarus, Belgium, Bulgaria, Canada, China (People's Republic of), Croatia, Cyprus, Czech Republic, Denmark, Estonia, Finland, France, Georgia, Germany, Greece, Hong Kong (China), Hungary, Iceland, India, Ireland, Israel, Italy, Japan, Kazakhstan, Korea, Kuwait, Kyrgyzstan, Lithuania, Luxembourg, Malta, Mexico, Moldova, Morocco, Netherlands, North Macedonia, Norway, Poland, Portugal, Qatar, Romania, Russia, Montenegro, Serbia, Singapore, Slovenia, Slovak Republic, Spain, Sweden, Switzerland, Tajikistan, Turkey, Turkmenistan, Ukraine, United Arab Emirates, United Kingdom, United States, Uzbekistan and Viet Nam.

Note by Turkey: The information in this document with reference to "Cyprus" relates to the southern part of the Island. There is no single authority representing both Turkish and Greek Cypriot people on the Island. Turkey recognises the Turkish Republic of Northern Cyprus (TRNC). Until a lasting and equitable solution is found within the context of the United Nations, Turkey shall preserve its position concerning the "Cyprus issue".

Note by all the European Union Member States of the OECD and the European Union. The Republic of Cyprus is recognised by all members of the United Nations with the exception of Turkey. The information in this document relates to the area under the effective control of the Government of the Republic of Cyprus.

Liberia

Liberia has met all aspects of the terms of reference (OECD, 2017[3]) (ToR) for the calendar year 2018 (year in review) that can be met in the absence of rulings being issued.

In the prior year report, Liberia did not receive any recommendations.

Liberia does not issue any type of ruling within the scope of the transparency framework. Theoretically, there is no impediment for Liberia to issue rulings, but in practice Liberia does not issue any rulings. As Liberia has adopted transfer pricing legislation in November 2016, it is now contemplating on implementing an APA framework. In the event that Liberia put in place the administrative process or develop the administrative capacity to issue rulings, Liberia notes that it would implement the transparency framework obligations.

As no exchanges were required to take place, no peer input was received in respect of the exchanges of information on rulings received from Liberia.

Introduction

This peer review covers Liberia's implementation of the BEPS Action 5 transparency framework for the year 2018. The report has four parts, each relating to a key part of the ToR. Each part is discussed in turn. A summary of recommendations is included at the end of this report.

A. The information gathering process

As no rulings are issued, this section is not assessed.

B. The exchange of information

As no rulings are issued, this section is not assessed.

C. Statistics (ToR IV)

As no rulings are issued, no statistics can be reported.

D. Matters related to intellectual property regimes (ToR I.4.1.3)

Liberia does not offer an intellectual property regime for which transparency requirements under the Action 5 Report (OECD, 2015[5]) were imposed.

Summary of recommendations on implementation of the transparency framework

Aspect of implementation of the transparency framework that should be improved	Recommendation for improvement
	No recommendations are made.

Liechtenstein

Liechtenstein has met all aspects of the terms of reference (OECD, 2017[3]) (ToR) for the calendar year 2018 (year in review) and no recommendations are made.

In the prior year report, Liechtenstein did not receive any recommendations.

Liechtenstein can legally issue four types of rulings within the scope of the transparency framework. In practice, Liechtenstein issued rulings within the scope of the transparency framework as follows:

- 18 past rulings;[1]
- For the period 1 April 2017 - 31 December 2017: six future rulings;
- For the year in review: five future rulings.

Peer input was received from two jurisdictions in respect of the exchanges of information on rulings received from Liechtenstein. The input was positive, noting that information was complete, in a correct format and received in a timely manner.

Introduction

This peer review covers Liechtenstein's implementation of the BEPS Action 5 transparency framework for the year 2018. The report has four parts, each relating to a key part of the ToR. Each part is discussed in turn. A summary of recommendations is included at the end of this report.

A. The information gathering process

Liechtenstein can legally issue the following four types of rulings within the scope of the transparency framework: (i) cross-border unilateral APAs and any other cross-border unilateral tax rulings (such as an advance tax ruling) covering transfer pricing or the application of transfer pricing principles; (ii) rulings providing for unilateral downward adjustments; (iii) permanent establishment rulings; and (iv) related party conduit rulings.

Past rulings (ToR I.4.1.1, I.4.1.2, I.4.2.1, I.4.2.2)

For Liechtenstein, past rulings are any tax rulings within scope that are issued either (i) on or after 1 January 2015 but before 1 April 2017; and (ii) on or after 1 January 2012 but before 1 January 2015, provided they were still in effect as at 1 January 2017.

In the prior year peer review report, it was determined that Liechtenstein's undertakings to identify past rulings and all potential exchange jurisdictions were sufficient to meet the minimum standard. Liechtenstein's implementation in this regard remains unchanged, and therefore continues to meet the minimum standard.

Future rulings (ToR I.4.1.1, I.4.1.2, I.4.2.1)

For Liechtenstein, future rulings are any tax rulings within scope that are issued on or after 1 April 2017.

In the prior year peer review report, it was determined that Liechtenstein's undertakings to identify future rulings and all potential exchange jurisdictions were sufficient to meet the minimum standard. Liechtenstein's implementation in this regard remains unchanged, and therefore continues to meet the minimum standard.

Review and supervision (ToR I.4.3)

In the prior year peer review report, it was determined that Liechtenstein's review and supervision mechanism was sufficient to meet the minimum standard. Liechtenstein's implementation in this regard remains unchanged, and therefore continues to meet the minimum standard.

Conclusion on section A

Liechtenstein has met all of the ToR for the information gathering process and no recommendations are made.

B. The exchange of information

Legal basis for spontaneous exchange of information (ToR II.5.1, II.5.2)

Liechtenstein has introduced the necessary domestic legal basis to exchange information spontaneously with effect of 1 January 2018 (Law on International Administrative Assistance in Tax Matters, LIAATM) that allows to exchange information on rulings issued as of 1 January 2012, provided they were still in effect on 1 January 2017. Liechtenstein notes that apart from this restriction on exchanging information on certain past rulings there are no legal or practical impediments that prevent the spontaneous exchange of information on rulings as contemplated in the Action 5 minimum standard.

Liechtenstein has international agreements permitting spontaneous exchange of information, including being a party to the (i) *Multilateral Convention on Mutual Administrative Assistance in Tax Matters: Amended by the 2010 Protocol* (OECD/Council of Europe, 2011[4]) ("the Convention"), and (ii) double tax agreements in force with fourteen jurisdictions.[2]

Completion and exchange of templates (ToR II.5.3, II.5.4, II.5.5, II.5.6, II.5.7)

In the prior year peer review report, it was determined that Liechtenstein's process for the completion and exchange of templates was sufficient to meet the minimum standard. Liechtenstein's implementation in this regard remains unchanged and therefore continues to meet the minimum standard.

The year in review was the first time exchanges were able to take place. For the year in review, the timeliness of exchanges is as follows:

Past rulings in the scope of the transparency framework	Number of exchanges transmitted by 31 December 2018	Delayed exchanges		
		Number of exchanges not transmitted by 31 December 2018	Reasons for the delays	Any other comments
	18	0	N/A	Information on past rulings has been exchanged within three months after the legal basis came into force.
Future rulings in the scope of the transparency framework	Number of exchanges transmitted within three months of the information becoming available to the competent authority or immediately after legal impediments have been lifted	Delayed exchanges		
		Number of exchanges transmitted later than three months of the information on rulings becoming available to the competent authority	Reasons for the delays	Any other comments
	11	0	N/A	N/A
Total	29	0		

Follow up requests received for exchange of the ruling	Number	Average time to provide response	Number of requests not answered
	0	N/A	N/A

Conclusion on section B

Liechtenstein has the necessary legal basis for spontaneous exchange of information, a process for completing the templates in a timely way and has completed all exchanges. Liechtenstein has met all of the ToR for the exchange of information process and no recommendations are made.

C. Statistics (ToR IV)

The statistics for the year in review are as follows:

Category of ruling	Number of exchanges	Jurisdictions exchanged with
Ruling related to a preferential regime	2	*De minimis* rule applies
Cross-border unilateral advance pricing agreements (APAs) and any other cross-border unilateral tax rulings (such as an advance tax ruling) covering transfer pricing or the application of transfer pricing principles	12	Curaçao, Israel, Switzerland, United Kingdom
Cross-border rulings providing for a unilateral downward adjustment to the taxpayer's taxable profits that is not directly reflected in the taxpayer's financial / commercial accounts	2	*De minimis* rule applies
Permanent establishment rulings	17	Austria, Germany, Israel, Luxembourg, Switzerland, United Kingdom
Related party conduit rulings	N/A	N/A
De minimis rule	N/A	N/A
IP regimes: total exchanges on taxpayers benefitting from the third category of IP assets, new entrants benefitting from grandfathered IP regimes; and taxpayers making use of the option to treat the nexus ratio as a rebuttable presumption	0	N/A
Total	33[3]	

D. Matters related to intellectual property regimes (ToR I.4.1.3)

Liechtenstein does not offer an intellectual property regime for which transparency requirements under the Action 5 Report (OECD, 2015[5]) were imposed.

Summary of recommendations on implementation of the transparency framework

Aspect of implementation of the transparency framework that should be improved	**Recommendation for improvement**
	No recommendations are made.

Notes

[1] Including four that fell into more than one category under the BEPS Action 5 report.

[2] Parties to the Convention are available here: www.oecd.org/tax/exchange-of-tax-information/convention-on-mutual-administrative-assistance-in-tax-matters.htm. Liechtenstein also has bilateral agreements with Andorra, Austria, Czech Republic, Germany, Hungary, Iceland, Jersey, Lithuania, Luxembourg, Monaco, San Marino, Singapore, United Arab Emirates, and United Kingdom.

[3] Including four that fell into more than one category under the BEPS Action 5 report.

Lithuania

Lithuania has met all aspects of the terms of reference (OECD, 2017[3]) (ToR) for the calendar year 2018 (year in review) and no recommendations are made.

In the prior year report, Lithuania did not receive any recommendations.

Lithuania can legally issue five types of rulings within the scope of the transparency framework. In practice, Lithuania issued rulings within the scope of the transparency framework as follows:

- Five past rulings;
- For the calendar year 2017: six future rulings, and
- For the year in review: five future rulings.

No peer input was received in respect of the exchanges of information on rulings received from Lithuania.

Introduction

This peer review covers Lithuania's implementation of the BEPS Action 5 transparency framework for the year 2018. The report has four parts, each relating to a key part of the ToR. Each part is discussed in turn. A summary of recommendations is included at the end of this report.

A. The information gathering process

Lithuania can legally issue the following five types of rulings within the scope of the transparency framework: (i) preferential regimes;[1] (ii) cross-border unilateral APAs and any other cross-border unilateral tax rulings (such as an advance tax ruling) covering transfer pricing or the application of transfer pricing principles; (iii) rulings providing for unilateral downward adjustments, (iv) permanent establishment rulings; and (v) related party conduit rulings. In the prior year peer review report, it was not noted that Lithuania can legally issue related party conduit rulings. However, Lithuania notes that after an internal review it was concluded that there is no legal impediment to issue all five types of rulings in scope of the Action 5 transparency framework. It should be noted that in the prior year, Lithuania did not issue any related party conduit rulings.

Past rulings (ToR I.4.1.1, I.4.1.2, I.4.2.1, I.4.2.2)

For Lithuania, past rulings are any tax rulings within scope that are issued either (i) on or after 1 January 2015 but before 1 April 2017; and (ii) on or after 1 January 2012 but before 1 January 2015, provided they were still in effect as at 1 January 2015.

In the prior year peer review report, it was determined that Lithuania's undertakings to identify past rulings and all potential exchange jurisdictions were sufficient to meet the minimum standard. Lithuania's implementation in this regard remains unchanged, and therefore continues to meet the minimum standard.

Future rulings (ToR I.4.1.1, I.4.1.2, I.4.2.1)

For Lithuania, future rulings are any tax rulings within scope that are issued on or after 1 April 2017.

In the prior year peer review report, it was determined that Lithuania's undertakings to identify future rulings and all potential exchange jurisdictions was sufficient to meet the minimum standard. Lithuania's implementation in this regard remains unchanged, and therefore continues to meet the minimum standard.

Review and supervision (ToR I.4.3)

In the prior year peer review report, it was determined that Lithuania's review and supervision mechanism was sufficient to meet the minimum standard. Lithuania's implementation in this regard remains unchanged, and therefore continues to meet the minimum standard.

Conclusion on section A

Lithuania has met all of the ToR for the information gathering process and no recommendations are made.

B. The exchange of information

Legal basis for spontaneous exchange of information (ToR II.5.1, II.5.2)

Lithuania has the necessary domestic legal basis to exchange information spontaneously. Lithuania notes that there are no legal or practical impediments that prevent the spontaneous exchange of information on rulings as contemplated in the Action 5 minimum standard.

Lithuania has international agreements permitting spontaneous exchange of information, including being a party to (i) the *Multilateral Convention on Mutual Administrative Assistance in Tax Matters: Amended by the 2010 Protocol* (OECD/Council of Europe, 2011) ("the Convention"), (ii) the Directive 2011/16/EU with all other European Union Member States and (iii) double tax agreements in force with 55 jurisdictions.[2]

Completion and exchange of templates (ToR II.5.3, II.5.4, II.5.5, II.5.6, II.5.7)

In the prior year peer review report, it was determined that Lithuania's process for the completion and exchange of templates were sufficient to meet the minimum standard. Lithuania's implementation in this regard remains unchanged and therefore continues to meet the minimum standard.

For the year in review, the timeliness of exchanges is as follows:

Past rulings in the scope of the transparency framework	Number of exchanges transmitted by 31 December 2018	Delayed exchanges		
		Number of exchanges not transmitted by 31 December 2018	Reasons for the delays	Any other comments
	0	0	N/A	N/A
Future rulings in the scope of the transparency framework	Number of exchanges transmitted within three months of the information becoming available to the competent authority or immediately after legal impediments have been lifted	Delayed exchanges		
		Number of exchanges transmitted later than three months of the information on rulings becoming available to the competent authority	Reasons for the delays	Any other comments
	5	0	N/A	N/A
Total	5	0		

Follow up requests received for exchange of the ruling	Number	Average time to provide response	Number of requests not answered
	0	N/A	N/A

Conclusion on section B

Lithuania has the necessary legal basis for spontaneous exchange of information, a process for completing the templates in a timely way and has completed all exchanges. Lithuania has met all of the ToR for the exchange of information process and no recommendations are made.

C. Statistics (ToR IV)

The statistics for the year in review are as follows:

Category of ruling	Number of exchanges	Jurisdictions exchanged with
Ruling related to a preferential regime	0	N/A
Cross-border unilateral advance pricing	*De minimis* rule applies	N/A

agreements (APAs) and any other cross-border unilateral tax rulings (such as an advance tax ruling) covering transfer pricing or the application of transfer pricing principles		
Cross-border rulings providing for a unilateral downward adjustment to the taxpayer's taxable profits that is not directly reflected in the taxpayer's financial / commercial accounts	0	N/A
Permanent establishment rulings	0	N/A
Related party conduit rulings	*De minimis* rule applies	N/A
De minimis rule	5	N/A
IP regimes: total exchanges on taxpayers benefitting from the third category of IP assets, new entrants benefitting from grandfathered IP regimes; and taxpayers making use of the option to treat the nexus ratio as a rebuttable presumption	0	N/A
Total	5	

D. Matters related to intellectual property regimes (ToR I.4.1.3)

Lithuania offers an intellectual property regime (IP regime) which came into effect from 1 January 2018. It is noted that this regime is not subject to transparency requirements under the Action 5 report (OECD, 2015[5]), because:

- ***New entrants benefitting from the grandfathered IP regime***: as this is a new IP regime rather than a grandfathered IP regime, transparency on new entrants was not relevant.
- ***Third category of IP assets***: not applicable as the regime does not allow the third category of IP assets to qualify for the benefits.
- ***Taxpayers making use of the option to treat the nexus ratio as a rebuttable presumption***: not applicable as the regime does not allow the nexus ratio to be treated as a rebuttable presumption.

Summary of recommendations on implementation of the transparency framework

Aspect of implementation of the transparency framework that should be improved	Recommendation for improvement
	No recommendations are made.

Notes

[1] With respect to the following preferential regimes: 1) Free economic zone taxation regime, 2) Tonnage tax regime and 3) IP regime.

[2] Parties to the Convention are available here: http://www.oecd.org/tax/exchange-of-tax-information/convention-on-mutual-administrative-assistance-in-tax-matters.htm. Lithuania also has bilateral agreements with Armenia, Austria, Azerbaijan, Belarus, Belgium, Bulgaria, Canada, China (People's Republic of), Croatia, Czech Republic, Cyprus, Denmark, Estonia, Finland, France, Georgia, Germany, Greece, Hungary, Iceland, India, Ireland, Israel, Italy, Japan, Kazakhstan, Korea, Kuwait, Kyrgyzstan, Latvia, Luxembourg, Malta, Mexico, Moldova, Netherlands, North Macedonia, Norway, Poland, Portugal, Romania, Russia, Serbia, Singapore, Slovak Republic, Slovenia, Spain, Sweden, Switzerland, Turkey, Turkmenistan, Ukraine, United Arab Emirates, United Kingdom, United States and Uzbekistan.

Note by Turkey: The information in this document with reference to "Cyprus" relates to the southern part of the Island. There is no single authority representing both Turkish and Greek Cypriot people on the Island. Turkey recognises the Turkish Republic of Northern Cyprus (TRNC). Until a lasting and equitable solution is found within the context of the United Nations, Turkey shall preserve its position concerning the "Cyprus issue".

Note by all the European Union Member States of the OECD and the European Union. The Republic of Cyprus is recognised by all members of the United Nations with the exception of Turkey. The information in this document relates to the area under the effective control of the Government of the Republic of Cyprus.

Luxembourg

Luxembourg has met all aspects of the terms of reference (OECD, 2017[3]) (ToR) for the calendar year 2018 (year in review) and no recommendations are made.

In the prior year report, Luxembourg did not receive any recommendations.

Luxembourg can legally issue four types of rulings within the scope of the transparency framework. In practice, Luxembourg issued rulings within the scope of the transparency framework as follows:

- 1 922 past rulings;
- For the period 1 April 2016 - 31 December 2016: 73 future rulings;
- For the calendar year 2017: 18 future rulings, and
- For the year in review: nine future rulings.[1]

Peer input was received from five jurisdictions in respect of the exchanges of information on rulings received from Luxembourg. The input was generally positive, noting that information was complete, in a correct format and received in a timely manner. One peer suggested to include more details in the template. Luxembourg has reviewed the particular case and has committed to make additional efforts to further improve the information in the template by including more details in the short summary of the issue covered by the ruling.

Introduction

This peer review covers Luxembourg's implementation of the BEPS Action 5 transparency framework for the year 2018. The report has four parts, each relating to a key part of the ToR. Each part is discussed in turn. A summary of recommendations is included at the end of this report.

A. The information gathering process

Luxembourg can legally issue the following four types of rulings within the scope of the transparency framework: (i) preferential regimes;[2] (ii) cross-border unilateral APAs and any other cross-border unilateral tax rulings (such as an advance tax ruling) covering transfer pricing or the application of transfer pricing principles; (iii) rulings providing for unilateral downward adjustments; and (iv) permanent establishment rulings. To the extent that related party conduit rulings are provided, they are already covered under the second category.

Past rulings (ToR I.4.1.1, I.4.1.2, I.4.2.1, I.4.2.2)

For Luxembourg, past rulings are any tax rulings within the scope that are issued either: (i) on or after 1 January 2014 but before 1 April 2016; or (ii) on or after 1 January 2010 but before 1 January 2014, provided they were still in effect as at 1 January 2014.

In the prior year peer review report, it was determined that Luxembourg's undertakings to identify past rulings and all potential exchange jurisdictions were sufficient to meet the minimum standard. Luxembourg's implementation in this regard remains unchanged, and therefore continues to meet the minimum standard.

Future rulings (ToR I.4.1.1, I.4.1.2, I.4.2.1)

For Luxembourg, future rulings are any tax rulings within scope that are issued on or after 1 April 2016.

In the prior years' peer review reports, it was determined that Luxembourg's implementation of a new system to identify future rulings and all potential exchange jurisdictions was sufficient to meet the minimum standard. Luxembourg's implementation in this regard remains unchanged, and therefore continues to meet the minimum standard.

Review and supervision (ToR I.4.3)

In the prior years' peer review reports, it was determined that Luxembourg's review and supervision mechanism was sufficient to meet the minimum standard. Luxembourg's implementation in this regard remains unchanged, and therefore continues to meet the minimum standard.

Conclusion on section A

Luxembourg has met all of the ToR for the information gathering process and no recommendations are made.

B. The exchange of information

Legal basis for spontaneous exchange of information (ToR II.5.1, II.5.2)

Luxembourg has the necessary domestic legal basis to exchange information spontaneously. Luxembourg notes that there are no legal or practical impediments that prevent the spontaneous exchange of information on rulings as contemplated in the Action 5 minimum standard.

Luxembourg has international agreements permitting spontaneous exchange of information, including being a party to the (i) *Multilateral Convention on Mutual Administrative Assistance in Tax Matters: Amended by the 2010 Protocol* (OECD/Council of Europe, 2011[4]) ("the Convention"), (ii) the Directive 2011/16/EU with all other European Union Member States and (iii) double tax agreements in force with 79 jurisdictions.[3]

Completion and exchange of templates (ToR II.5.3, II.5.4, II.5.5, II.5.6, II.5.7)

In the prior year peer review report, it was determined that Luxembourg's process for the completion and exchange of templates were sufficient to meet the minimum standard. Luxembourg's implementation in this regard remains unchanged and therefore continues to meet the minimum standard.

For the year in review, the timeliness of exchanges is as follows:

Past rulings in the scope of the transparency framework	Number of exchanges transmitted by 31 December 2018	Delayed exchanges		
		Number of exchanges not transmitted by 31 December 2018	Reasons for the delays	Any other comments
	0	0	N/A	N/A
Future rulings in the scope of the transparency framework	Number of exchanges transmitted within three months of the information becoming available to the competent authority or immediately after legal impediments have been lifted	Delayed exchanges		
		Number of exchanges transmitted later than three months of the information on rulings becoming available to the competent authority	Reasons for the delays	Any other comments
	17	0	N/A	N/A
Total	17[4]	0		

Follow up requests received for exchange of the ruling	Number	Average time to provide response	Number of requests not answered
	59	Six weeks	0

Conclusion on section B

Luxembourg has the necessary legal basis for spontaneous exchange of information, a process for completing the templates in a timely way and has completed all exchanges. Luxembourg has met all of the ToR for the exchange of information process and no recommendations are made.

C. Statistics (ToR IV)

The statistics for the year in review are as follows:

Category of ruling	Number of exchanges	Jurisdictions exchanged with
Ruling related to a preferential regime	0	N/A
Cross-border unilateral advance pricing agreements (APAs) and any other cross-border unilateral tax rulings (such as an advance tax ruling) covering transfer pricing or the application of transfer pricing principles	7	Italy, Netherlands, Spain, Switzerland, United Kingdom, United States
Cross-border rulings providing for a unilateral downward adjustment to the taxpayer's taxable profits that is not directly reflected in the taxpayer's financial / commercial accounts	10	Belgium, Germany, Guernsey, Ireland, Isle of Man, United Kingdom, United States
Permanent establishment rulings	0	N/A
Related party conduit rulings	N/A	N/A
De minimis rule	N/A	N/A
IP regimes: total exchanges on taxpayers benefitting from the third category of IP assets, new entrants benefitting from grandfathered IP regimes; and taxpayers making use of the option to treat the nexus ratio as a rebuttable presumption	38	Belgium, China (People's Republic of), Denmark, France, Germany, Hungary, India, Italy, Japan, Monaco, Netherlands, Norway, Poland, Portugal, Slovak Republic, Sweden, Switzerland, United States
Total	55[5]	

D. Matters related to intellectual property regimes (ToR I.4.1.3)

Luxembourg offered an intellectual property regime (IP regime)[6] that was abolished as of 1 July 2016 and is subject to transparency requirements under the Action 5 Report (OECD, 2015[5]). It states that the identification of the benefitting taxpayers will occur as follows:

- ***New entrants benefitting from the grandfathered IP regime***: during the previous peer review year, an IT research application was launched with the aim of identifying the taxpayers who requested the application of the IP regime in their tax return. Some taxpayers only filed their tax return for the fiscal years 2015 and 2016 by late 2017 or in 2018. Information on these remaining new entrants and new IP assets from existing taxpayers was exchanged in 2018, with a small number of additional exchanges taking place in early 2019. Exchanges took place generally within one month of receipt of the information.
- ***Third category of IP assets***: not applicable as the IP regime has been abolished.
- ***Taxpayers making use of the option to treat the nexus ratio as a rebuttable presumption***: not applicable as the IP regime has been abolished.

In addition, Luxembourg offers an IP regime that not is subject to the transparency requirements under the Action 5 Report (OECD, 2015[5]), because:

- ***New entrants benefitting from the grandfathered IP regime***: as this is a new IP regime rather than a grandfathered IP regime, transparency on new entrants is not relevant.
- ***Third category of IP assets***: not applicable as the regime does not allow the third category of IP assets to qualify for the benefits.

- ***Taxpayers making use of the option to treat the nexus ratio as a rebuttable presumption***: not applicable as the regime does not allow the nexus ratio to be treated as a rebuttable presumption.

Summary of recommendations on implementation of the transparency framework

Aspect of implementation of the transparency framework that should be improved	Recommendation for improvement
	No recommendations are made.

Notes

[1] In addition to the rulings in the scope of the transparency framework Luxembourg issued and exchanged in the year of review 28 rulings relating to "other types of rulings". These "other types of rulings" cover an additional category of rulings that Luxembourg identified, related to intragroup financing activities which in the absence of transparency may cause BEPS concerns. These rulings are not otherwise covered by one of the five categories within the scope of the transparency framework and are therefore defined as "other type of rulings". Luxembourg exchanged these rulings with the relevant Inclusive Framework members using the transparency framework.

[2] With respect to the following preferential regimes: 1) Private asset management company, 2) Investment company in risk capital, 3) Provision for fluctuations in reinsurance companies, and 4) Informal capital and partial exemption for income/gains derived from certain IP rights.

[3] Parties to the Convention are available here: http://www.oecd.org/tax/exchange-of-tax-information/convention-on-mutual-administrative-assistance-in-tax-matters.htm. Luxembourg also has double tax agreements with Andorra, Armenia, Austria, Azerbaijan, Bahrain, Bailiwick of Guernsey, Barbados, Belgium, Brazil, Brunei Darussalam, Bulgaria, Canada, China (People's Republic of), Croatia, Czech Republic, Denmark, Estonia, Finland, France, Georgia, Germany, Greece, Hungary, Iceland, India, Indonesia, Ireland, Isle of Man, Israel, Italy, Japan, Jersey, Kazakhstan, Korea, Lao People's Democratic Republic, Latvia, Liechtenstein, Lithuania, Malaysia, Malta, Mauritius, Mexico, Moldova, Monaco, Morocco, Netherlands, North Macedonia, Norway, Panama, Poland, Portugal, Qatar, Romania, Russia, San Marino, Saudi Arabia, Serbia, Seychelles, Singapore, Slovak Republic, Slovenia, South Africa, Spain, Sri Lanka, Sweden, Switzerland, Chinese Taipei, Tajikistan, Thailand, Trinidad and Tobago, Tunisia, Turkey, Ukraine, United Arab Emirates, United Kingdom, United States, Uruguay, Uzbekistan and Viet Nam.

[4] In addition to the rulings in the scope of the transparency framework Luxembourg transmitted 43 exchanges relating to "other types of rulings" during the year in review.

[5] An additional 43 exchanges of "other types of rulings" were transmitted by 31 December 2018 inter alia to the following countries: Belgium, Canada, China (People's Republic of), Germany, France, Guernsey, Japan, Jersey, Netherlands, Norway, Spain, Switzerland, United Kingdom, and United States.

[6] Partial exemption for income/gains derived from certain IP rights.

Macau (China)

Macau (China) ("Macau") has met all aspects of the terms of reference (OECD, 2017[3]) (ToR) for the calendar year 2018 (year in review) that can be met given in the absence of rulings being issued.

In the prior year report, Macau did not receive any recommendations.

Macau cannot legally issue any type of ruling within the scope of the transparency framework.

As no exchanges were required to take place, no peer input was received in respect of the exchanges of information on rulings received from Macau.

Introduction

This peer review covers Macau's implementation of the BEPS Action 5 transparency framework for the year 2018. The report has four parts, each relating to a key part of the ToR. Each part is discussed in turn. A summary of recommendations is included at the end of this report.

A. The information gathering process

As no rulings are issued, this section is not assessed.

B. The exchange of information

As no rulings are issued, this section is not assessed.

C. Statistics (ToR IV)

As no rulings are issued, no statistics can be reported.

D. Matters related to intellectual property regimes (ToR I.4.1.3)

Macau offered an intellectual property regime (IP regime)[1] that was abolished from 1 July 2018. No transparency requirements under the Action 5 Report (OECD, 2015) were relevant, because:

- ***New entrants benefitting from the grandfathered IP regime***: not applicable as the regime has been concluded as "abolished" and Macau reports that there have been no new entrants in the regime after the relevant date from which enhanced transparency obligations apply. Therefore, no enhanced transparency requirements apply.
- ***Third category of IP assets***: not applicable as the IP regime has been abolished.
- ***Taxpayers making the use of the option to treat the nexus ratio as a rebuttable presumption***: not applicable as the IP regime has been abolished.

Summary of recommendations on implementation of the transparency framework

Aspect of implementation of the transparency framework that should be improved	Recommendation for improvement
	No recommendations are made.

Notes

[1] Macau offshore institution.

Malaysia

Malaysia has met all aspects of the terms of reference (ToR) for the calendar year 2018 (year in review) except for timeliness in providing information on rulings to the Competent Authority and undertaking spontaneous exchange of information on all tax rulings within scope of the transparency framework (ToR II.5), and identifying and exchanging information on new entrants to the grandfathered IP regime (ToR I.4.1.3). Malaysia receives two recommendations on these points for the year in review.

In the prior year report, Malaysia received two recommendations. One of these recommendations has been addressed and is removed. The second recommendation has not been addressed and remains in place, and a new recommendation has been added.

Malaysia can legally issue five types of rulings within the scope of the transparency framework. In practice, Malaysia issued rulings within the scope of the transparency framework as follows:[1]

- 428 past rulings;
- For the period 1 September 2017 - 31 December 2017: 21 future rulings, and
- For the year in review: 54 future rulings.

Peer input was received from three jurisdictions in respect of the exchanges of information on rulings received from Malaysia. The input was generally positive, noting that information was complete, in a correct format and almost all received in a timely manner.

Introduction

This peer review covers Malaysia's implementation of the BEPS Action 5 transparency framework for the year 2018. The report has four parts, each relating to a key part of the ToR. Each part is discussed in turn. A summary of recommendations is included at the end of this report.

A. The information gathering process

Malaysia can legally issue the following five types of rulings within the scope of the transparency framework: (i) preferential regimes;[2] (ii) cross-border unilateral APAs and any other cross-border unilateral tax rulings (such as an advance tax ruling) covering transfer pricing or the application of transfer pricing principles; (iii) rulings providing for unilateral downward adjustments; (iv) permanent establishment rulings; and (v) related party conduit rulings.

Past rulings (ToR I.4.1.1, I.4.1.2, I.4.2.1, I.4.2.2)

For Malaysia, past rulings are any tax rulings within scope that are issued either (i) on or after 1 January 2015 but before 1 April 2017; and (ii) on or after 1 January 2012 but before 1 January 2015, provided they were still in effect as at 1 January 2015.

The prior year peer review report noted that Malaysia had a process for identifying all relevant past rulings and potential exchange jurisdictions that met the ToR, however Malaysia was still in the process of completing the identification under that process. Malaysia was recommended to finalise the information gathering process for past rulings.

Rulings related to preferential regimes are granted by the relevant Investment Promotional Agency. The promotional agencies identifies whether the rulings are in scope of the transparency framework as past rulings by reviewing the internal database of all rulings, and referring to the issue date. In addition, they identify the potential exchange jurisdictions by reviewing the internal database for the name and structure of the MNE group, and other group financial information if available, as well as utilising the "best efforts approach" and seeking further information from the taxpayer where relevant. These rulings and information is then transmitted to be processed by the Tax Incentive Advisory Division under the Tax Policy Department of Inland Revenue Board Malaysia (IRBM).

Rulings in relation to APAs or permanent establishments are issued by the Mutual Agreement Procedure and Transfer Pricing Policy Division under the Department of International Taxation in IRBM. Designated officers in the division identify whether the rulings are in scope of the transparency framework as past rulings by reviewing the internal records of all rulings, and by referring to the issue date. Potential exchange jurisdictions are identified based on the information contained in the ruling request and on file, consulting the internal database, as well as utilising the "best efforts approach" and seeking further information from the taxpayer where relevant.

During the year in review, Malaysia has completed the identification of past rulings and all potential exchange jurisdictions which meets the ToR and therefore the recommendation is now removed.

Future rulings (ToR I.4.1.1, I.4.1.2, I.4.2.1)

For Malaysia, future rulings are any tax rulings within scope that are issued on or after 1 September 2017.

In the prior year, Malaysia was still in the process of completing that information gathering. Malaysia was recommended to finalise the information gathering process for future rulings.

During the year in review, Malaysia has completed the identification of future rulings and all potential exchange jurisdictions, using the same information gathering process for future rulings as for past rulings. Future rulings are identified at the point of issue. All potential exchange jurisdictions are able to be identified from the information contained in the ruling, or by obtaining this from the taxpayer if necessary. This meets the ToR and therefore the recommendation is now removed.

Review and supervision (ToR I.4.3)

The prior year peer review report noted that Malaysia's review and supervision mechanism was implemented in 2018. During the year in review, Malaysia has implemented its review and supervision mechanism as described in the prior year peer review report. This meets the ToR and therefore the recommendation is now removed.

Conclusion on section A

Malaysia has met all of the ToR for the information gathering process and no recommendations are made.

B. The exchange of information

Legal basis for spontaneous exchange of information (ToR II.5.1, II.5.2)

Malaysia has the necessary domestic legal basis to exchange information spontaneously. Malaysia notes that there are no legal or practical impediments that prevent the spontaneous exchange of information on rulings as contemplated in the Action 5 minimum standard.

Malaysia has international agreements permitting spontaneous exchange of information, including being a party to the (i) *Multilateral Convention on Mutual Administrative Assistance in Tax Matters: Amended by the 2010 Protocol* (OECD/Council of Europe, 2011[4]) ("the Convention") and (ii) double tax agreements in force with 71 jurisdictions.[3]

Completion and exchange of templates (ToR II.5.3, II.5.4, II.5.5, II.5.6, II.5.7)

In the prior year peer review report, it was noted that Malaysia was still in the process of implementing a process to complete the templates on relevant rulings, and making them available to the Competent Authority for exchange of information.

During the year in review, Malaysia has implemented this process as follows. Within the Inland Revenue Board of Malaysia, there are two divisions responsible for the exchange of information on tax rulings.

The first division, the Tax Incentive Advisory Division within the Tax Policy Department, is responsible for the exchange of information on rulings relating to preferential regimes and cooperates with the promotional agencies to gather all the data required to complete the template as contained in Annex C of the 2015 Action 5 report (OECD, 2015[5]). The designated officers are supervised by a manager from each promotional agency. For the Pioneer status - contract R&D and the MSC Malaysia regimes, Malaysia uses a two-step approach whereby a letter of award for these regimes is issued which states eligibility for the regime, and taxpayers have 24 months within which to activate the incentive. Information will only be exchanged after the incentive is activated and becomes a ruling in scope of the transparency framework, and by which time related parties to transactions covered by the preferential treatment can be known. For all other preferential regimes, the letter of award (i.e. the approval letter pursuant to a preferential regime in Malaysia) is the ruling in scope of the transparency framework. For all preferential regime rulings, the Annex C template is sent to the applicable investors, who are required to provide the relevant information within six months of the activation of the incentive or the letter of award being issued, as applicable. The information is then reviewed within the division and the completed template is approved by a supervisor before transmission to the Competent Authority. Malaysia is aware that the current timelines in this process are not in line with the terms of reference to provide information on rulings to the Competent Authority without undue delay, and are in the process of amending their procedures to reduce these timelines.

Second, the Mutual Agreement Procedure and Transfer Pricing Policy Division within the International Tax Department is responsible for all other types of rulings. A process flow has been designed containing all steps to be undertaken for the exchange of information. These steps include that the information in the template in the form of Annex C of the 2015 Action 5 report (OECD, 2015[5]) is completed by the officer in charge at the point of issuing the ruling and afterwards verified and approved by a supervisor.

In all cases, the summary section of the template has to be completed in line with the internal FHTP suggested guidance. When the divisions have completed the templates for the exchanges, these will be sent to the Competent Authority for exchange.

The dedicated unit for the exchange of information has not yet been able to exchange information on all tax rulings, and therefore Malaysia still experienced significant delays in exchanges. Malaysia notes that a new officer has been hired for this dedicated unit, in order to expedite its exchange process.

For the year in review, the timeliness of exchanges is as follows:

Past rulings in the scope of the transparency framework	Number of exchanges transmitted by 31 December 2018	Delayed exchanges		
		Number of exchanges not transmitted by 31 December 2018	Reasons for the delays	Any other comments
	23	Approximately 405	Malaysia set up a unit for the exchange of information on tax rulings in September 2018 and is still in the process of collecting all data for exchange.	There are approximately 405 past rulings yet to be exchanged. The precise number of delayed exchanges will be reviewed in the subsequent year's peer review.
Future rulings in the scope of the transparency framework	Number of exchanges transmitted within three months of the information becoming available to the competent authority or immediately after legal impediments have been lifted	Delayed exchanges		
		Number of exchanges transmitted later than three months of the information on rulings becoming available to the competent authority	Reasons for the delays	Any other comments
	1	Approximately 74	Malaysia set up a unit for the exchange of information on tax rulings in September 2018 and is still in the process of collecting all data for exchange.	There are approximately 74 future rulings yet to be exchanged. The precise number of delayed exchanges will be reviewed in the subsequent year's peer review.
Total	24	Approximately 479		

Follow up requests received for exchange of the ruling	Number	Average time to provide response	Number of requests not answered
	0	N/A	N/A

Conclusion on section B

Malaysia has the necessary legal basis to undertake spontaneous exchange of information. Malaysia is recommended to continue its efforts to reduce the timelines for providing the information on rulings to the Competent Authority and to complete the templates for all relevant rulings and to ensure that the exchanges of information on rulings occur as soon as possible (ToR II.5).

C. Statistics (ToR IV)

The statistics for the year in review are as follows:

Category of ruling	Number of exchanges	Jurisdictions exchanged with
Ruling related to a preferential regime	23	Australia, Brunei Darussalam, France, Germany, Hong Kong (China), Iceland, Indonesia, Japan, Netherlands, New Zealand, Norway, Singapore, Thailand, Viet Nam
Cross-border unilateral advance pricing agreements (APAs) and any other cross-border unilateral tax rulings (such as an advance tax ruling) covering transfer pricing or the application of transfer pricing principles	1	*De minimis* rule applies
Cross-border rulings providing for a unilateral downward adjustment to the taxpayer's taxable profits that is not directly reflected in the taxpayer's financial / commercial accounts	0	N/A
Permanent establishment rulings	0	N/A
Related party conduit rulings	0	N/A
De minimis rule	N/A	N/A
IP regimes: total exchanges on taxpayers benefitting from the third category of IP assets, new entrants benefitting from grandfathered IP regimes; and taxpayers making use of the option to treat the nexus ratio as a rebuttable presumption	0	N/A
Total	24	

D. Matters related to intellectual property regimes (ToR I.4.1.3)

Malaysia offered three intellectual property regimes (IP regime)[4] that were abolished as of 1 July 2018 and are subject to transparency requirements under the Action 5 Report (OECD, 2015[5]). It states that the identification of the benefitting taxpayers will occur as follows:

- ***New entrants benefitting from the grandfathered IP regime***: Transparency obligations apply for the three regimes, because grandfathering is provided to entrants that entered the regime after the relevant date from which enhanced transparency obligations apply. Malaysia has not yet been able to identify these new entrants. Malaysia is therefore recommended to identify and exchange information on all new entrants to the grandfathered IP regime (ToR I.4.1.3).
- ***Third category of IP assets***: not applicable as the IP regime has been abolished.

- ***Taxpayers making use of the option to treat the nexus ratio as a rebuttable presumption***: not applicable as the IP regime has been abolished.

Summary of recommendations on implementation of the transparency framework

Aspect of implementation of the transparency framework that should be improved	Recommendation for improvement
Malaysia experienced delays in the provision of rulings to the Competent Authority and did not undertake spontaneous exchange of information on all tax rulings within scope of the transparency framework during the year in review.	Malaysia is recommended to continue its efforts to reduce the timelines for providing the information on rulings to the Competent Authority and to complete the templates for all relevant rulings and to ensure that the exchanges of information on rulings occur as soon as possible. This recommendation remains unchanged since the prior year peer review report.
Malaysia did not identify or exchange information on new entrants to the grandfathered IP regime.	Malaysia is recommended to identify and exchange information on all new entrants to the grandfathered IP regime.

Notes

[1] In September 2018, Malaysia set up a dedicated unit for the exchange of information on tax rulings. This unit reconciled the records of tax rulings issued for the purpose of implementing the transparency framework, as there were some rulings that were in fact not in scope of the Action 5 transparency framework, double-counted rulings, rulings without cross-border related party transactions and withdrawn rulings. Therefore, the statistics on issued rulings within the Action 5 transparency framework have been amended.

[2] With respect to the following preferential regimes: 1) Pioneer status – contract R&D, 2) Biotechnology industry, 3) Principal hub, 4) MSC Malaysia, 5) Green technology services and 6) Special economic regions.

[3] Parties to the Convention are available here: www.oecd.org/tax/exchange-of-tax-information/convention-on-mutual-administrative-assistance-in-tax-matters.htm. Malaysia also has bilateral agreements with Albania, Argentina, Australia, Austria, Bahrain, Bangladesh, Belgium, Bosnia and Herzegovina, Brunei, Canada, Chile, China (People's Republic of), Croatia, Czech Republic, Denmark, Egypt, Fiji, Finland, France, Germany, Hong Kong (China), Hungary, India, Indonesia, Iran, Ireland, Italy, Japan, Jordan, Kazakhstan, Korea, Kuwait, Kyrgyzstan, Laos, Lebanon, Luxembourg, Malta, Mauritius, Mongolia, Morocco, Myanmar, Namibia, Netherlands, New Zealand, Norway, Pakistan, Papua New Guinea, Philippines, Poland, Qatar, Romania, Russia, San Marino, Saudi Arabia, Seychelles, Singapore, South Africa, Spain, Slovak Republic, Sri Lanka, Sudan, Sweden, Switzerland, Syria, Thailand, Turkey, Turkmenistan, United Arab Emirates, United Kingdom, Uzbekistan, Venezuela, Viet Nam, Zimbabwe.

[4] These regimes are: 1) Biotechnology industry, 2) MSC Malaysia and 3) Principal hub.

Maldives

Maldives has met all aspects of the terms of reference (OECD, 2017[3]) (ToR) for the calendar year 2018 (year in review) that can be met in the absence of rulings being issued.

This is the first review of Maldives' implementation of the transparency framework.

Maldives does not issue any type of rulings within the scope of the transparency framework. Maldives issues public tax rulings, legally binding on the Maldives Inland Revenue Authority and on taxpayers. These documents are very general and do not cover the categories of rulings as defined in the Action 5 report (OECD, 2015). Theoretically, there is no legal impediment for Maldives to issue rulings, but in practice Maldives does not issue any rulings. In the event that Maldives put in place the administrative process to issue rulings, Maldives would be asked to implement the transparency framework obligations.

As no exchanges were required to take place, no peer input was received in respect of the exchanges of information on rulings received from Maldives.

Introduction

This peer review covers Maldives' implementation of the BEPS Action 5 transparency framework for the year 2018. The report has four parts, each relating to a key part of the ToR. Each part is discussed in turn. A summary of recommendations is included at the end of this report.

A. The information gathering process

As no rulings are issued, this section is not assessed.

B. The exchange of information

As no rulings are issued, this section is not assessed.

C. Statistics (ToR IV)

As no rulings are issued, no statistics can be reported.

D. Matters related to intellectual property regimes (ToR I.4.1.3)

Maldives does not offer an intellectual property regime for which transparency requirements under the Action 5 Report (OECD, 2015[5]) were imposed.

Summary of recommendations on implementation of the transparency framework

Aspect of implementation of the transparency framework that should be improved	Recommendation for improvement
	No recommendations are made.

Malta

Malta has met all aspects of the terms of reference (OECD, 2017[3]) (ToR) for the calendar year 2018 (year in review) and no recommendations are made.

In the prior year review report, Malta did not receive any recommendations.

Malta can legally issue four types of rulings within the scope of the transparency framework. In practice, Malta issued rulings within the scope of the transparency framework as follows:

- Seven past rulings;
- For the period 1 April 2017 - 31 December 2017: four future rulings, and
- For the year in review: seven future rulings.

No peer input was received in respect of the exchanges of information on rulings received from Malta.

Introduction

This peer review covers Malta's implementation of the BEPS Action 5 transparency framework for the year 2018. The report has four parts, each relating to a key part of the ToR. Each part is discussed in turn. A summary of recommendations is included at the end of this report.

A. The information gathering process

Malta can legally issue the following four types of rulings within the scope of the transparency framework: (i) cross-border unilateral APAs and any other cross-border unilateral tax rulings (such as an advance tax ruling) covering transfer pricing or the application of transfer pricing principles; (ii) rulings providing for unilateral downward adjustments; (iii) permanent establishment rulings; and (iv) related party conduit rulings.

Past rulings (ToR I.4.1.1, I.4.1.2, I.4.2.1, I.4.2.2)

For Malta, past rulings are any tax rulings within scope that are issued either (i) on or after 1 January 2015 but before 1 April 2017; and (ii) on or after 1 January 2012 but before 1 January 2015, provided they were still in effect as at 1 January 2015.

In the prior year peer review report, it was determined that Malta's undertakings to identify past rulings and all potential exchange jurisdictions were sufficient to meet the minimum standard. Malta's implementation in this regard remains unchanged, and therefore continues to meet the minimum standard.

Future rulings (ToR I.4.1.1, I.4.1.2, I.4.2.1)

For Malta, future rulings are any tax rulings within scope that are issued on or after 1 April 2017.

In the prior year peer review report, it was determined that Malta's implementation of a new system to identify future rulings and all potential exchange jurisdictions was sufficient to meet the minimum standard. Malta's implementation in this regard remains unchanged, and therefore continues to meet the minimum standard.

Review and supervision (ToR I.4.3)

In the prior year peer review report, it was determined that Malta's review and supervision mechanism was sufficient to meet the minimum standard. Malta's implementation in this regard remains unchanged, and therefore continues to meet the minimum standard.

Conclusion on section A

Malta has met all of the ToR for the information gathering process and no recommendations are made.

B. The exchange of information

Legal basis for spontaneous exchange of information (ToR II.5.1, II.5.2)

Malta has the necessary domestic legal basis to exchange information spontaneously. Malta notes that there are no legal or practical impediments that prevent the spontaneous exchange of information on rulings as contemplated in the Action 5 minimum standard.

Malta is a party to international agreements permitting spontaneous exchange of information, including (i) the *Multilateral Convention on Mutual Administrative Assistance in Tax Matters: Amended by the 2010 Protocol* (OECD/Council of Europe, 2011) ("the Convention") and (ii) double tax agreements in force with 75 jurisdictions.[1]

Completion and exchange of templates (ToR II.5.3, II.5.4, II.5.5, II.5.6, II.5.7)

In the prior year peer review report, it was determined that Malta's process for the completion and exchange of templates were sufficient to meet the minimum standard. Malta's implementation in this regard remains unchanged and therefore continues to meet the minimum standard.

For the year in review, the timeliness of exchanges is as follows:

Past rulings in the scope of the transparency framework	Number of exchanges transmitted by 31 December 2018	Delayed exchanges		
		Number of exchanges not transmitted by 31 December 2018	Reasons for the delays	Any other comments
	4	0	See below.	N/A
Future rulings in the scope of the transparency framework	Number of exchanges transmitted within three months of the information becoming available to the competent authority or immediately after legal impediments have been lifted	Delayed exchanges		
		Number of exchanges transmitted later than three months of the information on rulings becoming available to the competent authority	Reasons for the delays	Any other comments
	10	0	N/A	N/A
Total	14	0		

Follow up requests received for exchange of the ruling	Number	Average time to provide response	Number of requests not answered
	0	N/A	N/A

As noted in the previous year peer review report, there was a delay in exchanging the information on four past rulings. Malta experienced some technical issues in the implementation of the EU Directive for exchange of information on rulings within the EU and as a result, only exchanged information on rulings with EU jurisdictions. Steps were taken to exchange all outstanding information on rulings for the relevant period with the non-EU jurisdictions by April 2018.

Conclusion on section B

Malta has the necessary legal basis for spontaneous exchange of information, a process for completing the templates in a timely way and has completed all exchanges. Malta has met all of the ToR for the exchange of information process and no recommendations are made.

C. Statistics (ToR IV)

The statistics for the year in review are as follows:

Category of ruling	Number of exchanges	Jurisdictions exchanged with
Ruling related to a preferential regime	N/A	N/A
Cross-border unilateral advance pricing agreements (APAs) and any other cross-border unilateral tax rulings (such as an advance tax ruling) covering	0	N/A

transfer pricing or the application of transfer pricing principles		
Cross-border rulings providing for a unilateral downward adjustment to the taxpayer's taxable profits that is not directly reflected in the taxpayer's financial / commercial accounts	0	N/A
Permanent establishment rulings	4	*De minimis* rule applies
Related party conduit rulings	10	Belgium, Germany, Jersey, Netherlands, Panama, Singapore, Switzerland, United Kingdom, United States
De minimis rule	N/A	N/A
IP regimes: total exchanges on taxpayers benefitting from the third category of IP assets, new entrants benefitting from grandfathered IP regimes; and taxpayers making use of the option to treat the nexus ratio as a rebuttable presumption	0	N/A
Total	14	

D. Matters related to intellectual property regimes (ToR I.4.1.3)

Malta introduced a new IP regime which will come into effect by the end of 2019. Although this is after the year in review, it is noted that this regime is not subject to transparency requirements under the Action 5 Report (OECD, 2015[5]) for the year in review, because:

- ***New entrants benefitting from the grandfathered IP regime***: as this is a new IP regime rather than a grandfathered IP regime, transparency on new entrants is not relevant.
- ***Third category of IP assets***: the regime allows the third category of IP assets to qualify for the benefits. The transparency requirements on this will be reviewed during next year's peer review.
- ***Taxpayers making use of the option to treat the nexus ratio as a rebuttable presumption***: not applicable as the regime does not allow the nexus ratio to be treated as a rebuttable presumption.

Summary of recommendations on implementation of the transparency framework

Aspect of implementation of the transparency framework that should be improved	Recommendation for improvement
	No recommendations are made.

Notes

[1] Parties to the Convention are available here: http://www.oecd.org/tax/exchange-of-tax-information/convention-on-mutual-administrative-assistance-in-tax-matters.htm. Malta also has bilateral agreements in force with Albania, Andorra, Australia, Austria, Azerbaijan, Bahrain, Barbados, Belgium, Botswana, Bulgaria, Canada, China (People's Republic of), Croatia, Cyprus, Czech Republic, Denmark, Egypt, Estonia, Finland, France, Georgia, Germany, Greece, Guernsey, Hungary, Iceland, India, Ireland, Isle of Man, Israel, Italy, Jersey, Jordan, Korea, Kuwait, Latvia, Lebanon, Libya, Liechtenstein, Lithuania, Luxembourg, Malaysia, Mauritius, Mexico, Moldova, Monaco, Montenegro, Morocco, Netherlands, Norway, Pakistan, Poland, Portugal, Qatar, Romania, Russia, San Marino, Saudi Arabia, Serbia,

Singapore, Slovak Republic, Slovenia, South Africa, Spain, Sweden, Switzerland, Syria, Tunisia, Turkey, Ukraine, United Arab Emirates, United Kingdom, United States, Uruguay and Viet Nam.

Note by Turkey: The information in this document with reference to "Cyprus" relates to the southern part of the Island. There is no single authority representing both Turkish and Greek Cypriot people on the Island. Turkey recognises the Turkish Republic of Northern Cyprus (TRNC). Until a lasting and equitable solution is found within the context of the United Nations, Turkey shall preserve its position concerning the "Cyprus issue".

Note by all the European Union Member States of the OECD and the European Union. The Republic of Cyprus is recognised by all members of the United Nations with the exception of Turkey. The information in this document relates to the area under the effective control of the Government of the Republic of Cyprus.

Mauritius

Mauritius has met all aspects of the terms of reference (OECD, 2017[3]) (ToR) for the calendar year 2018 (year in review) and no recommendations are made.

In the prior year report, Mauritius did not receive any recommendations.

Mauritius can legally issue three types of rulings within the scope of the transparency framework. In practice, Mauritius issued rulings within the scope of the transparency framework as follows:

- 20 past rulings;
- For the period 1 September 2017 - 31 December 2017: no future rulings, and
- For the year in review: one future ruling.

Mauritius publishes taxpayer specific rulings in redacted form.[1]

Peer input was received from two jurisdictions in respect of the exchanges of information on rulings received from Mauritius. The input was generally positive, noting that information was complete, in a correct format and received in a timely manner.

Introduction

This peer review covers Mauritius' implementation of the BEPS Action 5 transparency framework for the year 2018. The report has four parts, each relating to a key part of the ToR. Each part is discussed in turn. A summary of recommendations is included at the end of this report.

A. The information gathering process

Mauritius can legally issue the following three types of rulings within the scope of the transparency framework: (i) preferential regimes;[2] (ii) cross-border unilateral APAs and any other cross-border unilateral tax rulings (such as an advance tax ruling) covering transfer pricing or the application of transfer pricing principles; and (iii) permanent establishment rulings.

Past rulings (ToR I.4.1.1, I.4.1.2, I.4.2.1, I.4.2.2)

For Mauritius, past rulings are any tax rulings within scope that are issued either: (i) on or after 1 January 2015 but before 1 September 2017; and (ii) on or after 1 January 2012 but before 1 January 2015, provided they were still in effect as at 1 January 2015.

In the prior year peer review report, it was determined that Mauritius' undertakings to identify past rulings and all potential exchange jurisdictions were sufficient to meet the minimum standard. Mauritius' implementation in this regard remains unchanged, and therefore continues to meet the minimum standard.

Future rulings (ToR I.4.1.1, I.4.1.2, I.4.2.1)

For Mauritius, future rulings are any tax rulings within scope that are issued on or after 1 September 2017.

In the prior year peer review report, it was determined that Mauritius' undertakings to identify future rulings and all potential exchange jurisdictions were sufficient to meet the minimum standard. Mauritius' implementation in this regard remains unchanged, and therefore continues to meet the minimum standard.

Review and supervision (ToR I.4.3)

In the prior year peer review report, it was determined that Mauritius' review and supervision mechanism was sufficient to meet the minimum standard. Mauritius' implementation in this regard remains unchanged, and therefore continues to meet the minimum standard.

Conclusion on section A

Mauritius has met all of the ToR for the information gathering process and no recommendations are made.

B. The exchange of information

Legal basis for spontaneous exchange of information (ToR II.5.1, II.5.2)

Mauritius has the necessary domestic legal basis to exchange information spontaneously. Mauritius notes that there are no legal or practical impediments that prevent the spontaneous exchange of information on rulings as contemplated in the Action 5 minimum standard.

Mauritius is a party to international agreements permitting spontaneous exchange of information, including (i) the *Multilateral Convention on Mutual Administrative Assistance in Tax Matters: Amended by the 2010*

Protocol (OECD/Council of Europe, 2011) ("the Convention") and (ii) double tax agreements in force with 45 jurisdictions.[3]

Completion and exchange of templates (ToR II.5.3, II.5.4, II.5.5, II.5.6, II.5.7)

In the prior year peer review report, it was determined that Mauritius' process for the completion and exchange of templates were sufficient to meet the minimum standard. Mauritius' implementation in this regard remains unchanged and therefore continues to meet the minimum standard.

For the year in review, the timeliness of exchanges is as follows:

Past rulings in the scope of the transparency framework	Number of exchanges transmitted by 31 December 2018	Delayed exchanges		
		Number of exchanges not transmitted by 31 December 2018	Reasons for the delays	Any other comments
	0	0	N/A	N/A
Future rulings in the scope of the transparency framework	Number of exchanges transmitted within three months of the information becoming available to the competent authority or immediately after legal impediments have been lifted	Delayed exchanges		
		Number of exchanges transmitted later than three months of the information on rulings becoming available to the competent authority	Reasons for the delays	Any other comments
	0	2	See below.	N/A
Total	0	2		

Follow up requests received for exchange of the ruling	Number	Average time to provide response	Number of requests not answered
	0	N/A	N/A

The two delayed exchanges relate to one ruling on a preferential regime, which was an intellectual property regime (IP regime). As of 1 July 2017, Mauritius had this new IP regime in place, to which Mauritius has made amendments in 2019 for the regime to be in line with the nexus approach, with retrospective effect. Mauritius notes that it was unaware that the regime was in fact an IP regime during the year in review, and therefore in respect of the one issued ruling, information was exchanged with a delay. The ruling was issued on 1 October 2018 and exchanged in early 2019. As this was an exceptional error, which was quickly remedied by Mauritius, and the resulting delay was relatively short, no recommendation has been made.

Conclusion on section B

Mauritius has the necessary legal basis for spontaneous exchange of information, a process for completing the templates in a timely way and has completed all exchanges. Mauritius has met all of the ToR for the exchange of information process and no recommendations are made.

C. Statistics (ToR IV)

As there was no information on rulings exchanged by Mauritius for the year in review, no statistics can be reported.

D. Matters related to intellectual property regimes (ToR I.4.1.3)

Mauritius offered two IP regimes[4] that are abolished as of 1 July 2018 and are subject to transparency requirements under the Action 5 Report (OECD, 2015[5]). It states that the identification of the benefitting taxpayers will occur as follows:

- ***New entrants benefitting from the grandfathered IP regime***:

  Transparency obligations apply for the two regimes, because grandfathering is provided to entrants that entered the regime after the relevant date from which enhanced transparency obligations apply.

  Global business licence 1: Mauritius is able to identify all new taxpayers, as they have to request a license in order to be a Global business company and to benefit from the regime. Taxpayers benefitting from the regime have to file a tax return, with a separate section for declaring royalty income. Information on those companies having declared royalty income and which are benefitting from the regime after the relevant date will be exchanged. With respect to new IP assets held by existing taxpayers, the tax authority will analyse the tax returns in order to determine whether there was an increase in net current assets and in income declared by the company. Based on this, there could be an indication that the company invested in new IP assets. These taxpayers have to provide additional information, and based on this Mauritius will perform exchanges.

  It should be noted that the first tax returns only became available after the year in review, and as such no exchanges could take place in the year in review.

  Global business licence 2: GBC2s are licensed by the Financial Services Commission (FSC). GBC2s are required to submit financial summaries to the FSC within six months after the end of the accounting period, including a profit and a loss account and a balance sheet. Based on the financial summaries, the FSC will retrieve a list of all GBC2s that derived income from IP and that benefitted from the regime after the relevant date. Information on those companies will provided to the tax authority and will be exchanged. With respect to new IP assets of existing taxpayers, the FSC will analyse the balance sheets in order to determine whether there was an increase in net current assets and in income declared by the company. Based on this, there could be an indication that the company invested in new IP assets. These companies have to provide additional information, and based on this Mauritius will perform exchanges.
- ***Third category of IP assets***: not applicable as the IP regime has been abolished.
- ***Taxpayers making use of the option to treat the nexus ratio as a rebuttable presumption***: not applicable as the IP regime has been abolished.

Mauritius introduced a new IP regime which came into effect from 1 July 2017.[5] Regulations for this regime have been issued in June 2019 and the regime now includes the nexus approach with retrospective effect. It states that the identification of the benefitting taxpayers will occur as follows:

- ***New entrants benefitting from the grandfathered IP regime***: as this is a new IP regime rather than a grandfathered IP regime, transparency on new entrants is not relevant.
- ***Third category of IP assets***: the regime allows the third category of IP assets to qualify for the benefits. However, as this regime has been amended in 2019 in order to introduce the nexus approach, taxpayers could only opt for the third category of IP assets in 2019 which is after the year in review. As such, this aspect will be assessed during next year's peer review.
- ***Taxpayers making use of the option to treat the nexus ratio as a rebuttable presumption***: not applicable as the regime does not allow the nexus ratio to be treated as a rebuttable presumption.

Summary of recommendations on implementation of the transparency framework

Aspect of implementation of the transparency framework that should be improved	Recommendation for improvement
Mauritius experienced some delays in exchanging information on one future ruling.	No recommendation is made because Mauritius completed exchanges on the delayed future ruling quickly after the issues were identified and resolved, and this is not a recurring issue.

Notes

[1] Available at: http://www.mra.mu/index.php/media-centre/rulings/income-tax-rulings.

[2] With respect to the following preferential regimes: 1) Global business license 1, 2) Global business license 2, 3) Global headquarters administration regime, 4) Global treasury activities, 5) Captive insurances, 6) Segment B banking, 7) Investment banking, 8) Freeport zone, 9) Shipping regime, 10) Innovation box and 11) Partial exemption system.

[3] Parties to the Convention are available here: http://www.oecd.org/tax/exchange-of-tax-information/convention-on-mutual-administrative-assistance-in-tax-matters.htm. Mauritius also has bilateral agreements in force with Bangladesh, Barbados, Belgium, Botswana, Cabo Verde, China (People's Republic of), Congo, Croatia, Cyprus, France, Germany, Ghana, Guernsey, India, Italy, Jersey, Kuwait, Latvia, Lesotho, Luxembourg, Madagascar, Malaysia, Malta, Monaco, Mozambique, Namibia, Nepal, Oman, Pakistan, Qatar, Rwanda, Senegal, Seychelles, Singapore, South Africa, Sri Lanka, Swaziland, Sweden, Thailand, Tunisia, Uganda, United Arab Emirates, United Kingdom, Zambia and Zimbabwe. In addition, Mauritius' TIEA with the United States permits for the spontaneous exchange of information.

Note by Turkey: The information in this document with reference to "Cyprus" relates to the southern part of the Island. There is no single authority representing both Turkish and Greek Cypriot people on the Island. Turkey recognises the Turkish Republic of Northern Cyprus (TRNC). Until a lasting and equitable solution is found within the context of the United Nations, Turkey shall preserve its position concerning the "Cyprus issue".

Note by all the European Union Member States of the OECD and the European Union. The Republic of Cyprus is recognised by all members of the United Nations with the exception of Turkey. The information in this document relates to the area under the effective control of the Government of the Republic of Cyprus.

[4] These regimes are: 1) Global business licence 1 and 2) Global business licence 2.

[5] Innovation box.

Mexico

Mexico has met all aspects of the terms of reference (OECD, 2017[3]) (ToR) for the calendar year 2018 (year in review) and no recommendations are made.

In the prior year report, Mexico received one recommendation. This recommendation has been addressed and is removed.

Mexico can legally issue two types of rulings within the scope of the transparency framework. In practice, Mexico issued rulings within the scope of the transparency framework as follows:

- 13 past rulings;
- For the period 1 April 2016 - 31 December 2016: one future ruling;
- For the calendar year 2017: 328 future rulings, and
- For the year in review: 294 future rulings.

Mexico publishes their tax rulings in redacted form.[1]

Peer input was received from four jurisdictions in respect of the exchanges of information on rulings received from Mexico. The input was generally positive, noting that information was complete, in correct format and received in a timely manner.

Introduction

This peer review covers Mexico's implementation of the BEPS Action 5 transparency framework for the year 2018. The report has four parts, each relating to a key part of the ToR. Each part is discussed in turn. A summary of recommendations is included at the end of this report.

A. The information gathering process

Mexico can legally issue the two following types of rulings within the scope of the transparency framework: (i) cross-border unilateral advance pricing arrangements (APAs) and any other cross-border unilateral tax rulings (such as an advance tax ruling) covering transfer pricing or the application of transfer pricing principles; and (ii) permanent establishment rulings.

Past rulings (ToR I.4.1.1, I.4.1.2, I.4.2.1, I.4.2.2)

For Mexico, past rulings are any tax rulings within scope that are issued either: (i) on or after 1 January 2014 but before 1 April 2016; or (ii) on or after 1 January 2010 but before 1 January 2014, provided they were still in effect as at 1 January 2014.

In the prior years' peer review reports, it was determined that Mexico's undertakings to identify past rulings and all potential exchange jurisdictions were sufficient to meet the minimum standard. Mexico's implementation in this regard remains unchanged, and therefore continues to meet the minimum standard.

Future rulings (ToR I.4.1.1, I.4.1.2, I.4.2.1)

For Mexico, future rulings are any tax rulings within scope that are issued on or after 1 April 2016.

In the prior years' peer review reports, it was determined that Mexico's undertakings to identify future rulings and all potential exchange jurisdictions was sufficient to meet the minimum standard. Mexico's implementation in this regard remains unchanged, and therefore continues to meet the minimum standard.

Review and supervision (ToR I.4.3)

In the prior years' peer review reports, it was determined that Mexico's review and supervision mechanism was sufficient to meet the minimum standard. Mexico's implementation in this regard remains unchanged, and therefore continues to meet the minimum standard.

Conclusion on section A

Mexico has met all of the ToR for the information gathering process and no recommendations are made.

B. The exchange of information

Legal basis for spontaneous exchange of information (ToR II.5.1, II.5.2)

Mexico has the necessary domestic legal basis to exchange information spontaneously. Mexico notes that there are no legal or practical impediments that prevent the spontaneous exchange of information on rulings as contemplated in the Action 5 minimum standard.

Mexico is a party to international agreements permitting spontaneous exchange of information, including (i) the *Multilateral Convention on Mutual Administrative Assistance in Tax Matters: Amended by the 2010*

Protocol (OECD/Council of Europe, 2011) ("the Convention"), (ii) double tax agreements in force with seven jurisdictions, and (iii) tax information exchange agreements in force with three jurisdictions.[2]

Completion and exchange of templates (ToR II.5.3, II.5.4, II.5.5, II.5.6, II.5.7)

In the prior year peer review report, it was determined that Mexico's process for the completion and exchange of templates were sufficient to meet the minimum standard, except for the timely exchange of future rulings (ToR II.5.6). During the year in review Mexico developed an internal procedure to improve the process for making available the information on the issued rulings to the Competent Authority. After implementing such procedure, the information is automatically segmented per country of destination, which in turn reduces the time necessary to complete the exchanges.

For the year in review, the timeliness of exchanges is as follows:

Past rulings in the scope of the transparency framework	Number of exchanges transmitted by 31 December 2018	Delayed exchanges		
		Number of exchanges not transmitted by 31 December 2018	Reasons for the delays	Any other comments
	0	0	N/A	N/A
Future rulings in the scope of the transparency framework	Number of exchanges transmitted within three months of the information becoming available to the competent authority or immediately after legal impediments have been lifted	Delayed exchanges		
		Number of exchanges transmitted later than three months of the information on rulings becoming available to the competent authority	Reasons for the delays	Any other comments
	654	0	N/A	N/A
Total	654	0		

Follow up requests received for exchange of the ruling	Number	Average time to provide response	Number of requests not answered
	1	30 days	0

Conclusion on section B

Mexico has the necessary legal basis for spontaneous exchange of information, a process for completing the templates in a timely way and has completed all exchanges. Mexico has met all of the ToR for the exchange of information process and no recommendations are made. As the issue regarding timely exchange of future rulings (ToR II.5.6) has been resolved, the recommendation is removed.

C. Statistics (ToR IV)

The statistics for the year in review are as follows:

Category of ruling	Number of exchanges	Jurisdictions exchanged with
Ruling related to a preferential regime	N/A	N/A
Cross-border unilateral advance pricing agreements (APAs) and any other cross-border unilateral tax rulings (such as an advance tax ruling) covering transfer pricing or the application of transfer pricing principles	654	Austria, Barbados, Belgium, Canada, China (People's Republic of), Denmark, France, Germany, Hong Kong (China), Ireland, Israel, Italy, Korea, Luxembourg, Netherlands, Singapore, Spain, Sweden, Switzerland, United Kingdom and United States.
Cross-border rulings providing for a	N/A	N/A

unilateral downward adjustment to the taxpayer's taxable profits that is not directly reflected in the taxpayer's financial / commercial accounts		
Permanent establishment rulings	0	N/A
Related party conduit rulings	N/A	N/A
De minimis rule	N/A	N/A
IP regimes: total exchanges on taxpayers benefitting from the third category of IP assets, new entrants benefitting from grandfathered IP regimes; and taxpayers making use of the option to treat the nexus ratio as a rebuttable presumption	N/A	N/A
Total	654	

D. Matters related to intellectual property regimes (ToR I.4.1.3)

Mexico does not offer an intellectual property regime for which transparency requirements under the Action 5 Report (OECD, 2015[5]) were imposed.

Summary of recommendations on implementation of the transparency framework

Aspect of implementation of the transparency framework that should be improved	Recommendation for improvement
	No recommendations are made.

Notes

[1] Available at: http://www2.sat.gob.mx/sitio_internet/sitio_aplicaciones/Resoluciones_Favorables/

[2] Parties to the Convention are available here: www.oecd.org/tax/exchange-of-tax-information/convention-on-mutual-administrative-assistance-in-tax-matters.htm. Mexico also has bilateral agreements in force with Austria, Canada, Hong Kong (China), Russian Federation, South Africa, Ukraine and the United States. In addition, Mexico has tax information exchange agreements permitting spontaneous exchange of information with Aruba, Canada and the United States.

Monaco

Monaco has met all aspects of the terms of reference (OECD, 2017[3]) (ToR) for the calendar year 2018 (year in review) and no recommendation is made.

In the prior year report, Monaco did not receive any recommendations.

Monaco does not issue any type of ruling within the scope of the transparency framework. In the event that Monaco puts in place the administrative process to issue rulings within the scope of the transparency framework, Monaco notes that it would implement the transparency framework obligations.

As no exchanges were required to take place, no peer input was received in respect of the exchanges of information on rulings received from Monaco.

Introduction

This peer review covers Monaco's implementation of the BEPS Action 5 transparency framework for the year 2018. The report has four parts, each relating to a key part of the ToR. Each part is discussed in turn. A summary of recommendations is included at the end of this report.

A. The information gathering process

As no rulings are issued, this section is not assessed.

B. The exchange of information

As no rulings are issued, this section is not assessed.

C. Statistics (ToR IV)

As no rulings are issued, no statistics can be reported.

D. Matters related to intellectual property regimes (ToR I.4.1.3)

Monaco does not offer an intellectual property regime for which transparency requirements under the Action 5 Report (OECD, 2015[5]) were imposed.

Summary of recommendations on implementation of the transparency framework

Aspect of implementation of the transparency framework that should be improved	Recommendation for improvement
	No recommendations are made.

Mongolia

Mongolia has met all aspects of the terms of reference (OECD, 2017[3]) (ToR) for the calendar year 2018 (year in review) that can be met in the absence of rulings being issued.

This is Mongolia's first review of implementation of the transparency framework. Mongolia does not issue any type of ruling within the scope of the transparency framework. Mongolia only issues interpretative rulings. These tax rulings are not binding for the tax authorities and are therefore not considered rulings as defined in the Action 5 Report (OECD, 2015[5]). In the event that Mongolia puts in place the administrative process to issue rulings within the scope of the transparency framework, Mongolia notes that it would implement the transparency framework obligations.

As no exchanges were required to take place, no peer input was received in respect of the exchanges of information on rulings received from Mongolia.

Introduction

This peer review covers Mongolia's implementation of the BEPS Action 5 transparency framework for the year 2018. The report has four parts, each relating to a key part of the ToR. Each part is discussed in turn. A summary of recommendations is included at the end of this report.

A. The information gathering process

As no rulings are issued, this section is not assessed.

B. The exchange of information

As no rulings are issued, this section is not assessed.

C. Statistics (ToR IV)

As no rulings are issued, no statistics can be reported.

D. Matters related to intellectual property regimes (ToR I.4.1.3)

Mongolia does not offer an intellectual property regime for which transparency requirements under the Action 5 Report (OECD, 2015[5]) were imposed.

Summary of recommendations on implementation of the transparency framework

Aspect of implementation of the transparency framework that should be improved	Recommendation for improvement
	No recommendations are made.

Montserrat

Montserrat has met all aspects of the terms of reference (OECD, 2017[3]) (ToR) for the calendar year 2018 (year in review) that can be met in the absence of rulings being issued.

In the prior year report, Montserrat did not receive any recommendations.

Montserrat cannot legally issue any type of rulings within the scope of the transparency framework.

As no exchanges were required to take place, no peer input was received in respect of the exchanges of information on rulings received from Montserrat.

Introduction

This peer review covers Montserrat's implementation of the BEPS Action 5 transparency framework for the year 2018. The report has four parts, each relating to a key part of the ToR. Each part is discussed in turn. A summary of recommendations is included at the end of this report.

A. The information gathering process

As no rulings are issued, this section is not assessed.

B. The exchange of information

As no rulings are issued, this section is not assessed.

C. Statistics (ToR IV)

As no rulings are issued, no statistics can be reported.

D. Matters related to intellectual property regimes (ToR I.4.1.3)

Montserrat does not offer an intellectual property regime for which transparency requirements under the Action 5 Report (OECD, 2015[5]) were imposed.

Summary of recommendations on implementation of the transparency framework

Aspect of implementation of the transparency framework that should be improved	Recommendation for improvement
	No recommendations are made.

The Netherlands

The Netherlands has met all aspects of the terms of reference (OECD, 2017[3]) (ToR) for the calendar year 2018 (year in review) and no recommendations are made.

In the prior year report, the Netherlands received one recommendation. This recommendation has been addressed and is removed.

The Netherlands can legally issue four types of rulings within the scope of the transparency framework. In practice, the Netherlands issued rulings within the scope of the transparency framework as follows:

- 2 204 past rulings;
- For the period 1 April 2016 - 31 December 2016: 297 future rulings;
- For the calendar year 2017: 214 future rulings, and
- For the year in review: 272 future rulings.

Peer input was received from ten jurisdictions in respect of the exchanges of information on rulings received from the Netherlands. The input was generally positive, noting that information was complete, mostly in a correct format and in general received in a timely manner.

Introduction

This peer review covers the Netherlands' implementation of the BEPS Action 5 transparency framework for the year 2018. The report has four parts, each relating to a key part of the ToR. Each part is discussed in turn. A summary of recommendations is included at the end of this report.

A. The information gathering process

The Netherlands can legally issue the following four types of rulings within the scope of the transparency framework: (i) preferential regimes;[1] (ii) cross-border unilateral APAs and any other cross-border unilateral tax rulings (such as an advance tax ruling) covering transfer pricing or the application of transfer pricing principles; (iii) rulings providing for unilateral downward adjustments; and (iv) permanent establishment rulings.

Past rulings (ToR I.4.1.1, I.4.1.2, I.4.2.1, I.4.2.2)

For the Netherlands, past rulings are any tax rulings within scope that are issued either: (i) on or after 1 January 2014 but before 1 April 2016; or (ii) on or after 1 January 2010 but before 1 January 2014, provided they were still in effect as at 1 January 2014.

In the prior year peer review report, it was determined that the Netherlands' undertakings to identify past rulings and all potential exchange jurisdictions were sufficient to meet the minimum standard. The Netherlands' implementation in this regard remains unchanged, and therefore continues to meet the minimum standard.

Future rulings (ToR I.4.1.1, I.4.1.2, I.4.2.1)

For the Netherlands, future rulings are any tax rulings within scope that are issued on or after 1 April 2016.

In the prior years' peer review reports, it was determined that the Netherlands' undertakings to identify future rulings and all potential exchange jurisdictions was sufficient to meet the minimum standard. The Netherlands' implementation in this regard remains unchanged, and therefore continues to meet the minimum standard.

Review and supervision (ToR I.4.3)

In the prior years' peer review reports, it was determined that the Netherlands' review and supervision mechanism was sufficient to meet the minimum standard. The Netherlands' implementation in this regard remains unchanged, and therefore continues to meet the minimum standard.

Conclusion on section A

The Netherlands has met all of the ToR for the information gathering process and no recommendations are made.

B. The exchange of information

Legal basis for spontaneous exchange of information (ToR II.5.1, II.5.2)

The Netherlands has the necessary domestic legal basis to exchange information spontaneously. The Netherlands notes that there are no legal or practical impediments that prevent the spontaneous exchange of information on rulings as contemplated in the Action 5 minimum standard.

The Netherlands has international agreements permitting spontaneous exchange of information, including being a party to the (i) *Multilateral Convention on Mutual Administrative Assistance in Tax Matters: Amended by the 2010 Protocol* (OECD/Council of Europe, 2011[4]) ("the Convention"), (ii) the Directive 2011/16/EU with all other European Union Member States and (iii) double tax agreements in force with 141 jurisdictions.[2]

Completion and exchange of templates (ToR II.5.3, II.5.4, II.5.5, II.5.6, II.5.7)

In the prior year peer review report, it was determined that the Netherlands' process for the completion and exchange of templates were sufficient to meet the minimum standard. The Netherlands' implementation in this regard remains unchanged and therefore continues to meet the minimum standard.

For the year in review, the timeliness of exchanges is as follows:

Past rulings in the scope of the transparency framework	Number of exchanges transmitted by 31 December 2018	Delayed exchanges		
		Number of exchanges not transmitted by 31 December 2018	Reasons for the delays	Any other comments
	2	0	During the year of review two past rulings have been identified that were mistakenly overlooked during the first review process.	N/A
Future rulings in the scope of the transparency framework	Number of exchanges transmitted within three months of the information becoming available to the competent authority or immediately after legal impediments have been lifted	Delayed exchanges		
		Number of exchanges transmitted later than three months of the information on rulings becoming available to the competent authority	Reasons for the delays	Any other comments
	442	0	N/A	N/A
Total	444	0		

Follow up requests received for exchange of the ruling	Number	Average time to provide response	Number of requests not answered
	12	41 days	Nil

With respect to the two exchanges on past rulings, these had not been identified in 2016 or 2017, owing to human error in the manual review process. The rulings were identified in the year in review in the course of other work on the relevant files. This is a relatively small error in the context of the Netherlands' exchange of information on rulings, given the substantial number of rulings issued, and the exchange took place within a very short period of the issue being identified. As such, no recommendation is made.

Conclusion on section B

The Netherlands has the necessary legal basis for spontaneous exchange of information, a process for completing the templates in a timely way and has completed all exchanges. The Netherlands has met all of the ToR for the exchange of information process and no recommendations are made.

C. Statistics (ToR IV)

The statistics for the year in review are as follows:

Category of ruling	Number of exchanges	Jurisdictions exchanged with
Ruling related to a preferential regime	233	Argentina, Aruba, Australia, Belarus, Brazil, Canada, Chile, China (People's Republic of), Colombia, Costa Rica, Curaçao, Egypt, Georgia, Ghana, Hong Kong (China), Iceland, India, Indonesia, Israel, Japan, Jordan, Kazakhstan, Korea, Malaysia, Mauritius, Mexico, Moldavia, Morocco, New Zealand, Nigeria, Norway, Panama, Philippines, Russia, Saudi Arabia, Serbia, Singapore, South Africa, Sri Lanka, Switzerland, Chinese Taipei, Thailand, Turkey, Ukraine, United States, Viet Nam
Cross-border unilateral advance pricing agreements (APAs) and any other cross-border unilateral tax rulings (such as an advance tax ruling) covering transfer pricing or the application of transfer pricing principles	190	Argentina, Australia, Barbados, Belarus, Brazil, Canada, Chile, China (People's Republic of), Colombia, Costa Rica, Curaçao, Egypt, Greenland, Hong Kong (China), India, Indonesia, Israel, Japan, Jersey, Korea, Malaysia, Malta, Mauritius, Mexico, New Zealand, Norway, Pakistan, Panama, Philippines, Russia, Saudi Arabia, Seychelles, Singapore, South Africa, Switzerland, Chinese Taipei, Thailand, Turkey, Ukraine, United States, Uruguay, Viet Nam
Cross-border rulings providing for a unilateral downward adjustment to the taxpayer's taxable profits that is not directly reflected in the taxpayer's financial / commercial accounts	14	Canada, Curaçao, Cyprus, Ireland, Israel, Italy, Kazakhstan, United Kingdom, United States
Permanent establishment rulings	7	Curaçao, Mexico, Switzerland, United States
Related party conduit rulings	N/A	N/A
De minimis rule	N/A	N/A
IP regimes: total exchanges on taxpayers benefitting from the third category of IP assets, new entrants benefitting from grandfathered IP regimes; and taxpayers making use of the option to treat the nexus ratio as a rebuttable presumption	0[3][4]	N/A
Total	444	

D. Matters related to intellectual property regimes (ToR I.4.1.3)

The Netherlands offers an intellectual property regime (IP regime)[5] that is subject to the transparency requirements under the Action 5 Report (OECD, 2015[5]). It states that the identification of the benefitting taxpayers will occur as follows:

- ***New entrants benefitting from the grandfathered IP regime***: the IP regime was in nearly all cases offered by way of ruling and this is how the Netherlands identified taxpayers entering new into the regime or bringing new assets into the regime.

    To the extent there could have been new entrants (both new taxpayers and new assets of existing taxpayers) who did not apply for a ruling, these were identified once they filed their corporate income tax returns, which had been amended for this purpose. If a taxpayer had indicated this in the return, the tax inspector verifies whether information had already been exchanged on the basis that a ruling has been issued. If not, the officer would have ensured that the template is filled out and submitted to the competent authority for exchange of information. In practice, all tax returns for the period of which new entrants could obtain grandfathering relating to 2017 will normally have been filed by the end of 2019. A complete review with final results will take place by end of 2019.

- ***Third category of IP assets***: the regime allows the third category of IP assets to benefit from the preferential tax treatment. Most taxpayers will seek a ruling in order to obtain this benefit, and information would be exchanged using the process for future rulings described above. However, as there is no requirement to apply for a ruling in order to benefit from the new innovation box, the Netherlands amended their tax return forms in 2017 and added a question to collect information on whether a taxpayer benefits from the third category of IP assets without having obtained a ruling. The Netherlands expects that all the tax returns relating to 2017 will normally be filed by the end of 2019. The Netherlands will then exchange information on any taxpayers that benefit from the third category in 2017 without applying for a ruling. The Netherlands notes that in practice because most taxpayers do apply for a ruling, the number of exchanges resulting from the amended tax returns is expected to be very low.
- ***Taxpayers making use of the option to treat the nexus ratio as a rebuttable presumption***: not applicable as the regime does not allow the nexus ratio to be treated as a rebuttable presumption.

Summary of recommendations on implementation of the transparency framework

Aspect of implementation of the transparency framework that should be improved	Recommendation for improvement
	No recommendations are made.

Notes

[1] With respect to the following preferential regimes: 1) Innovation box and 2) International shipping.

[2] Parties to the Convention are available here: www.oecd.org/tax/exchange-of-tax-information/convention-on-mutual-administrative-assistance-in-tax-matters.htm. The Netherlands also has bilateral agreements with Albania, Argentina, Armenia, Australia, Austria, Azerbaijan, Bahrain, Bangladesh, Barbados, Belarus, Belgium, Bermuda, Bosnia and Herzegovina, Brazil, Bulgaria, Canada, China (People's Republic of), Croatia, Curaçao, Czech Republic, Denmark, Egypt, Estonia, Ethiopia, Finland, France, Georgia, Germany, Ghana, Greece, Hong Kong (China), Hungary, Iceland, India, Indonesia, Ireland, Israel, Italy, Japan, Jordan, Kazakhstan, Kenya, Korea, Kuwait, Latvia, Lithuania, Luxembourg, Malaysia, Malta, Mexico, Moldova, Montenegro, Morocco, New Zealand, Nigeria, North Macedonia, Norway, Oman, Pakistan, Panama, Philippines, Poland, Portugal, Qatar, Romania, Russia, Saint Martin, Saudi Arabia, Serbia, Singapore, Slovak Republic, Slovenia, South Africa, Spain, Sri Lanka, Suriname, Sweden, Switzerland, Chinese Taipei, Tajikistan, Thailand, Tunisia, Turkey, Uganda, Ukraine, United Arab Emirates, United Kingdom, United States, Uzbekistan, Venezuela, Viet Nam, Zambia and Zimbabwe.

[3] It is noted that the Netherlands is using the same code to exchange information on new entrants of the grandfathered IP regime, entrants of the new innovation box, entrants of the new innovation box benefitting from the third category of assets, and beneficiaries of the shipping regime. Therefore exact figures of new entrants benefitting from the grandfathered regime and from the third category of assets as required for statistical purposes cannot yet be provided.

[4] The tax returns of the year 2017, in which taxpayers who did not apply for a ruling can opt for the continued application of the grandfathered regime (new entrants) or applying the new IP regime to the third category of IP asset, will normally have been filed by the end of 2019. The Netherlands will then exchange information about the application of the Innovation box if the taxpayers are grandfathered new entrants and/or have eligible profits with regard to third category IP assets, without having applied for a ruling. In practice, nearly all taxpayers request a ruling for the application of the Innovation box and therefore the number of additional taxpayers is expected to be very low.

[5] Innovation box.

New Zealand

New Zealand has met all aspects of the terms of reference (ToR) for the calendar year 2018 (year in review) and no recommendations are made.

In the prior year report, New Zealand did not receive any recommendations.

New Zealand can legally issue all five types of rulings within the scope of the transparency framework, but in practice only issues three types of rulings within the scope of the transparency framework. In practice, New Zealand has issued rulings within the scope of the transparency framework as follows:

- 69 past rulings;
- For the period 1 April 2016 - 31 December 2016: 14 future rulings;
- For the calendar year 2017: 15 future rulings, and
- For the year in review: eight future rulings.

Peer input was received from four jurisdictions in respect of the exchanges of information on rulings received from New Zealand. The input was generally positive, noting that information was complete, in a correct format and all received in a timely manner.

Introduction

This peer review covers New Zealand's implementation of the BEPS Action 5 transparency framework for the year 2018. The report has four parts, each relating to a key part of the ToR. Each part is discussed in turn. A summary of recommendations is included at the end of this report.

A. The information gathering process

New Zealand can legally all five types of rulings within the scope of the transparency framework, but in practice issues the three following types of rulings within the scope of the transparency framework: (i) cross-border unilateral advance pricing arrangements (APAs) and any other cross-border unilateral tax rulings (such as an advance tax ruling) covering transfer pricing or the application of transfer pricing principles; (ii) permanent establishment rulings; and (iii) related party conduit rulings.

Past rulings (ToR I.4.1.1, I.4.1.2, I.4.2.1, I.4.2.2)

For New Zealand, past rulings are any tax rulings within scope that are issued either: (i) on or after 1 January 2014 but before 1 April 2016; or (ii) on or after 1 January 2010 but before 1 January 2014, provided they were still in effect as at 1 January 2014.

In the prior years' peer review reports, it was determined that New Zealand's undertakings to identify past rulings and all potential exchange jurisdictions were sufficient to meet the minimum standard. New Zealand's implementation continues to meet the minimum standard.

Future rulings (ToR I.4.1.1, I.4.1.2, I.4.2.1)

For New Zealand, future rulings are any tax rulings within scope that are issued on or after 1 April 2016.

In the prior years' peer review reports, it was determined that New Zealand's undertakings to identify future rulings and all potential exchange jurisdictions was sufficient to meet the minimum standard.

Review and supervision (ToR I.4.3)

In the prior years' peer review reports, it was determined that New Zealand's review and supervision mechanism was sufficient to meet the minimum standard. New Zealand's implementation in this regard remains unchanged, and therefore continues to meet the minimum standard.

Conclusion on section A

New Zealand has met all of the ToR for the information gathering process and no recommendations are made.

B. The exchange of information

Legal basis for spontaneous exchange of information (ToR II.5.1, II.5.2)

New Zealand has the necessary domestic legal basis to exchange information spontaneously. New Zealand notes that there are no legal or practical impediments that prevent the spontaneous exchange of information on rulings as contemplated in the Action 5 minimum standard.

New Zealand is a party to international agreements permitting spontaneous exchange of information, including (i) the *Multilateral Convention on Mutual Administrative Assistance in Tax Matters: Amended by the 2010 Protocol* (OECD/Council of Europe, 2011) ("the Convention") and (ii) double tax agreements in force with 40 jurisdictions.[1]

Completion and exchange of templates (ToR II.5.3, II.5.4, II.5.5, II.5.6, II.5.7)

In the prior year peer review report, it was determined that New Zealand's completion and exchange of templates were sufficient to meet the minimum standard. New Zealand's implementation in this regard remains unchanged, and therefore continues to meet the minimum standard.

For the year in review, the timeliness of exchanges is as follows:

Past rulings in the scope of the transparency framework	Number of exchanges transmitted by 31 December 2018	Delayed exchanges		
		Number of exchanges not transmitted by 31 December 2018	Reasons for the delays	Any other comments
	0	0	N/A	N/A
Future rulings in the scope of the transparency framework	Number of exchanges transmitted within three months of the information becoming available to the competent authority or immediately after legal impediments have been lifted	Delayed exchanges		
		Number of exchanges transmitted later than three months of the information on rulings becoming available to the competent authority	Reasons for the delays	Any other comments
	21	0	N/A	N/A
Total	21	0		

Follow up requests received for exchange of the ruling	Number	Average time to provide response	Number of requests not answered
	0	N/A	N/A

Conclusion on section B

New Zealand has the necessary legal basis for spontaneous exchange of information, a process for completing the templates in a timely way and has completed all exchanges on time. New Zealand has met all of the ToR for the exchange of information process and no recommendations are made.

C. Statistics (ToR IV)

The statistics for the year in review are as follows:

Category of ruling	Number of exchanges	Jurisdictions exchanged with
Ruling related to a preferential regime	0	N/A
Cross-border unilateral advance pricing agreements (APAs) and any other cross-border unilateral tax rulings (such as an advance tax ruling) covering transfer pricing or the application of transfer pricing principles	21	Australia, Canada, France, Germany, Ireland, Japan, Malaysia, Netherlands, Singapore, Spain, Switzerland, United Kingdom, United States
Cross-border rulings providing for a unilateral downward adjustment to the taxpayer's taxable profits that is not directly reflected in the taxpayer's	0	N/A

financial / commercial accounts		
Permanent establishment rulings	0	N/A
Related party conduit rulings	0	N/A
De minimis rule	N/A	N/A
IP regimes: total exchanges on taxpayers benefitting from the third category of IP assets, new entrants benefitting from grandfathered IP regimes; and taxpayers making use of the option to treat the nexus ratio as a rebuttable presumption	N/A	N/A
Total	21	

D. Matters related to intellectual property regimes (ToR I.4.1.3)

New Zealand does not offer an intellectual property regime for which transparency requirements under the Action 5 Report (OECD, 2015[5]) were imposed.

Summary of recommendations on implementation of the transparency framework

Aspect of implementation of the transparency framework that should be improved	Recommendation for improvement
	No recommendations are made.

Notes

[1] Parties to the Convention are available here: www.oecd.org/tax/exchange-of-tax-information/convention-on-mutual-administrative-assistance-in-tax-matters.htm. New Zealand also has bilateral agreements in force with Fiji, Papua New Guinea, Philippines, Chinese Taipei, Thailand, United States and Viet Nam.

Nigeria

Nigeria has met all aspects of the terms of reference (OECD, 2017[3]) (ToR) for the calendar year 2018 (year in review).

In the prior year report, Nigeria did not receive any recommendations.

Nigeria does not issue any type of ruling within the scope of the transparency framework. Nigeria issues rulings on the tax consequences of a transaction which are binding for the tax authorities. However, the rulings issued by Nigeria do not relate to any of the categories of rulings in the scope of the Action 5 Report (OECD, 2015[5]). In the event that Nigeria puts in place the administrative process to issue rulings within the scope of the transparency framework, Nigeria notes that it would implement the transparency framework obligations.

As no exchanges were required to take place, no peer input was received in respect of the exchanges of information on rulings received from Nigeria.

Introduction

This peer review covers Nigeria's implementation of the BEPS Action 5 transparency framework for the year 2018. The report has four parts, each relating to a key part of the ToR. Each part is discussed in turn. A summary of recommendations is included at the end of this report.

A. The information gathering process

As no rulings are issued, this section is not assessed.

B. The exchange of information

As no rulings are issued, this section is not assessed.

C. Statistics (ToR IV)

As no rulings are issued, no statistics can be reported.

D. Matters related to intellectual property regimes (ToR I.4.1.3)

Nigeria does not offer an intellectual property regime for which transparency requirements under the Action 5 Report (OECD, 2015[5]) were imposed.

Summary of recommendations on implementation of the transparency framework

Aspect of implementation of the transparency framework that should be improved	Recommendation for improvement
	No recommendations are made.

Norway

Norway has met all aspects of the terms of reference (OECD, 2017[3]) (ToR) for the calendar year 2018 (year in review) and no recommendations are made.

In the prior year report, Norway did not receive any recommendations.

Norway can legally issue three types of rulings within the scope of the transparency framework. In practice, Norway issued rulings within the scope of the transparency framework as follows:

- One past ruling;
- For the period 1 April 2016 - 31 December 2016: no future rulings;
- For the calendar year 2017: one future ruling, and
- For the year in review: no future rulings.

As no exchanges were required to take place, no peer input was received in respect of the exchanges of information on rulings received from Norway.

Introduction

This peer review covers Norway's implementation of the BEPS Action 5 transparency framework for the year 2018. The report has four parts, each relating to a key part of the ToR. Each part is discussed in turn. A summary of recommendations is included at the end of this report.

A. The information gathering process

Norway can legally issue the three following types of rulings within the scope of the transparency framework: (i) rulings related to a preferential regimes;[1] (ii) cross-border unilateral advance pricing arrangements (APAs) covering transfer pricing or the application of transfer pricing principles in relation to realisation of natural gas for companies liable to tax under the Petroleum Tax Act; and (iii) related party conduit rulings.

Past rulings (ToR I.4.1.1, I.4.1.2, I.4.2.1, I.4.2.2)

For Norway, past rulings are any tax rulings within scope that are issued either: (i) on or after 1 January 2014 but before 1 April 2016; or (ii) on or after 1 January 2010 but before 1 January 2014, provided they were still in effect as at 1 January 2014.

In the prior years' peer review reports, it was determined that Norway's undertakings to identify past rulings and all potential exchange jurisdictions were sufficient to meet the minimum standard. Norway's implementation in this regard remains unchanged, and therefore continues to meet the minimum standard.

Future rulings (ToR I.4.1.1, I.4.1.2, I.4.2.1)

For Norway, future rulings are any tax rulings within scope that are issued on or after 1 April 2016.

In the prior years' peer review reports, it was determined that Norway's undertakings to identify future rulings and all potential exchange jurisdictions was sufficient to meet the minimum standard. Norway's implementation in this regard remains unchanged, and therefore continues to meet the minimum standard.

Review and supervision (ToR I.4.3)

In the prior years' peer review reports, it was determined that Norway's review and supervision mechanism was sufficient to meet the minimum standard. Norway's implementation in this regard remains unchanged, and therefore continues to meet the minimum standard.

Conclusion on section A

Norway has met all of the ToR for the information gathering process and no recommendations are made.

B. The exchange of information

Legal basis for spontaneous exchange of information (ToR II.5.1, II.5.2)

Norway has the necessary domestic legal basis to exchange information spontaneously. Norway notes that there are no legal or practical impediments that prevent the spontaneous exchange of information on rulings as contemplated in the Action 5 minimum standard.

Norway has international agreements permitting spontaneous exchange of information, including being a party to the (i) the *Multilateral Convention on Mutual Administrative Assistance in Tax Matters: Amended by the 2010 Protocol* (OECD/Council of Europe, 2011) ("the Convention"), (ii) the Nordic Convention on Assistance in Tax Matters and (iii) double tax agreements in force with 84 jurisdictions.[2]

Completion and exchange of templates (ToR II.5.3, II.5.4, II.5.5, II.5.6, II.5.7)

In the prior year peer review report, it was determined that Norway's process for the completion and exchange of templates were sufficient to meet the minimum standard. Norway's implementation in this regard remains unchanged and therefore continues to meet the minimum standard.

As Norway did not issue any future rulings in scope of the transparency framework in the relevant period, Norway was not required to exchange any information on rulings in the year in review and no data on the timeliness of exchanges can be reported.

Conclusion on section B

Norway has the necessary legal basis for spontaneous exchange of information, a process for completing the templates in a timely way and has completed all exchanges. Norway has met all of the ToR for the exchange of information process and no recommendations are made.

C. Statistics (ToR IV)

As there was no information on rulings exchanged by Norway for the year in review, no statistics can be reported.

D. Matters related to intellectual property regimes (ToR I.4.1.3)

Norway does not offer an intellectual property regime for which transparency requirements under the Action 5 Report (OECD, 2015[5]) were imposed.

Summary of recommendations on implementation of the transparency framework

Aspect of implementation of the transparency framework that should be improved	Recommendation for improvement
	No recommendations are made.

Notes

[1] With respect to the following regime: International shipping.

[2] Parties to the Convention are available here: http://www.oecd.org/tax/exchange-of-tax-information/convention-on-mutual-administrative-assistance-in-tax-matters.htm. Parties to the Nordic Convention on Assistance in Tax Matters are Denmark, Faroe Islands, Finland, Iceland and Sweden. Norway also has bilateral agreements in force with Albania, Argentina, Australia, Austria, Azerbaijan, Bangladesh, Barbados, Belgium, Benin, Bonaire, Bosnia and Herzegovina, Brazil, Bulgaria, Canada, Chile, China (People's Republic of), Croatia, Curaçao, Cyprus, Czech Republic, Egypt, Estonia, France, Gambia, Georgia, Germany, Greece, Hungary, India, Indonesia, Ireland, Israel, Italy, Ivory Coast, Jamaica, Japan, Kazakhstan, Kenya, Korea, Latvia, Lithuania, Luxembourg, Malawi, Malaysia, Malta, Mexico, Montenegro, Morocco, Nepal, Netherlands, New Zealand, North Macedonia, Pakistan, Philippines, Poland, Portugal, Qatar, Romania, Russia, Saba, Senegal, Serbia, Sierra Leone, Singapore, Saint Eustatius, Sint Maarten, Slovak Republic, Slovenia, South Africa, Spain, Sri Lanka, Switzerland, Tanzania, Thailand, Tunisia, Turkey, Uganda, Ukraine, United Kingdom, United States, Venezuela, Viet Nam, Zambia and Zimbabwe.

Note by Turkey: The information in this document with reference to "Cyprus" relates to the southern part of the Island. There is no single authority representing both Turkish and Greek Cypriot people on the Island. Turkey recognises the Turkish Republic of Northern Cyprus (TRNC). Until a lasting and equitable solution is found within the context of the United Nations, Turkey shall preserve its position concerning the "Cyprus issue".

Note by all the European Union Member States of the OECD and the European Union. The Republic of Cyprus is recognised by all members of the United Nations with the exception of Turkey. The information in this document relates to the area under the effective control of the Government of the Republic of Cyprus.

Oman

Oman has met all aspects of the terms of reference (OECD, 2017[3]) (ToR) for the calendar year 2018 (year in review).

This is the first review of Oman's implementation of the transparency framework.

Oman indicates that it cannot legally issue any type of rulings within the scope of the transparency framework.

As no rulings were issued, no exchange of information was required. No peer input was received in respect of the exchanges of information on rulings received from Oman.

Introduction

This peer review covers Oman's implementation of the BEPS Action 5 transparency framework for the year 2018. The report has four parts, each relating to a key part of the ToR. Each part is discussed in turn. A summary of recommendations is included at the end of this report.

A. The information gathering process

As no rulings are issued, this section is not assessed.

B. The exchange of information

As no rulings are issued, this section is not assessed.

C. Statistics (ToR IV)

As no rulings are issued, no statistics can be reported.

D. Matters related to intellectual property regimes (ToR I.4.1.3)

Oman does not offer an intellectual property regime for which transparency requirements under the Action 5 Report (OECD, 2015[5]) were imposed.

Summary of recommendations on implementation of the transparency framework

Aspect of implementation of the transparency framework that should be improved	Recommendation for improvement
	No recommendations are made.

Pakistan

Pakistan has met all aspects of the terms of reference (OECD, 2017[3]) (ToR) for the calendar year 2018 (year in review) that can be met in the absence of rulings in scope being issued and no recommendations are made.

In the prior year report, Pakistan did not receive any recommendations.

Pakistan does not issue any type of rulings within the scope of the transparency framework.

As no exchanges were required to take place, no peer input was received in respect of the exchanges of information on rulings received from Pakistan.

Introduction

This peer review covers Pakistan's implementation of the BEPS Action 5 transparency framework for the year 2018. The report has four parts, each relating to a key part of the ToR. Each part is discussed in turn. A summary of recommendations is included at the end of this report.

A. The information gathering process

As no rulings are issued, this section is not assessed.

B. The exchange of information

As no rulings are issued, this section is not assessed.

C. Statistics (ToR IV)

As no rulings are issued, no statistics can be reported.

D. Matters related to intellectual property regimes (ToR I.4.1.3)

Pakistan will be reviewed at future meetings of the Forum on Harmful Tax Practices ("FHTP") for potential IP regimes in scope of the FHTP work. However, for the year in review no transparency requirements were relevant.

Summary of recommendations on implementation of the transparency framework

Aspect of implementation of the transparency framework that should be improved	Recommendation for improvement
	No recommendations are made.

Panama

Panama has met all aspects of the terms of reference (OECD, 2017[3]) (ToR) for the calendar year 2018 (year in review) except for having in place an effective review and supervision mechanism to ensure that all relevant information is captured adequately (ToR I.4.3). Panama receives one recommendation on this point for the year in review.

In the prior year report, Panama did not receive any recommendations. For the year in review, a new recommendation has been added.

Panama can legally issue one type of rulings within the scope of the transparency framework. In practice, Panama issued rulings within the scope of the transparency framework as follows:

- One past ruling;
- For the period 1 April 2017 - 31 December 2017: no future rulings; and
- For the year in review: no future rulings.

As no exchanges took place during the year in review, no peer input was received in respect of the exchanges of information on rulings received from Panama.

Introduction

This peer review covers Panama's implementation of the BEPS Action 5 transparency framework for the year 2018. The report has four parts, each relating to a key part of the ToR. Each part is discussed in turn. A summary of recommendations is included at the end of this report.

A. The information gathering process

For the year in review, Panama could legally issue one type of ruling within the scope of the transparency framework: rulings related to preferential regimes.[1]

Past rulings (ToR I.4.1.1, I.4.1.2, I.4.2.1, I.4.2.2)

For Panama, past rulings are any tax rulings within scope that are issued either: (i) on or after 1 January 2015 but before 1 April 2017; or (ii) on or after 1 January 2012 but before 1 January 2015, provided they were still in effect as at 1 January 2015.

In the prior year peer review report, it was determined that Panama's process in place to identify past rulings and all potential exchange jurisdictions were sufficient to meet the minimum standard. However, during the year in review, Panama did not in practice identify the jurisdictions of residence of related parties to transactions for which a preferential treatment is granted or which gives rise to income from related parties benefiting from a preferential treatment. This was brought to Panama's attention in the course of the peer review process in August 2019. It is noted that Panama immediately took steps to identify the remaining exchange jurisdictions.

Future rulings (ToR I.4.1.1, I.4.1.2, I.4.2.1)

For Panama, future rulings are any tax rulings within scope that are issued on or after 1 April 2017.

In the prior year peer review report, it was determined that Panama's undertakings to identify future rulings and all potential exchange jurisdictions were sufficient to meet the minimum standard. Panama's implementation in this regard remains unchanged, and therefore continues to meet the minimum standard.

Review and supervision (ToR I.4.3)

In the prior year peer review report, it was determined that Panama's review and supervision mechanism was sufficient to meet the minimum standard. As noted above, during the year in review certain potential exchange jurisdictions were not identified, and this issue was not detected and resolved in the year in review through the review and supervision mechanism. Panama is therefore recommended to strengthen its review and supervision mechanism to ensure that the information gathering process is working effectively.

Conclusion on section A

For the year in review, Panama has met the ToR for the information gathering process, except for having in place a review and supervision mechanism to ensure that all relevant information is captured adequately (ToR I.4.3). Panama is recommended to strengthen its review and supervision mechanism to ensure that the information gathering process is working effectively.

B. The exchange of information

Legal basis for spontaneous exchange of information (ToR II.5.1, II.5.2)

Panama has the necessary domestic legal basis to exchange information spontaneously. Panama notes that there are no legal or practical impediments that prevent the spontaneous exchange of information on rulings as contemplated in the Action 5 minimum standard.

Panama has international agreements permitting spontaneous exchange of information, including being a party to the (i) *Multilateral Convention on Mutual Administrative Assistance in Tax Matters: Amended by the 2010 Protocol* (OECD/Council of Europe, 2011[4]) ("the Convention"), and (ii) double tax agreements in force with 17 jurisdictions,[2] however spontaneous exchange of information under these agreements is not authorised by Panama's domestic law.

Completion and exchange of templates (ToR II.5.3, II.5.4, II.5.5, II.5.6, II.5.7)

In the prior year peer review report, it was determined that Panama's process for the completion and exchange of templates was sufficient to meet the minimum standard in absence of a legal framework in place for spontaneously exchanging information on rulings. Domestic legislation implementing the Convention was introduced in 2017 and permits spontaneous exchange of information under the Convention for taxable periods beginning on or after 1 January 2018.

For the year in review, the timeliness of exchanges is as follows:

Past rulings in the scope of the transparency framework	Number of exchanges transmitted by 31 December 2018	Delayed exchanges		
		Number of exchanges not transmitted by 31 December 2018	Reasons for the delays	Any other comments
	0	3	Determination of the effective application of the information exchange instruments.	The information on the past ruling was exchanged in May 2019 with the jurisdiction of residence of the ultimate parent company. Exchanges with the jurisdictions of residence of two related parties have been performed in August 2019.
Future rulings in the scope of the transparency framework	Number of exchanges transmitted within three months of the information becoming available to the competent authority or immediately after legal impediments have been lifted	Delayed exchanges		
		Number of exchanges transmitted later than three months of the information on rulings becoming available to the competent authority	Reasons for the delays	Any other comments
	N/A	N/A		
Total	0	3		

Follow up requests received for exchange of the ruling	Number	Average time to provide response	Number of requests not answered
	0	N/A	N/A

During the year in review, Panama experienced some delays in the process of completing and exchanging the template for the one identified past ruling due to an error in the review and supervision mechanism with regard to the information gathering process identified in part A above, as well as uncertainty in determining whether the Convention allowed the spontaneous exchange of information on tax rulings, given the Convention applied for taxable periods from 1 January 2018. Information on the one identified past ruling was exchanged in May 2019 with the jurisdiction of residence of the ultimate parent company, as soon as the issue concerning the Convention was resolved. Exchanges with the jurisdictions of residence of two related parties have been performed in August 2019, quickly after the issue concerning the identification of the relevant exchange jurisdictions has been identified and resolved.

Conclusion on section B

Panama has the necessary legal basis for spontaneous exchange of information but experienced some delay in the process of completing and exchanging the templates in a timely way. However, given that these issues have been resolved, the exchanges were completed quickly after the underlying issues have been identified and resolved and as of 2019, Panama cannot legally issue any type of rulings within the scope of the transparency framework, it is concluded that Panama has met all of the ToR for the exchange of information process and no recommendations are made.

C. Statistics (ToR IV)

As there was no information on rulings exchanged by Panama for the year in review, no statistics can be reported.

D. Matters related to intellectual property regimes (ToR I.4.1.3)

Panama offers an intellectual property regime (IP regime)[3] that is not subject to the transparency requirements under the Action 5 Report (OECD, 2015[5]), because:

- ***New entrants benefitting from the grandfathered IP regime***: this regime has been amended by implementing the nexus approach from 27 December 2018. Taxpayers benefitting from the previous regime cannot benefit from grandfathering. As such, no enhanced transparency requirements apply.
- ***Third category of IP assets***: not applicable as the regime does not allow the third category of IP assets to qualify for the benefits.
- ***Taxpayers making use of the option to treat the nexus ratio as a rebuttable presumption***: not applicable as the regime does not allow the nexus ratio to be treated as a rebuttable presumption.

Panama introduced a new IP regime[4] which came into effect from 27 December 2018. It is noted that this regime is not subject to transparency requirements under the Action 5 Report (OECD, 2015[5]), because:

- ***New entrants benefitting from the grandfathered IP regime***: as this is a new IP regime rather than a grandfathered IP regime, transparency on new entrants is not relevant.
- ***Third category of IP assets***: not applicable as the regime does not allow the third category of IP assets to qualify for the benefits.

- ***Taxpayers making use of the option to treat the nexus ratio as a rebuttable presumption***: not applicable as the regime does not allow the nexus ratio to be treated as a rebuttable presumption.

Summary of recommendations on implementation of the transparency framework

Aspect of implementation of the transparency framework that should be improved	Recommendation for improvement
Panama did not identify the jurisdictions of residence of related parties to transactions for which a preferential treatment is granted or which gives rise to income from related parties benefiting from a preferential treatment with regard to the one identified past ruling. This issue was not identified through the review and supervision mechanism.	Panama is recommended to strengthen its review and supervision mechanism to ensure that the information gathering process is working effectively.
Panama experienced some delays in exchanging information on the one identified past ruling due to an error in the review and supervision mechanism with regard to the information gathering process as well as uncertainty in the determination of the effective application of the information exchange instruments.	No recommendation is made because Panama completed the exchanges on the one identified past ruling quickly after the issues were identified and resolved, and this is not a recurring issue.

Notes

[1] With respect to the following preferential regime: Multinational Companies Headquarters' regime (i.e. MHQ/SEM). These rulings are known as "fiscal agreements". Law 57 of 2018, entered into force on 1 January 2019, repealed the provision that included the possibility for Multinational headquarters (MHQ) Licensed Companies to obtain a fiscal agreement. Therefore as of 2019, Panama cannot legally issue any type of rulings within the scope of the transparency framework.

[2] Parties to the Convention are available here: www.oecd.org/tax/exchange-of-tax-information/convention-on-mutual-administrative-assistance-in-tax-matters.htm. Panama also has double tax agreements with Barbados, Czech Republic, France, Ireland, Israel, Italy, Korea, Luxembourg, Mexico, Netherlands, Portugal, Qatar, Singapore, Spain, United Arab Emirates, United Kingdom and Viet Nam.

[3] This regime is the City of knowledge technical zone.

[4] This regime is the General IP regime.

Papua New Guinea

Papua New Guinea has met all aspects of the terms of reference (OECD, 2017[3]) (ToR) for the calendar year 2018 (year in review) that can be met in the absence of rulings being issued.

In the prior year report, Papua New Guinea did not receive any recommendations.

Papua New Guinea cannot legally issue any type of rulings within the scope of the transparency framework.

As no exchanges were required to take place, no peer input was received in respect of the exchanges of information on rulings received from Papua New Guinea.

Introduction

This peer review covers Papua New Guinea's implementation of the BEPS Action 5 transparency framework for the year 2018. The report has four parts, each relating to a key part of the ToR. Each part is discussed in turn. A summary of recommendations is included at the end of this report.

A. The information gathering process

As no rulings are issued, this section is not assessed.

B. The exchange of information

As no rulings are issued, this section is not assessed.

C. Statistics (ToR IV)

As no rulings are issued, no statistics can be reported.

D. Matters related to intellectual property regimes (ToR I.4.1.3)

Papua New Guinea does not offer an intellectual property regime for which transparency requirements under the Action 5 Report (OECD, 2015[5]) were imposed.

Summary of recommendations on implementation of the transparency framework

Aspect of implementation of the transparency framework that should be improved	Recommendation for improvement
	No recommendations are made.

Paraguay

Paraguay has met all aspects of the terms of reference (OECD, 2017[3]) (ToR) for the calendar year 2018 (year in review) that can be met in the absence of rulings being issued.

In the prior year review, Paraguay received two recommendations, which have been addressed and are removed.

Paraguay does not issue any type of rulings within the scope of the transparency framework. In the prior year peer review report, it was noted that Paraguay could issue a ruling related to a preferential regime. However, it has since been confirmed that the preferential regime in question is not in the scope of the FHTP's work, and therefore is not a ruling to which the transparency framework applies. The two recommendations from the prior year report, relating to the identification and exchange of information on rulings, are no longer applicable. No other types of rulings that are in the scope of the transparency framework can be issued by Paraguay.

As no exchanges were required to take place, no peer input was received in respect of the exchanges of information on rulings received from Paraguay.

Introduction

This peer review covers Paraguay's implementation of the BEPS Action 5 transparency framework for the year 2018. The report has four parts, each relating to a key part of the ToR. Each part is discussed in turn. A summary of recommendations is included at the end of this report.

A. The information gathering process

As no rulings are issued, this section is not assessed.

B. The exchange of information

As no rulings are issued, this section is not assessed.

C. Statistics (ToR IV)

As no rulings are issued, no statistics can be reported.

D. Matters related to intellectual property regimes (ToR I.4.1.3)

Paraguay does not offer an intellectual property regime for which transparency requirements under the Action 5 Report (OECD, 2015[5]) were imposed.

Summary of recommendations on implementation of the transparency framework

Aspect of implementation of the transparency framework that should be improved	Recommendation for improvement
	No recommendations are made.

Peru

Peru has met all aspects of the terms of reference (OECD, 2017[3]) (ToR) for the calendar year 2018 (year in review) that can be met given in the absence of rulings being issued.

In the prior year report, Peru did not receive any recommendations.

Peru can legally issue five types of rulings within the scope of the transparency framework. In practice, Peru issued no rulings within the scope of the transparency framework.

Peru publishes the result of particular consultations.[1]

As no exchanges were required to take place, no peer input was received in respect of the exchanges of information on rulings received from Peru.

Introduction

This peer review covers Peru's implementation of the BEPS Action 5 transparency framework for the year 2018. The report has four parts, each relating to a key part of the ToR. Each part is discussed in turn. A summary of recommendations is included at the end of this report.

A. The information gathering process

Peru can legally issue the five following types of rulings within the scope of the transparency framework: (i) rulings relating to a preferential regime;[2] (ii) cross-border unilateral advance pricing arrangements (APAs) and any other cross-border unilateral tax rulings (such as an advance tax ruling) covering transfer pricing or the application of transfer pricing principles; (iii) rulings providing for unilateral downward adjustments; (iv) permanent establishment rulings; and (v) related party conduit rulings.[3]

Past rulings (ToR I.4.1.1, I.4.1.2, I.4.2.1, I.4.2.2)

For Peru, past rulings are any tax rulings within scope that are issued either: (i) on or after 1 January 2015 but before 1 September 2017; or (ii) on or after 1 January 2012 but before 1 January 2015, provided still in effect as at 1 January 2015.

In the prior year peer review report, it was determined that Peru's undertakings to identify past rulings were sufficient to meet the minimum standard. Peru's implementation in this regard remains unchanged, and therefore continues to meet the minimum standard.

Future rulings (ToR I.4.1.1, I.4.1.2, I.4.2.1)

For Peru, future rulings are any tax rulings within scope that are issued on or after 1 September 2017.

In the prior year peer review report, it was determined that Peru's undertakings to identify future rulings and all potential exchange jurisdictions were sufficient to meet the minimum standard, which involves reviewing information in the ruling, the taxpayer file or obtaining the information from the taxpayer directly. Peru's implementation in this regard remains unchanged, and therefore continues to meet the minimum standard in the absence of rulings being issued.

For the purpose of formalising the process, Peru notes its intention to put in place a procedure in the first half of 2020 for identifying the relevant exchange jurisdictions at the time of the taxpayer's request.

Review and supervision (ToR I.4.3)

In the prior year peer review report, it was determined that Peru's review and supervision mechanism was sufficient to meet the minimum standard. Peru's implementation in this regard remains unchanged, and therefore continues to meet the minimum standard.

Conclusion on section A

Peru has met all of the ToR for the information gathering process and no recommendations are made.

B. The exchange of information

Legal basis for spontaneous exchange of information (ToR II.5.1, II.5.2)

Peru has the necessary domestic legal basis to exchange information spontaneously. Peru notes that there are no legal or practical impediments that prevent the spontaneous exchange of information on rulings as contemplated in the Action 5 minimum standard.

Peru has international agreements permitting spontaneous exchange of information, including being a party to the (i) *Multilateral Convention on Mutual Administrative Assistance in Tax Matters: Amended by the 2010 Protocol* (OECD/Council of Europe, 2011[4]) ("the Convention"), (ii) double tax agreements in force with seven jurisdictions, and (iii) tax information exchange agreements in force with two jurisdictions.[4]

Completion and exchange of templates (ToR II.5.3, II.5.4, II.5.5, II.5.6, II.5.7)

In the prior year peer review report, it was determined that Peru's process for the completion and exchange of templates, which was based on an ad hoc process, was sufficient to meet the minimum standard. Peru's implementation in this regard remains unchanged and therefore continues to meet the minimum standard in the absence of rulings being issued and exchanged.

For the purpose of formalising the process, Peru notes that a formal procedure for the completion and exchange of templates will be established in the first half of 2020. As Peru did not issue any past or future rulings in scope of the transparency framework in the relevant periods, Peru was not required to exchange any information on rulings in the year in review and no data on the timeliness of exchanges can be reported.

Conclusion on section B

Peru has the necessary legal framework and administrative process in place for exchanging information on rulings. Peru has met all of the ToR for the exchange of information process that can be met in the absence of rulings being issued and exchanged in practice and no recommendations are made.

C. Statistics (ToR IV)

As no rulings are issued, no statistics can be reported.

D. Matters related to intellectual property regimes (ToR I.4.1.3)

Peru does not offer an intellectual property regime for which transparency requirements under the Action 5 Report (OECD, 2015[5]) were imposed.

Summary of recommendations on implementation of the transparency framework

Aspect of implementation of the transparency framework that should be improved	Recommendation for improvement
	No recommendations are made.

Notes

[1] Available at http://www.sunat.gob.pe/legislacion/oficios/Art95/2016/indcor.htm

[2] With respect to the following preferential regimes: 1) Special economic zone 1 (Ceticos) and 2) Special economic zone 2 (Zofratacna).

[3] Rulings other than APAs are known in Peru as "particular consultations."

[4] Parties to the Convention are available here: www.oecd.org/tax/exchange-of-tax-information/convention-on-mutual-administrative-assistance-in-tax-matters.htm. Peru also has double tax agreements in force with Brazil, Canada, Chile, Korea, Mexico, Portugal and Switzerland; and tax information exchange agreements in force with United States and Ecuador.

The Philippines

The Philippines is taking steps to implement the legal basis for the transparency framework by commencing administrative preparations to ensure that information on rulings will be exchanged once the new legal basis is in place. The Philippines has met all of the terms of reference (ToR) for the calendar year 2018 (year in review) except for identifying all potential exchange jurisdictions for both past and future rulings (ToR I.4.2.1 and ToR I.4.2.2), having in place a review and supervision mechanism (ToR I.4.3) and having in place a domestic legal framework allowing spontaneous exchange of information on rulings by ensuring the timely exchange of information on rulings in the form required by the transparency framework (ToR II.5). The Philippines receives four recommendations on these points for the year in review.

In the prior year report, the Philippines received the same four recommendations. As they have not been addressed, the recommendations remain in place.

The Philippines can legally issue one type of rulings within the scope of the transparency framework. In practice, the Philippines issued rulings within the scope of the transparency framework as follows:

- 78 past rulings;
- For the period 1 September 2017 - 31 December 2017: four future rulings, and
- For the year in review: 30 future rulings.

As no exchanges took place, no peer input was received in respect of the exchanges of information on rulings received from the Philippines.

Introduction

This peer review covers the Philippines' implementation of the BEPS Action 5 transparency framework for the year 2018. The report has four parts, each relating to a key part of the ToR. Each part is discussed in turn. A summary of recommendations is included at the end of this report.

A. The information gathering process

The Philippines can legally issue the following type of rulings within the scope of the transparency framework: permanent establishment rulings.

Past rulings (ToR I.4.1.1, I.4.1.2, I.4.2.1, I.4.2.2)

For the Philippines, past rulings are any tax rulings within scope that are issued either: (i) on or after 1 January 2015 but before 1 September 2017; or (ii) on or after 1 January 2012 but before 1 January 2015, provided they were still in effect as at 1 January 2015.

In the prior year peer review report, it was determined that the Philippines' undertakings to identify past rulings and all potential exchange jurisdictions met all the ToR, except for identifying potential exchange jurisdictions for all past rulings in the relevant categories (ToR I.4.2.2). Therefore, the Philippines was recommended to apply the "best efforts approach" to identify potential exchange jurisdictions for all past rulings. The only required information on potential exchange jurisdictions that was not provided by the taxpayer upon application was related to the ultimate parent company. However, during the year in review the Philippines experienced similar problems and therefore the prior year recommendation remains. The Philippines notes that it is currently addressing these issues, including capacity building and working in co-operation with the Department of Finance.

Future rulings (ToR I.4.1.1, I.4.1.2, I.4.2.1)

For the Philippines, future rulings are any tax rulings within scope that are issued on or after 1 September 2017.

In the prior year peer review report, it was determined that the Philippines' undertakings in respect of future rulings met the ToR, except for identifying all potential exchange jurisdictions (ToR I.4.2.1). The only required information on potential exchange jurisdictions that was not provided by the taxpayer upon application was related to the ultimate parent company. Therefore, the Philippines was recommended to ensure that all potential exchange jurisdictions are identified swiftly for future rulings. However, during the year in review the Philippines experienced similar problems and therefore the prior year recommendation remains. The Philippines notes that it is currently addressing these issues, including through capacity building.

Review and supervision (ToR I.4.3)

In the prior year peer review report, it was not clear whether the Philippines had a review and supervision process in place (ToR I.4.3). Therefore, the Philippines was recommended to have in place a review and supervision mechanism to ensure that all relevant information is captured adequately. The Philippines does not yet have a review and supervision process in place and therefore the prior year recommendation remains. The Philippines notes that it is currently addressing these issues.

Conclusion on section A

The Philippines has met the ToR for the information gathering process, except for applying the "best efforts approach" for past rulings (ToR I.4.2.2), identifying all potential exchange jurisdictions for all future rulings (ToR I.4.2.1) and having in place a review and supervision mechanism (ToR I.4.3). The Philippines is recommended to apply the best efforts approach for past rulings with respect to identifying the ultimate parent company, which was the only required information not provided by the taxpayer upon application to ensure that all potential exchange jurisdictions are identified swiftly for future rulings, and to have in place a review and supervision mechanism to ensure that the information gathering process is working effectively.

B. The exchange of information

Legal basis for spontaneous exchange of information (ToR II.5.1, II.5.2)

The Philippines does not have the necessary domestic legal basis to exchange information on rulings spontaneously. This is because the Philippines is legally prohibited from sharing information on, or copies of, rulings other than to the applicant taxpayer. The Philippines is currently in the process of issuing regulations to allow the Philippines to spontaneously exchange information on rulings.

The Philippines is a party to international agreements permitting spontaneous exchange of information, including double tax agreements with 43 jurisdictions.[1] The Philippines has signed the *Multilateral Convention on Mutual Administrative Assistance in Tax Matters: Amended by the 2010 Protocol* (OECD/Council of Europe, 2011) ("the Convention") which is currently with the Philippine Senate for concurrence. Once the Convention enters into force, the spontaneous exchange of information could also be undertaken with jurisdictions that are covered by the Convention.

Completion and exchange of templates (ToR II.5.3, II.5.4, II.5.5, II.5.6, II.5.7)

As the Philippines does not yet have the legal basis for exchanges, the process for the completion and exchange of templates has not been put in place. The Philippines is recommended to put in place a process for the completion and exchange of templates to ensure the exchanges can take place as soon as the legal basis is in force.

For the year in review, as there is no domestic legal basis for exchange, no data on the timeliness of exchanges can be reported.

Conclusion on section B

The Philippines is recommended to continue its efforts to put in place a domestic legal framework allowing spontaneous exchange of information on rulings and to ensure the timely exchange of information on rulings in the form required by the transparency framework (ToR II.5).

C. Statistics (ToR IV)

As there was no information on rulings exchanged by the Philippines for the year in review, no statistics can be reported.

D. Matters related to intellectual property regimes (ToR I.4.1.3)

The Philippines does not offer an intellectual property regime for which transparency requirements under the Action 5 Report (OECD, 2015[5]) were imposed.

Summary of recommendations on implementation of the transparency framework

Aspect of implementation of the transparency framework that should be improved	Recommendation for improvement
The Philippines does not currently collect information on all potential exchange jurisdictions, particularly the ultimate parent company for past rulings.	The Philippines is recommended to apply the "best efforts approach" to identify potential exchange jurisdictions for all past rulings.
The Philippines does not currently collect information on all potential exchange jurisdictions, particularly the ultimate parent company for future rulings.	The Philippines is recommended to ensure that all potential exchange jurisdictions are identified swiftly for all future rulings.
The Philippines does not have a review and supervision mechanism in place to ensure that all relevant information on the identification of rulings and potential exchange jurisdictions is captured adequately.	The Philippines is recommended to have in place a review and supervision mechanism to ensure that the information gathering process is working effectively.
The Philippines does not yet have the necessary domestic legal framework in place for exchanging information on rulings or a process in place to ensure the timely exchange of information on rulings in the form required by the transparency framework.	The Philippines is recommended to continue to put in place a domestic legal framework allowing spontaneous exchange of information on rulings and to ensure the timely exchange of information on rulings in the form required by the transparency framework.

Notes

[1] The Philippines has bilateral agreements in force with Australia, Austria, Bahrain, Bangladesh, Belgium, Brazil, Canada, China (People's Republic), Czech Republic, Denmark, Finland, France, Germany, Hungary, India, Indonesia, Israel, Italy, Japan, Korea, Kuwait, Malaysia, Mexico, Netherlands, New Zealand, Nigeria, Norway, Pakistan, Poland, Qatar, Romania, Russia, Singapore, Spain, Sri Lanka, Sweden, Switzerland, Thailand, Turkey, United Arab Emirates, United Kingdom, United States and Viet Nam.

Poland

Poland has met all aspects of the terms of reference (OECD, 2017[3]) (ToR) for the calendar year 2018 (year in review) except for identifying all potential exchange jurisdictions for future rulings other than APAs (ToR I.4.2.1). Poland receives one recommendation on this point for the year in review.

In the prior year report, Poland received the same recommendation. As it has not been addressed, the recommendation remains in place.

Poland can legally issue four types of rulings within the scope of the transparency framework. In practice, Poland issued rulings within the scope of the transparency framework as follows:

- 84 past rulings;
- For the period 1 April 2016 - 31 December 2016: six future rulings;
- For the calendar year 2017: 20 future rulings, and
- For the year in review: 16 future rulings.

Poland publishes their tax rulings, except for APA rulings, in redacted form on Poland's Ministry of Finance website.[1]

Peer input was received from three jurisdictions in respect of the exchanges of information on rulings received from Poland. The input was positive, noting that information was complete, in a correct format and received in a timely manner.

Introduction

This peer review covers Poland's implementation of the BEPS Action 5 transparency framework for the year 2018. The report has four parts, each relating to a key part of the ToR. Each part is discussed in turn. A summary of recommendations is included at the end of this report.

A. The information gathering process

Poland can legally issue the following four types of rulings within the scope of the transparency framework: (i) cross-border unilateral APAs and any other cross-border unilateral tax rulings (such as an advance tax ruling) covering transfer pricing or the application of transfer pricing principles; (ii) rulings providing for unilateral downward adjustments, (iii) permanent establishment rulings; and (iv) related party conduit rulings.

Past rulings (ToR I.4.1.1, I.4.1.2, I.4.2.1, I.4.2.2)

For Poland, past rulings are any tax rulings within scope that are issued either: (i) on or after 1 January 2014 but before 1 April 2016; or (ii) on or after 1 January 2010 but before 1 January 2014, provided they were still in effect as at 1 January 2014.

In the prior year peer review report, it was determined that Poland's undertakings to identify past rulings and all potential exchange jurisdictions were sufficient to meet the minimum standard. Poland's implementation in this regard remains unchanged, and therefore continues to meet the minimum standard.

Future rulings (ToR I.4.1.1, I.4.1.2, I.4.2.1)

For Poland, future rulings are any tax rulings within scope that are issued on or after 1 April 2016.

In the prior year peer review report, it was determined that Poland's undertakings to identify future rulings and all potential exchange jurisdictions have met the ToR, except for identifying all potential exchange jurisdictions for future rulings other than APAs (ToR I.4.2.1). Therefore, Poland was recommended to ensure that all potential exchange jurisdictions are identified swiftly for future rulings other than APAs. With effect from 30 April 2019, Poland addressed the recommendation by amending its legislation. According to the amended provisions, taxpayers requesting cross-border rulings are now obliged to include information related to all potentially affected jurisdictions in the ruling request form. However, during the year in review Poland still experienced problems in identifying the potential exchange jurisdictions and therefore the prior year recommendation remains. This is a continuing recommendation from the two prior years.

Review and supervision (ToR I.4.3)

In the prior years' peer review reports, it was determined that Poland's review and supervision mechanism was sufficient to meet the minimum standard. Poland's implementation in this regard remains unchanged, and therefore continues to meet the minimum standard.

Conclusion on section A

Poland has met all of the ToR for the information gathering process, except for identifying all potential exchange jurisdictions for all future rulings other than APAs (ToR I.4.2.1). As such, Poland is recommended to ensure that all potential exchange jurisdictions are identified swiftly for future rulings other than APAs.

B. The exchange of information

Legal basis for spontaneous exchange of information (ToR II.5.1, II.5.2)

Poland has the necessary domestic legal basis to exchange information spontaneously. Poland notes that there are no legal or practical impediments that prevent the spontaneous exchange of information on rulings as contemplated in the Action 5 minimum standard.

Poland has international agreements permitting spontaneous exchange of information, including being a party to the (i) *Multilateral Convention on Mutual Administrative Assistance in Tax Matters: Amended by the 2010 Protocol* (OECD/Council of Europe, 2011[4]) ("the Convention"), (ii) the Directive 2011/16/EU with all other European Union Member States and (iii) double tax agreements in force with 88 jurisdictions.[2]

Completion and exchange of templates (ToR II.5.3, II.5.4, II.5.5, II.5.6, II.5.7)

In the prior year peer review report, it was determined that Poland's process for the completion and exchange of templates were sufficient to meet the minimum standard. Poland's implementation in this regard remains unchanged and therefore continues to meet the minimum standard.

For the year in review, the timeliness of exchanges is as follows:

Past rulings in the scope of the transparency framework	Number of exchanges transmitted by 31 December 2018	Delayed exchanges		
		Number of exchanges not transmitted by 31 December 2018	Reasons for the delays	Any other comments
	8[3]	0		These exchanges relate to delayed exchanges reported in the prior year peer review report and were exchanged by February 2018.
Future rulings in the scope of the transparency framework	Number of exchanges transmitted within three months of the information becoming available to the competent authority or immediately after legal impediments have been lifted	Delayed exchanges		
		Number of exchanges transmitted later than three months of the information on rulings becoming available to the competent authority	Reasons for the delays	Any other comments
	23	2		The two delayed exchanges relate to delayed exchanges reported in the prior year peer review report and were exchanged by February 2018.
Total	31	2		

Follow up requests received for exchange of the ruling	Number	Average time to provide response	Number of requests not answered
	0	N/A	N/A

Conclusion on section B

Poland has the necessary legal basis for spontaneous exchange of information, and a process for completing the templates in a timely way. Poland addressed the delays and completed outstanding exchanges early in the year in review. All additional exchanges were completed in a timely way and the prior year recommendation is removed. Poland has met all the ToR for the exchange of information process and no recommendations are made.

C. Statistics (ToR IV)

The statistics for the year in review are as follows:

Category of ruling	Number of exchanges	Jurisdictions exchanged with
Ruling related to a preferential regime	N/A	N/A
Cross-border unilateral advance pricing agreements (APAs) and any other cross-border unilateral tax rulings (such as an advance tax ruling) covering transfer pricing or the application of transfer pricing principles	10	Austria, Belgium, Germany, Italy, Malta, Netherlands, United Kingdom
Cross-border rulings providing for a unilateral downward adjustment to the taxpayer's taxable profits that is not directly reflected in the taxpayer's financial / commercial accounts	1	*De minimis* rule applies
Permanent establishment rulings	4	*De minimis* rule applies
Related party conduit rulings	18	Canada, Chile, Korea, Switzerland, Turkey, United States
De minimis rule	N/A	N/A
IP regimes: total exchanges on taxpayers benefitting from the third category of IP assets, new entrants benefitting from grandfathered IP regimes; and taxpayers making use of the option to treat the nexus ratio as a rebuttable presumption	N/A	N/A
Total	33	

D. Matters related to intellectual property regimes (ToR I.4.1.3)

Poland introduced a new intellectual property regime (IP regime)[4] which came into effect from 1 January 2019. Although this is after the year in review, it is noted that this regime is not subject to transparency requirements under the Action 5 Report (OECD, 2015[5]), because:

- ***New entrants benefitting from the grandfathered IP regime***: as this is a new IP regime rather than a grandfathered IP regime, transparency on new entrants is not relevant.
- ***Third category of IP assets***: not applicable as the regime does not allow the third category of IP assets to qualify for the benefits.
- ***Taxpayers making use of the option to treat the nexus ratio as a rebuttable presumption***: not applicable as the regime does not allow the nexus ratio to be treated as a rebuttable presumption.

Summary of recommendations on implementation of the transparency framework

Aspect of implementation of the transparency framework that should be improved	Recommendation for improvement
During the year in review, Poland encountered delays in identifying all potential exchange jurisdictions for future rulings other than APAs.	Poland is recommended to ensure that all potential exchange jurisdictions are identified swiftly for all future rulings other than APAs. This recommendation remains unchanged since the prior year peer review report.

Notes

[1] Available at: http://sip.mf.gov.pl/

[2] Parties to the Convention are available here: www.oecd.org/tax/exchange-of-tax-information/convention-on-mutual-administrative-assistance-in-tax-matters.htm. Poland also has bilateral agreements with Albania, Armenia, Australia, Austria, Azerbaijan, Bangladesh, Belarus, Belgium, Bosnia and Herzegovina, Bulgaria, Canada, Chile, China (People's Republic of), Croatia, Cyprus, Czech Republic, Denmark, Egypt, Estonia, Finland, France, Georgia, Germany, Greece, Guernsey, Hungary, Iceland, India, Indonesia, Iran, Ireland, Isle of Man, Israel, Italy, Jamaica, Japan, Jersey, Jordan, Kazakhstan, Korea, Kuwait, Kyrgyzstan, Latvia, Lebanon, Lithuania, Luxembourg, Malaysia, Malta, Mexico, Moldova, Mongolia, Montenegro, Morocco, Netherlands, New Zealand, North Macedonia, Norway, Pakistan, Peru, Philippines, Portugal, Qatar, Romania, Russia, Saudi Arabia, Serbia, Singapore, Slovak Republic, Slovenia, South Africa, Spain, Sri Lanka, Sweden, Switzerland, Syria, Chinese Taipei, Tajikistan, Thailand, Tunisia, Turkey, Ukraine, United Arab Emirates, United Kingdom, United States, Uzbekistan, Vanuatu, Viet Nam and Zimbabwe.

Note by Turkey: The information in this document with reference to "Cyprus" relates to the southern part of the Island. There is no single authority representing both Turkish and Greek Cypriot people on the Island. Turkey recognises the Turkish Republic of Northern Cyprus (TRNC). Until a lasting and equitable solution is found within the context of the United Nations, Turkey shall preserve its position concerning the "Cyprus issue".

Note by all the European Union Member States of the OECD and the European Union. The Republic of Cyprus is recognised by all members of the United Nations with the exception of Turkey. The information in this document relates to the area under the effective control of the Government of the Republic of Cyprus.

[3] The prior year peer review report noted that there were nine delayed exchanges of past rulings, but Poland indicates that one of these rulings was not in the scope of the Action 5 transparency framework.

[4] IP box.

Portugal

Portugal has met all aspects of the terms of reference (ToR) for the calendar year 2018 (year in review) and no recommendations are made.

In the prior year report, Portugal received one recommendation. This recommendation has been addressed and is removed.

Portugal can legally issue two types of rulings within the scope of the transparency framework. In practice, Portugal has issued rulings within the scope of the transparency framework as follows:

- 24 past rulings;
- For the period 1 April 2016 - 31 December 2016: two future rulings;
- For the calendar year 2017: 11 future rulings, and
- For the year in review: 11 future rulings.

Peer input was received from one jurisdiction in respect of the exchanges of information on rulings received from Portugal. The input was generally positive, noting that information was complete, in a correct format and received in a timely manner.

Introduction

This peer review covers Portugal's implementation of the BEPS Action 5 transparency framework for the year 2018. The report has four parts, each relating to a key part of the ToR. Each part is discussed in turn. A summary of recommendations is included at the end of this report.

A. The information gathering process

Portugal can legally issue the following two types of rulings within the scope of the transparency framework: (i) cross-border unilateral APAs and any other cross-border unilateral tax ruling (such as an ATR) covering transfer pricing or the application of transfer pricing principles and (ii) permanent establishment rulings.

Past rulings (ToR I.4.1.1, I.4.1.2, I.4.2.1, I.4.2.2)

For Portugal, past rulings are any tax rulings within scope that are issued either: (i) on or after 1 January 2014 but before 1 April 2016; or (ii) on or after 1 January 2010 but before 1 January 2014, provided they were still in effect as at 1 January 2014.

In the prior year peer review report, it was determined that Portugal's undertakings to identify past rulings and all potential exchange jurisdictions were sufficient to meet the minimum standard. Portugal's implementation in this regard remains unchanged, and therefore continues to meet the minimum standard.

Future rulings (ToR I.4.1.1, I.4.1.2, I.4.2.1)

For Portugal, future rulings are any tax rulings within scope that are issued on or after 1 April 2016.

In the prior year peer review report, it was determined that Portugal's undertakings to identify future rulings and all potential exchange jurisdictions was sufficient to meet the minimum standard. Portugal's implementation in this regard remains unchanged, and therefore continues to meet the minimum standard.

Review and supervision (ToR I.4.3)

In the prior year peer review report, it was determined that Portugal's review and supervision mechanism was sufficient to meet the minimum standard. Portugal's implementation in this regard remains unchanged, and therefore continues to meet the minimum standard.

Conclusion on section A

Portugal has met all of the ToR for the information gathering process and no recommendations are made.

B. The exchange of information

Legal basis for spontaneous exchange of information (ToR II.5.1, II.5.2)

Portugal has the necessary domestic legal basis to exchange information spontaneously. Portugal notes that there are no legal or practical impediments that prevent the spontaneous exchange of information on rulings as contemplated in the Action 5 minimum standard.

Portugal is a party to international agreements permitting spontaneous exchange of information, including (i) the *Multilateral Convention on Mutual Administrative Assistance in Tax Matters: Amended by the 2010*

Protocol (OECD/Council of Europe, 2011) (the Convention), (ii) the Directive 2011/16/EU with all other European Union Member States and (iii) double tax agreements in force with 77 jurisdictions.[1]

Completion and exchange of templates (ToR II.5.3, II.5.4, II.5.5, II.5.6, II.5.7)

In the prior year peer review report, it was determined that Portugal's completion and exchange of templates was sufficient to meet the minimum standard, except for the timely exchange of information on future rulings (ToR II.5.6). Portugal received a recommendation to ensure the speedy exchange of all future rulings. Portugal has now addressed this issue, all future rulings have been exchange in a timely manner and the accordingly the recommendation is removed.

For the year in review, the timeliness of exchanges is as follows:

Past rulings in the scope of the transparency framework	Number of exchanges transmitted by 31 December 2018	Delayed exchanges		
		Number of exchanges not transmitted by 31 December 2018	Reasons for the delays	Any other comments
	0	0	N/A	N/A
Future rulings in the scope of the transparency framework	Number of exchanges transmitted within three months of the information becoming available to the competent authority or immediately after legal impediments have been lifted	Delayed exchanges		
		Number of exchanges transmitted later than three months of the information on rulings becoming available to the competent authority	Reasons for the delays	Any other comments
	11	0	N/A	N/A
Total	11	0		

Follow up requests received for exchange of the ruling	Number	Average time to provide response	Number of requests not answered
	0	N/A	N/A

Conclusion on section B

Portugal has the necessary legal basis for spontaneous exchange of information, a process for completing the templates in a timely way and has completed all exchanges on time. Portugal has met all of the ToR for the exchange of information process and no recommendations are made.

C. Statistics (ToR IV)

The statistics for the year in review are as follows:

Category of ruling	Number of exchanges	Jurisdictions exchanged with
Ruling related to a preferential regime	N/A	N/A
Cross-border unilateral advance pricing agreements (APAs) and any other cross-border unilateral tax rulings (such as an advance tax ruling) covering transfer pricing or the application of transfer pricing principles	9	Finland, Germany, Korea, Netherlands, Spain
Cross-border rulings providing for a unilateral downward adjustment to the	N/A	N/A

taxpayer's taxable profits that is not directly reflected in the taxpayer's financial / commercial accounts		
Permanent establishment rulings	2	*De minimis* rule applies
Related party conduit rulings	N/A	N/A
De minimis rule	N/A	N/A
IP regimes: total exchanges on taxpayers benefitting from the third category of IP assets, new entrants benefitting from grandfathered IP regimes; and taxpayers making use of the option to treat the nexus ratio as a rebuttable presumption	N/A	N/A
Total	11	

D. Matters related to intellectual property regimes (ToR I.4.1.3)

Portugal offers an intellectual property regime that is subject to transparency requirements under the Action 5 Report (OECD, 2015[5]).[2] It states that the identification of the benefitting taxpayers will occur as follows:

New entrants benefitting from the grandfathered IP regime: Portugal did not identify any new entrants benefitting from the grandfathered IP regime that should be subject to spontaneous exchange of information with other jurisdictions.

- ***Third category of assets***: not applicable as the regime does not allow the third category of IP assets to qualify for the benefits.
- ***Taxpayers making use of the option to treat the nexus ratio as a rebuttable presumption***: not applicable as the regime does not allow the nexus ratio to be treated as a rebuttable presumption.

Summary of recommendations on implementation of the transparency framework

Aspect of implementation of the transparency framework that should be improved	Recommendation for improvement
	No recommendations are made.

Notes

[1] Parties to the Convention are available here: www.oecd.org/tax/exchange-of-tax-information/convention-on-mutual-administrative-assistance-in-tax-matters.htm. Portugal also has bilateral agreements with Algeria, Andorra, Austria, Bahrain, Barbados, Belgium, Brazil, Bulgaria, Cabo Verde, Canada, Chile, China (People's Republic of), Colombia, Côte d'Ivoire, Croatia, Cuba, Cyprus, Czech Republic, Denmark, Estonia, Ethiopia, Finland, France, Georgia, Germany, Greece, Guinea-Bissau, Hong Kong (China), Hungary, Iceland, India, Indonesia, Ireland, Israel, Italy, Japan, Korea, Kuwait, Latvia, Lithuania, Luxembourg, Macau (China), Malta, Mexico, Moldova, Morocco, Mozambique, Netherlands, Norway, Oman, Pakistan, Panama, Peru, Poland, Qatar, Romania, Russia, San Marino, Sao Tome and Principe, Saudi Arabia, Senegal, Singapore, Slovak Republic, Slovenia, South Africa, Spain, Sweden, Switzerland, Tunisia, Turkey, Ukraine, United Arab Emirates, United Kingdom, United States, Uruguay, Venezuela and Viet Nam.

Note by Turkey: The information in this document with reference to "Cyprus" relates to the southern part of the Island. There is no single authority representing both Turkish and Greek Cypriot people on the Island. Turkey recognises the Turkish Republic of Northern Cyprus (TRNC). Until a lasting and equitable solution is found within the context of the United Nations, Turkey shall preserve its position concerning the "Cyprus issue".

Note by all the European Union Member States of the OECD and the European Union. The Republic of Cyprus is recognised by all members of the United Nations with the exception of Turkey. The information in this document relates to the area under the effective control of the Government of the Republic of Cyprus.

[2] Partial exemption for income from patents and other industrial property rights.

Qatar

Qatar has met all aspects of the terms of reference (OECD, 2017[3]) (ToR) for the calendar year 2018 (year in review).

This is Qatar's first review of implementation of the transparency framework.

Qatar can legally issue five types of rulings within the scope of the transparency framework. In practice, Qatar issued two rulings within the scope of the transparency framework. As the rulings were issued before 1 September 2018 they do not qualify as future rulings for Qatar and information on these rulings were not required to be exchanged under the terms of the peer review.

As no exchanges were required to take place, no peer input was received in respect of the exchanges of information on rulings received from Qatar.

Introduction

This peer review covers Qatar's implementation of the BEPS Action 5 transparency framework for the year 2018. The report has four parts, each relating to a key part of the ToR. Each part is discussed in turn. A summary of recommendations is included at the end of this report.

A. The information gathering process

Qatar can legally issue the following five types of rulings within the scope of the transparency framework: (i) preferential regimes; (ii) cross-border unilateral APAs and any other cross-border unilateral tax rulings (such as an advance tax ruling) covering transfer pricing or the application of transfer pricing principles; (iii) rulings providing for unilateral downward adjustments; (iv) permanent establishment rulings; and (v) related party conduit rulings. Currently all five types of rulings can be issued centrally only by the Qatar QFC Tax Department (QFC TD).

Past rulings (ToR I.4.1.1, I.4.1.2, I.4.2.1, I.4.2.2)

For Qatar, past rulings are any tax rulings issued prior to 1 September 2018. However, there is no obligation under the terms of the transparency framework for Qatar to spontaneously exchange information on past rulings.

Future rulings (ToR I.4.1.1, I.4.1.2, I.4.2.1)

For Qatar, future rulings are any tax rulings within scope that are issued on or after 1 September 2018.

The QFC TD can issue all five type of rulings to participants of the Qatar Financial Centre. For the year in review, all rulings are recorded in two databases, an excel file and on the E-Services of the QFC tax portal. Case officers have been instructed to review each ruling request to identify it as being relevant for the transparency framework. In order to identify potential exchange jurisdictions, information in the ruling request will be reviewed. If this does not contain all necessary information, the case officer can request additional information from the taxpayer before a ruling is issued, and the issuance of the ruling can be denied if requested information is not provided. As such, the procedure to identify future rulings and all potential exchange jurisdictions relating to rulings issued by the QFC TD is sufficient to meet the minimum standard.

Qatar notes that QFC's E-Services online system is being updated to ensure that it is automated and captures all necessary information with regard to the rulings, including all related party details and whether or not the ruling falls in the scope of the transparency framework. This is expected to be implemented in early 2020.

Review and supervision (ToR I.4.3)

The work of case officers conducting the information gathering is reviewed by the line manager in charge, who will review the information to confirm that the ruling is within the scope of Action 5 and to confirm that all information on potential exchange jurisdictions has been correctly identified. In addition, the two databases referred to above with the list of all ruling requests and their status is cross-checked to ensure all rulings have been identified for the purpose of Action 5. In addition, case officers have been made aware of the Action 5 requirements through the issuance of an instruction sheet and further training is foreseen for the responsible personnel. As rulings are generally granted for a two year period, upon renewal of the ruling, all relevant facts and information are checked again before the renewal is granted, following the same process.

Conclusion on section A

Qatar implemented procedures to identify and collect necessary information on rulings issued by the QFC TD. Qatar has therefore met all of the ToR for the information gathering process and no recommendations are made.

B. The exchange of information

Legal basis for spontaneous exchange of information (ToR II.5.1, II.5.2)

Qatar has the necessary domestic legal basis to exchange information spontaneously. Qatar notes that there are no legal or practical impediments that prevent the spontaneous exchange of information on rulings as contemplated in the Action 5 minimum standard.

Qatar has international agreements permitting spontaneous exchange of information, including being a party to the (i) *Multilateral Convention on Mutual Administrative Assistance in Tax Matters: Amended by the 2010 Protocol* (OECD/Council of Europe, 2011[4]) ("the Convention") and (ii) double tax agreements in force with 74 jurisdictions.[1]

Completion and exchange of templates (ToR II.5.3, II.5.4, II.5.5, II.5.6, II.5.7)

Qatar would use a form containing the relevant fields contained in the Annex C template to exchange information on rulings. The tax officer reviewing the ruling request completes the information in the form and a second tax officer will review the form before submitting it to the competent authority. Case officers have been instructed to fill in the template using the guide provided in the 2015 Action 5 Report. The form would then be forwarded to the competent authority within 30 days after a ruling has been issued. The competent authority is currently working on an IT system allowing for the exchange of such information, and which would take place within three months of the receipt of the form. In the event a ruling was issued prior to the finalisation of the IT system, the ruling would be exchanged manually.

As no relevant rulings were issued for the year in review, no exchanges were required to take place and no data on the timelines of exchanges is reported.

Conclusion on section B

Qatar has the necessary legal basis for spontaneous exchange of information and a process in place to exchange information on rulings issued by the QFC TD in a timely way. Qatar has therefore met all the ToR for the exchange of information process that can be met in the absence of rulings being issued and exchanged in practice and no recommendations are made.

C. Statistics (ToR IV)

As there were no rulings to be exchanged by Qatar for the year in review, no statistics can be reported.

D. Matters related to intellectual property regimes (ToR I.4.1.3)

Qatar does not offer an intellectual property regime for which transparency requirements under the Action 5 Report (OECD, 2015[5]) were imposed.

Summary of recommendations on implementation of the transparency framework

Aspect of implementation of the transparency framework that should be improved	Recommendation for improvement
	No recommendations are made.

Notes

[1] Parties to the Convention are available here: www.oecd.org/tax/exchange-of-tax-information/convention-on-mutual-administrative-assistance-in-tax-matters.htm. Qatar also has double tax agreements with Albania, Algeria, Armenia, Austria, Azerbaijan, Barbados, Belarus, Belgium, Bermuda, Bosnia and Herzegovina, Brunei Darussalam, Bulgaria, Chad, China (People's Republic of), Croatia, Cuba, Cyprus, Ecuador, Eritrea, Ethiopia, Fiji, France, Gambia, Georgia, Greece, Guernsey, Hong Kong (China), Hungary, India, Indonesia, Iran, Ireland, Isle of Man, Italy, Japan, Jersey, Jordan, Kazakhstan, Kenya, Korea, Kyrgyzstan, Latvia, Lebanon, Luxembourg, Malaysia, Malta, Mauritania, Mauritius, Mexico, Monaco, Morocco, Nepal, Netherlands, Nigeria, North Macedonia, Norway, Pakistan, Panama, Paraguay, Philippines, Poland, Portugal, Romania, Russia, San Marino, Senegal, Serbia, Seychelles, Singapore, Slovenia, South Africa, Spain, Sri Lanka, Sudan.

Note by Turkey: The information in this document with reference to "Cyprus" relates to the southern part of the Island. There is no single authority representing both Turkish and Greek Cypriot people on the Island. Turkey recognises the Turkish Republic of Northern Cyprus (TRNC). Until a lasting and equitable solution is found within the context of the United Nations, Turkey shall preserve its position concerning the "Cyprus issue".

Note by all the European Union Member States of the OECD and the European Union. The Republic of Cyprus is recognised by all members of the United Nations with the exception of Turkey. The information in this document relates to the area under the effective control of the Government of the Republic of Cyprus.

Romania

Romania has met all aspects of the terms of reference (OECD, 2017[3]) (ToR) for the calendar year 2018 (year in review) except for the timely exchange of information on past and future rulings (ToR II.5.6). Romania receives one recommendation on this point for the year in review.

In the prior year review, Romania received two recommendations. One recommendation has been addressed and is removed. The other recommendation has not been addressed and remains in place.

Romania can legally issue two types of ruling within the scope of the transparency framework. In practice, Romania issued rulings within the scope of the transparency framework as follows:

- 12 past rulings;
- For the period 1 April 2016 - 31 December 2016: no future rulings;
- For the calendar year 2017: five future rulings, and

For the year in review: seven future rulings.

As no exchanges took place, no peer input was received in respect of the exchanges of information on rulings received from Romania.

Introduction

This peer review covers Romania's implementation of the BEPS Action 5 transparency framework for the year 2018. The report has four parts, each relating to a key part of the ToR. Each part is discussed in turn. A summary of recommendations is included at the end of this report.

A. The information gathering process

Romania can legally issue the following two types of ruling within the scope of the transparency framework: (i) cross-border unilateral advance pricing arrangements (APAs) and any other cross-border unilateral tax rulings (such as an advance tax ruling) covering transfer pricing or the application of transfer pricing principles and (ii) permanent establishment rulings.

Past rulings (ToR I.4.1.1, I.4.1.2, I.4.2.1, I.4.2.2)

For Romania, past rulings are any tax rulings within scope that are issued either: (i) on or after 1 January 2015 but before 1 April 2017; or (ii) on or after 1 January 2012 but before 1 January 2015, provided they were still in effect as at 1 January 2015.

In the prior year peer review report, it was determined that Romania's undertakings to identify past rulings and all potential exchange jurisdictions were sufficient to meet the minimum standard. Romania's implementation in this regard remains unchanged, and therefore continues to meet the minimum standard.

Future rulings (ToR I.4.1.1, I.4.1.2, I.4.2.1)

For Romania, future rulings are any tax rulings within scope that are issued on or after 1 April 2017.

In the prior year peer review reports, it was determined that Romania's undertakings to identify future rulings and all potential exchange jurisdictions have met all the ToR. Romania's implementation in this regard remains unchanged, and therefore continues to meet the minimum standard.

Review and supervision (ToR I.4.3)

Romania did not yet have a review and supervision mechanism for past or future rulings under the transparency framework for the year in review. Therefore, Romania was recommended to implement a review and supervision mechanism.

During the year in review, Romania has introduced an internal written procedure for the exchange of information, which covers a review and supervision mechanism. Romania centralised the procedure to collect information with regard to the tax rulings, within the staff from the Directorate for transfer pricing and tax rulings. The head of the APA department performs a quality control check of the information completed. The Directorate for transfer pricing and tax rulings is then responsible for a final validation. In light of this, this aspect of the ToR is met and the recommendation is now removed.

Conclusion on section A

Romania met all of the ToR for the information gathering process and no recommendations are made.

B. The exchange of information

Legal basis for spontaneous exchange of information (ToR II.5.1, II.5.2)

Romania has the necessary domestic legal basis to exchange information spontaneously. Romania notes that there are no legal or practical impediments that prevent the spontaneous exchange of information on rulings as contemplated in the Action 5 minimum standard.

Romania has international agreements permitting spontaneous exchange of information, including being a party to the (I) *Multilateral Convention on Mutual Administrative Assistance in Tax Matters: Amended by the 2010 Protocol* (OECD/Council of Europe, 2011[4]) ("the Convention"), (ii) the Directive 2011/16/EU with all other European Union Member States and (iii) double tax agreements in force with 88 jurisdictions.[1]

Completion and exchange of templates (ToR II.5.3, II.5.4, II.5.5, II.5.6, II.5.7)

In the prior year peer review report, it was determined that Romania was still developing a process to complete the templates on relevant rulings, to make them available to the Competent Authority for exchange of information, and to exchange them with relevant jurisdictions. As described above, during the year in review, Romania has introduced an internal written procedure for the exchange of information. This includes the process to identify the information and to fill in the information required in the template in the form of Annex C, as well as a quality control process to ensure the information is complete and in the correct form. The information is verified by the head of the APA department and then a final validation prior to the exchange is made by the Director of the directorate for transfer pricing and tax rulings. Once the template is validated, it is uploaded into a central information management platform and submitted for spontaneous exchange of information. The written procedure provides that the timelines for submission to the Competent Authority is as soon as possible and the timeline for the Competent Authority to exchange is within three months of the issue of the ruling. In light of this, the ToRs II.5.3, II.5.4 and II.5.5 are met and the recommendation is now removed.

For the year in review, the timeliness of exchanges is as follows:

Past rulings in the scope of the transparency framework	Number of exchanges transmitted by 31 December 2018	Delayed exchanges		
		Number of exchanges not transmitted by 31 December 2018	Reasons for the delays	Any other comments
	0	12	Procedural delays	Partially sent by March 2019
Future rulings in the scope of the transparency framework	Number of exchanges transmitted within three months of the information becoming available to the competent authority or immediately after legal impediments have been lifted	Delayed exchanges		
		Number of exchanges transmitted later than three months of the information on rulings becoming available to the competent authority	Reasons for the delays	Any other comments
	0	7	Procedural delays	Partially sent by March 2019
Total	0	19		

Follow up requests received for exchange of the ruling	Number	Average time to provide response	Number of requests not answered
	N/A	N/A	N/A

During the year in review, there were delays in the exchange of information since Romania was still in the process of finalising the written procedure for spontaneous exchange of information. These delays include information that was noted as a delayed exchange in the prior year peer review report. Romania is recommended to ensure that all information on past and future rulings is exchanged as soon as possible.

Conclusion on section B

Romania has the necessary legal basis for spontaneous exchange of information. During the year of review, Romania experienced delays in the exchange of all past rulings and future rulings due to the absence of written procedures on exchange of information. Romania has since introduced these processes and started performing exchanges in the 2019. These actions taken will be review in the next year's peer review report. Romania is recommended to ensure that all information on past and future rulings is exchanged as soon as possible (ToR II.5.6).

C. Statistics (ToR IV)

As there was no information on rulings exchanged by Romania for the year in review, no statistics can be reported.

D. Matters related to intellectual property regimes (ToR I.4.1.3)

Romania does not offer an intellectual property regime for which transparency requirements under the Action 5 Report (OECD, 2015[5]) were imposed.

Summary of recommendations on implementation of the transparency framework

Aspect of implementation of the transparency framework that should be improved	Recommendation for improvement
Romania experienced delays in the exchange of all past rulings and future rulings since written procedures on exchange of information have only been recently introduced.	Romania is recommended to ensure that all information on past and future rulings is exchanged as soon as possible. This recommendation remains unchanged since the prior year peer review report.

Notes

[1] Parties to the Convention are available here: http://www.oecd.org/tax/exchange-of-tax-information/convention-on-mutual-administrative-assistance-in-tax-matters.htm

Romania also has double tax agreements with Albania, Algeria, Armenia, Australia, Austria, Azerbaijan, Bangladesh, Belarus, Belgium, Bosnia and Herzegovina, Bulgaria, Canada, China (People's Republic of), Croatia, Cyprus, Czech Republic, Democratic People's Republic of Korea, Denmark, Ecuador, Egypt, Estonia, Ethiopia, Finland, France, Georgia, Germany, Greece, Hong Kong (China), Hungary, Iceland, India, Indonesia, Iran, Ireland, Israel, Italy, Japan, Jordan, Kazakhstan, Korea, Kuwait, Latvia, Lebanon, Lithuania, Luxembourg, Malaysia, Malta, Mexico, Moldova, Montenegro, Morocco, Namibia, Netherlands, Nigeria, North Macedonia, Norway, Pakistan, Philippines, Poland, Portugal, Qatar, Russia, San Marino, Saudi Arabia, Serbia, Montenegro, Singapore, Slovenia, Slovak Republic, South Africa, Spain, Sri Lanka, Sudan, Sweden, Switzerland, Syrian Arab Republic, Tajikistan, Thailand, Tunisia, Turkey, Turkmenistan, Ukraine, United Arab Emirates, United Kingdom, United States, Uruguay, Uzbekistan, Viet Nam and Zambia.

Note by Turkey: The information in this document with reference to "Cyprus" relates to the southern part of the Island. There is no single authority representing both Turkish and Greek Cypriot people on the Island. Turkey recognises the Turkish Republic of Northern Cyprus (TRNC). Until a lasting and equitable solution is found within the context of the United Nations, Turkey shall preserve its position concerning the "Cyprus issue".

Note by all the European Union Member States of the OECD and the European Union. The Republic of Cyprus is recognised by all members of the United Nations with the exception of Turkey. The information in this document relates to the area under the effective control of the Government of the Republic of Cyprus.

Russian Federation

Russian Federation ("Russia") has met all aspects of the terms of reference (OECD, 2017[3]) (ToR) for the calendar year 2018 (year in review) and no recommendations are made.

In the prior year report, Russia did not receive any recommendations.

Russia can legally issue five types of rulings within the scope of the transparency framework. In practice, Russia issued rulings within the scope of the transparency framework as follows:

- One past ruling;
- For the period 1 April 2016 - 31 December 2016: no future rulings;
- For the calendar year 2017: no future rulings, and
- For the year in review: no future rulings.

As no exchanges were required to take place, no peer input was received in respect of the exchanges of information on rulings received from Russia.

Introduction

This peer review covers Russia's implementation of the BEPS Action 5 transparency framework for the year 2018. The report has four parts, each relating to a key part of the ToR. Each part is discussed in turn. A summary of recommendations is included at the end of this report.

A. The information gathering process

Russia can legally issue the following five types of rulings within the scope of the transparency framework: (i) preferential regimes;[1] (ii) cross-border unilateral APAs and any other cross-border unilateral tax rulings (such as an advance tax ruling) covering transfer pricing or the application of transfer pricing principles; (iii) rulings providing for unilateral downward adjustments; (iv) permanent establishment rulings; and (v) related party conduit rulings.

Past rulings (ToR I.4.1.1, I.4.1.2, I.4.2.1, I.4.2.2)

For Russia, past rulings are any tax rulings within scope that are issued either: (i) on or after 1 January 2014 but before 1 April 2016; or (ii) on or after 1 January 2010 but before 1 January 2014, provided they were still in effect as at 1 January 2014.

In the prior years' peer review reports, it was determined that Russia's undertakings to identify past rulings and all potential exchange jurisdictions were sufficient to meet the minimum standard in the absence of rulings being issued in practice. Russia's implementation in this regard remains unchanged, and therefore continues to meet the minimum standard.

Future rulings (ToR I.4.1.1, I.4.1.2, I.4.2.1)

For Russia, future rulings are any tax rulings within scope that are issued on or after 1 April 2016.

In the prior years' peer review reports, it was determined that Russia's undertakings to identify future rulings and all potential exchange jurisdictions was sufficient to meet the minimum standard in the absence of rulings being issued in practice. Russia's implementation in this regard remains unchanged, and therefore continues to meet the minimum standard.

Review and supervision (ToR I.4.3)

In the prior years' peer review reports, it was determined that Russia's review and supervision mechanism currently in place and the procedure to be implemented once a larger number of rulings are issued were sufficient to meet the minimum standard. Russia's implementation in this regard remains unchanged, and therefore continues to meet the minimum standard.

Conclusion on section A

Russia has met all of the ToR for the information gathering process and no recommendations are made.

B. The exchange of information

Legal basis for spontaneous exchange of information (ToR II.5.1, II.5.2)

Russia has the necessary domestic legal basis to exchange information spontaneously. Russia notes that there are no legal or practical impediments that prevent the spontaneous exchange of information on rulings as contemplated in the Action 5 minimum standard.

Russia has international agreements permitting spontaneous exchange of information, including being a party to the (i) *Multilateral Convention on Mutual Administrative Assistance in Tax Matters: Amended by the 2010 Protocol* (OECD/Council of Europe, 2011[4]) ("the Convention") and (ii) bilateral agreements in force with 83 jurisdictions.[2]

Completion and exchange of templates (ToR II.5.3, II.5.4, II.5.5, II.5.6, II.5.7)

In the prior year peer review report, it was determined that Russia's process for the completion and exchange of templates that would be applicable if rulings were issued in practice was sufficient to meet the minimum standard. Russia's implementation in this regard remains unchanged and therefore continues to meet the minimum standard.

As Russia did not issue any rulings in scope of the transparency framework in the relevant period, Russia was not required to exchange any information on rulings in the year in review and no data on the timeliness of exchanges can be reported.

Conclusion on section B

Russia has the necessary legal basis for spontaneous exchange of information, a process for completing the templates in a timely way. Russia has met all of the ToR for the exchange of information process that can be met in the absence of rulings being issued and exchanged in practice and no recommendations are made.

C. Statistics (ToR IV)

As there was no information on rulings exchanged by Russia for the year in review, no statistics can be reported.

D. Matters related to intellectual property regimes (ToR I.4.1.3)

Russia does not offer an intellectual property regime for which transparency requirements under the Action 5 Report (OECD, 2015[5]) were imposed.

Summary of recommendations on implementation of the transparency framework

Aspect of implementation of the transparency framework that should be improved	Recommendation for improvement
	No recommendations are made.

Notes

[1] With respect to the following preferential regimes: Special economic/industry zones.

[2] Parties to the Convention are available here: www.oecd.org/tax/exchange-of-tax-information/convention-on-mutual-administrative-assistance-in-tax-matters.htm. Russia has bilateral agreements in force with: Albania, Algeria, Argentina, Armenia, Australia, Austria, Azerbaijan, Belarus, Belgium, Botswana, Bulgaria, Canada, Chile, China (People's Republic of), Croatia, Cuba, Cyprus, Czech Republic, Democratic People's Republic of Korea, Denmark, Egypt, Finland, France, Georgia, Germany, Greece, Hungary, Iceland, India, Indonesia, Iran, Ireland, Israel, Italy, Japan, Kazakhstan, Korea, Kuwait, Kyrgyzstan, Latvia, Lebanon, Lithuania, Luxembourg, Malaysia, Mali, Malta, Morocco, Mexico, Moldova, Mongolia, Montenegro, Namibia, Netherlands, New Zealand, Nigeria, North Macedonia, Norway, Philippines, Poland, Portugal, Qatar, Romania, Saudi Arabia, Serbia, Singapore, Slovak Republic, Slovenia, South Africa, Spain, Sri Lanka, Sweden, Syria, Tajikistan, Thailand, Turkey, Turkmenia, Ukraine, United Arab Emirates, United Kingdom, United States, Uzbekistan, Venezuela, Viet Nam.

Note by Turkey: The information in this document with reference to "Cyprus" relates to the southern part of the Island. There is no single authority representing both Turkish and Greek Cypriot people on the Island. Turkey recognises the Turkish Republic of Northern Cyprus (TRNC). Until a lasting and equitable solution is found within the context of the United Nations, Turkey shall preserve its position concerning the "Cyprus issue".

Note by all the European Union Member States of the OECD and the European Union. The Republic of Cyprus is recognised by all members of the United Nations with the exception of Turkey. The information in this document relates to the area under the effective control of the Government of the Republic of Cyprus.

Saint Kitts and Nevis

Saint Kitts and Nevis has met all aspects of the terms of reference (OECD, 2017[3]) (ToR) for the calendar year 2018 (year in review).

This is Saint Kitts and Nevis' first review of implementation of the transparency framework.

Saint Kitts and Nevis' legal framework to issue taxpayer-specific rulings has been in force since 2005, but to date, Saint Kitts and Nevis has never received an application for a ruling from a taxpayer. Saint Kitts and Nevis can legally issue five types of rulings within the scope of the transparency framework but in practice has never issued any rulings.

As no exchanges were required to take place, no peer input was received in respect of the exchanges of information on rulings received from Saint Kitts and Nevis.

Introduction

This peer review covers Saint Kitts and Nevis' implementation of the BEPS Action 5 transparency framework for the year 2018. The report has four parts, each relating to a key part of the ToR. Each part is discussed in turn. A summary of recommendations is included at the end of this report.

A. The information gathering process

Saint Kitts and Nevis can legally issue the following five types of rulings within the scope of the transparency framework: (i) preferential regimes;[1] (ii) cross-border unilateral APAs and any other cross-border unilateral tax rulings (such as an advance tax ruling) covering transfer pricing or the application of transfer pricing principles; (iii) rulings providing for unilateral downward adjustments; and (iv) permanent establishment rulings; and (v) related party conduit rulings. Rulings are issued by the Comptroller of Inland Revenue upon appropriate application by a taxpayer.

Past rulings (ToR I.4.1.1, I.4.1.2, I.4.2.1, I.4.2.2)

For Saint Kitts and Nevis, past rulings are any tax rulings issued prior to 1 September 2018. However, there is no obligation under the terms of the transparency framework for Saint Kitts and Nevis to conduct spontaneous exchange of information on past rulings.

Future rulings (ToR I.4.1.1, I.4.1.2, I.4.2.1)

For Saint Kitts and Nevis, future rulings are any tax rulings within scope that are issued on or after 1 September 2018.

No rulings were issued by Saint Kitts and Nevis during the period in review. The Objections, Rulings and Interpretations Division is responsible for both the issuance and identification of whether any rulings issued fall into scope of the transparency framework. Although Saint Kitts and Nevis has not issued any future rulings, Saint Kitts and Nevis has indicated that potential exchange jurisdictions could be identified through analysing information from the annual corporate income tax return and supporting schedules. Where information cannot be directly obtained via the tax returns, a specific request may be made to the taxpayer or to any person who holds information for the taxpayer. These procedures are sufficient to meet the minimum standard.

Review and supervision (ToR I.4.3)

The accuracy of the information gathering process and the identification of rulings in scope of the transparency framework is supervised by the Assistant Comptroller of the Objections, Rulings and Interpretations Division.

Conclusion on section A

Saint Kitts and Nevis has met all of the ToR for the information gathering process and no recommendations are made.

B. The exchange of information

Legal basis for spontaneous exchange of information (ToR II.5.1, II.5.2)

Saint Kitts and Nevis has the necessary domestic legal basis to exchange information spontaneously. Saint Kitts and Nevis notes that there are no legal or practical impediments that prevent the spontaneous exchange of information on rulings as contemplated in the Action 5 minimum standard.

Saint Kitts and Nevis is a party to international agreements permitting spontaneous exchange of information, including (i) the *Multilateral Convention on Mutual Administrative Assistance in Tax Matters: Amended by the 2010 Protocol* (OECD/Council of Europe, 2011) ("the Convention").[2]

Completion and exchange of templates (ToR II.5.3, II.5.4, II.5.5, II.5.6, II.5.7)

Saint Kitts and Nevis notes that an officer of the Objections, Rulings and Interpretations Division would be responsible for the completion of the information required in the template contained in Annex C of the Action 5 Report (OECD, 2015[5]), which would include providing a detailed summary of the ruling following the instructions in Annex C. The template would then be quality checked by a supervisor in the Division, and thereafter sent to the Assistant Comptroller in collaboration with the Comptroller for final approval and exchange. The Inland Revenue Department is the Competent Authority in Saint Kitts and Nevis which is responsible for the identification, analysis and exchange of information on rulings. The Objections, Rulings, and Interpretations Division is a division within Inland Revenue Department which is a small, centralised office, and therefore all tax rulings would be readily available to the Competent Authority. Saint Kitts and Nevis notes that the Competent Authority would complete the required exchange within three months of receipt from the Objections, Rulings and Interpretations Division.

As Saint Kitts and Nevis did not issue any rulings in scope of the transparency framework in the relevant period, Saint Kitts and Nevis was not required to exchange any information on rulings in the year in review and no data on the timeliness of exchanges can be reported.

Conclusion on section B

Saint Kitts and Nevis has the necessary legal basis to undertake spontaneous exchange of information. Saint Kitts and Nevis has met all of the ToR for the exchange of information process that can be met in the absence of rulings being issued and exchanged in practice and no recommendations are made.

C. Statistics (ToR IV)

As there were no rulings required to be exchanged by Saint Kitts and Nevis for the year in review, no statistics can be reported.

D. Matters related to intellectual property regimes (ToR I.4.1.3)

Saint Kitts and Nevis offered three preferential regimes, which also provided benefits to income from intellectual property (IP regime).[3] However, for the year in review, no transparency requirements were relevant, as follows:

- ***New entrants benefitting from the grandfathered IP regime:*** not applicable for the year in review, because Saint Kitts and Nevis is currently in the process of finalising the grandfathering rules for all three regimes. The implementation of the enhanced transparency requirements, if required, will be taken into account during the subsequent peer review.

- ***Third category of IP assets***: not applicable to these regimes, which in 2018 were in the process of being amended.
- ***Taxpayers making use of the option to treat the nexus ratio as a rebuttable presumption***: not applicable to these regimes, which in 2018 were in the process of being amended.

Summary of recommendations on implementation of the transparency framework

Aspect of implementation of the transparency framework that should be improved	Recommendation for improvement
	No recommendations are made.

Notes

[1] With respect to the following preferential regimes: 1) Nevis LLC; 2) Nevis business corporation; and 3) Companies act – exempt companies.

[2] Parties to the Convention are available here: http://www.oecd.org/tax/exchange-of-tax-information/convention-on-mutual-administrative-assistance-in-tax-matters.htm.

[3] International business company, International trust and International partnership regimes.

Saint Lucia

Saint Lucia is taking steps to implement the legal basis for the transparency framework and to commence administrative preparations (in line with the terms of reference (OECD, 2017[3]) (ToR)) to ensure that it finalises its information gathering process (ToR I.4), information on rulings will be identified and exchanged in a timely manner (ToR II.5), to identify and exchange information on all new entrants to the IP regimes (ToR I.4.1.3). Saint Lucia receives three recommendations on these points for the year in review.

This is Saint Lucia's first review of implementation of the transparency framework.

Saint Lucia can legally issue two types of rulings within the scope of the transparency framework. In practice, Saint Lucia has issued no rulings in the year in review.

As no exchanges were required to take place, no peer input was received in respect of the exchanges of information on rulings received from Saint Lucia.

Introduction

This peer review covers Saint Lucia's implementation of the BEPS Action 5 transparency framework for the year 2018. The report has four parts, each relating to a key part of the ToR. Each part is discussed in turn. A summary of recommendations is included at the end of this report.

A. The information gathering process

Saint Lucia can legally issue two types of rulings within the scope of the transparency framework: (i) preferential regimes[1] and (ii) permanent establishment rulings. Rulings are issued by the Tax Administration Department.

Past rulings (ToR I.4.1.1, I.4.1.2, I.4.2.1, I.4.2.2)

For Saint Lucia, past rulings are any tax rulings issued prior to 1 September 2018. However, there is no obligation under the terms of the transparency framework for Saint Lucia to conduct spontaneous exchange information on past rulings.

Future rulings (ToR I.4.1.1, I.4.1.2, I.4.2.1)

For Saint Lucia, future rulings are any tax rulings within scope that are issued on or after 1 September 2018.

No rulings were issued by Saint Lucia during the future rulings period in the year of review. However, Saint Lucia indicates that there are not yet processes in place for the record keeping of rulings for the purposes of the transparency framework. It is noted that Saint Lucia intends to implement guidelines and practices to make sure the necessary information to meet the requirements of the transparency framework is required in all cases.

Review and supervision (ToR I.4.3)

Saint Lucia did not yet have a review and supervision mechanism under the transparency framework for the year in review. Saint Lucia is discussing the implementation of a revision and supervision mechanism for ensuring implementation of the transparency framework.

Conclusion on section A

Saint Lucia is recommended to finalise its information gathering process for identifying all future rulings and potential exchange jurisdictions, with a review and supervision mechanism, as soon as possible (ToR I.4).

B. The exchange of information

Legal basis for spontaneous exchange of information (ToR II.5.1, II.5.2)

Saint Lucia has the necessary domestic legal basis to exchange information spontaneously. Saint Lucia notes that there are no legal or practical impediments that prevent the spontaneous exchange of information on rulings as contemplated in the Action 5 minimum standard.

Saint Lucia has international agreements permitting spontaneous exchange of information, including being a party to the (i) *Multilateral Convention on Mutual Administrative Assistance in Tax Matters: Amended by the 2010 Protocol* (OECD/Council of Europe, 2011[4]) (the "Convention") and (ii) bilateral agreements in force with 16 jurisdictions.[2]

Completion and exchange of templates (ToR II.5.3, II.5.4, II.5.5, II.5.6, II.5.7)

Saint Lucia is still developing a process to complete the templates on relevant rulings, to make them available to the Competent Authority for exchange of information, and to exchange them with relevant jurisdictions.

As no exchanges were required to take place in the year of review, no data on the timeliness of exchanges can be reported.

Conclusion on section B

Saint Lucia is recommended to develop a process to complete the templates on relevant rulings and to ensure that the exchanges of information on rulings occur in accordance with the form and timelines under the transparency framework going forward (ToR II.5).

C. Statistics (ToR IV)

As no rulings are issued, no statistics can be reported.

D. Matters related to intellectual property regimes (ToR I.4.1.3)

Saint Lucia offered three intellectual property regimes (IP regime)[3] that were abolished from 1 December 2018 and are subject to the transparency requirements under the Action 5 Report (OECD, 2015[5]). It states that the identification of the benefitting taxpayers will occur as follows:

- ***New entrants benefitting from the grandfathered IP regime:*** Transparency obligations apply for the three regimes, because grandfathering is provided to entrants that entered the regime after the relevant date from which enhanced transparency obligations apply. Saint Lucia has not identified and exchanged information on new entrants to the IP regimes. Saint Lucia is therefore recommended to identify and exchange information on all new entrants to the grandfathered IP regimes (ToR I.4.1.3).
- ***Third category of IP assets***: not applicable to these regimes, which in 2018 were in the process of being abolished.
- ***Taxpayers making use of the option to treat the nexus ratio as a rebuttable presumption***: not applicable to these regimes, which in 2018 were in the process of being abolished.

Summary of recommendations on implementation of the transparency framework

Aspect of implementation of the transparency framework that should be improved	Recommendation for improvement
Saint Lucia has not yet finalised the steps to have in place its necessary information and gathering process.	Saint Lucia is recommended to finalise its information gathering process for identifying future rulings and potential exchange jurisdictions, with a review and supervision mechanism, as soon as possible.
Saint Lucia does not have a process to complete the templates on relevant rulings, to make them available to the Competent Authority for exchange of information, and to	Saint Lucia is recommended to develop a process to complete the templates on relevant rulings and to ensure that the exchanges of information on rulings occur in accordance with

exchange them with relevant jurisdictions.	the form and timelines under the transparency framework.
Saint Lucia did not identify or exchange information on new entrants to the IP regime or taxpayers benefitting from the third category of IP asset.	Saint Lucia is recommended to identify and exchange information on all new entrants to the IP regime, and to identify and exchange information on taxpayers benefitting from the third category of IP assets.

Notes

[1] With respect to the following preferential regimes: International business company, International trust and International partnership regimes

[2] Parties to the Convention are available here: www.oecd.org/tax/exchange-of-tax-information/convention-on-mutual-administrative-assistance-in-tax-matters.htm. Saint Lucia also has bilateral agreements in force with the CARICOM jurisdictions and the United States.

[3] International business company, International trust and International partnership regimes.

San Marino

San Marino's implementation of the transparency framework is still in development. San Marino is taking steps to implement the legal basis for the transparency framework and to commence administrative preparations (in line with the terms of reference (OECD, 2017[3]) (ToR)) to ensure that it finalises its information gathering process (ToR I.4), information on rulings will be identified and exchanged in a timely manner (ToR II.5) and to identify and exchange information on all new entrants to the IP regimes (ToR I.4.1.3). San Marino receives three recommendations on these points for the year in review.

In the prior year review, no recommendations were made, given that in that period no rulings in the scope of the transparency framework could legally be issued, and the implementation of grandfathering for the IP regime had not been finalised. As those circumstances have changed with respect to the year in review, recommendations have been made as relevant.

San Marino can legally issue one type of rulings within the scope of the transparency framework. In practice, San Marino issued no rulings within the scope of the transparency framework.

As no exchanges took place, no peer input was received in respect of the exchanges of information on rulings received from San Marino.

Introduction

This peer review covers San Marino's implementation of the BEPS Action 5 transparency framework for the year 2018. The report has four parts, each relating to a key part of the ToR. Each part is discussed in turn. A summary of recommendations is included at the end of this report.

A. The information gathering process

San Marino can legally issue the following type of rulings within the scope of the transparency framework: preferential regimes.[1] In the previous year peer review report, it was noted that San Marino cannot legally issue any rulings in scope of the transparency framework. However, in 2018, San Marino introduced a new IP regime that allows taxpayers to request benefits via a ruling. This also applies for the other two IP regimes that San Marino has in place.

Past rulings (ToR I.4.1.1, I.4.1.2, I.4.2.1, I.4.2.2)

For San Marino, past rulings are any tax rulings within scope that are issued either (i) on or after 1 January 2015 but before 1 April 2017; and (ii) on or after 1 January 2012 but before 1 January 2015, provided they were still in effect as at 1 January 2015. San Marino has the legal basis to issue rulings, but it requires a decree to issue certain types of rulings in scope of the transparency framework. Currently, San Marino has only issued a decree regarding the IP regime. However, it should be noted that in the past, San Marino could issue permanent establishment rulings (using another legal instrument, aimed to provide taxpayers with clarifications in case of objective uncertainties in the interpretation or in the application of specific tax provisions). San Marino is currently examining whether in practice it did issue any permanent establishment ruling in scope of the transparency framework.

Future rulings (ToR I.4.1.1, I.4.1.2, I.4.2.1)

For San Marino, future rulings are any tax rulings within scope that are issued on or after 1 April 2017.

San Marino can legally issue rulings from 2018. San Marino's tax office is in charge of issuing the rulings. San Marino notes that so far, no tax rulings have been issued in practice. However, San Marino acknowledges that it does not yet have an information gathering process in place to identify the rulings and all potential exchange jurisdictions. San Marino intends to implement this process as soon as possible.

Review and supervision (ToR I.4.3)

San Marino did not yet have a review and supervision mechanism in place for future rulings under the transparency framework for the year in review.

Conclusion on section A

San Marino is recommended to finalise its information gathering process for identifying all past and future rulings and potential exchange jurisdictions, with a review and supervision mechanism, as soon as possible (ToR I.4).

B. The exchange of information

Legal basis for spontaneous exchange of information (ToR II.5.1, II.5.2)

San Marino has the necessary domestic legal basis to exchange information spontaneously. San Marino notes that there are no legal or practical impediments that prevent the spontaneous exchange of information on rulings as contemplated in the Action 5 minimum standard.

San Marino has international agreements permitting spontaneous exchange of information, including being a party to the (i) *Multilateral Convention on Mutual Administrative Assistance in Tax Matters: Amended by the 2010 Protocol* (OECD/Council of Europe, 2011[4]) ("the Convention") and (ii) double tax agreements in force with 23 jurisdictions.[2]

Completion and exchange of templates (ToR II.5.3, II.5.4, II.5.5, II.5.6, II.5.7)

San Marino is still developing a process to complete the templates on the relevant rulings, to make them available to the Competent Authority for exchange of information and to exchange them with relevant jurisdictions.

As San Marino did not issue any future rulings in scope of the transparency framework in the relevant period, San Marino was not required to exchange any information on rulings in the year in review and no data on the timeliness of exchanges can be reported.

Conclusion on section B

San Marino is recommended to develop a process to complete the templates on relevant rulings and to ensure that the exchanges of information on rulings occur in accordance with the form and timelines under the transparency framework (ToR II.5).

C. Statistics (ToR IV)

As there was no information on rulings exchanged by San Marino for the year in review, no statistics can be reported.

D. Matters related to intellectual property regimes (ToR I.4.1.3)

San Marino offers three intellectual property regimes (IP regime)[3] that are subject to the transparency requirements under the Action 5 Report (OECD, 2015[5]). It states that the identification of the benefitting taxpayers will occur as follows:

IP regime

- ***New entrants benefitting from the grandfathered IP regime***: as this is a new IP regime rather than a grandfathered IP regime, transparency on new entrants is not relevant.
- ***Third category of IP assets***: not applicable as the regime does not allow the third category of IP assets to qualify for the benefits.
- ***Taxpayers making use of the option to treat the nexus ratio as a rebuttable presumption***: not applicable as the regime does not allow the nexus ratio to be treated as a rebuttable presumption.

New companies regime

- ***New entrants benefitting from the grandfathered IP regime***: Transparency obligations apply for this regime, because grandfathering is provided to entrants that entered the regime after the relevant date from which enhanced transparency obligations apply San Marino is currently putting in place a process to identify new entrants (both new taxpayers and IP assets) in the grandfathered regime. As such, San Marino is recommended to continue its efforts to identify and exchange information on new entrants to the grandfathered IP regime (ToR I.4.1.3).
- ***Third category of IP assets***: not applicable as the regime does not allow the third category of IP assets to qualify for the benefits.
- ***Taxpayers making use of the option to treat the nexus ratio as a rebuttable presumption***: not applicable as the regime does not allow the nexus ratio to be treated as a rebuttable presumption.

High tech regime

- ***New entrants benefitting from the grandfathered IP regime***: this is an amended regime. The amendments took effect from 29 June 2018, but before the amendments took effect there were no entrants in the regime, due to absence of administrative guidelines by San Marino which would operationalise the regime, and therefore the enhanced transparency requirements do not apply.
- ***Third category of IP assets***: not applicable as the regime does not allow the third category of IP assets to qualify for the benefits.
- ***Taxpayers making use of the option to treat the nexus ratio as a rebuttable presumption***: not applicable as the regime does not allow the nexus ratio to be treated as a rebuttable presumption.

San Marino is recommended to continue its efforts to identify and exchange information on new entrants to the grandfathered IP regime (ToR I.4.1.3).

Summary of recommendations on implementation of the transparency framework

Aspect of implementation of the transparency framework that should be improved	Recommendation for improvement
San Marino does not yet have in place a process to identify all information on potential exchange jurisdictions for future rulings.	San Marino is recommended to finalise its information gathering process for identifying all past and future rulings and potential exchange jurisdictions, with a review and supervision mechanism, as soon as possible.
San Marino does not yet have in place a process for completion of templates and exchange of information on rulings.	San Marino is recommended to develop a process to complete the templates on relevant rulings and to ensure that the exchanges of information on rulings occur in accordance with the form and timelines under the transparency framework.
San Marino has not exchanged all information on new taxpayers benefitting from the grandfathered IP regime, and new assets of existing taxpayers benefitting from the grandfathered regime as this information was not able to be collected during the year in review.	San Marino is recommended to continue its efforts to identify and exchange information on new entrants to the grandfathered IP regime.

Jurisdiction's response and recent developments

San Marino has already undertaken steps in 2019 to follow-up on the recommendations. It is currently designing a database for collecting issued rulings. In addition, an internal agreement was signed between the San Marino Tax Administration and the Competent Authority for the exchange of information on rulings. These two bodies are also currently developing internal manual for the implementation of the several elements of Action 5 transparency framework. San Marino notes that these steps will be finalised by the end of 2019. This will be assessed in the next year's peer review.

Notes

[1] With respect to the following preferential regimes: 1) New companies regime (New companies regime provided by art. 73, law no. 166/2013), 2) High tech regime (Regime for high-tech start-up companies under law no. 71/2013 and delegated decree no. 116/2014) and 3) IP regime.

[2] Parties to the Convention are available here: www.oecd.org/tax/exchange-of-tax-information/convention-on-mutual-administrative-assistance-in-tax-matters.htm. San Marino also has bilateral agreements in effect with: Austria, Azerbaijan, Barbados, Belgium, Croatia, Cyprus, Georgia, Greece, Hungary, Italy, Liechtenstein, Luxembourg, Malaysia, Malta, Portugal, Qatar, Romania, Saint Kitts and Nevis, Serbia, Seychelles, Singapore, United Arab Emirates and Viet Nam.

Note by Turkey: The information in this document with reference to "Cyprus" relates to the southern part of the Island. There is no single authority representing both Turkish and Greek Cypriot people on the Island. Turkey recognises the Turkish Republic of Northern Cyprus (TRNC). Until a lasting and equitable solution is found within the context of the United Nations, Turkey shall preserve its position concerning the "Cyprus issue".

Note by all the European Union Member States of the OECD and the European Union. The Republic of Cyprus is recognised by all members of the United Nations with the exception of Turkey. The information in this document relates to the area under the effective control of the Government of the Republic of Cyprus.

[3] 1) New companies regime (New companies regime provided by art. 73, law no. 166/2013), 2) High tech regime (Regime for high-tech start-up companies under law no. 71/2013 and delegated decree no. 116/2014) and 3) IP regime.

Saudi Arabia

Saudi Arabia has met all aspects of the terms of reference (ToR) for the calendar year 2018 (year in review) that can be met in the absence of rulings being issued.

In the prior year report, Saudi Arabia did not receive any recommendations.

Saudi Arabia cannot legally issue any type of rulings within the scope of the transparency framework.

As no exchanges took place, no peer input was received in respect of the exchanges of information on rulings received from Saudi Arabia.

Introduction

This peer review covers Saudi Arabia's implementation of the BEPS Action 5 transparency framework for the year 2018. The report has four parts, each relating to a key part of the ToR. Each part is discussed in turn. A summary of recommendations is included at the end of this report.

A. The information gathering process

As no rulings are issued, this section is not assessed.

B. The exchange of information

As no rulings are issued, this section is not assessed.

C. Statistics (ToR IV)

As no rulings are issued, no statistical data can be reported.

D. Matters related to intellectual property regimes (ToR I.4.1.3)

Saudi Arabia does not offer an intellectual property regime for which transparency requirements under the Action 5 Report (OECD, 2015[5]) were imposed.

Summary of recommendations on implementation of the transparency framework

Aspect of implementation of the transparency framework that should be improved	Recommendation for improvement
	No recommendations are made.

Senegal

Senegal is taking steps to implement the legal basis for the transparency framework and to commence administrative preparations to ensure that information on rulings will be exchanged in a timely manner, in line with the terms of reference (OECD, 2017[3]). Senegal is recommended to ensure that it has put in place an effective information gathering process and to implement a review and supervision mechanism, as soon as possible (ToR I.4). In addition, Senegal is recommended to develop a process to complete the templates on relevant rulings, to ensure that the exchanges of information on rulings occur in accordance with the form and timelines under the transparency framework going forward (ToR II.5).

This is Senegal's first review of implementation of the transparency framework.

Senegal can legally issue one type of rulings within the scope of the transparency framework. In practice, Senegal has issued no rulings in the year in review.

As no exchanges were required to take place, no peer input was received in respect of the exchanges of information on rulings received from Senegal.

Introduction

This peer review covers Senegal's implementation of the BEPS Action 5 transparency framework for the year 2018. The report has four parts, each relating to a key part of the ToR. Each part is discussed in turn. A summary of recommendations is included at the end of this report.

A. The information gathering process

Senegal can legally issue one type of rulings within the scope of the transparency framework: cross-border unilateral advance pricing agreements (APAs) and any other cross-border unilateral tax rulings (such as an advance tax ruling) covering transfer pricing or the application of transfer pricing principles. .

Past rulings (ToR I.4.1.1, I.4.1.2, I.4.2.1, I.4.2.2)

For Senegal, past rulings are any tax rulings within scope that are issued either (i) on or after 1 January 2016 but before 1 April 2018; and (ii) on or after 1 January 2014 but before 1 January 2016, provided still in effect as at 1 January 2016.

In Senegal, rulings are issued by the directorate of Legislation and International Cooperation, within the Tax Administration. This unit is responsible for storing and reviewing such rulings and has reviewed its files, being able to confirm that no past rulings have been issued. To date no rulings have been issued. As such there was no need to identify potential exchange jurisdictions.

Future rulings (ToR I.4.1.1, I.4.1.2, I.4.2.1)

For Senegal, future rulings are any tax rulings within scope that are issued on or after 1 April 2018.

No rulings were issued by Senegal during the future rulings period in the year of review. However, Senegal indicates that there are no processes in place for the record keeping of rulings for the purposes of the transparency framework. It is noted that Senegal intends to implement guidelines and practices to make sure the necessary information to meet the requirements of the transparency framework is required in all cases.

Review and supervision (ToR I.4.3)

Senegal did not yet have a review and supervision mechanism under the transparency framework for the year in review. Senegal is discussing the implementation of a revision and supervision mechanism for ensuring implementation of the transparency framework.

Conclusion on section A

Senegal is recommended to finalise its information gathering process, with a review and supervision mechanism, as soon as possible (ToR I.4).

B. The exchange of information

Legal basis for spontaneous exchange of information (ToR II.5.1, II.5.2)

Senegal has the necessary domestic legal basis to exchange information spontaneously. Senegal notes that there are no legal or practical impediments that prevent the spontaneous exchange of information on rulings as contemplated in the Action 5 minimum standard.

Senegal has international agreements permitting spontaneous exchange of information, including being a party to the (i) *Multilateral Convention on Mutual Administrative Assistance in Tax Matters: Amended by the 2010 Protocol* (OECD/Council of Europe, 2011[4]) (the "Convention") and (ii) bilateral agreements in force with 24 jurisdictions.[1]

Completion and exchange of templates (ToR II.5.3, II.5.4, II.5.5, II.5.6, II.5.7)

Senegal is still developing a process to complete the templates on relevant rulings, to make them available to the Competent Authority for exchange of information, and to exchange them with relevant jurisdictions.

As no exchanges were required to take place in the year of review, no data on the timeliness of exchanges can be reported.

Conclusion on section B

Senegal is recommended to develop a process to complete the templates on relevant rulings and to ensure that the exchanges of information on rulings occur in accordance with the form and timelines under the transparency framework going forward (ToR II.5).

C. Statistics (ToR IV)

As there were no rulings exchanged by Senegal for the year in review, no statistics can be reported here.

D. Matters related to intellectual property regimes (ToR I.4.1.3)

Senegal does not offer an intellectual property regime for which transparency requirements under the Action 5 Report (OECD, 2015[5]) were imposed.

Summary of recommendations on implementation of the transparency framework

Aspect of implementation of the transparency framework that should be improved	Recommendation for improvement
Senegal has not yet finalised the steps to have in place its necessary information and gathering process.	Senegal is recommended to finalise its information gathering process, with a review and supervision mechanism, as soon as possible.
Senegal does not have a process to complete the templates on relevant rulings, to make them available to the Competent Authority for exchange of information, and to exchange them with relevant jurisdictions.	Senegal is recommended to develop a process to complete the templates on relevant rulings and to ensure that the exchanges of information on rulings occur in accordance with the form and timelines under the transparency framework.

Notes

[1] Parties to the Convention are available here: www.oecd.org/tax/exchange-of-tax-information/convention-on-mutual-administrative-assistance-in-tax-matters.htm. Senegal also has bilateral agreements in force with African and Mauritian common organization, Belgium, Canada, Chinese Taipei, France, Italy, Lebanon, Luxembourg, Mauritania, Mauritius, Morocco, Norway, Portugal, Qatar, Spain, Tunisia, United Arab Emirates, United Kingdom, West African Economic and Monetary Union.

Serbia

Serbia has met all aspects of the terms of reference (OECD, 2017[3]) (ToR) for the calendar year 2018 (year in review) that can be met in the absence of rulings being issued.

This is Serbia's first review of implementation of the transparency framework.

Serbia cannot legally issue any type of rulings within the scope of the transparency framework.

As no exchanges took place, no peer input was received in respect of the exchanges of information on rulings received from Serbia.

Introduction

This peer review covers Serbia's implementation of the BEPS Action 5 transparency framework for the year 2018. The report has four parts, each relating to a key part of the ToR. Each part is discussed in turn. A summary of recommendations is included at the end of this report.

A. The information gathering process

As no rulings are issued, this section is not assessed.

B. The exchange of information

As no rulings are issued, this section is not assessed.

C. Statistics (ToR IV)

As no rulings are issued, no statistics can be reported.

D. Matters related to intellectual property regimes (ToR I.4.1.3)

Serbia does not offer an intellectual property regime for which transparency requirements under the Action 5 Report (OECD, 2015[5]) were imposed.

Summary of recommendations on implementation of the transparency framework

Aspect of implementation of the transparency framework that should be improved	Recommendation for improvement
	No recommendations are made.

Seychelles

Seychelles has met all aspects of the terms of reference (OECD, 2017[3]) (ToR) for the calendar year 2018 (year in review) and no recommendations are made.

In the prior year report, Seychelles did not receive any recommendations.

Seychelles can legally issue five types of rulings within the scope of the transparency framework. In practice, Seychelles issued no rulings within the scope of the transparency framework. In the year in review, Seychelles only provided general decisions, which are not binding on the tax administration.

As no exchanges were required to take place, no peer input was received in respect of the exchanges of information on rulings received from Seychelles.

Introduction

This peer review covers Seychelles' implementation of the BEPS Action 5 transparency framework for the year 2018. The report has four parts, each relating to a key part of the ToR. Each part is discussed in turn. A summary of recommendations is included at the end of this report.

A. The information gathering process

Seychelles can legally issue the five following types of rulings within the scope of the transparency framework: (i) rulings related to preferential regimes;[1] (ii) cross-border unilateral APAs and any other unilateral tax ruling (such as an advance tax ruling) covering transfer pricing or the application of transfer pricing principles; (iii) rulings providing for unilateral downward adjustments; (iv) permanent establishment rulings; and (v) related party conduit rulings.

Past rulings (ToR I.4.1.1, I.4.1.2, I.4.2.1, I.4.2.2)

For Seychelles, past rulings are any tax rulings within scope that are issued either: (i) on or after 1 January 2015 but before 1 April 2017; or (ii) on or after 1 January 2012 but before 1 January 2015, provided they were still in effect as at 1 January 2015.

In the prior year peer review report, it was determined that Seychelles' undertakings to identify past rulings were sufficient to meet the minimum standard. Seychelles' implementation in this regard remains unchanged, and therefore continues to meet the minimum standard.

Future rulings (ToR I.4.1.1, I.4.1.2, I.4.2.1)

For Seychelles, future rulings are any tax rulings within scope that are issued on or after 1 September 2017.

In the prior year peer review report, it was determined that Seychelles' undertakings to identify future rulings and all potential exchange jurisdictions was sufficient to meet the minimum standard. Seychelles' implementation in this regard remains unchanged, and therefore continues to meet the minimum standard. In order to identify potential exchange jurisdictions in the future, the Seychelles Revenue Commission (SRC) is planning to amend the existing form to request a private ruling to capture all the needed information. Until that takes place, Seychelles would continue to use its information gathering powers under the Revenue Administration Act to obtain information on all potential exchange jurisdictions, if needed.

Review and supervision (ToR I.4.3)

In the prior year peer review report, it was determined that Seychelles' review and supervision mechanism was sufficient to meet the minimum standard. Seychelles' implementation in this regard remains unchanged, and therefore continues to meet the minimum standard.

Conclusion on section A

Seychelles has met all of the ToR for the information gathering process and no recommendations are made.

B. The exchange of information

Legal basis for spontaneous exchange of information (ToR II.5.1, II.5.2)

Seychelles has the necessary domestic legal basis to exchange information spontaneously. Seychelles notes that there are no legal or practical impediments that prevent the spontaneous exchange of information on rulings as contemplated in the Action 5 minimum standard.

Seychelles has international agreements permitting spontaneous exchange of information, including being a party to the (i) *Multilateral Convention on Mutual Administrative Assistance in Tax Matters: Amended by the 2010 Protocol* (OECD/Council of Europe, 2011[4]) ("the Convention") and (ii) double tax agreements in force with 28 jurisdictions.[2]

Completion and exchange of templates (ToR II.5.3, II.5.4, II.5.5, II.5.6, II.5.7)

In the prior year peer review report, it was determined that Seychelles' process for the completion and exchange of templates were sufficient to meet the minimum standard. Seychelles' implementation in this regard remains unchanged and therefore continues to meet the minimum standard.

As Seychelles did not issue any past or future rulings in scope of Action 5 in the relevant periods, Seychelles did not exchange any information on rulings in the year in review and no data on the timeliness of exchanges can be reported.

Conclusion on section B

Seychelles has the necessary legal basis for spontaneous exchange of information. Seychelles has met all of the ToR for the exchange of information process and no recommendations are made.

C. Statistics (ToR IV)

As no rulings are issued, no statistics can be reported.

D. Matters related to intellectual property regimes (ToR I.4.1.3)

Seychelles offered three intellectual property regimes (IP regime)[3] that were abolished from 1 January 2019 and not subject to the transparency requirements under the Action 5 Report (OECD, 2015[5]), because:

- ***New entrants benefitting from the grandfathered IP regime***: the IP regimes have been abolished without grandfathering for taxpayers entering after the relevant date from which enhanced transparency obligations apply. As such, no enhanced transparency requirements apply.
- ***Third category of IP assets***: not applicable as the IP regimes have been abolished.
- ***Taxpayers making use of the option to treat the nexus ratio as a rebuttable presumption***: not applicable as the IP regimes have been abolished.

Summary of recommendations on implementation of the transparency framework

Aspect of implementation of the transparency framework that should be improved	Recommendation for improvement
	No recommendations are made.

Notes

[1] With respect to the following preferential regimes: 1) International business companies, 2) Companies special license, 3) International trade zone licensees, 4) Offshore banking, 5) Non-domestic insurance business, 6) Fund administration business, 7) Securities business under the securities act and 8) Reinsurance business.

[2] Parties to the Convention are available here: www.oecd.org/tax/exchange-of-tax-information/convention-on-mutual-administrative-assistance-in-tax-matters.htm. Seychelles also has double tax agreements with Bahrain, Barbados, Belgium, Bermuda, Botswana, China (People's Republic of), Cyprus, Ethiopia, Guernsey, Indonesia, Isle of Man, Jersey, Kenya, Luxembourg, Malaysia, Mauritius, Monaco, Oman, Qatar, San Marino, Singapore, South Africa, Sri Lanka, Swaziland, Thailand, United Arab Emirates, Viet Nam and Zambia.

Note by Turkey: The information in this document with reference to "Cyprus" relates to the southern part of the Island. There is no single authority representing both Turkish and Greek Cypriot people on the Island. Turkey recognises the Turkish Republic of Northern Cyprus (TRNC). Until a lasting and equitable solution is found within the context of the United Nations, Turkey shall preserve its position concerning the "Cyprus issue".

Note by all the European Union Member States of the OECD and the European Union. The Republic of Cyprus is recognised by all members of the United Nations with the exception of Turkey. The information in this document relates to the area under the effective control of the Government of the Republic of Cyprus.

[3] These regimes are: 1) International business companies; 2) Companies special license; and 3) International trade zone.

Sierra Leone

Sierra Leone has met all aspects of the terms of reference (OECD, 2017[3]) (ToR) for the calendar year 2018 (year in review) that can be met in the absence of rulings being issued.

In the prior year report, Sierra Leone did not receive any recommendations.

Sierra Leone indicates that it cannot legally issue any type of rulings within the scope of the transparency framework.

As no exchanges were required to take place, no peer input was received in respect of the exchanges of information on rulings received from Sierra Leone.

Introduction

This peer review covers Sierra Leone's implementation of the BEPS Action 5 transparency framework for the year 2018. The report has four parts, each relating to a key part of the ToR. Each part is discussed in turn. A summary of recommendations is included at the end of this report.

A. The information gathering process

As no rulings are issued, this section is not assessed.

B. The exchange of information

As no rulings are issued, this section is not assessed.

C. Statistics (ToR IV)

As no rulings are issued, no statistics can be reported.

D. Matters related to intellectual property regimes (ToR I.4.1.3)

Sierra Leone does not offer an intellectual property regime for which transparency requirements under the Action 5 Report (OECD, 2015[5]) were imposed.

Summary of recommendations on implementation of the transparency framework

Aspect of implementation of the transparency framework that should be improved	Recommendation for improvement
	No recommendations are made.

Singapore

Singapore has met all aspects of the terms of reference (OECD, 2017[3]) (ToR) for the calendar year 2018 (year in review) and no recommendations are made.

In the prior year report, Singapore did not receive any recommendations.

Singapore can legally issue five types of rulings within the scope of the transparency framework. In practice, Singapore issued rulings within the scope of the transparency framework as follows:

- 1 008 past rulings;[1]
- For the calendar year 2017: 85 future rulings; and
- For the year in review: 222 future rulings.

Peer input was received from five jurisdictions in respect of the exchanges of information on rulings received from Singapore. The input was generally positive, noting that information was complete, in a correct format and almost all received in a timely manner.

Introduction

This peer review covers Singapore's implementation of the BEPS Action 5 transparency framework for the year 2018. The report has four parts, each relating to a key part of the ToR. Each part is discussed in turn. A summary of recommendations is included at the end of this report.

A. The information gathering process

Singapore can legally issue the following five types of rulings within the scope of the transparency framework: (i) preferential regimes;[2] (ii) cross-border unilateral APAs and any other cross-border unilateral tax rulings (such as an advance tax ruling) covering transfer pricing or the application of transfer pricing principles; (iii) rulings providing for unilateral downward adjustments; (iv) permanent establishment rulings, and (v) related party conduit rulings.

Past rulings (ToR I.4.1.1, I.4.1.2, I.4.2.1, I.4.2.2)

For Singapore, past rulings are any tax rulings within scope that are issued either (i) on or after 1 January 2015 but before 1 April 2017; and (ii) on or after 1 January 2012 but before 1 January 2015, provided they were still in effect as at 1 January 2015.

In the prior year peer review report, it was determined that Singapore's undertakings to identify past rulings and all potential exchange jurisdictions were sufficient to meet the minimum standard. Singapore's implementation in this regard remains unchanged, and therefore continues to meet the minimum standard.

Future rulings (ToR I.4.1.1, I.4.1.2, I.4.2.1)

For Singapore, future rulings are any tax rulings within scope that are issued on or after 1 April 2017.

In the prior year peer review report, it was determined that Singapore's undertakings to identify future rulings and all potential exchange jurisdictions were sufficient to meet the minimum standard. Singapore's implementation in this regard remains unchanged, and therefore continues to meet the minimum standard.

Review and supervision (ToR I.4.3)

In the prior year peer review report, it was determined that Singapore's review and supervision mechanism was sufficient to meet the minimum standard. Singapore's implementation in this regard remains unchanged, and therefore continues to meet the minimum standard.

Conclusion on section A

Singapore has met all of the ToR for the information gathering process and no recommendations are made.

B. The exchange of information

Legal basis for spontaneous exchange of information (ToR II.5.1, II.5.2)

Singapore has the necessary domestic legal basis to exchange information spontaneously. Singapore notes that there are no legal or practical impediments that prevent the spontaneous exchange of information on rulings as contemplated in the Action 5 minimum standard.

Singapore has international agreements permitting spontaneous exchange of information, including being a party to the (i) *Multilateral Convention on Mutual Administrative Assistance in Tax Matters: Amended by the 2010 Protocol* (OECD/Council of Europe, 2011[4]) ("the Convention"), and (ii) double tax agreements in force with 80 jurisdictions.[3]

Completion and exchange of templates (ToR II.5.3, II.5.4, II.5.5, II.5.6, II.5.7)

In the prior year's peer review report, it was determined that Singapore's process for the completion and exchange of templates was sufficient to meet the minimum standard. Singapore's implementation in this regard remains unchanged and therefore continues to meet the minimum standard.

For the year in review, the timeliness of exchanges is as follows:

Past rulings in the scope of the transparency framework	Number of exchanges transmitted by 31 December 2018	Delayed exchanges		
		Number of exchanges not transmitted by 31 December 2018	Reasons for the delays	Any other comments
	269	0		These exchanges were reported as delayed exchanges in the prior year's peer review report and were exchanged by August 2018.
Future rulings in the scope of the transparency framework	Number of exchanges transmitted within three months of the information becoming available to the competent authority or immediately after legal impediments have been lifted	Delayed exchanges		
		Number of exchanges transmitted later than three months of the information on rulings becoming available to the competent authority	Reasons for the delays	Any other comments
	817	50	The delays occurred due to the need to seek clarification with regard to the reliance on the Convention as the legal basis for spontaneous exchange of information under the Action 5 transparency framework.	Clarifications were obtained in late April 2018 and the delayed exchanges were completed in May 2018.
Total	1 086	50		

Follow up requests received for exchange of the ruling	Number	Average time to provide response	Number of requests not answered
	0	N/A	N/A

Conclusion on section B

Singapore notes that further delays occurred when exchanging information on future rulings due to uncertainties about the application of the Convention as a legal basis for spontaneous exchange of information under the Action 5 transparency framework. These delayed exchanges have been completed by May 2018 and Singapore notes that it does not expect that further delays would occur in the future. Considering the amount of exchanges that occurred within the timeframe, that Singapore has addressed the issue and does not expect further delays in the future, and that the delayed exchanges were completed swiftly after the interpretive issue was resolved, it is determined that Singapore's process to exchange information still meets the minimum standard.

Conclusion on section B

Singapore has the necessary legal basis for spontaneous exchange of information, a process for completing the templates in a timely way and has completed all exchanges. Singapore has met all of the ToR for the exchange of information process and no recommendations are made.

C. Statistics (ToR IV)

The statistics for the year in review are as follows:

Category of ruling	Number of exchanges	Jurisdictions exchanged with
Ruling/letters of awards related to a preferential regime	1 134	Argentina, Australia, Austria, Belgium, Brazil, Canada, Chile, China (People's Republic of), Colombia, Denmark, Estonia, Finland, France, Germany, Greece, Guernsey, India, Ireland, Isle of Man, Israel, Italy, Japan, Jersey, Korea, Latvia, Liechtenstein, Luxembourg, Malaysia, Malta, Mauritius, Mexico, Netherlands, New Zealand, Norway, Poland, Portugal, Russia, Saudi Arabia, Slovak Republic, South Africa, Spain, Sweden, Switzerland, Turkey, United Kingdom, Uruguay
Cross-border unilateral advance pricing agreements (APAs) and any other cross-border unilateral tax rulings (such as an advance tax ruling) covering transfer pricing or the application of transfer pricing principles	2	*De minimis* rule applies
Cross-border rulings providing for a unilateral downward adjustment to the taxpayer's taxable profits that is not directly reflected in the taxpayer's financial / commercial accounts	0	N/A
Permanent establishment rulings	0	N/A
Related party conduit rulings	0	N/A
De minimis rule	N/A	N/A
IP regimes: total exchanges on taxpayers benefitting from the third category of IP assets, new entrants benefitting from grandfathered IP regimes; and taxpayers making use of the option to treat the nexus ratio as a rebuttable presumption	7	France, Germany, India, Japan, Korea, Malaysia, Switzerland
Total	1 143	

D. Matters related to intellectual property regimes (ToR I.4.1.3)

Singapore offered two preferential regimes, which also provided benefits to income from intellectual property (IP regime).[4] The IP parts of both regimes were abolished as of 30 June 2018 and are subject to transparency requirements under the Action 5 Report (OECD, 2015[5]). It states that the identification of the benefitting taxpayers will occur as follows:

- ***New entrants benefitting from the grandfathered IP regime***: Transparency obligations apply for the two regimes, because grandfathering is provided to entrants that entered the regime after the relevant date from which enhanced transparency obligations apply. New entrants include both (i) new taxpayers not previously benefitting from the regimes and (ii) new IP assets owned by taxpayers already benefitting from the regimes. Singapore's approach is described in detail in the prior year's report and which meets the ToR. Seven exchanges occurred in the year in review.
- ***Third category of IP assets***: not applicable as the IP regimes have been abolished.
- ***Taxpayers making use of the option to treat the nexus ratio as a rebuttable presumption***: not applicable as the IP regimes have been abolished.

Singapore introduced a new IP regime[5] which came into effect from 1 July 2018. It is noted that this regime is not subject to transparency requirements under the Action 5 Report (OECD, 2015[5]), because:

- ***New entrants benefitting from the grandfathered IP regime***: as this is a new IP regime rather than a grandfathered IP regime, transparency on new entrants is not relevant.
- ***Third category of IP assets***: not applicable as the regime does not allow the third category of IP assets to qualify for the benefits.
- ***Taxpayers making use of the option to treat the nexus ratio as a rebuttable presumption***: not applicable as the regime does not allow the nexus ratio to be treated as a rebuttable presumption.

Summary of recommendations on implementation of the transparency framework

Aspect of implementation of the transparency framework that should be improved	Recommendation for improvement
	No recommendations are made.

Notes

[1] Including two that fell into more than one category under the BEPS Action 5 report.

[2] With respect to the following preferential regimes: 1) Development and expansion incentive - services, 2) Pioneer service company, 3) Aircraft leasing scheme, 4) Finance and treasury centre, 5) Insurance business development, 6) Financial sector incentive, 7) Global trader programme.

[3] Parties to the Convention are available here: www.oecd.org/tax/exchange-of-tax-information/convention-on-mutual-administrative-assistance-in-tax-matters.htm. Singapore also has double tax agreements with Albania, Australia, Bahrain, Bangladesh, Barbados, Belarus, Belgium, Brunei Darussalam, Bulgaria, Cambodia, Canada, China (People's Republic of), Cyprus, Czech Republic, Denmark, Ecuador, Egypt, Estonia, Ethiopia, Fiji, Finland, France, Georgia, Germany, Guernsey, Hungary, India, Indonesia, Ireland, Isle of Man, Israel, Italy, Japan, Jersey, Kazakhstan, Korea, Kuwait, Lao People's Democratic Republic, Latvia, Libya, Lithuania, Luxembourg, Malaysia, Malta, Mauritius, Mexico, Mongolia, Morocco, Myanmar, Netherlands, New Zealand, Nigeria, Norway, Oman, Pakistan, Papua New Guinea, Philippines, Poland, Portugal, Qatar, Romania, Russia, Rwanda, San Marino, Saudi Arabia, Seychelles, Slovak Republic,

Slovenia, South Africa, Spain, Sri Lanka, Sweden, Thailand, Turkey, Ukraine, United Arab Emirates, United Kingdom, Uruguay, Uzbekistan and Viet Nam.

Note by Turkey: The information in this document with reference to “Cyprus” relates to the southern part of the Island. There is no single authority representing both Turkish and Greek Cypriot people on the Island. Turkey recognises the Turkish Republic of Northern Cyprus (TRNC). Until a lasting and equitable solution is found within the context of the United Nations, Turkey shall preserve its position concerning the “Cyprus issue”.

Note by all the European Union Member States of the OECD and the European Union. The Republic of Cyprus is recognised by all members of the United Nations with the exception of Turkey. The information in this document relates to the area under the effective control of the Government of the Republic of Cyprus.

[4] These regimes are: 1) Pioneer service company and 2) Development and expansion incentive – services.

[5] This regime is the IP development incentive.

Slovak Republic

The Slovak Republic has met all aspects of the terms of reference (OECD, 2017[3]) (ToR) for the calendar year 2018 (year in review) and no recommendations are made.

In the prior year report, the Slovak Republic did not receive any recommendations.

The Slovak Republic can legally issue two types of rulings within the scope of the transparency framework. In practice, the Slovak Republic issued rulings within the scope of the transparency framework as follows:

- One past ruling;
- For the period 1 April 2016 - 31 December 2016: two future rulings;
- For the calendar year 2017: five future rulings, and
- For the year in review: three future rulings.

No peer input was received in respect of the exchanges of information on rulings received from the Slovak Republic.

Introduction

This peer review covers the Slovak Republic's implementation of the BEPS Action 5 transparency framework for the year 2018. The report has four parts, each relating to a key part of the ToR. Each part is discussed in turn. A summary of recommendations is included at the end of this report.

A. The information gathering process

The Slovak Republic can legally issue the following two types of rulings within the scope of the transparency framework: (i) cross-border unilateral APAs and any other cross-border unilateral tax rulings (such as an advance tax ruling) covering transfer pricing or the application of transfer pricing principles and (ii) permanent establishment rulings.

Past rulings (ToR I.4.1.1, I.4.1.2, I.4.2.1, I.4.2.2)

For the Slovak Republic, past rulings are any tax rulings within scope that are issued either: (i) on or after 1 January 2014 but before 1 April 2016; or (ii) on or after 1 January 2010 but before 1 January 2014, provided they were still in effect as at 1 January 2014.

In the prior years' peer review reports, it was determined that the Slovak Republic's undertakings to identify past rulings and all potential exchange jurisdictions were sufficient to meet the minimum standard. The Slovak Republic's implementation in this regard remains unchanged, and therefore continues to meet the minimum standard.

Future rulings (ToR I.4.1.1, I.4.1.2, I.4.2.1)

For the Slovak Republic, future rulings are any tax rulings within scope that are issued on or after 1 April 2016.

In the prior years' peer review reports, it was determined that the Slovak Republic's undertakings to identify future rulings and all potential exchange jurisdictions were sufficient to meet the minimum standard. The Slovak Republic's implementation in this regard remains unchanged, and therefore continues to meet the minimum standard.

Review and supervision (ToR I.4.3)

In the prior years' peer review reports, it was determined that the Slovak Republic's review and supervision mechanism was sufficient to meet the minimum standard. The Slovak Republic's implementation in this regard remains unchanged, and therefore continues to meet the minimum standard.

Conclusion on section A

The Slovak Republic has met all of the ToR for the information gathering process and no recommendations are made.

B. The exchange of information

Legal basis for spontaneous exchange of information (ToR II.5.1, II.5.2)

The Slovak Republic has the necessary domestic legal basis to exchange information spontaneously. Slovak Republic notes that there are no legal or practical impediments that prevent the spontaneous exchange of information on rulings as contemplated in the Action 5 minimum standard.

The Slovak Republic is a party to international agreements permitting spontaneous exchange of information, including (i) the *Multilateral Convention on Mutual Administrative Assistance in Tax Matters: Amended by the 2010 Protocol* (OECD/Council of Europe, 2011) ("the Convention"), (ii) the Directive 2011/16/EU with all other European Union Member States and (iii) double tax agreements in force with 70 jurisdictions.[1]

Completion and exchange of templates (ToR II.5.3, II.5.4, II.5.5, II.5.6, II.5.7)

In the prior year peer review report, it was determined that the Slovak Republic's process for the completion and exchange of templates were sufficient to meet the minimum standard. The Slovak Republic's implementation in this regard remains unchanged and therefore continues to meet the minimum standard.

For the year in review, the timeliness of exchanges is as follows:

Past rulings in the scope of the transparency framework	Number of exchanges transmitted by 31 December 2018	Delayed exchanges		
		Number of exchanges not transmitted by 31 December 2018	Reasons for the delays	Any other comments
	0	0	N/A	N/A
Future rulings in the scope of the transparency framework	Number of exchanges transmitted within three months of the information becoming available to the competent authority or immediately after legal impediments have been lifted	Delayed exchanges		
		Number of exchanges transmitted later than three months of the information on rulings becoming available to the competent authority	Reasons for the delays	Any other comments
	3	0	N/A	N/A
Total	3	0		

Follow up requests received for exchange of the ruling	Number	Average time to provide response	Number of requests not answered
	0	N/A	N/A

Conclusion on section B

The Slovak Republic has the necessary legal basis for spontaneous exchange of information, a process for completing the templates in a timely way and has completed all exchanges. The Slovak Republic has met all of the ToR for the exchange of information process and no recommendations are made.

C. Statistics (ToR IV)

The statistics for the year in review are as follows:

Category of ruling	Number of exchanges	Jurisdictions exchanged with
Ruling related to a preferential regime	N/A	N/A
Cross-border unilateral advance pricing agreements (APAs) and any other cross-border unilateral tax rulings (such as an advance tax ruling) covering transfer pricing or the application of transfer pricing principles	*De minimis* rule applies	N/A
Cross-border rulings providing for a unilateral downward adjustment to the taxpayer's taxable profits that is not directly reflected in the taxpayer's financial / commercial accounts	N/A	N/A
Permanent establishment rulings	0	N/A
Related party conduit rulings	N/A	N/A
De minimis rule	3	N/A
IP regimes: total exchanges on taxpayers benefitting from the third category of IP assets, new entrants benefitting from grandfathered IP regimes; and taxpayers making use of the option to treat the nexus ratio as a rebuttable presumption	N/A	N/A
Total	3	

D. Matters related to intellectual property regimes (ToR I.4.1.3)

The Slovak Republic offers an intellectual property regime (IP regime)[2] that is not subject to the transparency requirements under the Action 5 Report (OECD, 2015[5]), because:

- ***New entrants benefitting from the grandfathered IP regime***: the regime is a new nexus-compliant regime and therefore there is no grandfathered IP regime for which enhanced transparency requirements will apply.
- ***Third category of IP assets***: not applicable as the regime does not allow the third category of IP assets to qualify for the benefits.
- ***Taxpayers making the use of the option to treat the nexus ratio as a rebuttable presumption***: not applicable the regime does not allow the nexus ratio to be treated as a rebuttable presumption.

Summary of recommendations on implementation of the transparency framework

Aspect of implementation of the transparency framework that should be improved	Recommendation for improvement
	No recommendations are made.

Notes

[1] Parties to the Convention are available here: http://www.oecd.org/tax/exchange-of-tax-information/convention-on-mutual-administrative-assistance-in-tax-matters.htm. The Slovak Republic also has bilateral agreements with Armenia, Australia, Austria, Belarus, Belgium, Bosnia and Herzegovina, Brazil, Bulgaria, Canada, China (People's Republic of), Croatia, Cyprus, Czech Republic, Denmark, Estonia, Ethiopia, Finland, France, Georgia, Germany, Greece, Hungary, Iceland, India, Indonesia, Iran, Ireland, Israel, Italy, Japan, Kazakhstan, Korea, Kuwait, Latvia, Libya, Lithuania, Luxembourg, Malaysia, Malta, Mexico, Moldova, Mongolia, Montenegro, Netherlands, Nigeria, North Macedonia, Norway, Poland, Portugal, Romania, Russia, Serbia, Singapore, Slovenia, South Africa, Spain, Sri Lanka, Sweden, Switzerland, Syrian Arab Republic, Chinese Taipei, Tunisia, Turkey, Turkmenistan, Ukraine, United Arab Emirates, United Kingdom, United States, Uzbekistan and Viet Nam.

Note by Turkey: The information in this document with reference to "Cyprus" relates to the southern part of the Island. There is no single authority representing both Turkish and Greek Cypriot people on the Island. Turkey recognises the Turkish Republic of Northern Cyprus (TRNC). Until a lasting and equitable solution is found within the context of the United Nations, Turkey shall preserve its position concerning the "Cyprus issue".

Note by all the European Union Member States of the OECD and the European Union. The Republic of Cyprus is recognised by all members of the United Nations with the exception of Turkey. The information in this document relates to the area under the effective control of the Government of the Republic of Cyprus.

[2] Patent-box.

Slovenia

Slovenia has met all aspects of the terms of reference (OECD, 2017[3]) (ToR) for the calendar year 2018 (year in review) and no recommendations are made.

In the prior year report, Slovenia did not receive any recommendations.

Slovenia can legally issue three types of rulings within the scope of the transparency framework. In practice, Slovenia issued rulings within the scope of the transparency framework as follows:

- Eight past rulings;
- For the period 1 April 2016 - 31 December 2016: no future rulings;
- For the calendar year 2017: one future ruling, and
- For the year in review: one future ruling.

No peer input was received in respect of the exchanges of information on rulings received Slovenia.

Introduction

This peer review covers Slovenia's implementation of the BEPS Action 5 transparency framework for the year 2018. The report has four parts, each relating to a key part of the ToR. Each part is discussed in turn. A summary of recommendations is included at the end of this report.

A. The information gathering process

Slovenia can legally issue the following three types of rulings within the scope of the transparency framework: (i) cross-border unilateral APAs and any other cross-border unilateral tax rulings (such as an advance tax ruling) covering transfer pricing or the application of transfer pricing principles; (ii) permanent establishment rulings, and (iii) related party conduit rulings.

Past rulings (ToR I.4.1.1, I.4.1.2, I.4.2.1, I.4.2.2)

For Slovenia, past rulings are any tax rulings within scope that are issued either: (i) on or after 1 January 2014 but before 1 April 2016; or (ii) on or after 1 January 2010 but before 1 January 2014, provided they were still in effect as at 1 January 2014.

In the prior years' peer review reports, it was determined that Slovenia's undertakings to identify past rulings and all potential exchange jurisdictions were sufficient to meet the minimum standard. Slovenia's implementation in this regard remains unchanged, and therefore continues to meet the minimum standard.

Future rulings (ToR I.4.1.1, I.4.1.2, I.4.2.1)

For Slovenia, future rulings are any tax rulings within scope that are issued on or after 1 April 2016.

In the prior years' peer review reports, it was determined that Slovenia's undertakings to identify future rulings and all potential exchange jurisdictions were sufficient to meet the minimum standard. Slovenia's implementation in this regard remains unchanged, and therefore continues to meet the minimum standard.

Review and supervision (ToR I.4.3)

In the prior years' peer review reports, it was determined that Slovenia's review and supervision mechanism was sufficient to meet the minimum standard. Slovenia's implementation in this regard remains unchanged, and therefore continues to meet the minimum standard.

Conclusion on section A

Slovenia has met all of the ToR for the information gathering process and no recommendations are made.

B. The exchange of information

Legal basis for spontaneous exchange of information (ToR II.5.1, II.5.2)

Slovenia has the necessary domestic legal basis to exchange information spontaneously. Slovenia notes that there are no legal or practical impediments that prevent the spontaneous exchange of information on rulings as contemplated in the Action 5 minimum standard.

Slovenia is a party to international agreements permitting spontaneous exchange of information, including (i) the *Multilateral Convention on Mutual Administrative Assistance in Tax Matters: Amended by the 2010*

Protocol (OECD/Council of Europe, 2011) ("the Convention"), (ii) the Directive 2011/16/EU with all other European Union Member States and (iii) double tax agreements in force with 60 jurisdictions.[1]

Completion and exchange of templates (ToR II.5.3, II.5.4, II.5.5, II.5.6, II.5.7)

In the prior year peer review report, it was determined that Slovenia's process for the completion and exchange of templates were sufficient to meet the minimum standard. Slovenia's implementation in this regard remains unchanged and therefore continues to meet the minimum standard.

For the year in review, the timeliness of exchanges is as follows:

Past rulings in the scope of the transparency framework	Number of exchanges transmitted by 31 December 2018	Delayed exchanges		
		Number of exchanges not transmitted by 31 December 2018	Reasons for the delays	Any other comments
	0	0	N/A	N/A
Future rulings in the scope of the transparency framework	Number of exchanges transmitted within three months of the information becoming available to the competent authority or immediately after legal impediments have been lifted	Delayed exchanges		
		Number of exchanges transmitted later than three months of the information on rulings becoming available to the competent authority	Reasons for the delays	Any other comments
	1	0	N/A	N/A
Total	1	0		

Follow up requests received for exchange of the ruling	Number	Average time to provide response	Number of requests not answered
	0	N/A	N/A

Conclusion on section B

Slovenia has the necessary legal basis for spontaneous exchange of information, a process for completing the templates in a timely way and has completed all exchanges. Slovenia has met all of the ToR for the exchange of information process and no recommendations are made.

C. Statistics (ToR IV)

The statistics for the year in review are as follows:

Category of ruling	Number of exchanges	Jurisdictions exchanged with
Ruling related to a preferential regime	N/A	N/A
Cross-border unilateral advance pricing agreements (APAs) and any other cross-border unilateral tax rulings (such as an advance tax ruling) covering transfer pricing or the application of transfer pricing principles	0	N/A
Cross-border rulings providing for a unilateral downward adjustment to the taxpayer's taxable profits that is not directly reflected in the taxpayer's financial / commercial accounts	N/A	N/A

Permanent establishment rulings	*De minimis* rule applies	N/A
Related party conduit rulings	0	N/A
De minimis rule	1	N/A
IP regimes: total exchanges on taxpayers benefitting from the third category of IP assets, new entrants benefitting from grandfathered IP regimes; and taxpayers making use of the option to treat the nexus ratio as a rebuttable presumption	N/A	N/A
Total	1	

D. Matters related to intellectual property regimes (ToR I.4.1.3)

Slovenia does not offer an intellectual property regime for which transparency requirements under the Action 5 Report (OECD, 2015[5]) were imposed.

Summary of recommendations on implementation of the transparency framework

Aspect of implementation of the transparency framework that should be improved	Recommendation for improvement
	No recommendations are made.

Notes

1 Parties to the Convention are available here: http://www.oecd.org/tax/exchange-of-tax-information/convention-on-mutual-administrative-assistance-in-tax-matters.htm. Slovenia also has bilateral agreements with Albania, Armenia, Austria, Azerbaijan, Belgium, Belarus, Bosnia and Herzegovina, Bulgaria, Canada, China (People's Republic of), Croatia, Cyprus, Czech Republic, Denmark, Estonia, Finland, France, Georgia, Germany, Greece, Hungary, Iceland, India, Iran, Ireland, Isle Of Man, Israel, Italy, Japan, Kazakhstan, Korea, Kosovo, Kuwait, Latvia, Lithuania, Luxembourg, Malta, Moldova, Netherlands, North Macedonia, Norway, Poland, Portugal, Qatar, Romania, Russia, Serbia, Montenegro, Singapore, Slovak Republic, Spain, Sweden, Switzerland, Thailand, Turkey, Ukraine, United Arab Emirates, United Kingdom, United States and Uzbekistan.

Note by Turkey: The information in this document with reference to "Cyprus" relates to the southern part of the Island. There is no single authority representing both Turkish and Greek Cypriot people on the Island. Turkey recognises the Turkish Republic of Northern Cyprus (TRNC). Until a lasting and equitable solution is found within the context of the United Nations, Turkey shall preserve its position concerning the "Cyprus issue".

Note by all the European Union Member States of the OECD and the European Union. The Republic of Cyprus is recognised by all members of the United Nations with the exception of Turkey. The information in this document relates to the area under the effective control of the Government of the Republic of Cyprus.

South Africa

South Africa has met all aspects of the terms of reference (OECD, 2017[3]) (ToR) for the calendar year 2018 (year in review) and no recommendations are made.

In the prior year report, South Africa did not receive any recommendations.

South Africa can legally issue one type of rulings within the scope of the transparency framework. In practice, South Africa issued rulings within the scope of the transparency framework as follows:

- One past ruling;
- For the period 1 April 2016 - 31 December 2016: no future rulings;
- For the calendar year 2017: no future rulings, and
- For the year in review: no future rulings.

South Africa publishes their tax rulings in redacted form on South Africa Revenue Service's website.[1]

As no exchanges were required to take place, no peer input was received in respect of the exchanges of information on rulings received from South Africa.

Introduction

This peer review covers South Africa's implementation of the BEPS Action 5 transparency framework for the year 2018. The report has four parts, each relating to a key part of the ToR. Each part is discussed in turn. A summary of recommendations is included at the end of this report.

A. The information gathering process

South Africa can legally issue one type of rulings within the scope of the transparency framework: preferential regimes.[2]

Past rulings (ToR I.4.1.1, I.4.1.2, I.4.2.1, I.4.2.2)

For South Africa, past rulings are any tax rulings within scope that are issued either: (i) on or after 1 January 2014 but before 1 April 2016; or (ii) on or after 1 January 2010 but before 1 January 2014, provided they were still in effect as at 1 January 2014.

In the prior year peer review report, it was determined that South Africa's undertakings to identify past rulings and all potential exchange jurisdictions were sufficient to meet the minimum standard. South Africa's implementation in this regard remains unchanged, and therefore continues to meet the minimum standard.

Future rulings (ToR I.4.1.1, I.4.1.2, I.4.2.1)

For South Africa, future rulings are any tax rulings within scope that are issued on or after 1 April 2016.

In the prior year peer review report, it was determined that South Africa's implementation of a new system to identify future rulings and all potential exchange jurisdictions was sufficient to meet the minimum standard. South Africa's implementation in this regard remains unchanged, and therefore continues to meet the minimum standard.

Review and supervision (ToR I.4.3)

In the prior year peer review reports, it was determined that South Africa's review and supervision mechanism was sufficient to meet the minimum standard. South Africa's implementation in this regard remains unchanged, and therefore continues to meet the minimum standard.

Conclusion on section A

South Africa has met all of the ToR for the information gathering process and no recommendations are made.

B. The exchange of information

Legal basis for spontaneous exchange of information (ToR II.5.1, II.5.2)

South Africa has the necessary domestic legal basis to exchange information spontaneously. South Africa notes that there are no legal or practical impediments that prevent the spontaneous exchange of information on rulings as contemplated in the Action 5 minimum standard.

South Africa has international agreements permitting spontaneous exchange of information, including being a party to the (i) *Multilateral Convention on Mutual Administrative Assistance in Tax Matters: Amended by the 2010 Protocol* (OECD/Council of Europe, 2011[4]) ("the Convention") and (ii) double tax agreements in force with 67 jurisdictions.[3]

Completion and exchange of templates (ToR II.5.3, II.5.4, II.5.5, II.5.6, II.5.7)

In the prior year peer review report, it was determined that South Africa's process for the completion and exchange of templates were sufficient to meet the minimum standard. South Africa's implementation in this regard remains unchanged and therefore continues to meet the minimum standard.

As South Africa did not issue any past or future rulings in scope of the transparency framework in the relevant period, South Africa was not required to exchange any information on rulings in the year in review and no data on the timeliness of exchanges can be reported.

Conclusion on section B

South Africa has the necessary legal basis for spontaneous exchange of information, a process for completing the templates in a timely way and has completed all exchanges. South Africa has met all of the ToR for the exchange of information process and no recommendations are made.

C. Statistics (ToR IV)

As no rulings are issued, no statistics can be reported.

D. Matters related to intellectual property regimes (ToR I.4.1.3)

South Africa does not offer an intellectual property regime for which transparency requirements under the Action 5 Report (OECD, 2015[5]) were imposed.

Summary of recommendations on implementation of the transparency framework

Aspect of implementation of the transparency framework that should be improved	Recommendation for improvement
	No recommendations are made.

Notes

[1] Available at: https://www.sars.gov.za/Pages/default.aspx

[2] With respect to the following preferential regimes: 1) Shipping regime and 2) Headquarters regime.

[3] Parties to the Multilateral Convention are available here: http://www.oecd.org/tax/exchange-of-tax-information/convention-on-mutual-administrative-assistance-in-tax-matters.htm. South Africa also has bilateral agreements with Algeria, Australia, Austria, Belarus, Belgium, Botswana, Brazil, Bulgaria, Cameroon, Canada, Chile, China (People's Republic of), Croatia, Cyprus, Czech Republic, Democratic Republic of Congo, Denmark, Egypt, Ethiopia, Finland, France, Ghana, Greece, Hong Kong (China), Hungary, India, Indonesia, Iran, Ireland, Italy, Japan, Kenya, Korea, Lesotho, Luxembourg, Malaysia, Malta, Mauritius, Mexico, Mozambique, Namibia, Netherlands, New Zealand, Nigeria, Norway, Oman, Pakistan, Poland, Portugal, Qatar, Rwanda, Samoa, Saudi Arabia, Seychelles, Singapore, Slovak

Republic, Spain, Swaziland, Sweden, Tanzania, Turkey, Uganda, Ukraine, United Arab Emirates, United Kingdom, United States and Zimbabwe.

Note by Turkey: The information in this document with reference to "Cyprus" relates to the southern part of the Island. There is no single authority representing both Turkish and Greek Cypriot people on the Island. Turkey recognises the Turkish Republic of Northern Cyprus (TRNC). Until a lasting and equitable solution is found within the context of the United Nations, Turkey shall preserve its position concerning the "Cyprus issue".

Note by all the European Union Member States of the OECD and the European Union. The Republic of Cyprus is recognised by all members of the United Nations with the exception of Turkey. The information in this document relates to the area under the effective control of the Government of the Republic of Cyprus.

Spain

Spain has met all aspects of the terms of reference (OECD, 2017[3]) (ToR) for the calendar year 2018 (year in review) except for collecting and exchanging information on new assets of existing taxpayers benefitting from the grandfathered IP regime (ToR I.4.1.3). Spain receives one recommendation on this point for the year in review.

In the prior year report, Spain received the same recommendation. As it has not been addressed, the recommendation remains in place.

Spain can legally issue three types of rulings within the scope of the transparency framework. In practice, Spain issued rulings within the scope of the transparency framework as follows:

- 146 past rulings;
- For the period 1 April 2016 - 31 December 2016: 28 future rulings;
- For the calendar year 2017: 46 future rulings, and
- For the year in review: 22 future rulings.

Rulings excluding APAs are published in anonymised form.[1]

Peer input was received from four jurisdictions in respect of the exchanges of information on rulings received from Spain. The input was generally positive, noting that information was complete, in a correct format and received in a timely manner.

Introduction

This peer review covers Spain's implementation of the BEPS Action 5 transparency framework for the year 2018. The report has four parts, each relating to a key part of the ToR. Each part is discussed in turn. A summary of recommendations is included at the end of this report.

A. The information gathering process

Spain can legally issue the following three types of rulings within the scope of the transparency framework: (i) preferential regimes;[2] (ii) cross-border unilateral APAs and any other cross-border unilateral tax rulings (such as an advance tax ruling) covering transfer pricing or the application of transfer pricing principles; and (iii) permanent establishment rulings.

Past rulings (ToR I.4.1.1, I.4.1.2, I.4.2.1, I.4.2.2)

For Spain, past rulings are any tax rulings within scope that are issued either: (i) on or after 1 January 2014 but before 1 April 2016; or (ii) on or after 1 January 2010 but before 1 January 2014, provided they were still in effect as at 1 January 2014.

In the prior year peer review report, it was determined that Spain's undertakings to identify past rulings and all potential exchange jurisdictions were sufficient to meet the minimum standard. Spain's implementation in this regard remains unchanged, and therefore continues to meet the minimum standard.

Future rulings (ToR I.4.1.1, I.4.1.2, I.4.2.1)

For Spain, future rulings are any tax rulings within scope that are issued on or after 1 April 2016.

In the prior year peer review report, it was determined that Spain's undertakings to identify future rulings and all potential exchange jurisdictions were sufficient to meet the minimum standard. Spain's implementation in this regard remains unchanged, and therefore continues to meet the minimum standard.

Review and supervision (ToR I.4.3)

In the prior year peer review reports, it was determined that Spain's review and supervision mechanism was sufficient to meet the minimum standard. Spain's implementation in this regard remains unchanged, and therefore continues to meet the minimum standard.

Conclusion on section A

Spain has met all of the ToR for the information gathering process and no recommendations are made.

B. The exchange of information

Legal basis for spontaneous exchange of information (ToR II.5.1, II.5.2)

Spain has the necessary domestic legal basis to exchange information spontaneously. Spain notes that there are no legal or practical impediments that prevent the spontaneous exchange of information on rulings as contemplated in the Action 5 minimum standard.

Spain is a party to international agreements permitting spontaneous exchange of information, including (i) the *Multilateral Convention on Mutual Administrative Assistance in Tax Matters: Amended by the 2010*

Protocol (OECD/Council of Europe, 2011) ("the Convention"), (ii) the Directive 2011/16/EU with all other European Union Member States and (iii) double tax agreements in force with 93 jurisdictions.[3]

Completion and exchange of templates (ToR II.5.3, II.5.4, II.5.5, II.5.6, II.5.7)

In the prior year peer review report, it was determined that Spain's process for the completion and exchange of templates were sufficient to meet the minimum standard. Spain's implementation in this regard remains unchanged and therefore continues to meet the minimum standard.

For the year in review, the timeliness of exchanges is as follows:

Past rulings in the scope of the transparency framework	Number of exchanges transmitted by 31 December 2018	Delayed exchanges		
		Number of exchanges not transmitted by 31 December 2018	Reasons for the delays	Any other comments
	2	0	N/A	The exchanges took place with a jurisdiction with whom the Convention came into force in 2018.
Future rulings in the scope of the transparency framework	Number of exchanges transmitted within three months of the information becoming available to the competent authority or immediately after legal impediments have been lifted	Delayed exchanges		
		Number of exchanges transmitted later than three months of the information on rulings becoming available to the competent authority	Reasons for the delays	Any other comments
	75	0	N/A	N/A
Total	77	0		

Follow up requests received for exchange of the ruling	Number	Average time to provide response	Number of requests not answered
	0	N/A	N/A

Conclusion on section B

Spain has the necessary legal basis for spontaneous exchange of information, a process for completing the templates in a timely way and has completed all exchanges. Spain has met all of the ToR for the exchange of information process and no recommendations are made.

C. Statistics (ToR IV)

The statistics for the year in review are as follows:

Category of ruling	Number of exchanges	Jurisdictions exchanged with
Ruling related to a preferential regime	0	N/A
Cross-border unilateral advance pricing agreements (APAs) and any other cross-border unilateral tax rulings (such as an advance tax ruling) covering transfer pricing or the application of transfer pricing principles	57	Austria, Belgium, Canada, China (People's Republic of), Czech Republic, Denmark, France, Germany, Greece, Hungary, Indonesia, Ireland, Italy, Japan, Korea, Latvia, Luxembourg, Malaysia, Netherlands, Poland, Portugal, Romania, Russia,

		Singapore, Slovak Republic, Sweden, Switzerland, United Kingdom, United States
Cross-border rulings providing for a unilateral downward adjustment to the taxpayer's taxable profits that is not directly reflected in the taxpayer's financial / commercial accounts	N/A	N/A
Permanent establishment rulings	20	Andorra, Belgium, Colombia, France, Germany, Ireland, Luxembourg, Malta, Netherlands, United Kingdom
Related party conduit rulings	N/A	N/A
De minimis rule	N/A	N/A
IP regimes: total exchanges on taxpayers benefitting from the third category of IP assets, new entrants benefitting from grandfathered IP regimes; and taxpayers making use of the option to treat the nexus ratio as a rebuttable presumption	21	Argentina, Belgium, Brazil, Chile, Colombia, Germany, India, Ireland, Italy, Luxembourg, Mexico, Netherlands, Portugal, Turkey, United Kingdom, Uruguay
Total	98	

D. Matters related to intellectual property regimes (ToR I.4.1.3)

Spain offers three intellectual property regimes (IP regime)[4] that are subject to the transparency requirements under the Action 5 Report (OECD, 2015[5]). It states that the identification of the benefitting taxpayers will occur as follows:

- ***New entrants benefitting from the grandfathered IP regime***: Transparency obligations apply for the regime, because grandfathering is provided to entrants that entered the regime after the relevant date from which enhanced transparency obligations apply. In the previous year peer review report, it was explained that Spain adopted a new tax form in August 2017 so that it could identify the new taxpayers for which the enhanced transparency requirements apply. However, Spain was not able to identify new IP assets entering the regime after the relevant date and benefiting from grandfathering. Spain was therefore recommended to identify and exchange relevant information on new assets of existing taxpayers benefitting from the grandfathered IP regime.

  In order to act on this recommendation, Spain tried to include a new reporting obligation in the tax form that was adopted in August 2017. However, in October 2017 the tax form was the subject of an appeal before the National Court and the judicial procedure is still under way. As such, this information has not been able to be collected for exchange. Therefore, the prior year recommendation remains.
- ***Third category of IP assets***: not applicable as the regimes do not allow the third category of IP assets to qualify for the benefits.
- ***Taxpayers making use of the option to treat the nexus ratio as a rebuttable presumption***: not applicable as the regimes do not allow the nexus ratio to be treated as a rebuttable presumption.

Summary of recommendations on implementation of the transparency framework

Aspect of implementation of the transparency framework that should be improved	Recommendation for improvement
Spain has not exchanged information on new assets of existing taxpayers benefitting from the grandfathered regime as this information was not available during the year in review. It is noted that Spain has already started to take steps to amend the tax form adopted in August 2017 to address this, but the tax form was appealed before the National Court and proceedings remained underway for the year in review.	Spain is recommended to continue its efforts to identify and exchange relevant information on new assets of existing taxpayers benefitting from the grandfathered IP regime. This recommendation remains unchanged since the prior year peer review report.

Notes

1 Rulings issued by the General Directorate of Taxation are available at http://petete.minhafp.gob.es/consultas.

2 With respect to the following preferential regimes: 1) Partial exemption for income from certain intangible assets and 2) Shipping regime.

3 Parties to the Convention are available here: http://www.oecd.org/tax/exchange-of-tax-information/convention-on-mutual-administrative-assistance-in-tax-matters.htm. Spain also has double tax agreements with: Albania, Algeria, Andorra, Argentina, Armenia, Australia, Austria, Barbados, Belarus, Belgium, Bolivia, Bosnia and Herzegovina, Brazil, Bulgaria, Canada, Chile, China (People's Republic of), Colombia, Costa Rica, Croatia, Cuba, Cyprus, Czech Republic, Dominican Republic, Ecuador, Egypt, El Salvador, Estonia, Finland, France, Georgia, Germany, Greece, Hong Kong (China), Hungary, Iceland, India, Indonesia, Iran, Ireland, Israel, Italy, Jamaica, Japan, Kazakhstan, Korea, Kuwait, Kyrgyzstan, Latvia, Lithuania, Luxembourg, Malaysia, Malta, Mexico, Moldova, Morocco, Netherlands, New Zealand, Nigeria, North Macedonia, Norway, Oman, Pakistan, Panama, Philippines, Poland, Portugal, Qatar, Romania, Russia, Saudi Arabia, Senegal, Serbia, Singapore, Slovak Republic, Slovenia, South Africa, Sweden, Switzerland, Tajikistan, Thailand, Trinidad and Tobago, Tunisia, Turkey, Turkmenistan, Ukraine, United Arab Emirates, United Kingdom, United States, Uruguay, Uzbekistan, Venezuela and Viet Nam.

Note by Turkey: The information in this document with reference to "Cyprus" relates to the southern part of the Island. There is no single authority representing both Turkish and Greek Cypriot people on the Island. Turkey recognises the Turkish Republic of Northern Cyprus (TRNC). Until a lasting and equitable solution is found within the context of the United Nations, Turkey shall preserve its position concerning the "Cyprus issue".

Note by all the European Union Member States of the OECD and the European Union. The Republic of Cyprus is recognised by all members of the United Nations with the exception of Turkey. The information in this document relates to the area under the effective control of the Government of the Republic of Cyprus.

4 These regimes are the partial exemptions for income from certain intangible assets for: 1) Federal regime, 2) Basque country and 3) Navarra.

Sri Lanka

Sri Lanka did not provide a completed peer review questionnaire to the Secretariat. It is not known whether Sri Lanka has implemented the transparency framework in line with the terms of reference (OECD, 2017[3]). Sri Lanka receives two recommendations covering the information gathering process (ToR I.4) and exchange of information (ToR II.5) for the year in review.

In the prior year report, Sri Lanka received the same two recommendations. As they have not been addressed, the recommendations remain in place.

It is not known whether Sri Lanka can legally issue any types of ruling within the scope of the transparency framework, or whether in practice Sri Lanka issued any such rulings.

No peer input was received in respect of the exchanges of information on rulings received from Sri Lanka.

Introduction

This peer review covers Sri Lanka's implementation of the BEPS Action 5 transparency framework for the year 2018. The report has four parts, each relating to a key part of the ToR. Each part is discussed in turn. A summary of recommendations is included at the end of this report.

A. The information gathering process

Sri Lanka was not yet able to complete the peer review questionnaire. It is not known whether Sri Lanka has implemented the transparency framework during the year in review.

Conclusion on section A

Sri Lanka is recommended to ensure that it has put in place an effective information gathering process to identify all relevant past and future rulings and all potential exchange jurisdictions and to implement a review and supervision mechanism, as soon as possible (ToR I.4).

B. The exchange of information

Legal basis for spontaneous exchange of information (ToR II.5.1, II.5.2)

It is not known whether Sri Lanka has the necessary domestic legal basis to exchange information spontaneously. Sri Lanka is recommended to put in place a domestic legal framework allowing spontaneous exchange of information on rulings if needed (ToR II.5.1).

Sri Lanka has international agreements permitting spontaneous exchange of information, including being a party to the (i) *Multilateral Convention on Mutual Administrative Assistance in Tax Matters: Amended by the 2010 Protocol* (OECD/Council of Europe, 2011[4]) ("the Convention"), (ii) bilateral agreements in force with 44 jurisdictions.[1]

Completion and exchange of templates (ToR II.5.3, II.5.4, II.5.5, II.5.6, II.5.7)

It is not known whether Sri Lanka has put in place a process to exchange information on rulings in accordance with the form and timelines required by the transparency framework. Sri Lanka is recommended to ensure the timely exchange of information on rulings in the form required by the transparency framework.

Conclusion on section B

Sri Lanka is recommended to continue to put in place a domestic legal framework allowing spontaneous exchange of information on rulings and to continue its efforts to complete the templates for all relevant rulings and to ensure that the exchanges of information on rulings occur as soon as possible (ToR II.5).

C. Statistics (ToR IV)

As the Secretariat is not aware whether information on rulings was exchanged by Sri Lanka for the year in review, no statistics can be reported here.

D. Matters related to intellectual property regimes (ToR I.4.1.3)

Sri Lanka does not offer an intellectual property regime for which transparency requirements under the Action 5 Report (OECD, 2015[5]) were imposed.

Summary of recommendations on implementation of the transparency framework

Aspect of implementation of the transparency framework that should be improved	Recommendation for improvement
It is not known whether Sri Lanka has an information gathering process in place.	Sri Lanka is recommended to ensure that it has put in place an effective information gathering process to identify all relevant past and future rulings and all potential exchange jurisdictions and to implement a review and supervision mechanism, as soon as possible. This recommendation remains unchanged since the prior year peer review report.
It is not known whether Sri Lanka has a domestic legal framework allowing spontaneous exchange of information on rulings if needed and has a process in place to ensure the timely exchange of information on rulings in the form required by the transparency framework.	Sri Lanka is recommended to put in place a domestic legal framework allowing spontaneous exchange of information on rulings if needed and to ensure the timely exchange of information on rulings in the form required by the transparency framework. This recommendation remains unchanged since the prior year peer review report.

Notes

[1] Parties to the Convention are available here: www.oecd.org/tax/exchange-of-tax-information/convention-on-mutual-administrative-assistance-in-tax-matters.htm. Sri Lanka also has bilateral agreements in force with Australia, Bangladesh, Bahrain, Belarus, Belgium, Canada, China (People's Republic of), Czech Republic, Denmark, Finland, France, Germany, Hong Kong (China), India, Indonesia, Iran, Italy, Japan, Korea, Kuwait, Luxembourg, Malaysia, Mauritius, Nepal, Netherlands, Norway, Oman, Pakistan, Palestinian Authority, Philippines, Poland, Qatar, Romania, Russia, Saudi Arabia, Seychelles, Singapore, Sweden, Switzerland, Thailand, United Arab Emirates, United Kingdom, United States, and Viet Nam.

Sweden

Sweden has met all aspects of the terms of reference (ToR) for the calendar year 2018 (year in review) except for identifying all potential exchange jurisdictions for future rulings (ToR I.4.2.1). Sweden receives one recommendation on this point for the year in review.

In the prior year report, as well as in the 2016 peer review, Sweden received the same recommendation. As it has not yet been addressed, the recommendation remains in place.

Sweden can legally issue three types of rulings within the scope of the transparency framework. In practice, Sweden issued rulings within the scope of the transparency framework as follows:

- 28 past rulings;
- For the period 1 April 2016 - 31 December 2016: five future rulings;
- For the calendar year 2017: three future rulings, and
- For the year in review: six future rulings.

Sweden publishes some of their tax rulings in redacted form on Swedish Board of Advanced Tax Rulings' website.[1]

Peer input was received from one jurisdiction in respect of the exchanges of information on rulings received from Sweden. The input was generally positive, noting that information was complete, in a correct format and received in a timely manner.

Introduction

This peer review covers Sweden's implementation of the BEPS Action 5 transparency framework for the year 2018. The report has four parts, each relating to a key part of the ToR. Each part is discussed in turn. A summary of recommendations is included at the end of this report.

A. The information gathering process

Sweden can legally issue the following three types of rulings within the scope of the transparency framework: (i) preferential regimes;[2] (ii) permanent establishment rulings; and (iii) related party conduit rulings.

Past rulings (ToR I.4.1.1, I.4.1.2, I.4.2.1, I.4.2.2)

For Sweden, past rulings are any tax rulings within scope that are issued either: (i) on or after 1 January 2014 but before 1 April 2016; or (ii) on or after 1 January 2010 but before 1 January 2014, provided they were still in effect as at 1 January 2014.

In the prior years' peer review reports, it was determined that Sweden's undertakings to identify past rulings and all potential exchange jurisdictions were sufficient to meet the minimum standard. Sweden's implementation in this regard remains unchanged, and therefore continues to meet the minimum standard.

Future rulings (ToR I.4.1.1, I.4.1.2, I.4.2.1)

For Sweden, future rulings are any tax rulings within scope that are issued on or after 1 April 2016.

In the prior years' peer review reports, Sweden was recommended to amend its rulings practice in order to be able to identify all potential exchange jurisdictions for future rulings.

In the year of review, there was no change from the prior year process adopted by the STA to identify the information on potential exchange jurisdictions for the relevant future rulings, which consisted in consulting the text of the ruling. This recommendation was included in the 2016 peer review report and the 2017 peer review report, and has not yet been implemented, and the recommendation is therefore retained.

It should be noted that to respond to this recommendation, the Swedish Ministry of Finance is currently drafting new legislation in order to fulfil the BEPS Action 5 minimum standard. The proposed legislation is scheduled to be approved by parliament by June 2020. It should furthermore be noted that the Swedish Tax Agency ("the STA") is working on amendments to its rulings practice and routine regarding written answers to external legal questions. However, the routine cannot be finalised until the legislation on tax rulings has been approved by the Swedish parliament. According to the new legislation and the new routine, the STA will be able to identify all potential exchange jurisdictions regarding future rulings, and this will be taken into account in the next year's peer review.

Review and supervision (ToR I.4.3)

In the prior years' peer review reports, it was determined that Sweden's review and supervision mechanism was sufficient to meet the minimum standard. Sweden's implementation in this regard remains unchanged, and therefore continues to meet the minimum standard.

Conclusion on section A

Sweden has met all of the ToR for the information gathering process except for identifying all potential exchange jurisdictions for future rulings (ToR I.4.2). Sweden is recommended to continue its efforts to amend its rulings practice to require taxpayers to provide information on all potential exchange jurisdictions for future rulings as soon as possible.

B. The exchange of information

Legal basis for spontaneous exchange of information (ToR II.5.1, II.5.2)

Sweden has the necessary domestic legal basis to exchange information spontaneously. Sweden notes that there are no legal or practical impediments that prevent the spontaneous exchange of information on rulings as contemplated in the Action 5 minimum standard.

Sweden is a party to international agreements permitting spontaneous exchange of information, including (i) the *Multilateral Convention on Mutual Administrative Assistance in Tax Matters: Amended by the 2010 Protocol* (OECD/Council of Europe, 2011) ("the Convention"), (ii) the Directive 2011/16/EU with all other European Union Member States, (iii) the Nordic Convention on Assistance in Tax Matters and (iv) double tax agreements in force with 62 jurisdictions.[3]

Completion and exchange of templates (ToR II.5.3, II.5.4, II.5.5, II.5.6, II.5.7)

In the prior year peer review report, it was determined that Sweden's process for the completion and exchange of templates were sufficient to meet the minimum standard. Sweden's implementation in this regard remains unchanged and therefore continues to meet the minimum standard.

For the year in review, the timeliness of exchanges is as follows:

Past rulings in the scope of the transparency framework	Number of exchanges transmitted by 31 December 2018	Delayed exchanges		
		Number of exchanges not transmitted by 31 December 2018	Reasons for the delays	Any other comments
	0	0	N/A	N/A
Future rulings in the scope of the transparency framework	Number of exchanges transmitted within three months of the information becoming available to the competent authority or immediately after legal impediments have been lifted	Delayed exchanges		
		Number of exchanges transmitted later than three months of the information on rulings becoming available to the competent authority	Reasons for the delays	Any other comments
	6	0	N/A	N/A
Total	6	0		

Follow up requests received for exchange of the ruling	Number	Average time to provide response	Number of requests not answered
	0	N/A	N/A

Conclusion on section B

Sweden has the necessary legal basis for spontaneous exchange of information, a process for completing the templates in a timely way and has completed all exchanges. Sweden has met all of the ToR for the exchange of information process and no recommendations are made.

C. Statistics (ToR IV)

The statistics for the year in review are as follows:

Category of ruling	Number of exchanges	Jurisdictions exchanged with
Ruling related to a preferential regime	1	*De minimis* rule applies
Cross-border unilateral advance pricing agreements (APAs) and any other cross-border unilateral tax rulings (such as an advance tax ruling) covering transfer pricing or the application of transfer pricing principles	N/A	N/A
Cross-border rulings providing for a unilateral downward adjustment to the taxpayer's taxable profits that is not directly reflected in the taxpayer's financial / commercial accounts	N/A	N/A
Permanent establishment rulings	4	*De minimis* rule applies
Related party conduit rulings	1	*De minimis* rule applies
De minimis rule	N/A	N/A
IP regimes: total exchanges on taxpayers benefitting from the third category of IP assets, new entrants benefitting from grandfathered IP regimes; and taxpayers making use of the option to treat the nexus ratio as a rebuttable presumption	N/A	N/A
Total	6	

D. Matters related to intellectual property regimes (ToR I.4.1.3)

Sweden does not offer an intellectual property regime for which transparency requirements under the Action 5 Report (OECD, 2015[5]) were imposed.

Summary of recommendations on implementation of the transparency framework

Aspect of implementation of the transparency framework that should be improved	Recommendation for improvement
Sweden experienced delays in identifying all potential exchange jurisdictions for future rulings.	Sweden is recommended to continue its efforts to amend its rulings practice to require taxpayers to provide information on all potential exchange jurisdictions for future rulings as soon as possible. This recommendation remains unchanged since the 2016 peer review report and the 2017 peer review report.

Notes

[1] Available at: https://www.skatterattsnamnden.se/.

[2] With respect to the following preferential regime: Tonnage tax regime.

[3] Parties to the Convention are available here: www.oecd.org/tax/exchange-of-tax-information/convention-on-mutual-administrative-assistance-in-tax-matters.htm. Parties to the Nordic Convention on Assistance in Tax Matters are Denmark, Faroe Islands, Finland, Iceland, Norway and Sweden. Sweden also has bilateral agreements with Argentina, Armenia, Australia, Austria, Barbados, Belgium, Botswana, Brazil, Bulgaria, Canada, Chile, China (People's Republic of), Croatia, Czech Republic, Egypt, Estonia, France, Georgia, Germany, Greece, Hungary, India, Indonesia, Ireland, Israel, Italy, Jamaica, Japan, Kazakhstan, Kenya, Korea, Latvia, Lithuania, Luxembourg, Malaysia, Malta, Mauritius, Mexico, Netherlands, New Zealand, Nigeria, North Macedonia, Pakistan, Poland, Portugal, Romania, Russia, Saudi Arabia, Serbia, Singapore, Slovak Republic, Slovenia, South Africa, Spain, Sri Lanka, Switzerland, Thailand, Trinidad and Tobago, Tunisia, Turkey, Ukraine, United Kingdom, United States, Viet Nam and Zambia.

Switzerland

Switzerland has met all aspects of the terms of reference (OECD, 2017[3]) (ToR) for the calendar year 2018 (year in review) and no recommendations are made.

In the prior year report, Switzerland did not receive any recommendations.

Switzerland can legally issue four types of rulings within the scope of the transparency framework. In practice, Switzerland issued rulings within the scope of the transparency framework as follows:

- 831 past rulings;
- For the calendar year 2017: 300 future rulings, and
- For the year in review: 228 future rulings.

Peer input was received from eight jurisdictions in respect of the exchanges of information on rulings received from Switzerland. The input was generally positive. The majority of jurisdictions noted that the information was complete and received in a timely manner, but some jurisdictions have stated that they have not received information from Switzerland in a timely manner. However, this appears to be a misunderstanding about the timelines that Switzerland followed to conduct the spontaneous exchange of information which reflect the applicable domestic and international legal framework, including on rulings that were issued in prior years. Follow-up communications with these jurisdictions has taken place to clarify the issue.

Introduction

This peer review covers Switzerland's implementation of the BEPS Action 5 transparency framework for the year 2018. The report has four parts, each relating to a key part of the ToR. Each part is discussed in turn. A summary of recommendations is included at the end of this report.

A. The information gathering process

Switzerland can legally issue the following four types of rulings within the scope of the transparency framework: (i) preferential regimes;[1] (ii) cross-border unilateral APAs and any other cross-border unilateral tax rulings (such as an advance tax ruling) covering transfer pricing or the application of transfer pricing principles; (iii) related party conduit rulings; and (iv) permanent establishment rulings.

Past rulings (ToR I.4.1.1, I.4.1.2, I.4.2.1, I.4.2.2)

For Switzerland, past rulings are any tax rulings within scope that are issued on or after 1 January 2010 until 31 December 2016, provided they were still in effect as at 1 January 2018.

In the prior years' peer review reports, it was determined that Switzerland's process to identify past rulings and all potential exchange jurisdictions were sufficient to meet the minimum standard. Switzerland's implementation in this regard remains unchanged, and therefore continues to meet the minimum standard.

Future rulings (ToR I.4.1.1, I.4.1.2, I.4.2.1)

For Switzerland, future rulings are any tax rulings within scope that are issued on or after 1 January 2017, provided they are still in effect on or after 1 January 2018.

In the prior years' peer review reports, it was determined that Switzerland's process to identify future rulings and all potential exchange jurisdictions was sufficient to meet the minimum standard. Switzerland's implementation in this regard remains unchanged, and therefore continues to meet the minimum standard.

Review and supervision (ToR I.4.3)

In the prior years' peer review reports, it was determined that Switzerland's review and supervision mechanism was sufficient to meet the minimum standard. Switzerland's implementation in this regard remains unchanged, and therefore continues to meet the minimum standard.

Conclusion on section A

Switzerland has met all of the ToR for the information gathering process and no recommendations are made.

B. The exchange of information

Legal basis for spontaneous exchange of information (ToR II.5.1, II.5.2)

Switzerland has the necessary domestic legal basis to exchange information spontaneously. Switzerland notes that there are no legal or practical impediments that prevent the spontaneous exchange of information on rulings as contemplated in the Action 5 minimum standard.

Switzerland has international agreements permitting spontaneous exchange of information, including being a party to the *Multilateral Convention on Mutual Administrative Assistance in Tax Matters: Amended by the 2010 Protocol* (OECD/Council of Europe, 2011[4]) ("the Convention").[2] The necessary domestic and international legal framework for spontaneous exchange of information entered into force on 1 January 2017, allowing for exchanges from 1 January 2018.

Completion and exchange of templates (ToR II.5.3, II.5.4, II.5.5, II.5.6, II.5.7)

In the prior year peer review report, it was determined that Switzerland had put in place a process to exchange information on rulings in accordance with the forms and timelines required by the transparency framework. This includes the use of an IT tool that facilitates the collection of information from taxpayers. This information is verified and / or completed by the responsible tax authority. For past rulings, the Tax Administrative Assistance Ordinance (TAAO), which governs the exchange of information on rulings, provides for the submission of the information to the competent authority within nine months after the entry into force of the legal basis enabling spontaneous exchange of information (i.e. 30 September 2018). For future rulings, the TAAO provides for the submission of the information to the competent authority by 60 days after issuing a ruling. The Swiss competent authority provides for a final check before sending the information. Information is to be exchanged within three months of receiving the information from the responsible tax authority.

Switzerland has started exchanging information on its rulings on 1 January 2018, meaning that this is the first year this section is assessed with regard to Switzerland. The IT tool was developed in order to facilitate the completion and exchange of templates. In most cases, taxpayers entered the required information in the IT system. This information was then checked and, if necessary, completed by the responsible tax authority prior to forwarding the information to the competent authority for information exchange with the relevant jurisdictions. The templates were thus reviewed twice in order to ensure the completeness of the templates and the adherence with the Action 5 minimum standard. In order to ensure a harmonised approach, meetings and training sessions were organized for the concerned units. Guidance on how to fill out the summary is also available and included directly in this IT tool.

Switzerland has ensured that the information on rulings is made available to the competent authority in a timely way by means of the domestic legal basis which provides for fixed deadlines for the transmission to the competent authority. The IT system enabled the tracking of ruling reports and their current status (for example, to be transmitted by the cantonal tax authorities / transmitted to the competent authority etc.). In case of incomplete or incorrect templates, the competent authority reverted to the responsible tax authorities. The transmission of the templates occurred periodically, on average every 3-4 weeks.

For the year in review, the timeliness of exchanges is as follows:

Past rulings in the scope of the transparency framework [3]	Number of exchanges transmitted by 31 December 2018	Delayed exchanges		
		Number of exchanges not transmitted by 31 December 2018	Reasons for the delays	Any other comments
	2 149	352	Need to substantiate summaries and revert to cantonal tax authorities; finalisation of IT system.	352 exchanges were transmitted in the first quarter of 2019.
Future rulings in the scope of the transparency framework	Number of exchanges transmitted within three months of the information becoming available to the competent authority or immediately after legal	Delayed exchanges		
		Number of exchanges transmitted later than three months of the information on rulings becoming available to	Reasons for the delays	Any other comments

	impediments have been lifted	the competent authority		
	400	0	N/A	N/A
Total	2 549	352		

Follow up requests received for exchange of the ruling	Number	Average time to provide response	Number of requests not answered
	5[4]	127 days	0

Switzerland encountered some delays with respect to past rulings. This was on account of the volume of exchanges on past rulings in this first year that exchanges were permitted to take place, some technical issues encountered with the IT system, as well as cases where the information provided by the cantonal authorities in the ruling template needed to be verified. As the information was ultimately exchanged within the first three months of the 2019, and this is not a recurring issue, no recommendation is made. In addition, Switzerland encountered some delays in responding to the follow up request for further information. This was a reflection of the increased workload of the competent authority in managing with the volume of exchanges in 2018 and is not expected to be a recurring issue.

Conclusion on section B

Switzerland has the necessary legal basis for spontaneous exchange of information, a process for completing the templates in a timely way and has completed all exchanges within a short time after the end of the year in review. Switzerland has met all of the ToR for the exchange of information process and no recommendations are made.

C. Statistics (ToR IV)

The statistics for the year in review are as follows:

Category of ruling	Number of exchanges	Jurisdictions exchanged with
Ruling related to a preferential regime	1 381	Argentina, Armenia, Aruba, Austria, Azerbaijan, Barbados, Belgium, Brunei Darussalam, Bulgaria, Cameroon, Canada, Chile, China (People's Republic of), Colombia, Costa Rica, Croatia, Curaçao, Cyprus, Czech Republic, Denmark, Finland, France, Georgia, Germany, Ghana, Greece, Guatemala, Guernsey, Hong Kong (China), Hungary, Iceland, India, Indonesia, Ireland, Isle of Man, Israel, Italy, Japan, Jersey, Kazakhstan, Korea, Latvia, Liechtenstein, Lithuania, Luxembourg, Malaysia, Malta, Mauritius, Mexico, Moldova, Netherlands, New Zealand, Nigeria, Norway, Pakistan, Panama, Peru, Poland, Portugal, Romania, Russia, Saint Kitts and Nevis, Saudi Arabia, Seychelles, Singapore, Slovak Republic, Slovenia, South Africa, Spain, Sweden, Tunisia, Turkey, Ukraine, United Kingdom, Uruguay
Cross-border unilateral advance pricing agreements (APAs) and any other cross-border unilateral tax rulings (such	1 330	Argentina, Armenia, Aruba, Austria, Azerbaijan, Barbados, Belgium, Bulgaria, Brunei Darussalam,

as an advance tax ruling) covering transfer pricing or the application of transfer pricing principles		Cameroon, Canada, Chile, China (People's Republic of), Colombia, Costa Rica, Croatia, Curaçao, Cyprus, Czech Republic, Denmark, Finland, France, Germany, Gibraltar, Ghana, Greece, Guernsey, Hong Kong (China), Hungary, Iceland, India, Indonesia, Ireland, Isle of Man, Israel, Italy, Japan, Jersey, Kazakhstan, Korea, Latvia, Liechtenstein, Lithuania, Luxembourg, Malaysia, Malta, Mauritius, Mexico, Moldova, Netherlands, New Zealand, Nigeria, Norway, Pakistan, Panama, Peru, Poland, Portugal, Romania, Russia, Saint Kitts and Nevis, Samoa, Saudi Arabia, Seychelles, Singapore, Slovak Republic, Slovenia, South Africa, Spain, Sweden, Tunisia, Turkey, Ukraine, United Kingdom, Uruguay
Cross-border rulings providing for a unilateral downward adjustment to the taxpayer's taxable profits that is not directly reflected in the taxpayer's financial / commercial accounts	N/A	N/A
Permanent establishment rulings	323	Albania, Argentina, Australia, Austria, Barbados, Belgium, Brazil, Canada, Chile, China (People's Republic of), Colombia, Costa Rica, Cyprus, Czech Republic, Denmark, Finland, France, Georgia, Germany, Gibraltar, Greece, Hong Kong (China), Hungary, India, Ireland, Italy, Japan, Jersey, Korea, Liechtenstein, Luxembourg, Malta, Mexico, Netherlands, Nigeria, Norway, Pakistan, Poland, Portugal, Romania, Russia, Saint Kitts and Nevis, Singapore, Slovak Republic, South Africa, Sweden, Tunisia, Ukraine, United Kingdom
Related party conduit rulings	8	Belgium, Cyprus, France, Germany, Isle of Man, Liechtenstein, United Kingdom
De minimis rule	N/A	N/A
IP regimes: total exchanges on taxpayers benefitting from the third category of IP assets, new entrants benefitting from grandfathered IP regimes; and taxpayers making use of the option to treat the nexus ratio as a rebuttable presumption	0	0
Total	3 042[5]	

D. Matters related to intellectual property regimes (ToR I.4.1.3)

Switzerland offered one intellectual property regime (Canton of Nidwalden – License box) that was amended as of 1 January 2016 and is subject to transparency requirements under the Action 5 Report (OECD, 2015[5]). It states that the identification of the benefitting taxpayers occur as follows:

- ***New entrants benefitting from the grandfathered IP regime***: No enhanced transparency requirements apply, as follows. The Canton of Nidwalden is a grandfathered IP regime, but there were no new entrants in the period after the relevant date from which the enhanced transparency obligations apply.

- ***Third category of IP assets***: not applicable as the regime does not allow the third category of IP assets to qualify for the benefits.
- ***Taxpayers making use of the option to treat the nexus ratio as a rebuttable presumption***: not applicable as the regime does not allow the nexus ratio to be treated as a rebuttable presumption.

Summary of recommendations on implementation of the transparency framework

Aspect of implementation of the transparency framework that should be improved	Recommendation for improvement
Switzerland experienced some delays in exchanging information on past rulings.	No recommendation is made because Switzerland completed exchanges on the delayed past rulings in early 2019 and this is not a recurring issue.

Notes

[1] With respect to the following preferential regimes: 1) Auxiliary company regime (previously referred to as domiciliary company regime, 2) Mixed company regime, 3) Commissionaire ruling regime, 4) Holding company regime (cantonal level), 5) Licence box (Canton of Nidwalden only).

[2] Parties to the Convention are available here: www.oecd.org/tax/exchange-of-tax-information/convention-on-mutual-administrative-assistance-in-tax-matters.htm.

[3] For the purposes of the year in review, exchanges relating to rulings issued in 2017 are included in this table in the column relating to past rulings. Although such rulings would fall in the category of future rulings for the purposes of the timelines for the transparency framework, the information on these rulings was not permitted to be exchanged by Switzerland until 2018, due to legal impediments. Therefore such rulings were exchanged alongside other past rulings.

[4] The five requests all concern the same ruling.

[5] Switzerland explained that in many cases the rulings templates identified in the statistics on exchanges above fall in two or more categories which has led to some multiple counting in this table. For the year in review, 2 549 individual exchanges took place.

Thailand

Thailand has met all aspects of the terms of reference (ToR) for the calendar year 2018 (year in review) except for undertaking spontaneous exchange of information on tax rulings (ToR II.5). Thailand receives one recommendation on this point for the year in review.

This is Thailand's first review of implementation of the transparency framework.

Thailand can legally issue one type of ruling within the scope of the transparency framework. In practice, Thailand issued rulings within the scope of the transparency framework as follows:

- 182 past rulings;
- For the period 1 April 2018 - 31 December 2018: 36 future rulings.

As no exchanges took place, no peer input was received in respect of the exchanges of information on rulings received from Thailand.

Introduction

This peer review covers Thailand's implementation of the BEPS Action 5 transparency framework for the year 2018. The report has four parts, each relating to a key part of the ToR. Each part is discussed in turn. A summary of recommendations is included at the end of this report.

A. The information gathering process

Thailand can legally issue the following type of rulings within the scope of the transparency framework: preferential regimes.[1] The rulings consist of confirmation letters for taxpayers to state that they can benefit from the preferential tax regime. These letters are issued by the Large Business Tax Administration Division in the tax administration.

Past rulings (ToR I.4.1.1, I.4.1.2, I.4.2.1, I.4.2.2)

For Thailand past rulings are any tax rulings within scope that are issued either (i) on or after 1 January 2016 but before 1 April 2018; and (ii) on or after 1 January 2014 but before 1 January 2016, provided still in effect as at 1 January 2016.

Thailand issues confirmation letters with respect to their preferential tax regimes. Each time a letter is issued, it is stored in a central database. This database was consulted in order to identify all past rulings.

When a taxpayer requests access to a preferential regime, it has to identify all relevant related parties, including the ultimate parent entity, the immediate parent entity and the related parties with which the taxpayer entered into a transaction. This information is available in the same database where the confirmation letters are stored. As such, Thailand was able to obtain information on all potential exchange jurisdictions and did not need to use the "best efforts approach."

Future rulings (ToR I.4.1.1, I.4.1.2, I.4.2.1)

For Thailand, future rulings are any tax rulings within scope that are issued on or after 1 April 2018.

The process for identifying future rulings and potential exchange jurisdictions is the same as to the process regarding the past rulings. Each time a ruling is issued, the relevant official is aware that it will be relevant for the transparency framework and is flagged as such.

Review and supervision (ToR I.4.3)

The team responsible for issuing rulings consists of ten members. This team is supervised by the Director of the Large Business Tax Administration Division. Only these persons have access to the database, and the Director is responsible for making sure that all information is captured accurately. The team has also received training on the transparency framework from the FHTP Secretariat.

Conclusion on section A

Thailand has met all of the ToR for the information gathering process and no recommendations are made.

B. The exchange of information

Legal basis for spontaneous exchange of information (ToR II.5.1, II.5.2)

Thailand has the necessary domestic legal basis to exchange information spontaneously. Thailand notes that there are no legal or practical impediments that prevent the spontaneous exchange of information on rulings as contemplated in the Action 5 minimum standard.

Thailand has international agreements permitting spontaneous exchange of information, including double tax agreements in force with 61 jurisdictions.[2]

Completion and exchange of templates (ToR II.5.3, II.5.4, II.5.5, II.5.6, II.5.7)

The Large Business Tax Administration Division gathers, verifies, and then sends the information relating to rulings to the Tax Policy and Planning Division. The Director of the Large Business Tax Administration Division supervises this process. The Tax Policy Group under the Tax Policy and Planning Division completes the template using Annex C of the Action 5 Report (OECD, 2015[5]), and the summary section of the template is completed in line with the internal FHTP suggested guidance. The template is then sent to the International Tax Group under the Tax Policy and Planning Division which is the assistant to the Competent Authority. This takes place once a month. Subsequently, the International Tax Group presents the information in the template to the Competent Authority for exchange. The Competent Authority then sends the templates within three months to the relevant jurisdictions.

For the year in review, the timeliness of exchanges is as follows:

Past rulings in the scope of the transparency framework	Number of exchanges transmitted by 31 December 2018	Delayed exchanges		
		Number of exchanges not transmitted by 31 December 2018	Reasons for the delays	Any other comments
	0	182	See below.	N/A
Future rulings in the scope of the transparency framework	Number of exchanges transmitted within three months of the information becoming available to the competent authority or immediately after legal impediments have been lifted	Delayed exchanges		
		Number of exchanges transmitted later than three months of the information on rulings becoming available to the competent authority	Reasons for the delays	Any other comments
	0	36	See below.	N/A
Total	0	218		

Follow up requests received for exchange of the ruling	Number	Average time to provide response	Number of requests not answered
	0	N/A	N/A

Thailand explains that delays have occurred in the exchange of information on rulings was because there was a misunderstanding of the definition of rulings. When Thailand became aware that the confirmation letters for the regime fall under the first category of rulings in scope of the transparency framework, immediate action was taken to commence the exchanges. This process is underway as of mid-2019 in order to conduct exchanges as soon as possible.

Conclusion on section B

Thailand has the necessary legal basis to undertake spontaneous exchange of information. Thailand is recommended to continue its efforts to complete the templates on relevant rulings and to ensure that the exchanges of information on rulings occur as soon as possible (ToR II.5).

C. Statistics (ToR IV)

As there was no information on rulings exchanged by Thailand for the year in review, no statistics can be reported.

D. Matters related to intellectual property regimes (ToR I.4.1.3)

Thailand offers three intellectual property regimes (IP regime)[3] that are not subject to the transparency requirements under the Action 5 Report (OECD, 2015[5]), because:

- ***New entrants benefitting from the grandfathered IP regime***: the regimes are not operational and in practice, no taxpayer has benefitted from any of the regimes. As such, there were no entrants on which information was required to be exchanged.
- ***Third category of IP assets***: not applicable as the regimes do not allow the third category of IP assets to qualify for the benefits.
- ***Taxpayers making the use of the option to treat the nexus ratio as a rebuttable presumption***: not applicable the regimes do not allow the nexus ratio to be treated as a rebuttable presumption.

Summary of recommendations on implementation of the transparency framework

Aspect of implementation of the transparency framework that should be improved	Recommendation for improvement
Thailand did not undertake spontaneous exchange of information on all tax rulings within scope of the transparency framework during the year in review.	Thailand is recommended to continue its efforts to complete the templates on relevant rulings and to ensure that the exchanges of information on rulings occur as soon as possible.

Notes

[1] With respect to the following preferential regimes: 1) International headquarters and treasury centre, 2) International trading centre and 3) International business centre.

[2] Thailand has bilateral agreements with: Armenia, Australia, Austria, Bahrain, Bangladesh, Belarus, Belgium, Bulgaria, Cambodia, Canada, Chile, China (People's Republic of), Cyprus, Czech Republic, Denmark, Estonia, Finland, France, Germany, Hong Kong (China), Hungary, India, Indonesia, Ireland, Israel, Italy, Japan, Korea, Kuwait, Laos, Luxembourg, Malaysia, Mauritius, Myanmar, Nepal, Netherlands, New Zealand, Norway, Oman, Pakistan, Philippines, Poland, Romania, Russia, Seychelles, Singapore, Slovenia, South Africa, Spain, Sri Lanka, Sweden, Switzerland, Chinese Taipei, Tajikistan, Turkey, Ukraine, United Arab Emirates, United Kingdom, United States, Uzbekistan and Viet Nam.

Note by Turkey: The information in this document with reference to "Cyprus" relates to the southern part of the Island. There is no single authority representing both Turkish and Greek Cypriot people on the Island. Turkey recognises the Turkish Republic of Northern Cyprus (TRNC). Until a lasting and equitable solution is found within the context of the United Nations, Turkey shall preserve its position concerning the "Cyprus issue".

Note by all the European Union Member States of the OECD and the European Union. The Republic of Cyprus is recognised by all members of the United Nations with the exception of Turkey. The information in this document relates to the area under the effective control of the Government of the Republic of Cyprus.

[3] These regimes are: 1) International headquarters and treasury centre, 2) Regional operating headquarters 1 and 3) Regional operating headquarters 2.

Trinidad & Tobago

Trinidad & Tobago has met all aspects of the terms of reference (OECD, 2017[3]) (ToR) for the calendar year 2018 (year in review) that can be met in the absence of rulings being issued.

In the prior year report, Trinidad & Tobago did not receive any recommendations.

Trinidad & Tobago indicates that it cannot legally issue any type of rulings within the scope of the transparency framework.

As no exchanges were required to take place, no peer input was received in respect of the exchanges of information on rulings received from Trinidad & Tobago.

Introduction

This peer review covers Trinidad & Tobago's implementation of the BEPS Action 5 transparency framework for the year 2018. The report has four parts, each relating to a key part of the ToR. Each part is discussed in turn. A summary of recommendations is included at the end of this report.

A. The information gathering process

As no rulings are issued, this section is not assessed.

B. The exchange of information

As no rulings are issued, this section is not assessed.

C. Statistics (ToR IV)

As no rulings are issued, no statistics can be reported.

D. Matters related to intellectual property regimes (ToR I.4.1.3)

Trinidad & Tobago does not offer an intellectual property regime for which transparency requirements under the Action 5 Report (OECD, 2015[5]) were imposed.

Summary of recommendations on implementation of the transparency framework

Aspect of implementation of the transparency framework that should be improved	Recommendation for improvement
	No recommendations are made.

Tunisia

Tunisia has met all aspects of the terms of reference (OECD, 2017[3]) (ToR) for the calendar year 2018 (year in review) that can be met in the absence of rulings being issued.

This is Tunisia's first review of implementation of the transparency framework.

Tunisia indicates that it cannot legally issue any type of rulings within the scope of the transparency framework.

As no exchanges were required to take place, no peer input was received in respect of the exchanges of information on rulings received from Tunisia.

Introduction

This peer review covers Tunisia's implementation of the BEPS Action 5 transparency framework for the year 2018. The report has four parts, each relating to a key part of the ToR. Each part is discussed in turn. A summary of recommendations is included at the end of this report.

A. The information gathering process

As no rulings are issued, this section is not assessed.

B. The exchange of information

As no rulings are issued, this section is not assessed.

C. Statistics (ToR IV)

As no rulings are issued, no statistics can be reported.

D. Matters related to intellectual property regimes (ToR I.4.1.3)

Tunisia does not offer an intellectual property regime for which transparency requirements under the Action 5 Report (OECD, 2015[5]) were imposed.

Summary of recommendations on implementation of the transparency framework

Aspect of implementation of the transparency framework that should be improved	Recommendation for improvement
	No recommendations are made.

Turkey

Turkey has met all aspects of the terms of reference (ToR) for the calendar year 2018 (year in review) except for identifying and exchanging information on new entrants to the grandfathered IP regime and exchanging information on all taxpayers benefitting from the third category of assets in the IP regime (ToR I.4.1.3). Turkey receives one recommendation on this point for the year in review.

In the prior year report, Turkey received the same recommendation. As it has not been addressed, the recommendation remains in place.

Turkey can legally issue one type of ruling within the scope of the transparency framework.

In practice, Turkey issued rulings within the scope of the transparency framework as follows:

- Three past rulings;
- For the period 1 April 2016 - 31 December 2016: no future rulings;
- For the calendar year 2017: eight future rulings, and
- For the year in review: no future rulings.

As no exchanges took place in the year in review, no peer input was received in respect of the exchanges of information on rulings received from Turkey.

Introduction

This peer review covers Turkey's implementation of the BEPS Action 5 transparency framework for the year 2018. The report has four parts, each relating to a key part of the ToR. Each part is discussed in turn. A summary of recommendations is included at the end of this report.

A. The information gathering process

Turkey can legally issue one type of rulings within the scope of the transparency framework: cross-border unilateral APAs and any other cross-border unilateral tax rulings (such as an advance tax ruling) covering transfer pricing or the application of transfer pricing principles.

Past rulings (ToR I.4.1.1, I.4.1.2, I.4.2.1, I.4.2.2)

For Turkey, past rulings are any tax rulings within scope that are issued either: (i) on or after 1 January 2014 but before 1 April 2016; or (ii) on or after 1 January 2010 but before 1 January 2014, provided they were still in effect as at 1 January 2014.

In the prior years' peer review reports, it was determined that Turkey's undertakings to identify past rulings and all potential exchange jurisdictions were sufficient to meet the minimum standard. Turkey's implementation in this regard remains unchanged, and therefore continues to meet the minimum standard.

Future rulings (ToR I.4.1.1, I.4.1.2, I.4.2.1)

For Turkey, future rulings are any tax rulings within scope that are issued on or after 1 April 2016.

In the prior years' peer review reports, it was determined that Turkey's undertakings to identify future rulings and all potential exchange jurisdictions were sufficient to meet the minimum standard. Turkey's implementation in this regard remains unchanged, and therefore continues to meet the minimum standard.

Review and supervision (ToR I.4.3)

In the prior years' peer review reports, it was determined that Turkey's review and supervision mechanism was sufficient to meet the minimum standard. Turkey's implementation in this regard remains unchanged, and therefore continues to meet the minimum standard.

Conclusion on section A

Turkey has met all of the ToR for the information gathering process and no recommendations are made.

B. The exchange of information

Legal basis for spontaneous exchange of information (ToR II.5.1, II.5.2)

Turkey has the necessary domestic legal basis to exchange information spontaneously. Turkey notes that there are no legal or practical impediments that prevent the spontaneous exchange information on rulings as contemplated in the Action 5 minimum standard.

Turkey has bilateral agreements in force with 86 jurisdictions.[1] In addition, Turkey has signed the *Multilateral Convention on Mutual Administrative Assistance in Tax Matters: Amended by the 2010 Protocol* (OECD/Council of Europe, 2011) ("the Convention") and it was ratified by the Turkish Parliament on 20 May 2017. The Convention entered into force on 1 July 2018 and will have effect from 1 January 2019.

Completion and exchange of templates (ToR II.5.3, II.5.4, II.5.5, II.5.6, II.5.7)

In the prior year peer review report, it was determined that Turkey's process for the completion and exchange of templates were sufficient to meet the minimum standard. Turkey's implementation in this regard remains unchanged and therefore continues to meet the minimum standard.

As Turkey did not issue any rulings in scope of the transparency framework in the relevant period, Turkey was not required to exchange any information on rulings in the year in review and no data on the timeliness of exchanges can be reported.

Conclusion on section B

Turkey has the necessary legal basis for spontaneous exchange of information, a process for completing the templates in a timely way and has completed all exchanges. Turkey has met all of the ToR for the exchange of information process and no recommendations are made.

C. Statistics (ToR IV)

As there was no information on rulings exchanged by Turkey for the year in review, no statistics can be reported.

D. Matters related to intellectual property regimes (ToR I.4.1.3)

Turkey has two intellectual property regimes that are subject to transparency requirements under the Action 5 Report (OECD, 2015[5]).[2] It states that the identification of the benefitting taxpayers will occur as follows:

Technology development zone regime

- ***New entrants***: Transparency obligations apply for the regime, because grandfathering is provided to entrants that entered the regime after the relevant date from which enhanced transparency obligations apply. Turkey has not yet been able to identify and exchange information on new entrants to the grandfathered IP regime, and the regime has been found to be actually harmful to the extent of extended grandfathering to taxpayers that entered the regime between 1 July 2016 and 19 October 2017. Therefore the period for enhanced transparency for new entrants on the grandfathered regime is from 6 February 2015 until 19 October 2017. Turkey has obliged taxpayers to declare their exempted IP income earned in this period in a temporary tax return, to be filed in 2018. This information will include the identification of both new taxpayers and new IP assets of existing taxpayers entering the regime in this period. This information was expected to be available to the Turkish Revenue Administration in August 2018. It is not known whether this information was received. In addition, no information has yet been exchanged. Therefore, Turkey is recommended to continue its efforts to identify and exchange information on new entrants to the grandfathered IP as soon as possible.
- ***Third category of IP assets***: In order for taxpayers to benefit from the third category of IP assets, the Ministry of Industry and Technology issues project completion documents, after the research-development project is completed and the assets have been created. A company requests the completion document electronically and the Ministry of Industry and Technology assesses the

application to determine whether the relevant IP assets have been created in the zone and the resulting income is therefore eligible for the tax benefit. After the document is approved and issued electronically by the Ministry, it is provided to the taxpayer. It is then expected that the Ministry of Industry and Technology will report to the tax administration for the purposes of completing the exchange of information. However, Turkey has not exchanged information on these taxpayers and therefore, it is recommended to exchange information on taxpayers benefitting from the third category of IP assets as soon as possible.

- ***Rebuttable presumption***: not applicable as the regime does not allow the nexus ratio to be treated as a rebuttable presumption.

5/B regime

- ***New entrants***: as this is a new IP regime rather than a grandfathered IP regime, transparency on new entrants was not required.
- ***Third category of IP assets***: not applicable as the regime does not allow the third category of IP assets to qualify for the benefits.
- ***Rebuttable presumption***: not applicable as the regime does not allow the nexus ratio to be treated as a rebuttable presumption.

Summary of recommendations on implementation of the transparency framework

Aspect of implementation of the transparency framework that should be improved	Recommendation for improvement
Turkey has not been able to identify and exchange information on new entrants to the grandfathered IP regime or to exchange information on all taxpayers benefitting from the third category of assets in the IP regime.	Turkey is recommended to identify and exchange information on new entrants to the grandfathered IP regime and to exchange information on taxpayers benefitting from the third category of IP assets as soon as possible. This recommendation remains unchanged since the prior year peer review report.

Notes

[1] Albania, Algeria, Australia, Austria, Azerbaijan, Bahrain, Bangladesh, Belarus, Belgium, Bosnia and Herzegovina, Brazil, Bulgaria, Canada, China (People's Republic of), Croatia, Czech Republic, Denmark, Egypt, Estonia, Ethiopia, Finland, France, Gambia, Georgia, Germany, Greece, Hungary, India, Indonesia, Iran, Ireland, Israel, Italy, Japan, Jordan, Kazakhstan, Korea, Kosovo, Kuwait, Kyrgyzstan, Latvia, Lebanon, Lithuania, Luxembourg, Malaysia, Malta, Mexico, Moldova, Mongolia, Montenegro, Morocco, Netherlands, New Zealand, North Macedonia, Norway, Oman, Pakistan, Philippines, Poland, Portugal, Qatar, Romania, Russian Federation, Saudi Arabia, Serbia, Singapore, Slovak Republic, Slovenia, South Africa, Spain, Sudan, Sweden, Switzerland, Syria, Tajikistan, Thailand, Tunisia, Turkish Republic of Northern Cyprus, Turkmenistan, Ukraine, United Arab Emirates, United Kingdom, United States, Uzbekistan, Viet Nam and Yemen.

Note by Turkey: The information in this document with reference to "Cyprus" relates to the southern part of the Island. There is no single authority representing both Turkish and Greek Cypriot people on the Island. Turkey recognises the Turkish Republic of Northern Cyprus (TRNC). Until a lasting and equitable solution is found within the context of the United Nations, Turkey shall preserve its position concerning the "Cyprus issue".

Note by all the European Union Member States of the OECD and the European Union. The Republic of Cyprus is recognised by all members of the United Nations with the exception of Turkey. The information in this document relates to the area under the effective control of the Government of the Republic of Cyprus.

[2] These regimes are: 1) Technology development zone regime and 2) 5/B regime.

Ukraine

Ukraine has met all of the terms of reference (ToR) for the calendar year 2018 (year in review).

This is Ukraine's first review of implementation of the transparency framework.

Ukraine can legally issue one type of ruling within the scope of the transparency framework. In practice, Ukraine issued no rulings within the scope of the transparency framework. Ukraine notes that it has received two requests for unilateral APAs which are under review.

As no exchanges were required to take place, no peer input was received in respect of the exchanges of information on rulings received from Ukraine.

Introduction

This peer review covers Ukraine's implementation of the BEPS Action 5 transparency framework for the year 2018. The report has four parts, each relating to a key part of the ToR. Each part is discussed in turn. A summary of recommendations is included at the end of this report.

A. The information gathering process

Ukraine can legally issue the one type of ruling within the scope of the transparency framework: cross-border unilateral APAs and any other cross-border unilateral tax rulings (such as an advance tax ruling) covering transfer pricing or the application of transfer pricing principles.

Past rulings (ToR I.4.1.1, I.4.1.2, I.4.2.1, I.4.2.2)

For Ukraine, past rulings are any tax rulings within scope that are issued either (i) on or after 1 January 2016, but before 1 April 2018; and (ii) on or after 1 January 2014, but before 1 January 2016, provided still in effect as at 1 January 2016.

Ukraine has not issued any past ruling. Any issued rulings would be stored in a central database at the headquarters level and would be identifiable as relevant for the transparency framework, and no such rulings had been recorded. Therefore it was not relevant to identify any potential exchange jurisdictions for past rulings.

Future rulings (ToR I.4.1.1, I.4.1.2, I.4.2.1)

For Ukraine, future rulings are any tax rulings within scope that are issued on or after 1 April 2018.

During the year in review, Ukraine did not issue any future rulings. For the year in review, the State Fiscal Service (SFS) Legal Entities Taxation Department was responsible for treatment of APA requests and issuance of APAs. That team consists of five members. Any issued rulings would be stored in a central database at the headquarters level and would be identifiable as relevant for the transparency framework.

When a taxpayer applies for an APA, it has to provide information on the jurisdictions of residence of related parties with which the taxpayers enter into a transaction covered by the ruling. According to the existing procedure, the taxpayer shall also enclose with the APA request information on their subsidiaries, parent entities and other information about the multinational group. This would include information on all potential exchange jurisdictions for the purposes of the transparency framework. However, if any information was missing, Ukraine would ask the taxpayer before issuing the ruling, in accordance with the procedure stipulated in Ukraine's internal regulation.

Review and supervision (ToR I.4.3)

The accuracy of the information gathering process and the identification of rulings in scope is supervised by a working group, which is in charge of APA negotiation. Ukraine noted that is currently receiving support from the OECD Secretariat as part of an induction programme and working to have in place a more formal procedure with respect to its review and supervision mechanism to make sure that all relevant information is captured adequately and submitted to all relevant jurisdictions without delay.

Conclusion on section A

Ukraine has met all of the ToR for the information gathering process and no recommendation is made.

B. The exchange of information

Legal basis for spontaneous exchange of information (ToR II.5.1, II.5.2)

Ukraine has the necessary domestic legal basis to exchange information spontaneously. Ukraine notes that there are no legal or practical impediments that prevent the spontaneous exchange of information on rulings as contemplated in the Action 5 minimum standard.

Ukraine has international agreements permitting spontaneous exchange of information, including being a party to the (i) *Multilateral Convention on Mutual Administrative Assistance in Tax Matters: Amended by the 2010 Protocol* (OECD/Council of Europe, 2011[4]) ("the Convention") and (ii) double tax agreements in force with 75 jurisdictions.[1]

Completion and exchange of templates (ToR II.5.3, II.5.4, II.5.5, II.5.6, II.5.7)

As there is a representative of the acting Competent Authority (the Strategic Development and International Cooperation Department) in the working group responsible for the issuance of rulings, the Competent Authority is immediately aware of the issuance of APAs. The head of the APA working group would ensure that the template is filled out and provided to the Competent Authority as soon as possible, but no later than three months after the issuance of the ruling. After this, the Competent Authority will then be responsible for reviewing the template for completeness, translating it and sending the template to all relevant jurisdictions as soon as possible, but no later than three months after the tax ruling becomes available to it. Ukraine confirms that it would refer to the FHTP internal guidance on completing the summary section.

As no rulings have been issued, no exchanges were required for the year in review and no data on timeliness can be reported.

Conclusion on section B

Ukraine has the necessary legal basis to undertake spontaneous exchange of information and a process for completion of templates and exchange of information on rulings. Ukraine has met all of the ToR for the exchange of information process and no recommendations are made.

C. Statistics (ToR IV)

As no rulings have been issued, no statistics can be reported.

D. Matters related to intellectual property regimes (ToR I.4.1.3)

Ukraine does not offer an intellectual property regime for which transparency requirements under the Action 5 Report (OECD, 2015[5]) were imposed.

Summary of recommendations on implementation of the transparency framework

Aspect of implementation of the transparency framework that should be improved	Recommendation for improvement
	No recommendations are made.

Notes

[1] Parties to the Convention are available here: www.oecd.org/tax/exchange-of-tax-information/convention-on-mutual-administrative-assistance-in-tax-matters.htm. Ukraine also has double tax agreements with Algeria, Armenia, Austria, Azerbaijan, Belarus, Belgium, Brazil, Bulgaria, Canada, China (People's Republic of), Croatia, Cyprus, Czech Republic, Denmark, Egypt, Estonia, Finland, France, Georgia, Germany, Greece, Hungary, Iceland, India, Indonesia, Iran, Ireland, Israel, Italy, Japan, Jordan, Kazakhstan, Korea, Kuwait, Kyrgyzstan, Latvia, Lebanon, Libya, Lithuania, Luxembourg, Malaysia, Malta, Mexico, Moldova, Mongolia, Montenegro, Morocco, Netherlands, North Macedonia, Norway, Pakistan, Poland, Portugal, Qatar, Romania, Russia, Saudi Arabia, Serbia, Singapore, Slovak Republic, Slovenia, South Africa, Spain, Sweden, Switzerland, Syria, Tajikistan, Thailand, Turkey, Turkmenistan, United Arab Emirates, United Kingdom, United States, Uzbekistan and Viet Nam.

Note by Turkey: The information in this document with reference to "Cyprus" relates to the southern part of the Island. There is no single authority representing both Turkish and Greek Cypriot people on the Island. Turkey recognises the Turkish Republic of Northern Cyprus (TRNC). Until a lasting and equitable solution is found within the context of the United Nations, Turkey shall preserve its position concerning the "Cyprus issue".

Note by all the European Union Member States of the OECD and the European Union. The Republic of Cyprus is recognised by all members of the United Nations with the exception of Turkey. The information in this document relates to the area under the effective control of the Government of the Republic of Cyprus.

United Kingdom

The United Kingdom has met all aspects of the terms of reference (OECD, 2017[3]) (ToR) for the calendar year 2018 (year in review) and no recommendations are made.

In the prior year report, the United Kingdom received one recommendation. This recommendation has been addressed and is removed.

The United Kingdom can legally issue three types of rulings within the scope of the transparency framework. In practice, the United Kingdom issued rulings within the scope of the transparency framework as follows:

- 599 past rulings;
- For the period 1 April 2016 - 31 December 2016: 71 future rulings;
- For the calendar year 2017: 16 future rulings, and
- For the year in review: 19 future rulings.

Peer input was received from five jurisdictions in respect of the exchanges of information on rulings received from the United Kingdom. The input was generally positive, noting that information was complete, in a correct format and received in a timely manner.

Introduction

This peer review covers the United Kingdom's implementation of the BEPS Action 5 transparency framework for the year 2018. The report has four parts, each relating to a key part of the ToR. Each part is discussed in turn. A summary of recommendations is included at the end of this report.

A. The information gathering process

The United Kingdom can legally issue the three following types of rulings within the scope of the transparency framework: (i) rulings related to preferential regimes;[1] (ii) cross-border unilateral advance pricing agreements (APAs) and any other cross-border unilateral tax rulings (such as an advance tax ruling) covering transfer pricing or the application of transfer pricing principles; and (iii) permanent establishment rulings.

Past rulings (ToR I.4.1.1, I.4.1.2, I.4.2.1, I.4.2.2)

For the United Kingdom, past rulings are any tax rulings within scope that are issued either: (i) on or after 1 January 2014 but before 1 April 2016; or (ii) on or after 1 January 2010 but before 1 January 2014, provided they were still in effect as at 1 January 2016.

In the prior years' peer review reports, it was determined that the United Kingdom's undertakings to identify past rulings and all potential exchange jurisdictions were sufficient to meet the minimum standard. The United Kingdom's implementation in this regard remains unchanged, and therefore continues to meet the minimum standard.

Future rulings (ToR I.4.1.1, I.4.1.2, I.4.2.1)

For the United Kingdom, future rulings are any tax rulings within scope that are issued on or after 1 April 2016.

In the prior years' peer review reports, it was determined that the United Kingdom's undertakings to identify future rulings and all potential exchange jurisdictions was sufficient to meet the minimum standard. The United Kingdom's implementation in this regard remains unchanged, and therefore continues to meet the minimum standard.

Review and supervision (ToR I.4.3)

In the prior years' peer review reports, it was determined that the United Kingdom tax administration's review and supervision mechanisms were sufficient to meet the minimum standard. The United Kingdom tax administration's implementation in this regard remains unchanged, and therefore continues to meet the minimum standard.

Conclusion on section A

The United Kingdom has met all of the ToR for the information gathering process and no recommendations are made.

B. The exchange of information

Legal basis for spontaneous exchange of information (ToR II.5.1, II.5.2)

United Kingdom has the necessary domestic legal basis to exchange information spontaneously. United Kingdom notes that there are no legal or practical impediments that prevent the spontaneous exchange of information on rulings as contemplated in the Action 5 minimum standard.

The United Kingdom is a party to international agreements permitting spontaneous exchange of information, including (i) the *Multilateral Convention on Mutual Administrative Assistance in Tax Matters: Amended by the 2010 Protocol* (OECD/Council of Europe, 2011) ("the Convention"), (ii) the Directive 2011/16/EU with all other European Union Member States and (iii) double tax agreements in force with 121 jurisdictions.[2]

Completion and exchange of templates (ToR II.5.3, II.5.4, II.5.5, II.5.6, II.5.7)

In the prior year peer review reports, it was determined that the United Kingdom's completion and exchange of templates were sufficient to meet the minimum standard. The United Kingdom's implementation in this regard remains unchanged and therefore continues to meet the minimum standard.

For the year in review, the timeliness of exchanges is as follows:

Past rulings in the scope of the transparency framework	Number of exchanges transmitted by 31 December 2018	Delayed exchanges		
		Number of exchanges not transmitted by 31 December 2018	Reasons for the delays	Any other comments
	0	0	N/A	N/A
Future rulings in the scope of the transparency framework	Number of exchanges transmitted within three months of the information becoming available to the competent authority or immediately after legal impediments have been lifted	Delayed exchanges		
		Number of exchanges transmitted later than three months of the information on rulings becoming available to the competent authority	Reasons for the delays	Any other comments
	13	11	Delays resulting from resourcing issues and a misunderstanding between timing under the Action 5 standard and the EU Directive.	All rulings have now been exchanged.
Total	13	11		

Follow up requests received for exchange of the ruling	Number	Average time to provide response	Number of requests not answered
	0	N/A	N/A

The United Kingdom experienced some delays exchanging information on future rulings. The delays were a result of resourcing issues, and a misunderstanding between the time limits under the Action 5 standard and the EU directive which are typically longer. HMRC has clarified its instructions for the exchange of rulings under the Action 5 standard to ensure this misunderstanding does not continue to occur, and all exchanges were completed within the year in review. As such, no recommendation is made.

Conclusion on section B

The United Kingdom has the necessary legal basis for spontaneous exchange of information, a process for completing the templates in a timely way and has completed exchanges mostly on time. The United Kingdom has met all of the ToR for the exchange of information process and no recommendations are made.

C. Statistics (ToR IV)

The statistics for the year in review are as follows:

Category of ruling	Number of exchanges	Jurisdictions exchanged with
Ruling related to a preferential regime	0	N/A
Cross-border unilateral advance pricing agreements (APAs) and any other cross-border unilateral tax rulings (such as an advance tax ruling) covering transfer pricing or the application of transfer pricing principles	15	Canada, Hong Kong (China), Ireland, Japan, Luxembourg, Netherlands, Sweden, Switzerland, United States
Cross-border rulings providing for a unilateral downward adjustment to the taxpayer's taxable profits that is not directly reflected in the taxpayer's financial / commercial accounts	N/A	N/A
Permanent establishment rulings	9	Australia, Austria, Belgium, Hong Kong (China), Ireland, Mexico, United States
Related party conduit rulings	N/A	N/A
De minimis rule	N/A	N/A
IP regimes: total exchanges on taxpayers benefitting from the third category of IP assets, new entrants benefitting from grandfathered IP regimes; and taxpayers making use of the option to treat the nexus ratio as a rebuttable presumption	177	Australia, Austria, Belgium, Canada, China (People's Republic of), Curaçao, Denmark, Finland, France, Germany, Greece, Hong Kong (China), India, Israel, Italy, Japan, Luxembourg, Mexico, Netherlands, Norway, Panama, Philippines, Spain, Sweden, Switzerland, United States
Total	201	

D. Matters related to intellectual property regimes (ToR I.4.1.3)

The United Kingdom offers an intellectual property regime (IP regime)[3] that is subject to transparency requirements under the Action 5 Report (OECD, 2015[5]). It states that the identification of the benefitting taxpayers occurs as follows:

- ***New entrants benefitting from the grandfathered IP regime***: Transparency obligations apply for the regime, because grandfathering is provided to entrants that entered the regime after the relevant date from which enhanced transparency obligations apply. In the prior year peer review report, it was determined that the United Kingdom's implementation regarding matters related to intellectual property regime was sufficient to meet the minimum standard except for identifying and exchanging information on new IP assets of existing taxpayers benefitting from the grandfathered IP regime, for which the United Kingdom received a recommendation to exchange such information. Given the need to respect domestic law limitations on obtaining specific information on new IP assets as noted in the prior year report, the United Kingdom identified all taxpayers able to benefit from grandfathering during the relevant period. The United Kingdom has exchanged this information in 2018 with 26 jurisdictions. Accordingly, the prior year recommendation is removed.

- ***Third category of IP assets***: not applicable as the regime does not allow the third category of IP assets to qualify for the benefits.
- ***Taxpayers making use of the option to treat the nexus ratio as a rebuttable presumption***: the United Kingdom confirms that no taxpayer elected to treat the nexus approach as a rebuttable presumption and as such no exchanges were required for the year in review.

Summary of recommendations on implementation of the transparency framework

Aspect of implementation of the transparency framework that should be improved	Recommendation for improvement
The United Kingdom experienced some delays in exchanging information on future rulings.	No recommendation is made because the United Kingdom has remedied the issue and completed exchanges on the delayed future rulings in the year in review and this is not expected to be a recurring issue.

Notes

[1] With respect to the following preferential regimes: 1) Patent box and 2) Shipping regime.

[2] Parties to the Convention are available here: www.oecd.org/tax/exchange-of-tax-information/convention-on-mutual-administrative-assistance-in-tax-matters.htm. The United Kingdom also has bilateral agreements with Albania, Algeria, Antigua and Barbuda, Argentina, Armenia, Australia, Azerbaijan, Bahrain, Bangladesh, Barbados, Belarus, Belize, Bolivia, Bosnia and Herzegovina, Botswana, British Virgin Islands, Brunei, Bulgaria, Cayman Islands, Chile, China (People's Republic of), Colombia, Côte d'Ivoire, Croatia, Cyprus, Czech Republic, Denmark, Egypt, Estonia, Ethiopia, Falkland Islands, Faroe Islands, Fiji, Finland, Gambia, Georgia, Ghana, Greece, Grenada, Guernsey, Guyana, Hong Kong (China), Hungary, Iceland, India, Indonesia, Ireland, Isle of Man, Israel, Jamaica, Japan, Jersey, Jordan, Kazakhstan, Kenya, Kiribati, Korea, Kosovo, Kuwait, Latvia, Lesotho, Libya, Lithuania, Malawi, Malaysia, Malta, Mauritius, Mexico, Moldova, Mongolia, Montenegro, Montserrat, Morocco, Myanmar, Namibia, New Zealand, Nigeria, North Macedonia, Norway, Oman, Pakistan, Panama, Papua New Guinea, Philippines, Poland, Portugal, Qatar, Romania, Russia, Saudi Arabia, Senegal, Serbia, Sierra Leone, Singapore, Slovak Republic, Slovenia, Solomon Islands, South Africa, Spain, Sri Lanka, Saint Kitts and Nevis, Sudan, Swaziland, Chinese Taipei, Tajikistan, Thailand, Trinidad and Tobago, Tunisia, Turkey, Turkmenistan, Tuvalu, Uganda, Ukraine, United Arab Emirates, United States, Uruguay, Uzbekistan, Venezuela, Viet Nam, Zambia and Zimbabwe.

Note by Turkey: The information in this document with reference to "Cyprus" relates to the southern part of the Island. There is no single authority representing both Turkish and Greek Cypriot people on the Island. Turkey recognises the Turkish Republic of Northern Cyprus (TRNC). Until a lasting and equitable solution is found within the context of the United Nations, Turkey shall preserve its position concerning the "Cyprus issue".

Note by all the European Union Member States of the OECD and the European Union. The Republic of Cyprus is recognised by all members of the United Nations with the exception of Turkey. The information in this document relates to the area under the effective control of the Government of the Republic of Cyprus.

[3] Patent box.

United States

The United States has met all aspects of the terms of reference (OECD, 2017[3]) (ToR) for the calendar year 2018 (year in review) and no recommendations are made.

In the prior year report, the United States did not receive any recommendations.

The United States can legally issue four types of rulings within the scope of the transparency framework. In practice, the United States issued rulings within the scope of the transparency framework as follows:

- 114 past rulings;
- For the period 1 April 2016 - 31 December 2016: 21 future rulings;
- For the calendar year 2017: 30 future rulings;[1] and
- For the year in review: 27 future rulings.[2]

Peer input was received from six jurisdictions in respect of the exchanges of information on rulings received from the United States. The input was generally positive, noting that information was complete, in a correct format and received in a timely manner.

Introduction

This peer review covers the United States' implementation of the BEPS Action 5 transparency framework for the year 2018. The report has four parts, each relating to a key part of the ToR. Each part is discussed in turn. A summary of recommendations is included at the end of this report.

A. The information gathering process

The United States can legally issue the following four types of rulings within the scope of the transparency framework: (i) preferential regimes;[3] (ii) cross-border unilateral APAs and any other cross-border unilateral tax rulings (such as an advance tax ruling) covering transfer pricing or the application of transfer pricing principles; (iii) permanent establishment rulings; and (iv) related party conduit rulings.

Past rulings (ToR I.4.1.1, I.4.1.2, I.4.2.1, I.4.2.2)

For the United States, past rulings are any tax rulings within scope that are issued either: (i) on or after 1 January 2014 but before 1 April 2016; or (ii) on or after 1 January 2010 but before 1 January 2014, provided they were still in effect as at 1 January 2014.

In the prior years' peer review reports, it was determined that the United States' undertakings to identify past rulings and all potential exchange jurisdictions were sufficient to meet the minimum standard. The United States' implementation in this regard remains unchanged, and therefore continues to meet the minimum standard.

Future rulings (ToR I.4.1.1, I.4.1.2, I.4.2.1)

For the United States, future rulings are any tax rulings within scope that are issued on or after 1 April 2016.

In the prior years' peer review reports, it was determined that the United States' undertakings to identify future rulings and all potential exchange jurisdictions was sufficient to meet the minimum standard. The United States' implementation in this regard remains unchanged, and therefore continues to meet the minimum standard.

Review and supervision (ToR I.4.3)

In the prior years' peer review reports, it was determined that the United States' review and supervision mechanism was sufficient to meet the minimum standard. The United States' implementation in this regard remains unchanged, and therefore continues to meet the minimum standard.

Conclusion on section A

The United States has met all of the ToR for the information gathering process and no recommendations are made.

B. The exchange of information

Legal basis for spontaneous exchange of information (ToR II.5.1, II.5.2)

The United States has the necessary domestic legal basis to exchange information spontaneously. The United States notes that there are no legal or practical impediments that prevent the spontaneous exchange of information on rulings as contemplated in the Action 5 minimum standard.

The United States has international agreements permitting spontaneous exchange of information, including being a party to the (i) *Multilateral Convention on Mutual Administrative Assistance in Tax Matters* (OECD/Council of Europe, 2011[4]) ("the Convention"), (ii) tax information exchange agreements and (iii) double tax agreements in force with 48 jurisdictions.[4]

Completion and exchange of templates (ToR II.5.3, II.5.4, II.5.5, II.5.6, II.5.7)

In the prior year peer review report, it was determined that the Unites States' process for the completion and exchange of templates were sufficient to meet the minimum standard. The United States' implementation in this regard remains unchanged and therefore continues to meet the minimum standard.

For the year in review, the timeliness of exchanges is as follows:

Past rulings in the scope of the transparency framework	Number of exchanges transmitted by 31 December 2018	Delayed exchanges		
		Number of exchanges not transmitted by 31 December 2018	Reasons for the delays	Any other comments
	0	0	N/A	N/A
Future rulings in the scope of the transparency framework	Number of exchanges transmitted within three months of the information becoming available to the competent authority or immediately after legal impediments have been lifted	Delayed exchanges		
		Number of exchanges transmitted later than three months of the information on rulings becoming available to the competent authority	Reasons for the delays	Any other comments
	122	0	N/A	N/A
Total	122	0		

Follow up requests received for exchange of the ruling	Number	Average time to provide response	Number of requests not answered
	0	N/A	N/A

Conclusion on section B

The United States has the necessary legal basis for spontaneous exchange of information, a process for completing the templates in a timely way and has completed all exchanges. The United States has met all of the ToR for the exchange of information process and no recommendations are made.

C. Statistics (ToR IV)

The statistics for the year in review are as follows:

Category of ruling	Number of exchanges	Jurisdictions exchanged with
Ruling related to a preferential regime	N/A	N/A
Cross-border unilateral advance pricing agreements (APAs) and any other cross-border unilateral tax rulings (such as an advance tax ruling) covering transfer pricing or the application of transfer pricing principles	122	Argentina, Australia, Austria, Belgium, Brazil, Canada, Chin a9People's republic of), Colombia, Costa Rica, Czech Republic, Denmark, Egypt, Finland, France, Germany, Greece, Hungary, India, Indonesia, Ireland, Israel, Italy, Japan, Kazakhstan, Luxembourg, Mauritius, Mexico, Netherlands, New Zealand, Norway, Pakistan, Peru, Poland, Portugal, Romania, Russia, Slovenia, South Africa, Spain, Sweden, Thailand, Turkey, Ukraine, United Kingdom.
Cross-border rulings providing for a unilateral downward adjustment to the taxpayer's taxable profits that is not directly reflected in the taxpayer's financial / commercial accounts	N/A	N/A
Permanent establishment rulings	3	*De minimis* rule applies
Related party conduit rulings	N/A	N/A
De minimis rule	N/A	N/A
IP regimes: total exchanges on taxpayers benefitting from the third category of IP assets, new entrants benefitting from grandfathered IP regimes; and taxpayers making use of the option to treat the nexus ratio as a rebuttable presumption	N/A	N/A
Total	122[5]	

D. Matters related to intellectual property regimes (ToR I.4.1.3)

The United States offers an intellectual property regime (IP regime).[6] The regime was under review by the FHTP from late in the year in review. No transparency requirements applied for the year in review.

Summary of recommendations on implementation of the transparency framework

Aspect of implementation of the transparency framework that should be improved	Recommendation for improvement
	No recommendations are made.

Notes

[1] One of them qualifying both as an APA and as a PE ruling.

[2] Three of them qualifying both as an APA and as a PE ruling.

[3] With respect to the following preferential regime: Foreign derived intangible income regime.

[4] Parties to the Convention are available here: www.oecd.org/tax/exchange-of-tax-information/convention-on-mutual-administrative-assistance-in-tax-matters.htm. The United States also has double tax agreements with Australia, Austria, Barbados, Belgium, Bulgaria, Canada, China (People's Republic of), Czech Republic, Denmark, Egypt, Estonia, Finland, France, Germany, Greece, Hungary, Iceland, India, Indonesia, Ireland, Israel, Italy, Jamaica, Japan, Kazakhstan, Latvia, Lithuania, Luxembourg, Malta, Mexico, Netherlands, New Zealand, Norway, Pakistan, Poland, Portugal, Romania, Russia, Slovak Republic, Slovenia, South Africa, Spain, Sri Lanka, Sweden, Thailand, Turkey, Ukraine and United Kingdom.

[5] The three exchanges on PE rulings also qualified as unilateral APAs and were exchanged on templates that identified those two categories of rulings. As these were included on combined templates, the PE rulings were excluded from the total to avoid double counting.

[6] This is the Foreign derived intangible income regime.

Uruguay

Uruguay has met all aspects of the terms of reference (OECD, 2017[3]) (ToR) for the calendar year 2018 (year in review) and no recommendations are made.

This is Uruguay's first review of implementation of the transparency framework.

Uruguay can legally issue one type of ruling within the scope of the transparency framework. In practice, Uruguay issued rulings within the scope of the transparency framework as follows:

- One past ruling, and
- For the period 1 April 2018 - 31 December 2018: no future rulings.

No peer input was received in respect of the exchanges of information on rulings received from Uruguay.

Introduction

This peer review covers Uruguay's implementation of the BEPS Action 5 transparency framework for the year 2018. The report has four parts, each relating to a key part of the ToR. Each part is discussed in turn. A summary of recommendations is included at the end of this report.

A. The information gathering process

Uruguay can legally issue the following type of rulings within the scope of the transparency framework: cross-border unilateral APAs and any other cross-border unilateral tax rulings (such as an advance tax ruling) covering transfer pricing or the application of transfer pricing principles. APAs are issued by the International Tax Department (DFI), which is a part of the Large Taxpayer Division within the Tax Administration (DGI).

Past rulings (ToR I.4.1.1, I.4.1.2, I.4.2.1, I.4.2.2)

For Uruguay, past rulings are any tax rulings within scope that are issued either (i) on or after 1 January 2016 but before 1 April 2018; and (ii) on or after 1 January 2014 but before 1 January 2016, provided still in effect as at 1 January 2016.

There are ten people working within the DFI in charge of issuing APAs. This specific unit was also responsible for identifying the past rulings. When an APA is issued, the information is filed and a copy of the ruling is stored within the DFI and another copy is stored within the General Director's office. These central files were reviewed to identify rulings issued within the period defined as past rulings, and the results were also cross-checked with the second copy. Based on this verification process, one past ruling was identified.

With respect to the identified past ruling, the DFI used the best efforts approach in order to identify the potential exchange jurisdictions. This was done by firstly identifying jurisdictions from the information contained in the APA and secondly by checking additional information from the taxpayer's transfer pricing documentation. Uruguay confirms that it was able to identify all potential exchange jurisdictions.

Future rulings (ToR I.4.1.1, I.4.1.2, I.4.2.1)

For Uruguay, future rulings are any tax rulings within scope that are issued on or after 1 April 2018.

The process for identifying the future rulings is similar to the process of identifying the past rulings. The process for identifying the potential exchange jurisdictions is similar as to the process used for past rulings. Uruguay notes that when requesting an APA, the taxpayer must identify all transactions that will be covered by the agreement and provide all necessary information about these related parties. The transfer pricing documentation that the taxpayer has to provide includes more detailed information on these transactions, as well as the group structure including the immediate parent and ultimate parent. As such, Uruguay has sufficient data to identify all potential exchange jurisdictions.

Review and supervision (ToR I.4.3)

On a quarterly basis, the Director of the Large Taxpayer Division requests the DFI to submit a report that contains detailed information regarding the rulings that were issued during this period. The Director then verifies that all relevant information is captured adequately and submitted to all relevant jurisdictions without delay.

The people in charge of implementing the procedures with respect to the transparency framework are provided with a training and instructions.

Conclusion on section A

Uruguay has met all of the ToR for the information gathering process and no recommendations are made.

B. The exchange of information

Legal basis for spontaneous exchange of information (ToR II.5.1, II.5.2)

Uruguay has the necessary domestic legal basis to exchange information spontaneously. Uruguay notes that there are no legal or practical impediments that prevent the spontaneous exchange of information on rulings as contemplated in the Action 5 minimum standard.

Uruguay has international agreements permitting spontaneous exchange of information, including being a party to the (i) *Multilateral Convention on Mutual Administrative Assistance in Tax Matters: Amended by the 2010 Protocol* (OECD/Council of Europe, 2011[4]) ("the Convention") and (ii) double tax agreements in force with 20 jurisdictions.[1]

Completion and exchange of templates (ToR II.5.3, II.5.4, II.5.5, II.5.6, II.5.7)

The DFI, which is responsible for identifying rulings, is also the competent authority. The DFI is responsible for completing the templates, in the form of Annex C of the 2015 Action 5 report (OECD, 2015[5]). The summary section of the template has to be completed in line with the internal FHTP suggested guidance. After approval of the template by the General Director, the DFI proceeds to exchange the information on the APA with the relevant jurisdictions. Uruguay ensures that exchanges take place within three months of issuing the ruling. To verify this is occurring, the Director requires a report on a quarterly basis including detailed information regarding the issued rulings and the timelines for the exchange.

For the year in review, the timeliness of exchanges is as follows:

Past rulings in the scope of the transparency framework	Number of exchanges transmitted by 31 December 2018	Delayed exchanges		
		Number of exchanges not transmitted by 31 December 2018	Reasons for the delays	Any other comments
	11	0	N/A	N/A
Future rulings in the scope of the transparency framework	Number of exchanges transmitted within three months of the information becoming available to the competent authority or immediately after legal impediments have been lifted	Delayed exchanges		
		Number of exchanges transmitted later than three months of the information on rulings becoming available to the competent authority	Reasons for the delays	Any other comments
	N/A	N/A	N/A	N/A
Total	11	0		

Follow up requests received for exchange of the ruling	Number	Average time to provide response	Number of requests not answered
	0	N/A	N/A

Conclusion on section B

Uruguay has the necessary legal basis for spontaneous exchange of information, a process for completing the templates in a timely way and has completed all exchanges. Uruguay has met all of the ToR for the exchange of information process and no recommendations are made.

C. Statistics (ToR IV)

The statistics for the year in review are as follows:

Category of ruling	Number of exchanges	Jurisdictions exchanged with
Ruling related to a preferential regime	N/A	N/A
Cross-border unilateral advance pricing agreements (APAs) and any other cross-border unilateral tax rulings (such as an advance tax ruling) covering transfer pricing or the application of transfer pricing principles	*De minimis* rule applies	N/A
Cross-border rulings providing for a unilateral downward adjustment to the taxpayer's taxable profits that is not directly reflected in the taxpayer's financial / commercial accounts	N/A	N/A
Permanent establishment rulings	N/A	N/A
Related party conduit rulings	N/A	N/A
De minimis rule	11	N/A
IP regimes: total exchanges on taxpayers benefitting from the third category of IP assets, new entrants benefitting from grandfathered IP regimes; and taxpayers making use of the option to treat the nexus ratio as a rebuttable presumption	N/A	N/A
Total	11	

D. Matters related to intellectual property regimes (ToR I.4.1.3)

In the year of review, Uruguay offered three intellectual property regimes (IP regime). However, these are not subject to the transparency requirements under the Action 5 Report (OECD, 2015[5]), because:

Benefits under law 16.906 for biotechnology

- ***New entrants benefitting from the grandfathered IP regime***: not applicable, as the IP regime has been abolished without grandfathering.
- ***Third category of IP assets***: not applicable as the IP regime has been abolished.
- ***Taxpayers making use of the option to treat the nexus ratio as a rebuttable presumption***: not applicable as the IP regime has been abolished.

Benefits under lit S art. 52 for biotechnology and for software

- ***New entrants benefitting from the grandfathered IP regime***: No enhanced transparency requirements apply, as follows. During the year in review, Uruguay amended the IP regime by implementing the nexus approach. The previous regime has been closed-off, and although grandfathering was provided, it only applies to entrants that benefited from the regime prior to the relevant date from which enhanced transparency obligations would apply.

- ***Third category of IP assets***: not applicable as the regime does not allow the third category of IP assets to qualify for the benefits.
- ***Taxpayers making use of the option to treat the nexus ratio as a rebuttable presumption***: not applicable as the regime does not allow the nexus ratio to be treated as a rebuttable presumption.

Free zones

- ***New entrants benefitting from the grandfathered IP regime***: not applicable, as the IP regime has been amended and no grandfathering was provided to existing taxpayers.
- ***Third category of IP assets***: not applicable as the regime does not allow the third category of IP assets to qualify for the benefits.
- ***Taxpayers making use of the option to treat the nexus ratio as a rebuttable presumption***: not applicable as the regime does not allow the nexus ratio to be treated as a rebuttable presumption.

Summary of recommendations on implementation of the transparency framework

Aspect of implementation of the transparency framework that should be improved	Recommendation for improvement
	No recommendations are made.

Notes

[1] Parties to the Convention are available here: www.oecd.org/tax/exchange-of-tax-information/convention-on-mutual-administrative-assistance-in-tax-matters.htm. Uruguay also has bilateral agreements in force with: Belgium, Chile, Ecuador, Finland, Germany, India, Korea, Liechtenstein, Luxembourg, Malta, Mexico, Paraguay, Portugal, Romania, Singapore, Spain, Switzerland, United Arab Emirates, United Kingdom and Viet Nam.

Viet Nam

Viet Nam has met all aspects of the terms of reference (ToR) for the calendar year 2017 (year in review), except for having in place a process for completion of templates and exchange of information on rulings (ToR II.5). Viet Nam receives one recommendation on this point for the year in review.

In the prior year report, Viet Nam received the same recommendation. As it has not been addressed, the recommendation remains in place.

Viet Nam can legally issue one type of ruling within the scope of the transparency framework. In practice, Viet Nam issued no rulings within the scope of the transparency framework. It has currently received three requests for unilateral APAs which are under review or in a pre-filing stage.

As no exchanges took place, no peer input was received in respect of the exchanges of information on rulings received from Viet Nam.

Introduction

This peer review covers Viet Nam's implementation of the BEPS Action 5 transparency framework for the year 2018. The report has four parts, each relating to a key part of the ToR. Each part is discussed in turn. A summary of recommendations is included at the end of this report.

A. The information gathering process

Viet Nam can legally issue one type of ruling within the scope of the transparency framework: cross-border unilateral advance pricing agreements (APAs) and any other cross-border unilateral tax rulings (such as an advance tax ruling) covering transfer pricing or the application of transfer pricing principles. The deputy Commissioner in charge of international taxation and affairs is responsible for issuing the APA, after approval by the Minister of Finance.

Past rulings (ToR I.4.1.1, I.4.1.2, I.4.2.1, I.4.2.2)

For Viet Nam, past rulings are any tax rulings within scope that are issued either: (i) on or after 1 January 2015 but before 1 September 2017; or (ii) on or after 1 January 2012 but before 1 January 2015, provided they were still in effect as at 1 January 2015.

In the prior year peer review report, it was determined that Viet Nam's undertakings to identify past rulings and all potential exchange jurisdictions were sufficient to meet the minimum standard. Viet Nam's implementation in this regard remains unchanged, and therefore continues to meet the minimum standard.

Viet Nam specified that the team in the large taxpayers' department referred to in the prior year report, which is assigned the APA requests, is the APA team. As noted in the prior year report, this APA team was also the team responsible for identifying when an APA is relevant for the purposes of the transparency framework and for identifying potential exchange jurisdictions.

Future rulings (ToR I.4.1.1, I.4.1.2, I.4.2.1)

For Viet Nam, future rulings are any tax rulings within scope that are issued on or after 1 September 2017.

In the prior year peer review report, it was determined that Viet Nam's system to identify future rulings and all potential exchange jurisdictions was sufficient to meet the minimum standard. Viet Nam's implementation in this regard remains unchanged, and therefore continues to meet the minimum standard. It is noted that no APAs have been issued within the period defined as "future rulings".

Review and supervision (ToR I.4.3)

In the prior year peer review report, it was determined that Viet Nam's review and supervision mechanism was sufficient to meet the minimum standard. Viet Nam's implementation in this regard remains unchanged, and therefore continues to meet the minimum standard.

Conclusion on section A

Viet Nam has met all of the ToR for the information gathering process and no recommendations are made.

B. The exchange of information

Legal basis for spontaneous exchange of information (ToR II.5.1, II.5.2)

Viet Nam has the necessary domestic legal basis to exchange information spontaneously. Viet Nam notes that there are no legal or practical impediments that prevent the spontaneous exchange of information on rulings as contemplated in the Action 5 minimum standard.

Viet Nam has international agreements permitting spontaneous exchange of information, including being a party to double tax agreements in force with 75 jurisdictions.[1]

Completion and exchange of templates (ToR II.5.3, II.5.4, II.5.5, II.5.6, II.5.7)

In the prior year peer review report, it was determined that Viet Nam's process for the completion and exchange of templates did not meet the ToR (ToR II.5). Therefore, Viet Nam was recommended to continue to put in place a process to complete the templates for all relevant rulings and to ensure the timely exchange of information on rulings in the form required by the transparency framework.

During the year in review, Viet Nam clarified that the APA team is also tasked with completing the templates in the form contained in Annex C of the Action 5 report (OECD, 2015). After completing the template, it would be sent to the Deputy Commissioner in charge of international taxation and affairs for approval, and afterwards to the Director of the international taxation department, designated as the Competent Authority for exchange of information, who would then exchange it with the relevant exchange jurisdictions. At this stage, timelines for the transmission of the template to the Competent Authority and for the completion of exchanges have not been established. Viet Nam is planning to issue internal guidance on this. Therefore the prior year recommendation remains.

As no rulings within the scope of the transparency framework have been issued in practice, Viet Nam was not required to complete any exchanges of information and there is no data to report on the timeliness of exchanges.

Conclusion on section B

Viet Nam has the necessary legal basis for spontaneous exchange of information. Viet Nam is currently putting in place a process for completion of templates and exchange of information on rulings (ToR II.5). Viet Nam is recommended to develop a process to complete the templates on relevant rulings and to ensure that the exchanges of information on rulings occur in accordance with the form and timelines under the transparency framework.

C. Statistics (ToR IV)

As no rulings are issued, no statistics can be reported.

D. Matters related to intellectual property regimes (ToR I.4.1.3)

During the year in review, the FHTP reviewed an intellectual property regime (IP regime)[2] offered by Viet Nam. At its June 2019 meeting, the FHTP concluded this regime as "out of scope" and therefore it is not subject to the transparency requirements under the Action 5 report (OECD, 2015[5]).

Summary of recommendations on implementation of the transparency framework

Aspect of implementation of the transparency framework that should be improved	Recommendation for improvement
Viet Nam is currently putting in place a process for completion of templates and exchange of information on rulings.	Viet Nam is recommended to develop a process to complete the templates on relevant rulings and to ensure that the exchanges of information on rulings occur in accordance with the form and timelines under the transparency framework. This recommendation remains unchanged since the prior year peer review report.

Notes

[1] Viet Nam has double tax agreements with Australia, Austria, Azerbaijan, Bangladesh, Belarus, Belgium, Brunei Darussalam, Bulgaria, Cambodia, Canada, China (People's Republic of), Cuba, Czech Republic, Democratic People's Republic of Korea, Denmark, Estonia, Finland, France, Germany, Hong Kong (China), Hungary, Iceland, India, Indonesia, Iran, Ireland, Israel, Italy, Japan, Kazakhstan, Korea, Kuwait, Lao People's Democratic Republic, Latvia, Luxembourg, Macau (China), Malaysia, Malta, Mongolia, Morocco, Mozambique, Myanmar, Netherlands, New Zealand, Norway, Oman, Pakistan, Palestinian Authority, Panama, Philippines, Poland, Portugal, Qatar, Romania, Russia, San Marino, Saudi Arabia, Serbia, Seychelles, Singapore, Slovak Republic, Spain, Sri Lanka, Sweden, Switzerland, Chinese Taipei, Thailand, Tunisia, Turkey, Ukraine, United Arab Emirates, United Kingdom, Uruguay, Uzbekistan and Venezuela.

[2] This regime is the Transfer of technology.

Zambia

Zambia has met all aspects of the terms of reference (OECD, 2017[3]) (ToR) for the calendar year 2018 (year in review) that can be met in the absence of rulings being issued.

This is Zambia's first review of implementation of the transparency framework.

Zambia indicates that it cannot legally issue any type of rulings within the scope of the transparency framework.

As no exchanges were required to take place, no peer input was received in respect of the exchanges of information on rulings received from Zambia.

Introduction

This peer review covers Zambia's implementation of the BEPS Action 5 transparency framework for the year 2018. The report has four parts, each relating to a key part of the ToR. Each part is discussed in turn. A summary of recommendations is included at the end of this report.

A. The information gathering process

As no rulings are issued, this section is not assessed.

B. The exchange of information

As no rulings are issued, this section is not assessed.

C. Statistics (ToR IV)

As no rulings are issued, no statistics can be reported.

D. Matters related to intellectual property regimes (ToR I.4.1.3)

Zambia does not offer an intellectual property regime for which transparency requirements under the Action 5 Report (OECD, 2015[5]) were imposed.

Summary of recommendations on implementation of the transparency framework

Aspect of implementation of the transparency framework that should be improved	Recommendation for improvement
	No recommendations are made.

References

OECD (2017), *BEPS Action 5 on Harmful Tax Practices – Terms of Reference and Methodology for the Conduct of the Peer Reviews of the Action 5 Transparency Framework*, http://www.oecd.org/tax/beps/beps-action-5-harmful-tax-practices-peer-review-transparency-framework.pdf (consulté le 20 janvier 2020). [3]

OECD (2017), *Harmful Tax Practices - 2017 Progress Report on Preferential Regimes: Inclusive Framework on BEPS: Action 5*, OECD/G20 Base Erosion and Profit Shifting Project, OECD Publishing, Paris, https://dx.doi.org/10.1787/9789264283954-en. [2]

OECD (2015), *Countering Harmful Tax Practices More Effectively, Taking into Account Transparency and Substance, Action 5 - 2015 Final Report*, OECD/G20 Base Erosion and Profit Shifting Project, OECD Publishing, Paris, https://dx.doi.org/10.1787/9789264241190-en. [5]

OECD (2015), *Countering Harmful Tax Practices More Effectively, Taking into Account Transparency and Substance, Action 5 - 2015 Final Report*, OECD/G20 Base Erosion and Profit Shifting Project, OECD Publishing, Paris, https://dx.doi.org/10.1787/9789264241190-en. [1]

OECD/Council of Europe (2011), *The Multilateral Convention on Mutual Administrative Assistance in Tax Matters: Amended by the 2010 Protocol*, OECD Publishing, Paris, https://dx.doi.org/10.1787/9789264115606-en. [4]

www.ingramcontent.com/pod-product-compliance
Ingram Content Group UK Ltd.
Pitfield, Milton Keynes, MK11 3LW, UK
UKHW051456290926
15471UKWH00008B/1233

9 789264 529458